A Balanced Introduction
to Computer Science

Third Edition

A Balanced Introduction to Computer Science

Third Edition

David Reed

Creighton University

Prentice Hall

Boston   Columbus   Indianapolis   New York   San Francisco   Upper Saddle River
Amsterdam   Cape Town   Dubai   London   Madrid   Milan   Munich   Paris   Montreal   Toronto
Delhi   Mexico City   Sao Paulo   Sydney   Hong Kong   Seoul   Singapore   Taipei   Tokyo

Vice President/Editorial Director: Marcia Horton
Editor-in-Chief: Michael Hirsch
Executive Editor: Tracy Dunkelberger
Assistant Editor: Melinda Haggerty
Editorial Assistant: Allison Michael
Vice President of Marketing: Patrice Jones
Marketing Manager: Yezan Alayan
Marketing Coordinator: Kathryn Ferranti
Vice President, Production: Vince O'Brien
Managing Editor: Jeff Holcomb

Senior Operations Supervisor: Alan Fischer
Art Director: Kristine Carney
Cover Designer: Marta Samsel
Cover Image: big/Shutterstock Images
Media Editor: Dan Sandin
Project Management: Peggy Kellar, Aptara®, Inc.
Composition and Illustration: Aptara®, Inc.
Printer/Binder: Edwards Brothers
Cover Printer: Coral Graphics

Credits and acknowledgments borrowed from other sources and reproduced, with permission, appear on the Credits page in the endmatter of this textbook.

Microsoft® and Windows® are registered trademarks of the Microsoft Corporation in the U.S.A. and other countries. Screen shots and icons reprinted with permission from the Microsoft Corporation. This book is not sponsored or endorsed by or affiliated with the Microsoft Corporation.

Many of the designations by manufacturers and sellers to distinguish their products are claimed as trademarks. Where those designations appear in this book, and the publisher was aware of a trademark claim, the designations have been printed in initial caps or all caps and appear on the Trademark Information page in the endmatter of this textbook.

Library of Congress Cataloging-in-Publication Data available upon request.

10 9 8 7 6 5 4 3 2 1—EB—14 13 12 11 10

Prentice Hall
is an imprint of

www.pearsonhighered.com

ISBN 10: 0-13-216675-5
ISBN 13: 978-0-13-216675-1

Dedicated to Laura, Charlie, and Jack —
with all my love and thanks.

Contents

Preface

Welcome to *A Balanced Introduction to Computer Science*. There are a number of reasons why you might be reading this text. Perhaps you have had limited experience with computers and would like to know more about how they work and how to control them. Or perhaps you recognize the marketability of programming and computer literacy, and would like to expand your skills for the future job market. Or perhaps you are just curious about the World Wide Web and want to know how you can create your own Web presence. In any case, you are embarking on what I hope will be an exciting, challenging, and rewarding experience.

Balancing Breadth and Depth

This text is different from most introductory computing texts in that it attempts to maintain a balance between computing breadth and programming depth. Traditionally, introductory texts have focused almost exclusively on one approach or the other. Breadth-based texts have emphasized a broad understanding of computers and computer science. By surveying a wide range of topics such as computer organization, graphics, networking, and technology in society, the intent is for students to experience the breadth of the field and develop a perspective to later understand and appreciate the role of technology in their lives. Alternatively, depth-based texts have focused more deeply on the role of programming in computing. The discipline of programming not only develops problem-solving skills, but also is central to many areas of computer science and thus important to appreciating their significance.

Each of these approaches has merit, but there are potential weaknesses to either extreme. A breadth-based survey of computing can be too superficial, presenting a broad perspective to students who lack the context or experience to fully comprehend it. And although programming depth can provide experience with many computing concepts, developing proficiency as a programmer and problem-solver requires extensive hands-on experience (especially when learning a complex language such as C++ or Java), and may not be directly relevant to all students.

The approach taken by this text is to balance breadth and depth. Chapters are included on concepts and issues in computing that are most relevant to the beginning student, including computer terminology, the Internet and World Wide Web, the history of computing, the organization and manufacture of computer technology, and technology's impact on society. Mixed among these breadth topics are chapters that introduce fundamental programming concepts and skills in a hands-on, tutorial format. Using the programming language JavaScript, students will develop skills in designing and implementing interactive Web pages. JavaScript's simplicity, natural interfaces, and seamless integration with the Web make it possible for novices to develop interesting and engaging programs quickly. In addition, JavaScript is always available (for free!) for anyone with a Web browser, making it easy to apply programming skills learned from this text to everyday problems.

In striking a balance between breadth and depth, the intent of this text is not to be a complete and exhaustive survey of computing or a reference on Web development. Breadth chapters focus on key ideas and concepts that are relevant to beginning students as they attempt to understand computing technology and the field of computer science. Likewise, programming chapters focus on JavaScript features that demonstrate fundamental programming concepts while also allowing for interesting and engaging applications. Links to other sources are provided for the interested reader, including supplemental material and exercises at the end of each programming chapter. This provides a broad perspective on computing as well as enough problem solving and programming depth to appreciate the significance of computer science.

Text Goals

There are three main goals to this text and its accompanying resources. First, it serves to expose the student to the breadth that is the field of computer science. Computer science is more than just the study of computers—it focuses on all facets of computation, from the design and analysis of algorithms (step-by-step sequences of instructions for carrying out tasks), to the engineering and manufacture of computer components, to the development of software systems. Through readings and the use of online resources, the student will study topics such as the history of computer technology, the underlying architecture of modern computers, the translation and execution sequence of programs, and the capabilities and limitations of computation. Using software simulators, the student will build virtual components of a computer and watch the flow of information as a program is translated and executed on the low-level machinery. Through this combination of reading and experimentation, hopefully these concepts will come alive for the student and provide a sense of what computer science is all about.

The second main goal of this text is to teach the student the fundamentals of programming. *Programming is the process of solving problems on the computer* , that is, devising solutions to specific tasks and formalizing those solutions in a language the computer can understand and execute. Programming is the central activity in computer science, providing an inroad to many of the interesting facets and challenges of the field. In learning to program, the student will be learning to analyze problems, think logically, formalize his or her thoughts, and solve problems. It is a discipline, because a systematic approach must be learned, but it is also a creative process, since novel approaches must be found to attack new problems. And because many of the skills developed in programming apply to problem solving in general, experience gained through this text should carry over to other disciplines as well. Finally, the fact that programs are written in the context of interactive Web pages highlights the relevance of programming to applications students use everyday.

The third main goal of this text is to demonstrate the scientific and interdisciplinary nature of computing. Research in various fields of study, most notably the mathematical and natural sciences, is becoming increasingly dependent on computers and programming. By studying and investigating applications in fields such as biology, physics, psychology, and even economics, the student will learn to apply his or her programming skills to a wide range of problems. In addition, the student will develop empirical skills that are common to all scientific endeavors.

Text Features

The balanced approach to computer science and programming taken by this text is evident in the layout of its chapters. There are two types of chapters in the text, those that use narrative to introduce key concepts of computing (i.e., the computer science breadth chapters: 1, 3, 6, 8, 10, 12, 14, 16, and 18) and those that use a tutorial style to develop problem-solving and programming skills (i.e., the programming depth chapters: 2, 4, 5, 7, 9, 11, 13, 15, and 17). The interleaving of these chapters is both intentional and important. It provides variety in the types of activities students will undertake, and thus may be more accommodating to students with different learning styles. Readings and classroom discussions serve as buffers between programming tutorials, allowing the student more time to assimilate programming concepts and skills before beginning the next tutorial. Finally, and perhaps most importantly, the interleaving of chapters supports the student's understanding and appreciation of the content. For example, after developing their own home pages in Chapter 2, students are better prepared to understand what the Web is and how it works in Chapter 3.

Features of the computer science breadth chapters (which are highlighted by a color bleed across the top edge of pages):

- They focus on topics that are most relevant to a beginning student. The goal is not to inundate the student with details, but instead to emphasize the central ideas of that topic.

- Illustrations are used whenever possible to illuminate key points.

- Web-based visualization tools (accessible at the book's Web page: `http://balance3e.com`) are provided to complement many of the chapters and support active learning. For example, Chapter 14 integrates a suite of simulators that allows the student to explore the internal workings of computers.

- Each chapter ends with a Chapter Summary and Review Questions that encourage reflection and the integration of content from that chapter.

Features of the programming depth chapters (which are highlighted by a color bleed down the outer edge of pages):

- They are presented in a tutorial style, recognizing that the only way to learn programming (and, more generally, problem solving) is to actually do it.

- Exercises follow an incremental approach, allowing students to master programming concepts by first studying existing programs (which are accessible at the book's Web page: `http://balance3e.com`) and then making modifications using new tools and constructs. Eventually, students create new programs for solving interesting and hopefully engaging problems.

- In addition to incremental exercises, each depth chapters contains at least one motivational application—a larger programming example that is familiar and relevant to students (such as rotating banner ads, embedded countdown clocks, and text encryption).

- Common errors and points of confusion are identified and discussed in special sections called "Common Errors to Avoid . . ."

- Problem-solving and program design advice is provided in special sections called "Designer Secrets."

- Each chapter includes a Chapter Summary that presents the key concepts and programming tools in a concise bullet list.

- Supplemental material and exercises are provided at the end of each chapter for further study.

Appendices are provided at the end of this text as references. Appendices A and B provide tutorials on Web browsers and common text editors, which may be useful for students who are not already familiar with computers and the Web. Appendix C is an HTML reference, collecting all of the HTML elements used throughout the text in a table. Appendix D is a JavaScript reference, which similarly collects all of the JavaScript programming constructs. Appendices E through G provide full listings of the library files that are introduced in chapter exercises.

Online Resources

The book's Web site, `http://balance3e.com`, contains many resources that can assist the student using the text. These resources include:

- Source code for all examples listed in the text. These Web pages can be viewed directly through the Web site, or they can be downloaded to allow the student to edit and experiment with the pages.

- All of the visualization pages from the chapters, linked together on a single page for ease of access.

- A collection of additional self-study exercises that complement the existing chapter exercises. Solutions are provided so that the student can check his or her answers and receive hints as needed.

In addition, password-protected resources are available for the instructor teaching with the text. The password is available from any Pearson sales representative or online through `http://www.pearsonhighered.com/educator`. These resources include:

- Solutions to all of the exercises and review questions in the text.

- Nine laboratory assignments that complement the material in the programming depth chapters. They emphasize experimentation, analysis, and the use of programs for solving interdisciplinary problems.

- Lecture notes in PowerPoint format corresponding to each chapter of the book.

- Images of many of the figures from the book in a ZIP file for easy download.
- Sample syllabi for organizing a course based on the book.

Changes in the Third Edition

The third edition of this text is significantly different from the previous two editions. The structure and main topics of the text are similar, but much of the content has been reorganized and augmented to reflect the current state of computing. The most notable changes are:

- HTML and JavaScript code throughout the book has been revised to match the latest HTML5 draft standard.
- The programming depth chapters have been reorganized to take advantage of changes to HTML5. In particular, Chapters 4 and 5 introduce event-driven pages earlier, using buttons, text boxes, and page divisions for controlling images and text within a page. Chapter 7 focuses on functions and abstraction, using randomness as a common thread through numerous examples.
- In addition to incremental exercises, each programming depth chapter has at least one larger, motivational application that demonstrates programming concepts in a setting familiar to students. These include interacting help buttons (Chapter 4), online form letters (Chapter 5), rotating banner ads (Chapter 7), embedded countdown clocks (Chapter 9), a slot machine simulation (Chapter 11), dice simulations (Chapter 13), text encryption (Chapter 15), and ASCII animations (Chapter 17).
- New material has been added throughout the book on recent developments and important technologies, such as multi-core processors and operating systems (Chapter 1), cascading style sheets (Chapter 2), HTML5 standards (Chapter 3), wireless networking (Chapter 6), parallel processing (Chapter 10), digital media (Chapter 12), and social networking (Chapter 18).
- Statistics on the Internet/Web and computer specifications have been updated to match the current state of technology.

Advice for the Student

This text does not assume any previous experience with computer applications or programming. Certainly, familiarity with computers is a plus (e.g., word processing or email), but is not necessary. Basic computer terminology will be covered in the text as needed, and appendices are provided to assist the novice with simple computer skills, such as using a text editor, saving files to a disk, and browsing the Web. The goal is not to teach you everything you could ever want to know about computers and programming, but instead to provide you with a working set of skills and knowledge. Whenever possible, links to further readings will be provided in case you are interested in a topic and would like to learn more.

Through the use of readings, exercises, and experiments, this text aspires to provide you with a broad sense of what computer science is all about, while simultaneously developing depth as a problem-solver and programmer. The choice of JavaScript as the medium for developing programming skills was specifically made to make this task simpler and more relevant to students. JavaScript was designed to be a simple scripting language for controlling pages on the World Wide Web. Using JavaScript, you can control actions with the click of the mouse or generate dynamic images on a page. As such, learning JavaScript opens the door for many exciting applications on the Web. Similarities between JavaScript and the programming languages Java and C++ also mean that experience with JavaScript programming can be a stepping-stone to larger-scale programming in these industry-strength languages.

Whether you choose to continue studies in computer science, or merely wish to apply computing skills to your everyday life, the balanced coverage of computing topics as found in this text should prove valuable to you. As always, enjoy and learn.

Advice for the Instructor

The layout of the chapters in this text is designed to provide maximum flexibility for the instructor. Depending on the preferences of the instructor and the goals of the particular course, the right balance and order of the material can be determined for your needs. If you are teaching a traditional nonmajor course, then a roughly even balance between breadth and depth probably makes sense. If the students are computer knowledgeable and taking this course as part of a computer science sequence, then some breadth topics may be skipped or shortened to allow for greater programming depth. This text has been used in both nonmajors' (CS0) courses and introductory majors' courses (CS1) at a variety of institutions. Sample syllabi that demonstrate possible course organizations are available online as supplements.

One of the strengths of this book is the flexibility that it provides the instructor. An instructor might choose to emphasize the breadth chapters, while only covering the first few programming chapters, or emphasize the programming chapters while selecting a few breadth chapters of interest, or perhaps find a balance in between. The interleaving of breadth and depth chapters throughout the text is specifically designed to support the content and vary the types of learning activities students engage in. Although the relative order in which the programming depth chapters are covered is constrained by their content, it is certainly possible to omit or move some of the computer science breadth chapters. For example, some instructors might prefer covering the history of computers (Chapter 6) earlier in the course, or perhaps covering the chapters on how computers work (Chapter 14) and are built (Chapter 16) together.

As always, enjoy, teach, and learn.

Acknowledgments

This book is the culmination of a long process of thinking, experimenting, implementing, classroom testing, rethinking, reexperimenting, and so on. There are numerous people who have contributed to this book during its development, both tangibly and with moral support. The people at Prentice Hall have been outstanding, including editors Petra Recter, Kate Hargett, and Tracy Dunkelberger. I would also like to thank the following outside reviewers, whose insightful comments were a great help:

Debra Burhans, *Canisius College*
Martin Chetlen, *Moorpark College*
Donald Costello, *University of Nebraska*
Lionel Craddock, *Bluefield State College*
Scott Dexter, *Brooklyn College*
Linda DuHadway, *Utah State University*
Buster Dunsmore, *Purdue University*
Erica Eddy, *University of Wisconsin — Parkside*
Karen Ehrlich, *SUNY College at Fredonia*
Chaya Gurwitz, *Brooklyn College*
Dmitri Gusev, *Edinboro University of Pennsylvania*
Paul Helmer, *Hampden-Sydney College*
Michael Hennessy, *University of Oregon*
Mark Holliday, *Western Carolina University*
Ralph Hooper, *University of Alabama — Tuscaloosa*
Nancy Kinnersley, *University of Kansas – Main*
Hank Korth, *Lehigh University*
Rowan Lindley, *Westchester Community College*
Ronald Marsh, *University of North Dakota*
David Middleton, *Arkansas Tech University*
Arnie Miles, *Georgetown University*

Jenna Miley, *Bainbridge College*
Vince Offenback, *North Seattle Community College*
Jeff Parker, *Merrimack College*
Roger Priebe, *University of Texas — Austin*
Mary Ann May-Pumphrey, *DeAnza College*
Charles Riedesel, *University of Nebraska—Lincoln*
Anton Riedl, *Christopher Newport University*
Jerry Ross, *Lane Community College*
Jim Schmolze, *Tufts University*
Patrick Sebrechts, *California State University—San Marcos*
Gene Sheppard, *Georgia Perimeter College*
David Valentine, *Slippery Rock University*
Mark Williams, *Lane Community College*

The concepts behind this book were initially formed while I was at Dickinson College in the late 1990s. Numerous colleagues at Dickinson taught early versions of the material and contributed new ideas, especially Grant Braught and Craig Miller. In addition to those early colleagues, I would like to thank colleagues at Creighton University, who have also been supportive of the course and its material, especially Brian Kokensparger. As a general inspiration and source for great ideas, I gratefully acknowledge my good friend Owen Astrachan, who served as my early role model in teaching as well as embarrassing me in public on numerous occasions.

On a personal note, I would like to thank my parents who raised me to value knowledge and learning, and supported me in my studies. My wife Laura has probably suffered the most during the development of this book—losing me to many late nights of work and having to listen to endless stories about what did and didn't work in class. Her willingness to listen, provide keen insights, and pick up the slack for me at home has made this book possible. Finally, special thanks go to our boys, Charlie and Jack, who have grown up along with the evolution of this book. While I am proud of this book, they are without a doubt my best work.

Dave Reed
Creighton University

A Balanced Introduction to Computer Science

Third Edition

Computer Basics

This chapter uses narrative, illustrations, and review questions to introduce computer science and technology concepts.

Computers are incredibly fast, accurate, and stupid: humans are incredibly slow, inaccurate and brilliant; together they are powerful beyond imagination.

Albert Einstein

Computers are to computing as instruments are to music. Software is the score whose interpretations amplifies our reach and lifts our spirits. Leonardo da Vinci called music the shaping of the invisible, and his phrase is even more apt as a description of software.

Alan Kay
Scientific American, 1984

The easiest way to tell the difference between hardware and software is to kick it. If it hurts your toe, it's hardware.

Anonymous

The computer, at least in the form we think of it today, is a relatively new technological development. The first electronic computers were built in the 1940s, and desktop computers accessible to average people date back only to the late 1970s. In a very short time, computers have become integral to nearly every aspect of our society, from business transactions to personal communications. However, although many people use them for work and pleasure every day, few have even a basic understanding of how computers work.

This chapter presents an overview of computer technology, focusing on what computers are, how they are organized, and what they can do. The coverage is not meant to be exhaustive—many of the topics introduced here will be revisited in later chapters. However, this overview should provide a framework for understanding computing concepts as you encounter them throughout the book, as well as making you a wiser consumer of computer technology.

What Is a Computer?

When you think of the word "computer," you probably picture a machine that sits on a desk and is used to create documents, send email, or explore the World Wide Web. This type of computer is often referred to as a ***personal computer*** (***PC***), as it is designed for

Figure 1.1 Various types of computers.

use by one person at a time, or as a ***desktop computer***, since it is small enough to fit on top of a desk. Or, perhaps you think of a ***laptop*** computer, a small, portable device that integrates all of the computer components into one unit. When people contemplate computers today, many think only of these types of machines; however, a wide variety of computers are used to fulfill different needs. Some, known as ***supercomputers***, are large enough to fill entire rooms and can perform trillions of calculations per second. Researchers involved in complex tasks, such as modeling weather patterns or testing engineering designs, are the primary users of supercomputers. More recently, smaller handheld devices, sometimes referred to as ***palmtops***, have been growing in popularity. These devices often combine the functionality of a computer with another technology, such as a cell phone or personal music player, and enable the user to perform basic tasks such as electronic mail and Web surfing. In addition, millions of tiny computers are embedded in (e.g., built into) and used to control everyday devices, such as automobiles, air conditioners, and microwave ovens. Figure 1.1 depicts four diverse types of computers, ranging from a supercomputer that takes up a room to an Apple iPad that fits in a person's hand.

In general, we will define a ***computer*** as a device that receives, stores, and processes information. Although the computers described in the previous paragraph may look different and perform diverse functions, they all fit this general definition. For example, a supercomputer is able to receive data on current weather patterns, store that data, and process it to predict when storm conditions will arise. A personal computer is able to recognize characters typed by the user, store these characters in files, and process them to produce a document, spreadsheet, or email message. Likewise, a computer embedded in a car's antilock brake system is able to sense the spin of the wheels, process that data to compute the optimal braking pattern, and bring the car to a safe stop.

Although computers are pervasive in everyday life, few people truly comprehend how they are organized and perform their tasks. Even purchasing a personal computer can be an overwhelming experience involving highly technical information and obscure computer jargon. For example, Figure 1.2 compares the advertised specifications of two desktop computer systems marketed by a major computer manufacturer (May 2010). System 1 is a ***low-end*** computer system, indicating that it is inexpensive but provides limited features and uses older technology. System 2 is a ***high-end*** computer, which maximizes performance by incorporating the latest technology, but at a higher cost. Understanding the trade-offs between these two models requires a significant amount of computer knowledge—and this is a streamlined version of only one table of options for one category of computer system marketed by one company!

The remainder of this chapter will define key terms from Figure 1.2, as well as describe the basic workings of computers. Supplementing the explanations of many of the computing concepts, the chapter provides "Technical Details . . ." relating those concepts to the systems in Figure 1.2. Thus, after completing this chapter, you should be able to appreciate many of the differences between these two systems.

A first step toward understanding the table in Figure 1.2—and, by extension, computers in general—is to distinguish between hardware and software. ***Hardware*** refers to the physical components of the computer, such as the monitor, keyboard, and hard drive. ***Software*** refers to the programs that execute (i.e., run) on the computer, carrying out tasks such as word processing or

	Desktop System 1	Desktop System 2
CPU	2.2 GHz Intel Celeron 450	3.2 GHz Intel Core i5
Memory		
Cache	512 KB cache	4 MB cache
RAM	4 GB RAM	8 GB RAM
Hard Drive	320 GB hard drive	1 TB hard drive
CD-ROM/DVD	DVD+/−RW drive	DVD+/−RW drive
Input/Output		
Keyboard	USB multifunction keyboard	wireless multifunction keyboard
Pointing Device	USB optical mouse	wireless optical mouse
Screen	20" HD flatscreen monitor	24" HD flatscreen monitor
Speakers	Multimedia Speaker System	Dolby Surround Sound Speakers
Network Adapter	Integrated 10/100/1000 Ethernet	Integrated 10/100/1000 Ethernet Integrated wireless card & antenna
Operating System	Windows 7 Home Premium	Windows 7 Professional
Web Browser	Internet Explorer 8	Internet Explorer 8
Productivity Suite	Microsoft Works 9	Microsoft Office Professional 2007
Security	McAfee Security Center	McAfee Security Center

Figure 1.2 Two different desktop computer systems. (Based on actual advertisements, May 2010.)

accessing the Web. In Figure 1.2, the first three sections (labeled CPU, Memory, and Input/Output) refer to the systems' various hardware components. The last section refers to software components.

Hardware

Given the diversity of modern computers, it is difficult to describe a "typical" computer hardware system. However, certain features are common to most desktop machines, as shown in Figure 1.3.

Although specific components and their appearance may vary from computer to computer, virtually all modern computers have the same underlying structure. This structure is known as the *von Neumann architecture*, named after computer science pioneer John von Neumann, who formalized his method of computer organization in the early 1950s. The von Neumann architecture identifies three essential components that work together to function as a computer (i.e., a device that receives, stores, and processes information). *Input/output devices* allow the user to communicate with the computer by entering commands and then viewing the results. *Memory* stores information for the computer to process, as well as *programs*, or instructions specifying the steps necessary to complete specific tasks. Finally, the *central processing unit* (*CPU*) carries out programmatic steps in order to process data. These three components are connected by *buses*, collections of wires that carry information in the form of electrical signals. (See Chapter 14 for more details about the underlying hardware of computers.)

Computers that use the von Neumann architecture are known as *stored-program computers*, which means that they can initiate different tasks by retrieving different programs from memory. For example, to complete such actions as creating a text document or performing a computation, the CPU accesses the associated program instructions from memory and executes them in order. If the computer user wishes to perform a new task, he simply loads a new program into memory and instructs the CPU to execute that program. In fact, the von Neumann architecture enables multiple

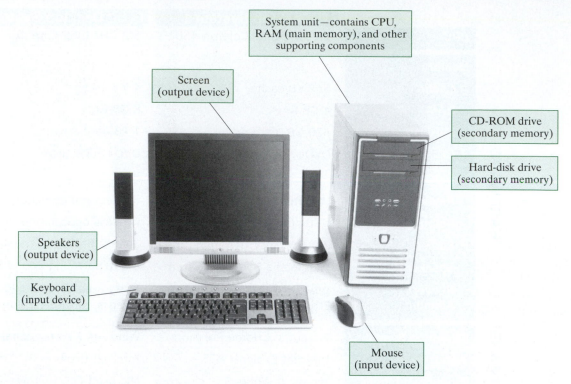

Figure 1.3 A common desktop computer system.

programs to reside in memory at the same time, allowing the CPU to juggle multiple tasks, such as switching back and forth between a Web browser and a text editor.

Figure 1.4 outlines the relationships among the three components of the von Neumann architecture. Additional details regarding how each component works and interacts within the computer are provided in subsequent subsections.

Central Processing Unit (CPU)

The CPU is the brains of the computer, responsible for controlling the internal workings of the machine. You will learn more about how the CPU works in Chapter 14. For now, we note that the CPU is made of *circuitry*, or electronic components wired together to control the flow of electrical signals. The CPU is by far the most complex part of a computer system. The Intel Core 2 Duo processor, first introduced in 2006, for example, contains circuitry comprised of more than 291 million individual components. All of this circuitry is packaged onto a small silicon chip encased in plastic, with metal pins for connecting the chip to other hardware components (Figure 1.5). Introduced in 2010, the 8-core Intel Xeon contains an astounding 2.3 billion components. Other CPUs commonly found in personal computers include the Intel Celeron 450, Intel Core i3, AMD Sempron, and AMD Athlon^{TM} 64 X2.

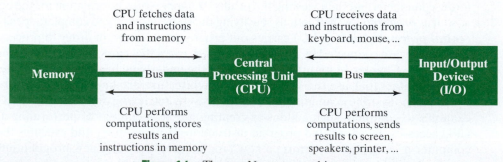

Figure 1.4 The von Neumann architecture.

Figure 1.5   Core Duo circuitry and packaging (Intel Corporation, 2006).

In controlling the workings of the computer, the CPU has two key tasks: (1) fetching program instructions from memory, and (2) executing those instructions. As the ultimate behavior of computer programs can be complex, you might expect that the individual instructions executed by the CPU would be complex, but they are not. Even programs with advanced capabilities are broken into sequences of very simple instructions, such as "add two numbers" or "copy a value from one location to another." Of course, it may require thousands or even millions of such low-level instructions to specify the behavior of a Web browser or word processor. Fortunately, CPUs can process instruction sequences extremely quickly, which enables the processors to handle these immense programs. CPU speed is generally measured in gigahertz (GHz), which indicates how many *billions* of instructions a CPU can execute *in a second*. For example, a 3.2GHz CPU can execute approximately 3.2 billion simple instructions in a second, thus producing complex behavior at a speed that appears almost instantaneous to the human user.

Technical Details

The first row of the table in Figure 1.2 lists the type of CPU contained in each system. Both System 1 and System 2 utilize CPUs manufactured by Intel, the world's largest manufacturer of processors. However, the particular models used in the two systems differ in cost and performance. These variations are similar to the disparity between two car models manufactured by the same automobile company.

- System 2 contains a Core i5 processor, which is one of Intel's high-end processors. The Core i5 provides a broad range of capabilities and is marketed to advanced users who require a high level of performance in processing data and operations. For example, it has special features that allow it to process images and video very quickly, making it well suited for running graphic-arts applications and interactive games. The Core i5 belongs to a new generation of processors that contain duplicate control circuitry, in this case a quad-core. In many ways, it works like four processors packaged on one chip, although some resources are shared between the four cores. As a result, the quad-core processor is able to execute four different sets of instructions at the same time, and thus complete tasks faster than a single processor.

- System 1 contains a Celeron 450 processor, which is one of Intel's economy processors. In the same way that an economy car costs less because features such as weight or horsepower have been diminished, the capabilities of the less expensive, single-core Celeron 450 processor are limited in comparison to those of the Core i5. The Celeron 450 is marketed to casual users for whom price is the primary concern.

- If we simply compared numbers, it would appear that the 3.2GHz Core i5 from System 2 would be around 45% faster than the 2.2GHz Celeron 450 from System 1 (3.2 billion instructions per second vs. 2.2 billion instructions per second). However, direct comparisons based on CPU speed alone can be misleading. Since the Core i5 is a quad-core processor it is capable of executing four different instructions simultaneously, producing the effect of up to 12.8 billion instructions per second. (Note, however, that not all tasks can be easily divided into four independent executions sequences, and so the 4x speedup may not always occur in practice.) In addition, it is important to note that different CPUs provide different sets of basic instructions. For example, the Celeron 450 processor, with its more limited set of instructions, might require several steps to carry out a task that could be accomplished in one step using a Core i5. Thus, the Core i5 might perform tasks more than six times as fast than the Celeron 450 does. It is also important to note that a faster CPU does not always translate to a faster application. The speed of many applications is constrained by other factors. For example, a word processing program is limited by the speed at which a person can type characters and the speed at which the monitor can display them—a faster processor will generally not improve its performance.

Memory

The **memory** is the part of a computer that stores programs and data. Modern computers are **digital** devices, which means that they store and process information as **binary digits**, or **bits**—units of data that correspond to one of two potential values. Because bits represent one of only two possibilities, they are referred to as **discrete** values—this is in contrast to **continuous** values (such as those used to store analog audio), which are represented on a scale containing an infinite range of possibilities. Bits are the building blocks of digital memory; usually, the two possible values of a bit are written as 0 and 1, but the values could just as easily be represented as off and on, open and closed, volts and no volts, and so on.

Of course, a single bit is not very useful for storing information, as it can only differentiate between two different values. If you combine two bits, however, there are four different patterns that can be used to represent values: 00, 01, 10, and 11. Similarly, three bits are able to represent eight values using the following patterns: 000, 001, 010, 011, 100, 101, 110, and 111. Each additional bit of storage doubles the range of potential values that can be stored, as shown in Figure 1.6. In general, N bits can represent 2^N different values.

Although the bit is the building block of digital memory, memory capacity is usually specified in bytes. A **byte** is a collection of 8 bits, and thus is capable of representing $2^8 = 256$ different values. Because that is sufficient for expressing many ranges of data, including every character on a keyboard, the byte is a more practical unit of measure. Collections of bytes can be identified using prefixes; for example, a **kilobyte** (*KB*) is roughly 1,000 bytes of storage, a **megabyte** (*MB*) is roughly one million bytes of storage, a **gigabyte** (*GB*) is roughly one billion bytes of storage, and a **terabyte** (*TB*) is roughly one trillion bytes of storage (Figure 1.7).

```
1 bit   → 2 values      0 1
2 bits  → 4 values      00 01 10 11
3 bits  → 8 values      000 001 010 011 100 101 110 111
4 bits  → 16 values     0000 0001 0010 0011 0100 0101 0110 0111 1000 1001 1010 1011 1100 1101 1111
5 bits  → 32 values     00000 00001 00010 00011 00100 00101 00110 00111 01000 01001 01010 ...
6 bits  → 64 values     000000 000001 000010 000011 000100 000101 000110 000111 001000 ...
7 bits  → 128 values    0000000 0000001 0000010 0000011 0000100 0000101 0000110 0000111 ...
8 bits  → 256 values    00000000 00000001 00000010 00000011 00000100 00000101 00000110 ...
9 bits  → 512 values    000000000 000000001 000000010 000000011 000000100 000000101 ...
10 bits → 1,024 values  0000000000 0000000001 0000000010 0000000011 0000000100 0000000101 ...
.
.
.
N bits  → 2^N values
```

Figure 1.6 Bit patterns.

byte	→ 8 bits		
kilobyte (KB)	→ 2^{10} bytes	= 1,024 bytes	(= 8,192 bits)
megabyte (MB)	→ 2^{20} bytes	= 1,048,576 bytes	(= 8,388,608 bits)
gigabyte (GB)	→ 2^{30} bytes	= 1,073,741,824 bytes	(= 8,589,934,592 bits)
terabyte (TB)	→ 2^{40} bytes	= 1,099,511,627,776 bytes	(= 8,796,093,022,208 bits)

Figure 1.7   Common data storage units.

As a byte is sufficient to represent a single character, it may be instructive to think of memory capacity in terms of text. A kilobyte is capable of storing more than 1,000 characters of text (e.g., a few paragraphs), a megabyte more than one million characters of text (e.g., a book), a gigabyte more than one billion characters of text (e.g., a small library), and a terabyte more than one trillion characters of text (e.g., a large book repository). Although these capacities may seem large with respect to text, storing other types of data can require extensive memory. For example, a high-resolution photograph might require several megabytes of storage, the audio track of a single song as much as 50 megabytes, and a full-length video perhaps gigabytes.

Although the von Neumann architecture portrays computer memory as a single component, modern computers use a combination of memory types, each with its own performance and cost characteristics. The memory technologies that enable the fastest transfer of bits to and from the CPU are those that use electronic circuitry, where 1 and 0 are represented as the presence or absence of voltage over wires. *Cache* and *RAM* (short for Random Access Memory) are examples of this type of electronic memory. Cache memory, which is usually built into the CPU chip itself, utilizes high-speed circuitry to provide extremely fast access to data. RAM memory, which is packaged on separate chips, communicates with the CPU using lower-speed circuitry; thus, data stored in RAM cannot be accessed as quickly as data in cache, but RAM is significantly less expensive to build. Computer designers balance cost and performance by including a small amount (usually measured in kilobytes) of cache for storing critical data and a larger amount (usually measured in megabytes) of RAM for storing additional data.

Cache and RAM together form a computer's *main memory* (or *primary memory*), holding any and all data that the CPU is actively using. Although main memory is crucial in that its data can be accessed very quickly, it is expensive in comparison to other technologies. In addition, main memory is *volatile*, meaning that it requires a constant flow of electricity to maintain its stored values. When you turn off a computer, the values stored in cache and RAM are lost. Thus, computers require *secondary memory*, which is less expensive and can provide permanent storage. Secondary memory comes in a variety of technologies. A *hard disk* is a metal platter that stores bits as magnetized and nonmagnetized spots. The disk rotates under a sensor, which detects the magnetized spots and interprets them as bits. Although this technology is considerably slower than that of memory built from circuitry, hard-disk storage is much less expensive and can retain data without power. A hard disk is capable of permanently storing vast amounts of information (usually measured in gigabytes), which can be transferred into main memory when needed.

CDs, DVDs, and flash drives are examples of inexpensive, portable secondary memory. A *CD* (*Compact Disk*) is a metal disk that stores up to 700MB of data as patterns on its reflective surface. Using *CD-ROM* (*Compact Disk—Read Only Memory*) technology, the patterns are burned onto the surface of the disk with a laser and therefore cannot be overwritten. Using *CD-RW* (*Compact Disk—ReWritable*) technology, patterns are formed in a photosensitive coating on the surface of the disk, allowing data to be overwritten repeatedly. *DVD* disks appear similar to CDs, but are able to store up to 8.5GB of data due to higher-density storage and more advanced compression algorithms. The most common DVD format, *DVD+RW*, allows for reading and repeated writing to the disk. Flash drives come in a variety of forms, including the thumb-sized sticks that are commonly referred to as memory sticks or thumb drives. They store data as electrical charges in a series of memory "cells" made up of non-volatile electronic circuitry. Flash drives connect to the computer

| RAM chips | Hard disk | Flash drive | Compact disk (CD) |

Figure 1.8 Various types of memory.

using a standard *USB* (*Universal Serial Bus*) interface, and may hold anywhere from 512MB to 320GB of data.

Input/Output Devices (I/O)

Clearly, a computer is not very useful if it is not able to communicate with people or other computers. *Input devices* allow the computer to receive data and instructions from an external source, such as a person entering commands at a keyboard. Examples of input devices are keyboards, mice, track pads, microphones, and scanners. Similarly, *output devices* allow the computer to display or broadcast its results. Examples of output devices are monitors, printers, and speakers. Devices that enable the computer to communicate with other computers are both input and output devices. Examples include modems, Ethernet adapters, and wireless networking adapters. (See Chapter 10 for more details on networking.)

Technical Details

Each example computer system described in Figure 1.2 contains and/or supports the full range of memory types, from cache and RAM down to a hard drive and CD drive. The primary differences between the systems are the amount of each memory type they contain and some technical details.

- System 2 contains eight times as much cache (512KB vs. 4MB) and twice as much RAM (4GB vs. 8GB) than System 1 does. As main memory is used to store active data, System 2 will provide higher performance for users processing large amounts of information or running multiple programs simultaneously.

- Similarly, System 2 contains more than 3 times the hard-disk space that System 1 does, which means that System 2 can permanently store much larger amounts of information.

- Both systems contain DVD+/–RW drives, which are able to read and write DVD disks (as well as older CD disks).

Input and output technology is constantly evolving, making it easier for users to interact with computers and for computers to interact with one another. For example, the introduction of the mouse as an input device was key to the popularization of personal computers in the 1980s. Similarly, improvements in flat-screen technology enabled smaller and lighter laptop computers to become affordable in the 1990s. Today, wireless-networking technology is becoming prevalent, allowing users to access email and the Web through cellular phones and other handheld devices (Figure 1.9).

Figure 1.9 Apple iPhone and Blackberry cellular phone.

Technical Details

Each example computer system in Figure 1.2 includes an assortment of input/output devices, including a keyboard and mouse for input, a screen and speakers for output, and an Ethernet adapter for network communications.

- The term multifunction keyboard refers to the fact that, in addition to standard typewriter keys, the keyboard includes special keys (e.g., F1, Print, Home) that provide shortcuts for performing various functions.

- An optical mouse uses a laser mechanism—as opposed to a roller—in order to control pointer movements on the screen. Optical mice tend to be easier to use and require less maintenance than mechanical mice.

- The keyboard and mouse for System 1 connect to the computer directly through wires that attach to the USB interface. In contrast, the keyboard and mouse for System 2 are wireless, transmitting information to and from the computer using a radio signal.

- The size of a display screen is measured diagonally, which means that the screen for System 1 is 20 inches from top-left corner to bottom-right corner. System 2 provides a larger 24-inch screen.

- Both systems include an Ethernet adapter to allow the computer to connect to a local network via a cable. Ethernet is a popular technology for connecting computers into a small-scale network, with connection speeds of 10Mbits, 100Mbits, or 1000Mbits per second, depending on the wiring used. In addition, System 2 includes an integrated wireless card and antenna to allow the computer to connect to a wireless network (see Chapter 10 for more details).

Software

Whereas **hardware** encompasses the physical components of the computer, **software** refers to the programs that execute on the hardware. A software program is a collection of instructions for the computer (more specifically, the CPU) to carry out in order to complete some task. For example, word processors such as Microsoft Word and Corel® WordPerfect® contain instructions for creating and managing documents; graphics programs such as Adobe® Photoshop® and Flash contain instructions for creating and displaying graphical images; and Web browsers such as Microsoft Internet

Explorer® and Mozilla Firefox® contain instructions for accessing and displaying Web pages. Programs such as these are known as *applications software*, each being designed to carry out tasks within a particular application area, such as word processing, graphical design, or Web access. Since computers are used in many diverse application areas, it is not surprising that a wide variety of applications software is available.

Operating Systems

In contrast to applications software, *systems software* manages the resources and behavior of the computer itself. The largest and most integral systems software stored on a computer is its *operating system*, a collection of programs that controls how the CPU, memory, and I/O devices work together to execute programs. When a computer is turned on, or *booted*, a small part of the operating system is automatically loaded into memory. In turn, it loads other components of the operating system, which then execute continuously in the background to control the workings of the computer.

The most critical functionality of the computer is controlled by the component of the operating system known as its *kernel*. The kernel manages the CPU's operation, controlling how data and instructions are loaded from memory and accessed by the CPU. Most modern computers are *multitasking* machines, meaning that more than one program can reside in main memory at the same time, sharing the CPU's resources. For example, a personal computer user might perform several tasks simultaneously, such as downloading mail, viewing a Web page, and listening to music. By switching control of the CPU back and forth between active programs at a very fast rate, the kernel can produce the appearance of simultaneous execution. In addition to controlling the flow of programs and data between the CPU and memory, the kernel also coordinates other hardware components, allowing software applications to access memory and interact with the input/output devices. This allows a program being executed by the CPU to receive input from a keyboard, fetch data from a hard drive, display results on a screen, and even print the results to a laser printer.

Other components of the operating system perform specialized tasks that allow the computer to function. The *file system* manages the computer's memory, organizing storage into files and directories (or folders). A *file* is a document that stores information, such as text (e.g., a term paper), an image (e.g., a picture of your family), sound (e.g., a song), or a program (e.g., a Web browser). The file system component of the operating systems keeps track of where individual files are stored so that they can be accessed when needed. To make storage and retrieval easier for the user, memory is usually divided into directories (or folders). A *directory* is a collection of files that are organized together and labeled with a common name. For example, a student in an English class might place all of her term papers in a single directory and name it "Term Papers," so that she can easily locate any particular paper. Directories are hierarchical in nature, meaning that a directory can store other directories, as well as files. Thus, the student could organize all of her schoolwork in a hierarchical structure by creating a directory for each class and then adding subdirectories for papers and assignments within each class directory.

To make interacting with the computer easier for the user, most operating systems—including Microsoft Windows, Mac OS, and Linux—provide a *graphical user interface* (*GUI*). A GUI (pronounced *gooey*) uses intuitive, visual elements to simplify the process of viewing files and executing programs. Although their organization and appearance may differ, most modern GUIs have similar features and behaviors. Programs, directories, and files are represented as *icons*—small pictures that convey some aspect of the element they symbolize. By pointing the mouse and clicking on a program or file icon, the user can obtain information about or perform operations on that program or file. For example, the Mac OS X operating system uses a stamp icon (Figure 1.10) to represent its email application, whereas Microsoft Windows 7 uses an envelope icon (Figure 1.11). When a user clicks on one of these icons, the operating system opens the associated program, allowing the user to type and view email messages. In both GUIs, directories are represented as

Figure 1.10 Example GUI from Mac OS X. (Copyright © 2010 Apple Inc. All rights reserved.)

icons that look like folders, as a directory organizes files in the same way that a cardboard folder organizes papers.

By clicking the mouse on a folder icon, the user can open that directory and view its contents in a separate window. *Windows* represent separate work spaces that can be active at the same time, displaying files or executing programs. The Mac OS X screen in Figure 1.10 shows two different

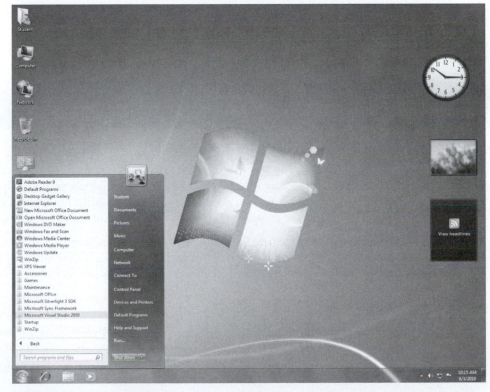

Figure 1.11 Example GUI from Microsoft Windows 7. (© 2009 Microsoft Corporation. All Rights Reserved. Courtesy of Mary Boucher.)

windows: a Finder windows for viewing files in a directory (labeled `davereed`) and a TextEdit window for editing a file (labeled `Preface.txt`). The Windows 7 screen in Figure 1.11 shows only one window: the Start window that lists common programs and directories (labeled by the user name `Student`). Most GUIs also use ***pull-down menus*** of commands, which allow the user to identify and select common commands easily. For example, Figure 1.10 shows a menu of commands across the top of the screen, with headings such as `TextEdit,  File`, and `Edit`. When the user clicks on one of these headings, a list of commands appears from which the user can select. In Figure 1.10, the commands associated with file manipulation in TextEdit are shown.

Internet and the Web

Chapter 3 will describe the history and underlying structure of the Internet and the World Wide Web. However, because you will begin developing Web pages in Chapter 2, a brief overview is worthwhile at this point.

Despite a common misconception, the Internet and the World Wide Web are not the same thing. The Internet is a vast, international network of computers. In the same way that an interstate highway crosses state borders and links cities, the Internet crosses geographic borders and links computers. The physical connections may vary from high-speed dedicated cables (such as cable-modem connections) to slow but inexpensive phone lines, but the effect is that a person sitting at a computer in Omaha, Nebraska (or wherever), is able to share information and communicate with a computer in Osaka, Japan (or wherever) (Figure 1.12). The Internet traces its roots back to 1969, when the first long-distance network was established to connect computers at the University of California at Los Angeles (UCLA), the University of California at Santa Barbara (UCSB), the Stanford Research Institute (SRI), and the University of Utah. Throughout the 1970s and 1980s, the network that would eventually be known as the Internet grew steadily; however, its use was limited primarily to government and academic institutions until the development of the World Wide Web in the 1990s.

Technical Details

Each example computer system in Figure 1.2 is packaged with the Microsoft Windows 7 operating system and a suite of applications software.

- System 1 comes with the Home version of Windows 7, which provides basic functionality; System 2 comes with the Professional version, which has additional features such as automatic backup tools and backward compatibility with many Windows XP programs.

- Both systems come with Internet Explorer, the Web browser freely distributed by Microsoft. As you will learn in the next section, a Web browser is a program that allows a user to view documents, images, and audio recordings from computers across the world.

- System 1 comes with Microsoft Works 9, a suite of basic programs for word processing, spreadsheets, and presentations; System 2 comes with Microsoft Office 2007, a high-powered suite of applications software that includes Word (word processing), Excel (spreadsheets), PowerPoint (presentations), and Access (databases).

- Both systems come with McAfee Security Center, a network security application that guards against viruses and other malicious software.

Figure 1.12   Internet users around the world.

Whereas the Internet is made up of hardware (computers and the connections that allow them to communicate), the World Wide Web is a collection of software that spans the Internet and enables the interlinking of documents and resources (Figure 1.13). The basic idea for the Web was proposed in 1989 by Tim Berners-Lee of the European Laboratory for Particle Physics (CERN). In order to allow distant researchers to share information more easily, Berners-Lee designed a system through which documents—even those containing multimedia elements, such as images and sound clips— could be interlinked over the Internet. Through the use of well-defined rules, or ***protocols***, that define how pages are formatted, documents could be shared across networks on various types of computers, allowing researchers to disseminate their research broadly. With the introduction of easy-to-use

THINK:

Internet is *hardware*
  • consists of computers around the world and the communications links that connect them

World Wide Web is *software*
  • consists of Web pages, images, sound files, etc., and the software that stores and retrieves these files

Figure 1.13   Internet = hardware, Web = software.

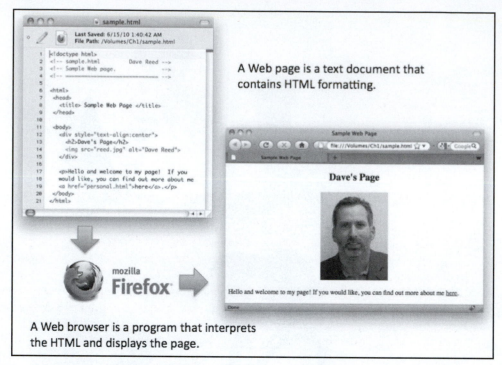

Figure 1.14 A Web browser interprets HTML instructions and formats text in a page. (Mozilla Firefox® is a registered trademark of Mozilla.org. All Rights Reserved.)

graphical browsers for viewing documents in the mid-1990s the Web became accessible to a broader public, resulting in the World Wide Web of today.

Web Browsers and Servers

A **Web page** is nothing more than a text document that contains additional formatting information in a language called **HTML** (**HyperText Markup Language**). As you will see in Chapter 2, all you need to create a Web page is a simple text editor and familiarity with the HTML language. To view a Web page in which HTML formatting is properly applied, however, you need a special kind of computer program called a **Web browser**. The job of a Web browser is to access a Web page, interpret the HTML formatting information, and display the formatted page accordingly (see Figure 1.14). The two most popular browsers on the market today are Microsoft Internet Explorer and Mozilla Firefox. Most modern computers are sold with one or both of these browsers already installed.

What makes the Web the "World Wide" Web is that, rather than being limited to a single computer, pages instead can be distributed to computers all across the Internet. A **Web server** is an Internet-enabled computer that executes software for providing access to certain Web documents. When you request a Web page, either by typing its name in your browser's Address box or by clicking a link, the browser sends a request over the Internet to the appropriate server. The server locates the specified page and sends it back to your computer.

Web Addresses

Web pages require succinct and specific names so that users can identify them and browsers can locate them. For this purpose, each page is assigned a **Uniform Resource Locator**, or **URL**. For example, the home page for this book has the following address, or URL:

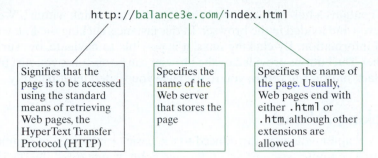

A URL begins with the protocol prefix `http://`, which specifies that the HyperText Transfer Protocol should be used in communications between the browser and server. Additional details on how the HTTP protocol works are provided in Chapter 3. The rest of the URL specifies the location of the desired page. Immediately following `http://` is the server name, identifying the Web server on which the page is stored followed by the file name. If the Web pages are organized into directories on the server, then the file name may be further broken down into components, based on the directory structure. For example, `http://balance3e.com/Images/reed.jpg` refers to the image file named `reed.jpg`, that is stored in the `Images` directory on the Web server `balance3e.com`.

Often, a user need not type every portion of a Web page's full URL. When using most browsers, if you omit the protocol prefix, then `http://` is assumed. Also, if the page name is omitted from the end of the URL, then the default name `index.html` is assumed. For this reason, Web designers often name home pages `index.html` so that users need to remember only the file's location, rather than its full name. Thus, the link to the book's home page provided earlier in this section can be written as:

```
balance3e.com
```

Accessing Local Pages

As you develop your own Web pages, you will most likely want to store them locally (on a disk or on the hard drive of your computer) while you are working on them. To load a local page into your Web browser, select `Open` under the `File` menu then browse to select the desired file. Alternatively, if you know the exact location of the file, you can enter the full directory path for the file directly in the Address box (Figure 1.15).

As the sample page demonstrates, Web pages can contain more than just text. This page includes an image (a picture) and a hyperlink. A *hyperlink* (or *link*, for short) represents a connection to another page and is usually displayed in a Web page as underlined, colored text. For example, the sample

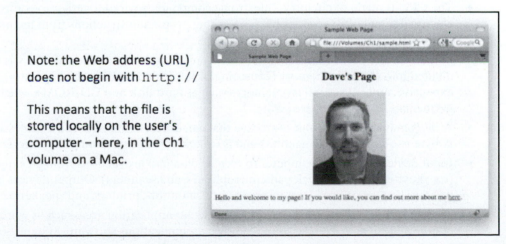

Figure 1.15 The browser Address box.

page contains a link labeled *here*. When a user clicks a link within a Web page, the connected page is retrieved and loaded in the browser. In this instance, clicking the link will load a separate page of personal information. By clicking links, it is possible to navigate, or "surf," the Web from one page to another. The buttons provided by the browser can be useful as you surf from page to page. For example, the Back button will return you to the page you visited most recently.

Looking Ahead...

In this chapter, you were introduced to the basic terminology of computers. Using the specifications of actual computer systems as a reference point, you learned the distinction between hardware and software and gained a basic understanding of how computers are organized. As you expand on this knowledge in subsequent chapters, you will revisit many of these concepts in greater depth. For example, Chapter 6 presents computers from a historical perspective and overviews the evolution of modern computer design. Chapter 8 emphasizes the software aspects of computing, discussing algorithms and their formalization as computer programs. Chapters 14 and 16 delve into the internal workings of computer hardware, focusing on the mechanisms of the CPU and how computer components are designed and manufactured.

The last section of this chapter introduced the World Wide Web, providing a level of understanding sufficient for accessing information on the Web. In the next chapter, you will advance to the next stage by learning how to create your own Web pages using the HTML language. The material in Chapter 2 is presented in a hands-on, tutorial style, so you will be encouraged to apply new concepts to the actual development of a Web page, which you may then display to the world.

Chapter Summary

- A computer is a device that receives, stores, and processes information.

- The term hardware refers to the physical components of the computer, such as the monitor, keyboard, hard drive, etc. Software refers to the programs that execute (i.e., run) on the computer, carrying out tasks such as word processing or accessing the Web.

- Virtually all modern computers have the same underlying structure, known as the von Neumann architecture. The three essential components are input/output devices, memory, and the central processing unit (CPU).

- The CPU is made of circuitry—electronic components wired together to control the flow of electrical signals. It is responsible for fetching program instructions from memory and executing those instructions.

- Memory is the part of the computer that stores programs and data. Memory is commonly divided into (1) main memory (consisting of RAM and cache), which is fast, volatile and expensive; and (2) secondary memory (such as hard disk and CD-ROM), which is slow but permanent and inexpensive.

- A bit (binary digit) is a unit of storage that can differentiate between 2 values, e.g., 0 and 1. A byte is a collection of eight bits and is sufficient for representing 256 different values.

- Input devices allow the computer to receive data and instructions from an external source (e.g., keyboards, mice, track pads, microphones, and scanners). Output devices allow the computer to display or broadcast its results (e.g., monitors, printers, and speakers).

- Programs that carry out tasks within a particular application area, such as word processing, graphical design, or Web access, are known as applications software. Systems software manages the resources and behavior of the computer itself.

- An operating system is a collection of systems software that controls how the CPU, memory, and input/output devices work together.

- The Internet is hardware—a vast, international network of computers that traces its roots back to the 1960s. The World Wide Web is a collection of software that spans the Internet and enables the interlinking of documents and resources.

- A Web page is a text document that contains additional formatting information in a language called HTML (HyperText Markup Language). Web pages are stored on computers known as Web servers, and viewed with programs known as Web browsers.

- A Web address, or Uniform Resource Locator (URL), uniquely identifies the Web server and location of a page so that it can be accessed by a browser.

Review Questions

1. TRUE or FALSE? In order to be classified as a "computer," a device must have a keyboard and display screen.

2. TRUE or FALSE? A bus is a collection of wires that carry information as electrical signals between the hardware components of a computer.

3. TRUE or FALSE? As computer programs can be complex and difficult to write, they are known as "hardware."

4. TRUE or FALSE? A bit is a unit of data that corresponds to one of two potential values (commonly written as 0 and 1).

5. TRUE or FALSE? A kilobyte of storage is $2^{10} = 1,024$ bytes, where a byte is a collection of 8 bits.

6. TRUE or FALSE? A hard disk is classified as volatile memory, because it requires a constant power supply in order to retain its information.

7. TRUE or FALSE? Keyboards and mice are examples of computer input devices.

8. TRUE or FALSE? A directory is a collection of files that are organized together and labeled with a common name.

9. TRUE or FALSE? The World Wide Web was developed in the early 1970s, shortly after the creation of the Internet.

10. TRUE or FALSE? A Web browser is an example of applications software.

11. Describe the difference between hardware and software and identify two examples of each.

12. Describe the three essential components of a computer that make up the von Neumann architecture. How do these components work together to produce a machine that can be programmed to complete different tasks?

13. Modern computers integrate several different types of memory, such as cache, RAM, hard disk, and flash drive. Why are different types of memory used, as opposed to the exclusive use of a particular technology? What would be the drawbacks, for example, of using only cache memory, or only hard disk?

14. Computer memory is usually grouped in bytes, which consist of 8 bits each. How many different values can be represented using a byte? How many different values can be represented using two bytes?

15. The Intel Core 2 Duo is an example of a processor, or CPU, as are the Intel Celeron and AMD Athlon. List the two main tasks that the CPU performs in controlling the computer's workings and provide a short explanation of each.

16. In what units are CPU speeds measured, and what does this measurement unit refer to? If one computer has a 2GHz Celeron processor and another has a 2GHz AMD Athlon processor, does that imply they will be able to execute the same program in the same amount of time? Explain.

17. Windows 7 is an example of an operating system, as are the Mac OS and Linux. List the three main tasks that the operating system performs in controlling the computer's resources and behavior. Provide a short explanation of each.

18. Describe three elements common to a graphical user interface (GUI). How do these elements make it easier for a user to interact with the computer?

19. Suppose you are shopping for a personal computer that you plan to use exclusively for email and Web access. Which would be a better use of your limited funds—a faster CPU or a larger hard drive? Why?

20. It has been said that the Internet could exist without the Web, but the Web couldn't exist without the Internet. Why is this true?

21. What is a Web server, and what role does it play in the World Wide Web?

22. Consider the following fictitious URL: `http://www.acme.com/products/info.html`. What does each part of this URL (separated by slashes) specify?

References

Berners-Lee, Tim, Mark Fischetti, and Michael L. Derouzos. *Weaving the Web: The Original Design and Ultimate Destiny of the World Wide Web*. New York: HarperBusiness, 2000.

Capron, H.L., and J. A. Johnson. *Computers: Tools for an Information Age*, 8th ed. Upper Saddle River, NJ: Prentice Hall, 2003.

Comer, Douglas E. *The Internet Book: Everything you need to know about computer networking and how the Internet works*, 4th ed. Upper Saddle River, NJ: Prentice Hall, 2006.

LaMorte, Christopher, and John Lilly. "Computers: History and Development." *Jones Telecommunications and Multimedia Encyclopedia*, 1999.

Malone, Michael. *The Microprocessor: A Biography*. New York: Springer-Verlag, 1995.

Petzold, Charles. *Code: The Hidden Language of Computer Hardware and Software*. Redmond, WA: Microsoft Press, 1999.

Silberschatz, Abraham, Peter Galvin, and Greg Gagne. *Operating System Concepts*, 8th ed. Hoboken, NJ: John Wiley & Sons, 2008.

HTML and Web Pages

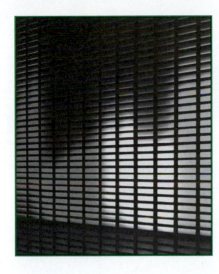

This chapter uses narrative, examples, and hands-on exercises to introduce programming concepts and Web development skills.

The goal of the Web was to be a shared information space through which people (and machines) could communicate. The intent was that this space should span from a private information system to a public information, from high value carefully checked and designed material, to off-the-cuff ideas which make sense only to a few people and never be read again.

Tim Berners-Lee
The World Wide Web: Past, Present and Future, 1996

If this were a traditional science, Berners-Lee would win a Nobel Prize. What he's done is that significant.

Eric Schmidt, CEO of Novell

The World Wide Web is probably the most pervasive and visible aspect of computing today. Initially designed as a way for researchers to share documents over the Internet, the Web has evolved into a widespread, dynamic medium for communication and commerce. Using a program called a Web browser, people can instantly access documents (commonly referred to as Web pages) stored on computers around the world. With just a few clicks of a mouse, Web users can read newspapers, check sports scores, send email, play interactive games, or interact with friends. In addition, the Web provides an easy-to-use interface for advertising and business transactions, as evidenced by the abundance of corporate Web addresses that appear in television and print ads.

In this chapter, we introduce the basics of Web design and its underlying language, HTML. As you read, you will gain hands-on experience by developing your own Web page, adding new features incrementally as you learn. By the end of the chapter, you will be able to join the Web community by making your Web page publicly available. This means that anyone with a Web browser and an Internet connection will be able to access the document you've created.

HTML Basics

A Web page is a text document that contains additional formatting information in a language called **HTML** (**HyperText Markup Language**). Using HTML, a Web page creator can identify various features of a page, such as a section heading, a centered table, or an image to be displayed. This information is then interpreted by a Web browser, which formats the page contents appropriately.

HTML Tags

HTML specifies formatting within a page using **tags**. In its simplest form, a tag is a word or symbol surrounded by angular brackets (<>). For example, every Web page must begin with the tag `<!doctype html>`, which specifies that the document contains HTML formatting information and that the browser should interpret the contents accordingly. The tags `<html>` and `</html>` mark the beginning and end of the page content, which is generally divided into two sections: a HEAD section, which is delimited by the tags `<head>` and `</head>`, and a BODY section, which is delimited by the tags `<body>` and `</body>`.

The HEAD section contains information that the browser uses to determine the look of the page. For now, the only information that we will place in the HEAD will be the title of the page, delimited by the tags `<title>` and `</title>`. When a browser renders the page, the text occurring between the TITLE tags is displayed in the title bar at the top of the browser window. The BODY section contains the text that will actually appear in the page.

For example, Figure 2.1 shows a simple Web page named `demo1.html`. In this example, the title of the page is "Title of the Page," which appears in the title bar of the Web browser (Figure 2.2). The text in the body, which is displayed within the browser window, is simply "Text that appears in

```
1.  <!doctype html>
2.  <!-- demo1.html                    Dave Reed -->
3.  <!-- This is a simple Web page.            -->
4.  <!-- ==================================== -->
5.
6.  <html>
7.    <head>
8.      <title> Title of the Page </title>
9.    </head>
10.
11.   <body>
12.     Text that appears in the page.
13.   </body>
14. </html>
```

Figure 2.1   A simple Web page.

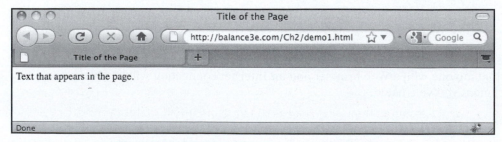

Figure 2.2   `demo1.html` rendered in a Web browser.

the page." In this and subsequent figures, HTML tags are highlighted in blue to differentiate them from text that appears in the rendered page.

HTML Elements

Most HTML tags come in pairs, with the first tag marking the beginning of a section and the second tag (which is identical to the first except for the slash /) marking the end of the section. For this reason, we will often refer to the first and second tags as *opening* and *closing tags*, respectively. For example, `<title>` is the opening tag for the TITLE and `</title>` is the closing tag. ***HTML elements***, which form the building blocks of Web pages, are made up of text and the tags that specify the text's role or purpose within the page. For example, `<title>Title of the Page </title>` can be referred to as a TITLE element, because it represents the piece of the Web page that specifies a title. Likewise, the HTML element that begins with the `<html>` opening tag and ends with the `</html>` closing tag itself contains HEAD and BODY elements.

Although most HTML tags come in pairs, some do not. For example, the `<!doctype html>` tag does not need a closing tag because the single tag suffices to identify the content type of the document. As such, it serves as a complete HTML element by itself. Similarly, a ***comment element***, or ***comment*** for short, is defined by a single tag, which begins with `<!--` and ends with `-->`. For example, the Web page in Figure 2.1 contains three comment elements, occurring immediately after the DOC-TYPE tag (lines 2–4). You may think of comments as notes to yourself, or to some future Web developer who might review your HTML text. By placing information such as the file name, last modification date, and general purpose of the page in comments, you ensure proper credit and simplify the process of updating or modifying the page. As Figure 2.2 shows, comments are ignored by the browser, so this additional text does not clutter up the page when it is rendered. You should always place a sequence of comments at the top of any HTML document you create to identify the file name, author, and purpose of the page.

Numerous software tools on the market allow you to design and create elaborate Web pages. To create simple pages, however, all you really need is a text editor. A ***text editor*** is a program in which you can type and edit text, then save that text in a file. Common examples are NotePad and WordPad, which come free with Microsoft Windows, and TextEdit, which comes free on Apple computers. Many software companies also offer free or low-cost text editors that provide special features, such as automatic indentation or color coding of HTML elements. Appendix B includes instructions on using some of these common editors.

To develop a Web page, all you need to do is create a text file containing the desired HTML elements. Then a browser can be used to render the page. To render a file stored locally using Internet Explorer, you select `Open` under the `File` menu and browse to select the desired file; using Mozilla Firefox, you select `Open File` under the `File` menu and select the desired file. Appendix A includes more detailed instructions on opening and viewing files in a browser.

Of course, a Web page rarely looks exactly the way its designer intended the first time it is displayed by a browser. For example, you may make a mistake in entering the contents of the page, or you may simply decide that the page would look better with different formatting. Thus, Web page development usually involves having two windows open at the same time—one running a text editor, which allows the creator to update the page contents, and another running a Web browser, which shows the creator the latest version of the rendered page. After each revision to the page in the editor, you must reload the page (i.e., by clicking on the browser's Reload icon) to view the changes.

EXERCISE 2.1

Create a simple home page for yourself using a text editor. Your page should have a title, such as "Dave's Home Page," and should contain some basic information about you. Save your page to a file under the name `index.html`.

Document Formatting

You may have found that, when you displayed your home page, the text didn't appear in the browser window exactly as you typed it. This is inevitable, as the size of the browser window in which the page is rendered may vary. The lines you typed might be too long to fit in the window or might leave wasted white space at the end. To ensure that Web page text looks attractive in various window sizes, the browser automatically adjusts the length of lines to fit the current window, wrapping text to the next line as needed. You may also have noted that, when the browser performs this automatic formatting, it ignores any blank lines, extra spaces, and tabs in your text. When displayed in the browser, any consecutive spaces, tabs, or blank lines will appear as a single space.

Text Spacing

Despite browsers' automatic formatting features, Web designers can control some text spacing by using additional HTML tags. A P element specifies text that is to be treated as a paragraph. Text enclosed within the opening tag <p> and the closing tag </p> will be displayed starting on a new line that is preceded by a blank line. If you wish to break text explicitly without inserting a blank line, you can place a BR element in the text. Unlike the paragraph element, which has opening and closing tags (because there is a logical beginning and end to the paragraph), a BR element is defined by a single tag: <br>. Text that follows a <br> tag will be displayed starting on a new line. In addition, if you don't want to begin a new line but would like to force consecutive spaces in the text, you can do so by inserting the special symbol   in the page. In general, a **special symbol** is a word in HTML that has special meaning to the browser when it renders the page. For example, the special symbol   represents a nonbreaking space. When a Web page is rendered by a browser, each occurrence of the special symbol   is displayed as a space, no matter where it appears in the text. Figure 2.3 demonstrates the use of tags and the   symbol to control spacing (with the page rendering shown in Figure 2.4).

```
1.  <!doctype html>
2.  <!-- demo2.html                          Dave Reed -->
3.  <!-- This page demos text spacing and layout. -->
4.  <!-- ======================================= -->
5.
6.  <html>
7.   <head>
8.    <title> Demo of text layout </title>
9.   </head>
10.
11.  <body>
12.   <p>
13.     Here is a paragraph
14.     that is broken across <br>
15.     two lines.
16.   </p>
17.
18.   <p>
19.        Here is another paragraph. <br>
20.     This time, the first line is indented two spaces.
21.   </p>
22.  </body>
23. </html>
```

Figure 2.3 A Web page that demonstrates text spacing and layout.

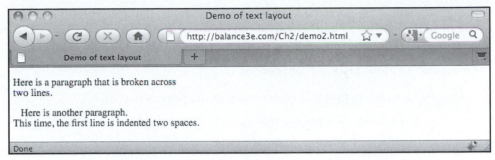

Figure 2.4 `demo2.html` rendered in a Web browser.

Common errors to avoid...

It is important to note that HTML tags are sequences of characters that are placed in a file along with the text they are intended to format. If you enter a malformed tag, omitting either the opening or closing braces, the tag will not be recognized as HTML and will be displayed as plain text within the page. For example, the text

```
<p>Hello, I'm Dave <br
My hobbies include hiking and baseball.</p>
```

would be displayed as

```
Hello, I'm Dave <br My hobbies include hiking and baseball.
```

By contrast, a browser will typically ignore a well-formed tag whose name is misspelled. For example, if you mistakenly type <bl> instead of the intended <br>, the tag will be ignored, and nothing will appear in its place in the page.

EXERCISE 2.2

Add additional paragraphs to your home page. If you are having trouble thinking of things to write about yourself, consider writing one paragraph that provides biographical data, another that describes your hobbies, and a third listing some favorite books or movies. Use <p></p>, <br>, and   appropriately to make your page readable and attractive.

Headings and Alignment

In a large document, it is often useful to divide the text into sections and then provide each with a heading describing the content that follows. HTML includes special tags that enable Web designers to specify headings of various sizes. For example, text enclosed between the tags <h1> and </h1> is displayed in large, bold letters above the text that follows it. The tags <h2> and </h2> can be used to display a heading in slightly smaller letters, <h3> and </h3> are used for even smaller letters, and so on down to <h6> and </h6>. To divide different parts of a document further, designers can separate sections with a horizontal line using the <hr> tag (where HR stands for horizontal rule).

By default, all text in a Web page is displayed left-justified on the page. This means that each heading, paragraph, or line of text begins at the page's left edge. However, it is possible to align text so that it is centered or even right-justified by including a STYLE attribute in the appropriate opening tag. In general, an **attribute** is an additional property that can be assigned to an HTML element as part of its tag. The STYLE attribute can be added to an opening tag to specify the alignment of that particular element. For example, the opening tag

```
<h2 style="text-align:center">
```

specifies a heading that will be centered in the page, whereas

```
<p style="text-align:right">
```

specifies a paragraph that will be right-justified in the page. Figure 2.5 demonstrates the alignment of headings and paragraphs within a page (with the page rendering shown in Figure 2.6). This page also incorporates DIV tags, which can be used to group multiple elements into a single page division. The advantage of arranging multiple elements inside a set of DIV tags is that you can format all enclosed elements at once, as opposed to formatting each individually. In this example, a heading and a paragraph are grouped together and right-justified using DIV tags (lines 28 through 34).

```
1.  <!doctype html>
2.  <!-- demo3.html                        Dave Reed -->
3.  <!-- This page demos headings and alignment. -->
4.  <!-- ======================================= -->
5.
6.  <html>
7.   <head>
8.     <title> Demo of headings </title>
9.   </head>
10.
11.  <body>
12.    <h1>Left-Justified Big Heading</h1>
13.    <p>
14.      left-justified text <br>
15.      and more left-justified text
16.    </p>
17.
18.    <hr>
19.
20.    <h2 style="text-align:center">Centered Medium Heading</h2>
21.    <p style="text-align:center">
22.      centered text <br>
23.      and more centered text
24.    </p>
25.
26.    <hr>
27.
28.    <div style="text-align:right">
29.      <h3>Right-Justified Small Heading</h3>
30.      <p>
31.        right-justified text <br>
32.        and more right-justified text
33.      </p>
34.    </div>
35.  </body>
36. </html>
```

Figure 2.5 A Web page that demonstrates the alignment of headings and text.

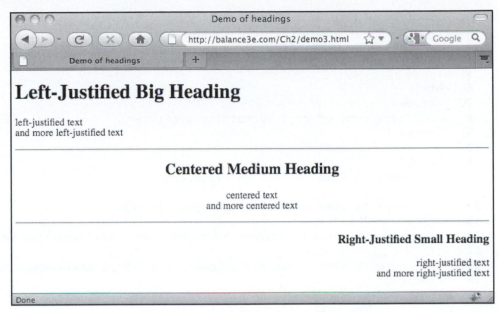

Figure 2.6 demo3.html rendered in a Web browser.

EXERCISE 2.3

Divide your home page into sections. Use a large heading (delimited by H1 tags) to list your name so that it is centered at the top of the page, followed by a horizontal line. For each subsequent text section, use a smaller heading—for example, H2 or H3. At least one section of your page should contain multiple paragraphs.

Font Formatting

In printing terminology, a **font** defines a particular typeface (such as Times New Roman, Courier, or Arial) and size (such as 11 pt. or 12 pt.) used to display characters in a document. In general, Web page creators have limited control over the fonts that are used to display their pages. Browsers allow the user to specify his or her own font preferences by selecting default fonts for viewing pages, so one browser may display a page very differently than another would. There is some font formatting that can be forced in a page, however. For example, text enclosed in the tags <b></b> will appear in bold, <i></i> indicate text in italics, <big></big> indicate text in a slightly larger font, and <small></small> indicate text in a slightly smaller font. In addition, you can change the color of text by enclosing it in SPAN tags of the following form:

```
<span style="color:DESIRED_COLOR"> ... </span>
```

In general, SPAN tags serve to group a block of text together for common formatting. The STYLE attribute of the form `style="color:DESIRED_COLOR"` specifies the color of the text within the SPAN tags, where DESIRED_COLOR is a color name such as `red`, `blue`, `darkblue`, or `purple`. A list of the most commonly used color names in HTML is provided in Appendix C. Figure 2.7 demonstrates text formatting within the page (with the page rendering shown in Figure 2.8).

EXERCISE 2.4

Augment your home page by coloring some of the text and using font formatting where appropriate. For example, if you listed favorite books or movies, you could italicize their titles.

```
1.  <!doctype html>
2.  <!-- demo4.html                     Dave Reed -->
3.  <!-- This page demos font formatting.       -->
4.  <!-- ==================================== -->
5.
6.  <html>
7.   <head>
8.     <title> Demo of font formatting </title>
9.   </head>
10.
11.  <body>
12.    <p>Here is some <b>bold text</b>.</p>
13.
14.    <p>Here is some <i>italicized text</i>.</p>
15.
16.    <p>Here is some <big>bigger text</big> and <small>smaller text</small>.</p>
17.
18.    <p>Here is some <span style="color:blue">blue text</span>.</p>
19.  </body>
20.  </html>
```

Figure 2.7 A Web page that demonstrates text formatting.

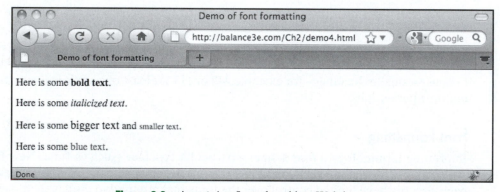

Figure 2.8 demo4.html rendered in a Web browser.

Common errors to avoid...

When specifying HTML elements with opening and closing tags, it is important to type both tags correctly. If you omit or misspell the opening tag of an element, the browser will ignore the closing tag, and no formatting will occur. On the other hand, if you specify the opening tag but forget or misspell the closing tag, the indicated formatting will continue throughout the document. For example, inexperienced programmers often forget to include the / in closing tags, which in effect specifies two opening tags. If you type <b>oops<b>, any text occurring after this tag set will appear in bold when rendered in a browser.

As previous examples have demonstrated, HTML elements can contain other elements nested inside them. For example, all HTML elements that format text in the page are nested inside the BODY element (<body>...</body>), which is itself nested inside <html> ...</html>. When nesting HTML elements, be sure that the order in which you specify the closing tags is exactly opposite to that in which you specified the opening tags. Misordering tags in a nested element, such as <b><i>oops</b></i>, is technically incorrect and may cause the browser to display the text in unintended ways.

In programming terminology, any error related to the format of a statement (such as a misspelled tag name or unmatched opening and closing tags) is known as a *syntax error*. In general, the browser will ignore any HTML syntax error it encounters and continue rendering the page contents as best it can.

Hypertext and Multimedia

Although it is always possible to retrieve a Web page by entering its URL into the browser's Address box, most pages are not accessed this way. The defining feature of the Web is its ability to link pages together through hyperlinks. A *hyperlink*, or *link* for short, is an element on a Web page, usually displayed as underlined text, which connects the page to another page or online resource. When a Web user clicks on a hyperlink, the browser loads the connected page, regardless of its physical location on the Web. Thus, by following a chain of hyperlinks, a user can explore related documents, even if the documents are stored on computers thousands of miles apart. Text that contains embedded hyperlinks is referred to as *hypertext*.

Hyperlinks

When inserting a hyperlink into a document, Web designers use the tags <a> and </a> to enclose the text that will represent the link. In this context, A is short for *anchor*, signifying that the hyperlink anchors (i.e., connects) separate documents together. The designer also must indicate the address of the page to which the link connects; this information is specified within the <a> tag via an attribute named HREF (short for Hypertext REFerence).

The general form of a hyperlink element is:

```
<a href="ADDRESS_OF_PAGE">TEXT LABEL FOR LINK</a>
```

Whatever text you type between <a> and </a> tags will appear as an underlined link when the page is rendered. If the user clicks that text, the browser will replace the current page with the page specified in the opening tag. The address listed in the HREF attribute can be either an *absolute address*, meaning that it specifies the URL of a page on the Web, or a *relative address*, meaning that it specifies a file stored in a location related to that of the Web page itself. For example, the Web page in Figure 2.9 contains three hyperlinks (with the page rendering shown in Figure 2.10). The first (spanning lines 13 and 14) uses an absolute address, specifying the URL (starting with http://) where that page can be found. When a visitor clicks the link labeled "Home Page for *A Balanced Introduction to Computer Science*," the browser will access the linked page and display it in the browser window. The second and third hyperlinks (on lines 18 and 19) use relative addresses, specifying only the file name of the desired page. Because the http:// prefix is omitted, the browser automatically assumes that this address refers to a file stored in the same directory as the current Web page.

By default, clicking on a link will cause the new page to overwrite the current page in the existing browser window. There are times, however, when it is preferable to have the new page open in a separate window so that the user can easily go back and forth between the pages. This is accomplished by adding the attribute target="_blank" to the opening A tag (line 19).

You might note that links within a Web page can appear in different colors. By default, a Web browser displays a link that has been previously visited in one color (usually purple), whereas an unvisited link appears in another color (usually blue).

EXERCISE 2.5

Add a section to your home page containing at least five hyperlinks to sites that you consider useful and/or interesting. To ensure that these hyperlinks work correctly, you should click each one and then view the linked page in your browser.

```
 1. <!doctype html>
 2. <!-- demo5.html                        Dave Reed -->
 3. <!-- This page demos hyperlinks.              -->
 4. <!-- ==================================== -->
 5.
 6. <html>
 7.   <head>
 8.     <title> Demo of hyperlinks </title>
 9.   </head>
10.
11.   <body>
12.     <p>
13.       <a href="http://balance3e.com">Home Page for
14.         <i>A Balanced Introduction to Computer Science</i></a>
15.     </p>
16.
17.     <p>
18.         Here is a <a href="local.html">local page</a> you might like. <br>
19.         Here it is <a href="local.html" target="_blank">again</a>, but
20.         opening in a different window.
21.     </p>
22.   </body>
23. </html>
```

Figure 2.9 A Web page that demonstrates hyperlinks.

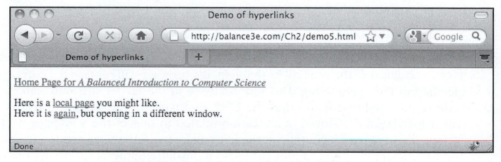

Figure 2.10 demo5.html rendered in a Web browser.

Images

So far, we have discussed ways to format text, font, and spacing within a Web page and to create links between your page and other Web resources. However, anyone who has surfed the Web realizes that pages contain much more than text and hyperlinks. The term *multimedia* refers to documents that integrate various communication media, such as text, images, movies, and sound clips. In HTML, images are loaded into a page using an <img> tag. Standard browsers have built-in capabilities for displaying images in GIF (Graphics Interchange Format), JPEG (Joint Photographic Experts Group), and PNG (Portable Network Graphics) formats, which are the most common methods of storing digital images. (The Graphics Interchange Format is the copyright property of CompuServe Incorporated. GIF is a service mark property of CompuServe Incorporated.) To render other types of image formats, the browser may require special-purpose extensions called *plug-ins*. Therefore, if you want an image to be viewable by the majority of Web users, it is advisable to limit yourself to GIF, JPEG, and PNG formats. (See Chapter 12 for more details on image formats.)

An IMG tag typically has two attributes associated with it. The SRC attribute specifies the location of the image file to be displayed, and the ALT attribute specifies alternate text that appears if the image can't be found or displayed properly. The ALT attribute is particularly crucial when a Web page is rendered by certain types of browsers, such as a text-to-speech browser for the visually impaired. Also, some browsers display the ALT text when the mouse moves over an image, enabling Web designers to provide additional context for images.

The general form of an image element is:

```
<img src="ADDRESS_OF_IMAGE" alt="TEXT_DESCRIPTION">
```

After encountering an image element when loading a Web page, the browser accesses the source file specified in the tag and displays that image in the page. As was the case with the HREF attribute for hyperlinks, the address assigned to the SRC attribute of an IMG can be either absolute (a complete URL) or relative (a file stored in a location related to that of the page). For example, the image element in Figure 2.11 (line 13) uses a relative address, specifying that the browser should display the image file named `reed.jpg` that is stored in the same directory or folder as the Web page (the page rendering is shown in Figure 2.12). Note that if the developer had chosen to store the image in a subfolder, say a dedicated folder for images named `Images`, then the source address would reflect that structure: `src="Images/reed.jpg"`.

```
1.  <!doctype html>
2.  <!-- demo6.html                    Dave Reed -->
3.  <!-- This page demos images.                -->
4.  <!-- ================================== -->
5.
6.  <html>
7.   <head>
8.     <title> Demo of images </title>
9.   </head>
10.
11.  <body>
12.    <div style="text-align:center">
13.       <img src="reed.jpg" alt="Dave Reed">
14.
15.       <p>This is a picture of the author.</p>
16.    </div>
17.  </body>
18. </html>
```

Figure 2.11 A Web page that demonstrates images.

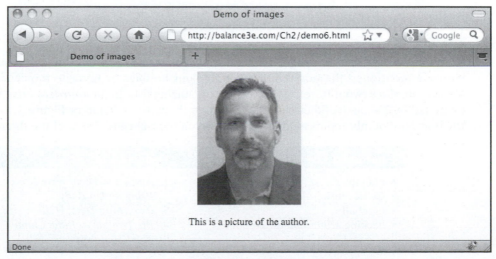

Figure 2.12 demo6.html rendered in a Web browser.

EXERCISE 2.6

Select a digital picture of your own, or choose a public-domain image from the Web that you would like to include on your Web page. You must be careful not to violate copyrights or otherwise infringe upon the rights of the owner (unless explicitly stated otherwise, you should assume that any image on the Web is private property). Once located, copy the image to your local directory (under Windows, click the right mouse button over the desired image and select Save Image from the resulting menu; under the Mac OS, click on the image while holding down the Control key, then select Save Image). After saving the image in the directory that contains `index.html`, incorporate the local image into your home page. Be sure to include alternate text for your image via the ALT attribute.

Designer Secrets

When the browser displays an image in a Web page, it will automatically adjust the page contents to fit the dimensions of the image. Thus, a small image (e.g., an icon) will take up very little space, whereas a large image (e.g., a digital photograph) will dominate the page. To adjust the size of an image in a Web page, you have two options. The first is to edit the image file itself, shrinking or expanding the image using a separate image processing program. The advantage of this approach is that the resulting image file is stored in the exact format you want. However, it requires access to the file itself, which may not be possible if the image is copyrighted or stored on a remote Web site. The second approach is to leave the image unchanged but add attributes to the IMG element to control how it is displayed. The HEIGHT and WIDTH attributes of an IMG element specify the dimensions (in *pixels*, or picture elements) that are used in displaying the image. For example, the following image would be displayed 200 pixels high and 300 pixels wide, regardless of the actual dimensions the image stored in `photo.jpg`:

```
<img src="photo.jpg" alt="My friends" height=200 width=300>
```

In general, you should be careful when resizing an image using HEIGHT and WIDTH. If you provide new dimensions that do not maintain the relative height and width of the image, the image will be distorted. For example, if you start with an image of a face that is 400 pixels high and 300 pixels wide, resizing it to 200 × 200 will flatten the face. However, resizing it to 200 × 150 will maintain the original ratio of height to width and result in an undistorted image that is half the original size.

It should be noted that adjusting the HEIGHT and WIDTH attributes of an IMG element only affects the way the image is displayed in the page. If the image is huge, say a 3,000 × 2,000–pixel photograph, the entire image (all 6 million pixels) must still be downloaded, regardless of the dimensions used for its display.

Lists

When organizing text in a page, it is often convenient to list similar items in sequence. For example, we have mentioned the possibility of listing your hobbies or favorite movies in your home page. HTML provides two different elements for organizing lists. In an ***unordered list***, individual items are preceded by bullets (solid circles), as shown on the left-hand side of Figure 2.13. In an ***ordered list***, the items are numbered in sequence, as shown on the right-hand side of the figure.

Unordered List	Ordered List
• old movies	*1. And Then There Were None*
• Celtic music	*2. Bringing Up Baby*
• baseball	*3. Crouching Tiger, Hidden Dragon*
• hacking around on the computer	*4. Big Trouble in Little China*
	5. The Usual Suspects

Figure 2.13 Examples of unordered and ordered lists.

In HTML, an unordered list is identified by the tags <ul> and </ul>, whereas an ordered list is identified by the tags <ol> and </ol>. In either type of list, the individual list items are delimited by the tags <li> and </li>. For example, the Web page in Figure 2.14 (rendered in Figure 2.15) contains list elements corresponding to the text lists in Figure 2.13.

```
1.  <!doctype html>
2.  <!-- demo7.html                                    Dave Reed -->
3.  <!-- This page demos unordered and ordered lists.          -->
4.  <!-- ================================================= -->
5.
6.  <html>
7.    <head>
8.      <title> Demo of lists </title>
9.    </head>
10.
11.   <body>
12.      <p>My Hobbies</p>
13.       <ul>
14.         <li> old movies </li>
15.         <li> Celtic music </li>
16.         <li> baseball </li>
17.         <li> hacking around on the computer </li>
18.       </ul>
19.
20.      <p>My Favorite Movies</p>
21.       <ol>
22.         <li> <i>And Then There Were None</i> </li>
23.         <li> <i>Bringing Up Baby</i> </li>
24.         <li> <i>Crouching Tiger, Hidden Dragon</i> </li>
25.         <li> <i>Big Trouble in Little China</i> </li>
26.         <li> <i>The Usual Suspects</i> </li>
27.       </ol>
28.   </body>
29. </html>
```

Figure 2.14   A Web page that demonstrates lists.

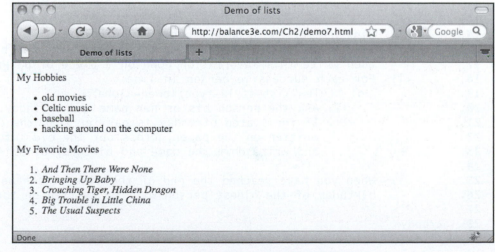

Figure 2.15   demo7.html rendered in a Web browser.

```
<ul style="list-style-type:square">       →  Items preceded by squares.
<ol style="list-style-type:lower-alpha">   →  Items preceded by lowercase
                                              letters (a, b, c, d, ...).
<ol style="list-style-type:upper-alpha">   →  Items preceded by uppercase
                                              letters (A, B, C, D, ...).
<ol style="list-style-type:lower-roman">   →  Items preceded by lowercase
                                              roman letters (i,ii,iii,iv,...).
<ol style="list-style-type:upper-roman">   →  Items preceded by uppercase
                                              roman letters (I, II, III, ...).
```

Figure 2.16 Style attributes to format lists.

Formatting Lists

By default, items in an unordered list are preceded by bullets, and items in an ordered list are numbered. However, the page designer can specify alternative formats using the STYLE attribute. Items in an unordered list will be preceded by squares, instead of bullets, if you add the attribute style="list-item-type:square" to the opening UL tag. Likewise, you can specify that an ordered list use letters or roman numerals instead of numbers to identify each list item. The style attributes that correspond to each of these formatting styles are listed in Figure 2.16.

The ability to specify an ordered list's format is especially useful when you wish to nest lists. For example, the Web page in Figure 2.17 (rendered in Figure 2.18) displays an algorithm for finding the oldest person in a room. As you will learn in Chapter 8, an *algorithm* is a step-by-step sequence of instructions for carrying out some task. In this case, the algorithm has four main steps, which appear

```
1.  <!doctype html>
2.  <!-- demo8.html                    Dave Reed -->
3.  <!-- This page demos formatted lists.       -->
4.  <!-- ==================================== -->
5.
6.  <html>
7.   <head>
8.     <title> Demo of lists </title>
9.   </head>
10.
11.  <body>
12.    <p>To find the oldest person in a room:</p>
13.
14.    <ol>
15.      <li> Line up all the people along one wall. </li>
16.      <li> Ask the first person to state his or her name and birthday,
17.           then write this information down on a piece of paper. </li>
18.      <li> For each successive person in line:
19.          <ol style="list-style-type:lower-alpha">
20.            <li> Ask the person his or her name and birthday. </li>
21.            <li> If the stated birthday is earlier than the date
22.                 written on the paper, cross out the old information
23.                 and write down the name and birthday of this person. </li>
24.          </ol> </li>
25.      <li> When you have reached the end of the line, the name and
26.           birthday of the oldest person will be written on the paper. </li>
27.    </ol>
28.  </body>
29. </html>
```

Figure 2.17 A Web page that demonstrates nested ordered lists.

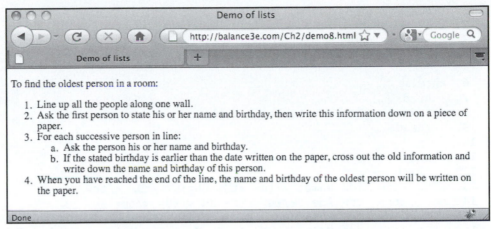

Figure 2.18 demo8.html rendered in a Web browser.

in the page as items in an ordered list. The creator of this page has broken the third step into parts "a" and "b" by nesting an ordered list (with appropriate STYLE attribute) inside the third list item.

EXERCISE 2.7

Add a list to your home page. For example, you might list your favorite CDs, your current courses, or the names of your siblings.

Tables

Although it is usually preferable to let the browser determine how text is laid out within a page, there are times when you want things to line up just so. For example, suppose that you want to display a collection of related information about a student. Aligning such data into columns can make a page more attractive and easier to read.

Name:	Chris
Age:	20
Hometown:	Chicago
Major:	Computer Science

In HTML, table elements are used to organize text and other elements into rows and columns. Elements in the same row appear on the same line when rendered by a browser (as is the case with "Name:" and "Chris" above). Elements in the same column are aligned on the left-hand side (as is the case with "Chris," "20," "Chicago," and "Computer Science"). Web designers specify a table element using the tags <table> and </table>. Individual rows in the table are identified by <tr></tr> (short for table row), and the number of columns is determined by the number of data items in the rows, as identified by <td></td> (short for table data). Every time you end one row element and begin another, the browser places the first data item in the first column of that new row. For example, the Web page in Figure 2.19 (rendered in Figure 2.20) contains a table element that displays the aligned text from our sample student information record.

As this example demonstrates, the browser automatically adjusts the width of each column to accommodate its largest entry. In this case, the width of the first column is determined by the space needed to fit the "Hometown:" entry. If the table included a fifth row containing a longer entry in the first column—say "Favorite Movie:"—then the browser would adjust the column size to fit that entry.

Table Borders

If you would like to insert borders between the rows and columns in a table, this is accomplished by adding a STYLE attribute assignment to the individual TD tags: style="border:solid". This

```
1.  <!doctype html>
2.  <!-- demo9.html                    Dave Reed -->
3.  <!-- This page demos a borderless table. -->
4.  <!-- ================================= -->
5.
6.  <html>
7.   <head>
8.     <title> Demo of tables </title>
9.   </head>
10.
11.  <body>
12.    <table>
13.       <tr> <td> Name: </td> <td> Chris </td> </tr>
14.       <tr> <td> Age: </td> <td> 20 </td> </tr>
15.       <tr> <td> Hometown: </td> <td> Chicago </td> </tr>
16.       <tr> <td> Major: </td> <td> Computer Science </td> </tr>
17.    </table>
18.  </body>
19. </html>
```

Figure 2.19   A Web page that demonstrates a borderless table.

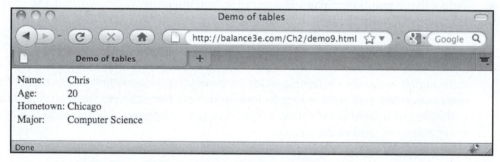

Figure 2.20   demo9.html rendered in a Web browser.

results in a solid box being drawn around the table data element when it is rendered. Adding the same STYLE attribute assignment to the opening TABLE tag will similarly draw a box around the entire table. For example, the page in Figure 2.21 (rendered in Figure 2.22) displays the same table as in Figure 2.19, except that the table and each entry is surrounded by a border.

Table Alignment

In addition to organizing text into columns, tables are useful for aligning a variety of HTML elements. For example, a common use of tables is to align an image with text that refers to it. The Web page in Figure 2.23 (rendered in Figure 2.24) contains a table with only one row. An image appears in the first column, and text appears in the second column. The result is that the text appears to the right of the image, centered vertically.

If you want to center a table in a page, you will find that adding the STYLE attribute style="text-align:center" will not suffice. Instead, it causes the text within the table to be centered in the columns. Placing the table in a DIV element with that STYLE attribute will not work either. If you want to center the entire table, you must use the somewhat odd combination style="margin-left:auto;margin-right:auto" in the opening TABLE tag.

```
1.  <!doctype html>
2.  <!-- demo10.html                Dave Reed -->
3.  <!-- This page demos a borderless table. -->
4.  <!-- ==================================== -->
5.
6.  <html>
7.   <head>
8.    <title> Demo of tables </title>
9.   </head>
10.
11.  <body>
12.   <table style="border:solid">
13.     <tr> <td style="border:solid"> Name: </td>
14.          <td style="border:solid"> Chris </td> </tr>
15.     <tr> <td style="border:solid"> Age: </td>
16.          <td style="border:solid"> 20 </td> </tr>
17.     <tr> <td style="border:solid"> Hometown: </td>
18.          <td style="border:solid"> Chicago </td> </tr>
19.     <tr> <td style="border:solid"> Major: </td>
20.          <td style="border:solid"> Computer Science </td> </tr>
21.   </table>
22.  </body>
23. </html>
```

Figure 2.21   A Web page that demonstrates a bordered table.

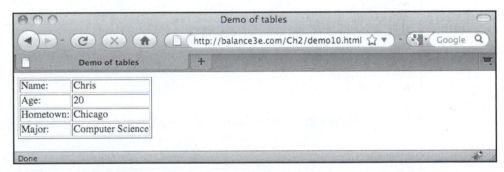

Figure 2.22   demo10.html rendered in a Web browser.

EXERCISE 2.8

Use a table to align text and/or images into rows and columns. For example, you might organize your class schedule into a table, designating a row for each class and columns for listing the course name, room number, and meeting times. Alternatively, you might align the names and email addresses of your friends into columns.

Designer Secrets

As we discussed in Chapter 1, the Web has become an important information and communication source for millions of people worldwide. When designing a Web page, it is important to keep all users in mind, especially those who might have disabilities that limit their accessibility to online content. The World Wide Web Consortium has founded a Web Accessibility Initiative to encourage the design of Web pages that are accessible to all users, including vision-impaired users who may utilize devices to read Web content aloud. In 2008, the initiative produced the *Web Content Accessibility Guidelines 2.0*, a document that provides practical advice on creating accessible Web pages (accessible online at http://www.w3.org/TR/WCAG20/). Guidelines from this document include the following:

1. Use appropriate HTML elements (e.g., headings, lists, tables) and consistent structure to organize the page.

2. For each document, the title element should identify its purpose or topic.

3. For each link, be sure to select text that makes sense when read out of context.

4. For each image, be sure to use the ALT attribute to describe its contents.

5. For each table, be sure that a line-by-line reading of the contents is sensible.

```
1.  <!doctype html>
2.  <!-- demo11.html                    Dave Reed -->
3.  <!-- This page demos a table for alignment. -->
4.  <!-- ==================================== -->
5.
6.  <html>
7.   <head>
8.     <title> Demo of tables </title>
9.   </head>
10.
11.  <body>
12.    <table>
13.      <tr>
14.        <td><img src="help.jpg" alt="help icon"></td>
15.        <td>Thanks for visiting my site. <br> Please contact
16.             <i>help@dave-reed.com</i> if you have any questions.</td>
17.      </tr>
18.    </table>
19.  </body>
20.  </html>
```

Figure 2.23 A Web page that demonstrates a table for image alignment.

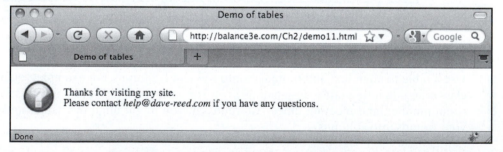

Figure 2.24 demo11.html rendered in a Web browser.

Making Pages Publicly Viewable

As you have learned in this chapter, developing Web pages does not require an Internet connection. You have been able to create pages, store them on your computer, and then view the pages in a browser. However, for your pages to be retrievable via the Web, you will need access to a Web server connected to the Internet. The easiest way to accomplish this will vary depending on your situation. If you are at a college or university, your school most likely has a Web server available for student use. After obtaining permission to store pages on such a server, you will receive specific instructions on how to copy your pages to the appropriate directories on that server. If your Internet access is supplied through an Internet service provider (ISP), such as a cable television or telephone company, the company will probably offer space on its Web servers for customers to use. You will need to contact the company's customer support to determine the steps for uploading your pages. When you copy a page to a publicly accessible Web server, remember that you must also copy any supporting pages or files needed by the page. For example, in Exercise 2.6 you copied an image onto your disk and incorporated that image into your page. Because you employed a relative address to identify the image, a browser will assume that the image is stored in the same location as the page, so it is necessary to copy the image along with the page.

EXERCISE 2.9

If you have access to a Web server, copy both your home page and the downloaded image file to the server. After you have done this, anyone should be able to view your page, regardless of his or her location on the Internet.

Common errors to avoid...

Most Web pages refer to supporting documents, such as images or other Web pages, that are stored in the original page's directory or folder. Whenever you move the page from one directory or folder to another, you must be sure to move the supporting documents along with it. If the browser is unable to locate an image file in the expected location, a box containing an X or ? will be displayed in its place, possibly accompanied by the text from the ALT attribute (depending on browser settings). If a supporting HTML document (e.g., a linked Web page) cannot be found, then a default screen containing an error message will appear when a user clicks the link.

Looking Ahead...

In this chapter, you learned to create your own Web pages with HTML. By using (1) HTML elements to format and align text, (2) images and links to incorporate visuals and related documents, and (3) lists and tables to organize elements, you created a home page comparable to most found on the Web. In fact, the act of placing your home page on a publicly accessible Web server has effected your transition from Web user to Web contributor. Your home page now serves to introduce you to the world, or at least to anyone in the world with Internet access. For future reference, a summary of the various HTML elements that you used in this chapter is found in Appendix C.

As you have learned via the chapter exercises, creating a Web page involves both artistry (in organizing the layout of elements in the page) and careful, logical thinking (in properly formatting the HTML tags). In practice, most Web designers use a variety of technologies in addition to HTML when developing their pages. These technologies include XML (an extension of HTML in which the Web designer can define his own tags), Macromedia Flash (a program that integrates moving images into a page), and programming languages such as PHP, Java, and JavaScript. Although the mastery of all of these technologies is beyond the scope of this book, in subsequent chapters you will learn the fundamentals of JavaScript, the simplest and most popular language for extending HTML. Building upon the skills you have developed in this chapter, you will learn to use JavaScript in the development of dynamic Web pages—pages that not only display text and images but also interact with the user and react to actions such as mouse clicks and keyboard entries. Before the book continues on to JavaScript, however, Chapter 3 gives an overview of the history and functionality of the Internet and the World Wide Web.

You may be comfortable using the Internet for email or surfing the Web, but chances are you have very little knowledge about how the Internet and the Web were created. Chapter 3 provides a historical context for understanding the evolution of these systems as well as the technical details concerning their workings.

Chapter Summary

- A Web page is a text document that contains additional formatting information in a language called HTML (HyperText Markup Language). A Web browser is a program that displays Web pages by interpreting the HTML and formatting the page accordingly. A Web server is a computer that runs special software for storing and retrieving pages. A Web address (formally known as a Uniform Resource Locator, or URL) specifies the location of a particular Web page.

- HTML specifies formatting within a page using tags. An HTML element, the building block of Web pages, is made up of text enclosed in tags that indicate the text's role or purpose within the page.

- Every HTML document must begin with the tag `<!doctype html>`.

- The content of an HTML document is contained between the tags `<html>` and `</html>`, and is divided into two sections. The HEAD contains the TITLE of the page, which appears at the top of the browser window when that page is displayed. The BODY contains the text and formatting that you want to appear within the page.

- Comments can be placed at any point in the page and are delimited by `<!--` and `-->`. By placing key information about a page in comments, you ensure proper credit and simplify the process of updating or modifying the page. The browser ignores comments when the page is loaded.

- Typically, a browser formats text to fit the current window, ignoring blank lines and extra spacing within the HTML document. Designers can control spacing in Web pages by using the `<br>` element, which explicitly breaks a line of text. Similarly, `<p>` and `</p>` tags specify a new paragraph (preceded by a blank line). In addition, the ` ` symbol inserts a space into text.

- The tags `<h1></h1>`, `<h2></h2>`, and `<h3></h3>` can be used to display section headings of decreasing sizes; `<hr>` draws a horizontal line across the page. Designers can add STYLE attributes to headings or paragraphs to control text alignment. For example, `<h2 style="text-align:center">` creates a centered heading.

- Numerous other HTML tags can be used to format text, such as `<b></b>` for bold text, `<i></i>` for italicized text, `<big></big>` for larger text, `<small></small>` for smaller text, and `<span style="color:red"></span>` for red text.

- Hyperlinks to other HTML documents can be embedded in a Web page using an anchor element—e.g., `<a href="http://balance3e.com">Book Site</a>`. The HREF attribute specifies the address of the linked page.

- GIF and JPEG images can be embedded in a Web page using an image tag—e.g., `<img src="reed.gif" alt="Dave Reed">`. The SRC attribute specifies the address of the image file to be displayed, and the ALT attribute specifies alternate text to be displayed if the image doesn't load.

- A list can be used to organize items in a page. By default, an unordered list (identified by `<ul></ul>`) displays each item (identified by `<li></li>`) preceded by a bullet. An ordered list (identified by `<ol></ol>`) displays each item (identified by `<li></li>`) preceded by a number.

- A table can be used to organize items into rows and columns. A table is identified by `<table></table>`, with individual rows identified by `<tr></tr>` and entries within that row identified by `<td></td>`.

Supplemental Material and Exercises

HTML Standards

To ensure that all browsers are able to read and display Web content consistently, the World Wide Web Consortium maintains language standards that all browsers must abide by. The latest proposed standard for HTML, which defines the different tags and their meaning, is HTML5. Thus, if you adhere to the HTML5 standard when you write your Web page, you can be assured that any standards-compliant browser will display it correctly.

The Web site for the World Wide Web Consortium includes a tool for verifying whether a Web page adheres to the HTML5 standard: `http://validator.w3.org`. Using this tool, you can validate your Web page by either specifying its URL or else by uploading the file itself.

EXERCISE 2.10

Test your home page at `http://validator.w3.org`, and make whatever revisions are necessary to successfully validate your page as HTML5 compliant.

When validating your page, you may receive a warning from the validator along the lines of "No character encoding declared at document level." By default, Web pages are assumed to use the 8-bit Unicode Transformation Format (UTF-8) for representing characters in the text. This default is sufficient for creating simple Web pages. To avoid this warning message, however, you can add the following META tag to the HEAD of the page:

```
<meta http-equiv="Content-type" content="text/html;charset=UTF-8" />
```

Browser Settings

A fundamental idea behind HTML is that, although the creator of a page can use tags to identify various text elements, the browser handles the text's final formatting. This increases the universal accessibility of Web documents—if each specific browser controls a page's formatting, the page can be viewed in different browsers running on different types of machines and operating systems. In addition, this approach allows individual users to customize the way in which pages are displayed in their personal browsers. For example, users can easily increase or decrease the size of text fonts through the `View` menu.

Users can also customize other viewing preferences, such as selecting default fonts and colors and a default home page. If you are using Firefox, select `Options` under the `Tools` menu to see all of the possible options. In Internet Explorer, you can change your preferences by selecting `Internet Options` under the `Tools` menu.

EXERCISE 2.11

If you are working on a private computer, customize the browser so that its settings match your personal preferences. If you are working on a publicly accessible computer, you may experiment with the settings, but be sure to reset them to their default values when you are done. It is inconsiderate to impose your preferences on others!

Background Color and Images

By default, most browsers display Web pages with a white background (although individual users can reset this default value via preferences). However, a little color can sometimes make a page more attractive and interesting. To change a page's background color, you must assign a specific color value within the STYLE attribute of the BODY tag. For example, the opening tag

```
<body style="background-color:lightgrey">
```

would cause the background of the page to appear light gray. Appendix C lists the most commonly used color names that are predefined by HTML.

When changing the background of a page, it is important to choose color carefully. Readability is the primary goal when designing a Web page—if users can't read the contents, it doesn't matter how pretty the page is! As such, subtle colors, such as lightgrey or lightblue, are usually preferable. If you really want a bold color as background, you may want to change the text color to provide contrast. This is done by adding a color to the STYLE attribute (using a semicolon to separate the two color settings):

```
<body style="background-color:darkblue;color:white">
```

EXERCISE 2.12

If desired, add a background color to your home page. Depending on your color choice, you may also need to change the text color to make the page readable and attractive.

As you surf the Web, you may have noticed that some Web pages have backgrounds comprising textured patterns or even photographic images. A Web designer can specify an image as the background of a Web page using the STYLE attribute of the BODY tag. For example, the opening tag

```
<body style="background-image:
          url(http://balance3e.com/Images/paper.jpg)">
```

would cause the image located at the specified URL to be displayed in the background of the page. In this case, the background would have a yellow, paperlike texture. Note that if the image is too small to fill the entire browser window (which is usually the case), then the image is repeated to fill the space. This is why simple, repetitive patterns make the best backgrounds.

EXERCISE 2.13

If desired, add a background image to your page (sample images can be found at various Web sites, such as http://www.free-backgrounds.com). However, be very selective when choosing your image. Plastering your picture in the background of your page might seem like a neat idea, but complex background images almost always detract from the page's readability.

Image Links and Video

In all the examples you have seen so far, links have been labeled with text—that is, only text appeared between the opening and closing A tags. However, Web designers can anchor a link to any HTML element, including an image. The following example defines an image link, in which an IMG element is placed inside the A tags.

```
<a href="http://balance3e.com">
 <img src="http://balance3e.com/cover.jpg"
      alt="A Balanced Introduction to Computer Science">
</a>
```

Images that serve as hyperlinks display the same behavior that hypertext does. When a user clicks the image, the browser loads the page specified in the HREF attribute. By default, images enclosed in A tags are surrounded by colored borders to identify the images as links. If you do not want the image to appear with a border, you can add attributes to the ANCHOR and IMG tags to remove the border, as in the following:

```
<a href="http://balance3e.com" style="text-decoration:none">
 <img src="http://balance3e.com/cover.jpg"
      alt="A Balanced Introduction to Computer Science" border=0>
</a>
```

Add images that serve as links to your home page. The images that you select should have relevance to the link destinations—don't use a picture unless a user could intuitively connect the image to the document represented by the link. Also, do not remove the borders from images unless you have a good reason for doing so. These borders help Web users identify and locate links.

In addition to images, Web pages are increasingly being used to embed video clips. The most well known example of this is YouTube (`http://www.youtube.com`), which stores millions of user-created videos for viewing. To embed a video clip in a Web page, you must use an OBJECT element, such as the example below that links to a video clip on YouTube. This particular video describes career opportunities in computer science and was produced by the University of Washington. However, by changing the URL in the OBJECT tag (and also in the embedded PARAM tag), you can link to any publicly accessible video clip.

```
<object type="application/x-shockwave-flash"
        data="http://www.youtube.com/v/RENVVTNsVHg&hl=en_US&fs=1&"
        width="480" height="385">
  <param name="movie"
        value="http://www.youtube.com/v/RENVVTNsVHg&hl=en_US&fs=1&"></param>
  <param name="allowFullScreen" value="true"></param>
  <param name="allowscriptaccess" value="always"></param>
</object>
```

EXERCISE 2.15

Add a video clip to your home page using an OBJECT element similar to the example shown. You may control the size of the clip by changing the WIDTH and HEIGHT attributes in the OBJECT tag.

Cascading Style Sheets

As we have seen, several of the tags shown in this chapter have an optional STYLE attribute that can be used to control the way the page element is displayed. For example, adding the attribute `style="text-align:center"` to an H1 tag causes that header to be centered on the page. Likewise, adding the attribute `style="color:red"` to a P or DIV tag causes the text in that paragraph or page division to appear in red.

When developing a Web site with numerous interconnected pages, consistency is important. Having some of your pages with centered headers and light blue background, while other pages have left-justified headers and a white background, produces a disconnected, unprofessional appearance. Fortunately, HTML provides a mechanism for applying consistent STYLE attributes across multiple files: cascading style sheets. A *cascading style sheet* is a text file that specifies page elements and the STYLE attributes they are to have. For example, the following text specifies that every H1 element in a page is to be centered, while the BODY of the page has a background color of blue and a text color of white:

```
h1 {text-align:center}
body {background-color:blue; color:white}
```

If this text were saved in a file named `mystyle.css`, it could then be linked into any HTML document by placing the following tag in the HEAD of the page:

```
<link href="mystyle.css" rel="stylesheet" type="text/css">
```

As a result, every page that linked this cascading style sheet would apply the STYLE attributes consistently. That is, all pages linking to `mystyle.css` would have a blue background, white text, and centered H1 elements. If you ever changed your mind about the appearance of your pages—say you decided you liked a dark blue background better than a blue one—you would simply need to update the STYLE attribute in `mystyle.css`. Each page that linked to this file would thus be updated automatically and in a consistent manner.

In addition to defining the global appearance of page elements across a Web site, style declarations can be applied selectively to classes of elements. For example, suppose you wanted some of the H1 elements in your Web site to be centered, but others not. You can use the CLASS attribute to identify those elements that are to be centered, giving them a common name such as "centered."

```
<h1 class="centered">My Page</h1>
```

Then, a style declaration can be selectively applied to only those elements by including the CLASS identifier in the style declaration:

```
h1.centered {text-align:center}
```

Using the CLASS attribute, you can create numerous looks for page elements and selectively apply those looks as appropriate throughout the Web site.

EXERCISE 2.16

Create a cascading style sheet that defines STYLE attributes for your home page. Add a LINK element to your page to link to that cascading style sheet and produce the desired appearance. Next, link that same cascading style sheet to another HTML document and verify that it maintains a consistent look to the page.

The Internet and the Web

This chapter uses narrative, illustrations, and review questions to introduce computer science and technology concepts.

It shouldn't be too much of a surprise that the Internet has evolved into a force strong enough to reflect the greatest hopes and fears of those who use it. After all, it was designed to withstand nuclear war, not just the puny huffs and puffs of politicians and religious fanatics.

Denise Caruso

There are two ages of the Internet—before Mosaic, and after. The combination of Tim Berners-Lee's Web protocols, which provided connectivity, and Marc Andreesen's browser, which provided a great interface, proved explosive. In twenty-four months, the Web has gone from being unknown to absolutely ubiquitous.

Mark Pesce
A Brief History of Cyberspace, 1995

When I took office, only high energy physicists had ever heard of what is called the Worldwide Web. . . . Now even my cat has its own page.

President Bill Clinton, 1996

The Internet is a vast network of computers that connects people all over the world. Using the Internet, a person in Indiana can communicate freely with a person in India, scientists at different universities can share computing power, and researchers can access libraries of information from the comfort of their own homes or offices. Over the past two decades, the World Wide Web has popularized the Internet by providing a simple, intuitive interface through which users can share and access information, thus enabling the Internet to become an essential medium for communication, research, and commerce.

In Chapter 1, we provided an overview of the Internet and the Web from a user's perspective. We emphasized the differences between the Internet and the Web, noting that the Internet encompasses hardware (such as computers, cable, and wires) for facilitating communication, whereas the Web is comprised of software (such as documents, images, and sound clips) stored on and accessed over the Internet. Chapter 2 continued our discussion of the Internet by introducing the basics of Web design and HTML, a language used to format Web documents. In this chapter, we provide additional information about the Internet and Web, including how they were developed, how they work, and their impact on society. The historical contexts that led to the development and growth of the Internet and Web are described, as well as the key technical ideas that shaped their evolution. Although not overly technical, this chapter does outline the protocols that define the Internet (TCP/IP) and Web (HTTP/HTML) and make their explosive growth possible.

History of the Internet

One of the most significant advancements in recent computing history is the Internet, the idea for which can be traced back to the early 1960s. While a professor at the Massachusetts Institute of Technology, J.C.R. Licklider (1915–1990) published a series of articles describing a "Galactic Network" of computers that would allow people worldwide to share and access information (Figure 3.1). Licklider was excited by computers' potential to influence scientific and engineering research, but was frustrated by the difficulties involved in accessing computers. Very few computers existed in the early 1960s, and those that were in use tended to be monopolized by a small number of researchers at major universities. Licklider believed that, if computers could be connected over long distances so that a researcher in one state could access a computer in another, then a larger group of researchers would be able to benefit from computers' capabilities. Such a network would also allow institutions to reduce computing costs by sharing resources.

In 1962, Licklider was appointed head of the computer research program at the U.S. Department of Defense's Advanced Research Project Agency (ARPA). As part of his job, he was asked to investigate how researchers—especially those working on defense-related projects—could better utilize computers. He immediately saw the opportunity to bring about his Galactic Network and began establishing relationships with the top computer research organizations in the country. Over the next few years, ARPA funded numerous network-related research initiatives, which generated the ideas and technology that would eventually lead to the Internet.

ARPANet

One of those inspired by Licklider's vision of a long-distance network was Larry Roberts (1937–), a computer researcher at MIT (Figure 3.2). In 1967, Roberts was named head of the ARPA project to design a long-distance computer network. Within a year, Roberts and his team had finalized plans for the network, which was to be called the ARPANet. In 1969, the ARPANet became a reality, linking four computers at the University of California at Los Angeles (UCLA), the University of California at Santa Barbara (UCSB), the Stanford Research Institute (SRI), and the University of Utah. The network employed dedicated cables, lines buried in the ground and used solely for communications between the computers. Researchers at the four institutions were able to connect to one another's computers and run programs remotely, meaning that researchers at multiple sites could share both

Figure 3.1 J.C.R. Licklider.

Figure 3.2 Larry Roberts.

hardware and software costs. In addition, researchers could share information by transferring text and data files from one location to another. It is interesting to note that the transfer rate between the computers—i.e., the speed at which data could be sent and received over the dedicated cables—was 56 Kbits/sec. This is roughly the same rate that today's Internet users can achieve with a modem and standard phone lines. However, at the time, the ARPANet's communication speed represented a dramatic increase over the 160 bits/sec transfer rate obtainable over standard phone lines.

Growth and Privatization

The U.S. Department of Defense originally intended the ARPANet to connect only military installations and universities participating in government projects. Throughout the 1970s and early 1980s, the ARPANet grew at a steady pace, as computers owned by various military contractors and research institutions were added to the network. For example, Figure 3.3 shows a map of the ARPANet in

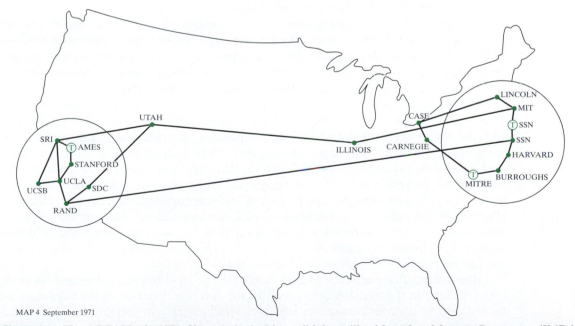

MAP 4 September 1971

Figure 3.3 The ARPANet in 1971. Sites marked with a solid dot utilized Interface Message Processors (IMPs), special-purpose computers that connected up to four terminals to the network. Sites marked with a T utilized Terminal Interface Processors (TIPs), which were introduced in 1971 and allowed up to 64 terminal connections.

ARPANET GEOGRAPHIC MAP, OCTOBER 1980

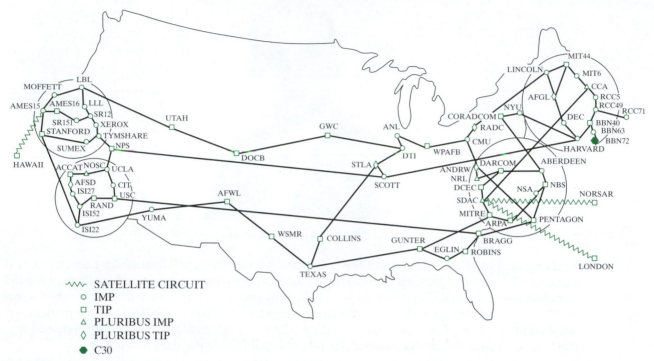

SATELLITE CIRCUIT
○ IMP
□ TIP
△ PLURIBUS IMP
◇ PLURIBUS TIP
● C30

Figure 3.4 The ARPANet in 1980, with the type of networking computer identified at each site. Pluribus IMP and Pluribus TIP were extensions of older IMP and TIP computers that utilized multiple processors to increase capacity. The C30 was a customized, high-speed computer developed by BBN, the original developers of IMP technology.

1971, when the system facilitated communication among 18 computers across the country. By 1980, close to 100 computers were connected to the ARPANet, and satellite connections provided links to select cities outside the continental United States (Figure 3.4).

After more than a decade of slow, steady expansion, the ARPANet experienced an astounding growth spurt in the 1980s. Attracted by network applications such as electronic mail (through which users can send messages and files over the network), newsgroups (through which users can share ideas and results), and remote logins (through which users can share computing power), researchers at virtually every college and university wanted to become a part of the ARPANet. By 1984, the ARPANet encompassed more than 1,000 computers, far exceeding the expectations of its original designers. To accommodate further growth, the National Science Foundation (NSF) became involved with the ARPANet in 1984. The NSF, an independent agency of the U.S. government that promotes the progress of science, funded the construction of high-speed transmission lines that would form the backbone of the expanding network. The term "Internet" was coined in recognition of the similarities between this computer network and the interstate highway system. The backbone connections were analogous to interstate highways, providing fast communications between principal destinations (Figure 3.5). Connected to the backbone were transmission lines, which provided slower, more limited capabilities and linked secondary destinations; these transmission lines could be compared to state highways. Additional connections were required to reach individual computers, in the same way that city and neighborhood roads are used to link individual houses.

Recognizing that continued growth would require an influx of funding and research, the government decided in the mid-1990s to privatize the Internet. Control of the network's hardware was turned over to telecommunications companies and research organizations, which were expected to implement new Internet technologies as they were developed. Today, most of the physical components that make up the Internet, including the high-speed backbone connections, are owned and maintained by commercial firms such as AT&T, Verizon, Sprint, and Qwest. Other aspects of the

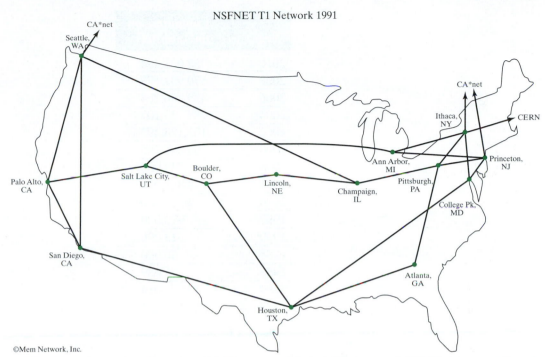

NSFNET T1 Network 1991

©Mem Network, Inc.

Figure 3.5   The Internet backbone in 1991. The arrows labeled **CA *net** and CERN are connections to the Canadian and European networks, respectively.

Internet are administered by the Internet Society, an international nonprofit organization founded in 1992. The Internet Society maintains and enforces standards, ensuring that all computers on the Internet are able to communicate with each other. (You will learn more about standards in the next section.) It also organizes committees that propose new Internet-related technologies and software and provides a managerial structure for determining when and how technologies are adopted. Key organizations within the Internet Society are identified in Figure 3.6.

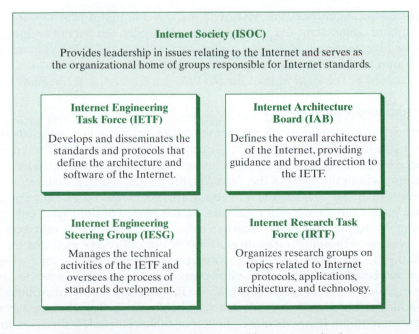

Internet Society (ISOC)

Provides leadership in issues relating to the Internet and serves as the organizational home of groups responsible for Internet standards.

Internet Engineering Task Force (IETF)

Develops and disseminates the standards and protocols that define the architecture and software of the Internet.

Internet Architecture Board (IAB)

Defines the overall architecture of the Internet, providing guidance and broad direction to the IETF.

Internet Engineering Steering Group (IESG)

Manages the technical activities of the IETF and oversees the process of standards development.

Internet Research Task Force (IRTF)

Organizes research groups on topics related to Internet protocols, applications, architecture, and technology.

Figure 3.6   The Internet Society and its key organizations.

Year	Computers on the Internet[1]
2010	758,081,484
2008	570,937,778
2006	439,286,364
2004	285,139,107
2002	162,128,493
2000	93,047,785
1998	36,739,000
1996	12,881,000
1994	3,212,000
1992	992,000
1990	313,000
1988	56,000
1986	5,089
1984	1,024
1982	235

Figure 3.7 Internet growth.

Figure 3.7 documents the increasing size of the Internet over the past three decades, as estimated by the Internet Software Consortium (another nonprofit organization involved in developing and disseminating Internet standards). These statistics indicate exponential growth, with the number of Internet-connected computers doubling every one to two years. Of course, this rate of expansion cannot continue indefinitely, and recent years have begun to show a reduction in rate of growth. Still, technological advances continue to accommodate increasing demand, and no immediate end to the growth of the Internet is foreseen.

How the Internet Works

As we have mentioned, the ARPANet was novel in that it provided the first efficient computer-to-computer connections over long distances. However, the network's inherent organization was also innovative, representing a significant departure from telephone systems and other communications schemes of that era. The design of the ARPANet—and hence of today's Internet—was strongly influenced by the ideas of Paul Baran (1926–), a researcher at the Rand Corporation in the 1960s.

Distributed Network

The first of Baran's ideas adopted for the ARPANet was that of a ***distributed network***. To fully understand the logic behind the Internet's structure, you must recall that funding for the ARPANet was provided by the U.S. Department of Defense, which had very specific objectives in mind. Given that the country was in the midst of the Cold War, the military wanted to develop a national communications network that would be resistant to attack. This goal required a design that allowed communication to take place even if parts of the network were damaged or destroyed, either by an enemy action or by normal mechanical failures. Clearly, a centralized network that relied on a small number of master computers to coordinate transmissions would not suffice. For example, the U.S. telephone network of the time relied on central hubs or switches that were responsible for routing service to entire regions. If a hub failed for some reason, entire cities or regions could lose service. Baran proposed a different architecture for a computer network, one in which control was distributed across a large number of machines. His design employed a lattice structure, in which each computer on the network was linked to several others. If a particular computer or connection failed, then communications could be routed around that portion of the network, and the network would continue to transmit data (Figure 3.8).

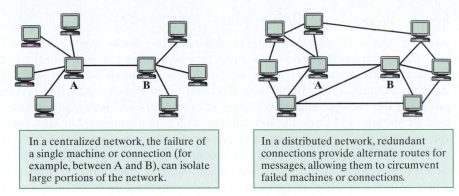

In a centralized network, the failure of a single machine or connection (for example, between A and B), can isolate large portions of the network.

In a distributed network, redundant connections provide alternate routes for messages, allowing them to circumvent failed machines or connections.

Figure 3.8 Centralized vs. distributed networks.

Packet Switching

Baran's other idea central to the ARPANet architecture was that of *packet switching*. In a packet-switching network, messages to be sent over the network are first broken into small pieces known as *packets*, and these packets are sent independently to their final destination (Figure 3.9). Transmitting messages in this way offers three key advantages. First, sending information in smaller units increases the efficient use of connections. If a large message were able to monopolize a connection, many smaller messages might be forced to wait. As a real-life example of this effect, think of a checkout line at a busy grocery store. If the customer at the front of the line has a full cart of groceries, then everyone else in line has to wait, even those who only need to purchase a few items. To avoid this, most grocery stores provide an express line where the number of items is limited. If purchases are limited to 10 items, for example, then each customer in the express line is guaranteed a turn in a reasonable amount of time. Similarly, limiting the size of network transmissions allows many users to share the connections in a more equitable manner. The second advantage of packet switching is that it allows the network to react to failures or congestion. As each packet works its way toward its destination, routers can recognize failures or network congestion and reroute the packet around trouble areas. The third advantage is that packet switching improves reliability. If a message is broken into packets and the packets are transmitted independently, it is probable that at least part of the message will arrive at its destination, even if some failures occur within the network. If the recipient receives only part of the message, software on her computer can acknowledge the partial message's receipt and request retransmission from the sender.

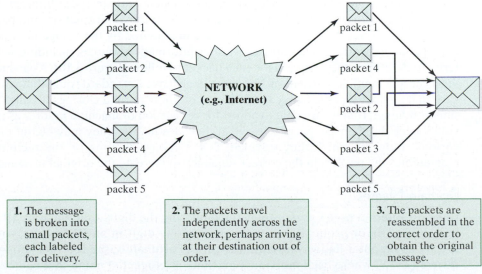

1. The message is broken into small packets, each labeled for delivery.

2. The packets travel independently across the network, perhaps arriving at their destination out of order.

3. The packets are reassembled in the correct order to obtain the original message.

Figure 3.9 A packet-switching network.

Internet Protocols: TCP/IP

Although the terms *distributed* and *packet-switching* can be used to describe the Internet's architecture, these characteristics do not address how computers connected to the Internet are able to communicate with one another. After all, just as people speak different languages and have different customs, computers are built using different technologies, operating systems, and computer languages. If the average American can't speak or understand Russian (and vice versa), how can we expect a computer in Minnesota to exchange data with a computer in Moscow? To solve this problem, the computing community must agree on *protocols*, sets of rules that describe how communication takes place. Internet protocols can be thought of as analogous to the postal service address system, which is used to route letters and packages (jokingly referred to as *snail mail* by some in the electronic community). If every state or country maintained its own method of labeling mail, sending a letter would be an onerous, if not impossible, task. Fortunately, protocols have been established for uniquely specifying addresses, including zip codes and country codes that allow letters to be sent easily across state and national borders. Similar protocols were established for the Internet to define how sending and receiving computers identify each other, as well as the form in which messages must be labeled for delivery.

Just as houses are assigned addresses that distinguish them from their neighbors, computers on the Internet are assigned unique identifiers known as *IP addresses*. An IP address is a number, usually written as a dotted sequence such as 147.134.2.84. When a new computer is connected to the Internet, the owner's Internet Service Provider (ISP) or equivalent organization must assign the computer an IP address. Once the computer obtains its IP address and is physically linked to the network, the computer can send and receive messages, as well as access other Internet services. The manner in which messages are sent and received over the Internet is defined by a pair of protocols called the *Transmission Control Protocol* (*TCP*) and *Internet Protocol* (*IP*), which were co-developed in the early 1970s by Vinton Cerf and Robert Kahn. TCP controls the method by which messages are broken down into packets and then reassembled when they reach their final destination. IP, on the other hand, is concerned with labeling the packets for delivery and controlling the packets' paths from sender to recipient. The combination of these two protocols, written as TCP/IP, is often referred to as the language of the Internet. Any computer that is able to "speak" the language defined by TCP/IP will be able to communicate with any other computer on the Internet.

When a person sends a message over the Internet, specialized software using the rules of TCP breaks that message into packets (no bigger than 1,500 characters each) and labels the packets according to their sequence (for example, packet 2 of 5). Next, software following the rules of IP labels those packets with routing information, including the IP addresses of the source and destination computers. Once labeled, the packets are sent independently over the Internet. Special-purpose machines called *routers* receive the packets, access the routing information, and pass the packets on toward their destination. The routers, which are maintained by the companies and organizations that manage the network connections, use various information sources, including statistics on traffic patterns, to determine the best path for each packet to follow (Figure 3.10). As an analogy, consider driving a car to a familiar destination. You most likely have a standard route that you take, but you might vary that route if you see heavy traffic ahead or know of road closings because of construction. In a similar manner, routers are able to adjust for congestion or machine failures as they direct each individual packet. When the packets arrive at their destination, they may be out of order, owing to the various routes by which they traveled. TCP software running on the recipient's computer then reassembles the packets in the correct sequence to recreate the original message.

Domain Names

From an Internet user's perspective, remembering the digits that make up IP addresses would be tedious and error prone. If you mistype only one digit in an IP address, you might mistakenly specify a computer halfway around the world. Fortunately, the Internet supports a *domain-name system* (*DNS*) where each individual machine is assigned a name that can be used in place of its IP address. For example, the computer with IP address 147.134.2.84 can be referred to by the

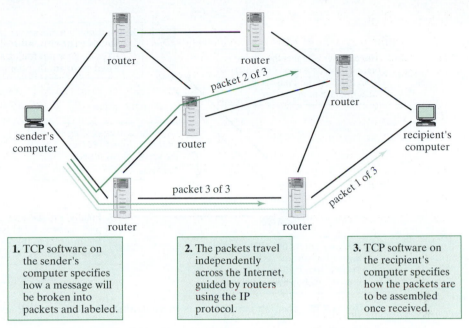

1. TCP software on the sender's computer specifies how a message will be broken into packets and labeled.

2. The packets travel independently across the Internet, guided by routers using the IP protocol.

3. TCP software on the recipient's computer specifies how the packets are to be assembled once received.

Figure 3.10   Transmitting a message over the Internet.

name `www.creighton.edu`. Such names, commonly referred to as ***domain names***, are hierarchical in nature, which makes them easier to remember. The leftmost part of a domain name specifies the name of the machine, whereas the subsequent parts indicate the organization (and possibly suborganizations) to which the computer belongs. The rightmost part of the domain name is known as the ***top-level domain*** and identifies the type of organization with which the computer is associated. For example, the computer `www.creighton.edu` is named www (a common name for Web servers) and belongs to Creighton University, which is an educational institution. Similarly, `www.sales.acme.com` is a computer named www belonging to the sales department of a fictitious Acme Corporation, which is a commercial business. Since 1998, the assignment of domain names and IP addresses has been coordinated by the Internet Corporation for Assigned Names and Numbers (ICANN), a nonprofit coalition of businesses, academic institutions, and individuals. ICANN accredits companies, known as ***domain-name registrars***, which sell domain-name rights directly to consumers.

Figure 3.11 lists examples of common top-level domains. However, Internet users should be aware that these top-level domains are used primarily by American companies and organizations. Computers located in other countries are often identified by country-specific top-level domains, such as `ca` (Canada), `uk` (United Kingdom), `cn` (China), and `in` (India).

Domain names help Internet users identify specific computers efficiently, because these names are much easier to remember than numeric IP addresses are. However, any communication that

Top-Level Domain	Primary Use
edu	U.S. educational institutions
com	Commercial organizations
org	Nonprofit organizations
mil	U.S. military
gov	U.S. government
net	Network providers and businesses

Figure 3.11   Top-level domain names.

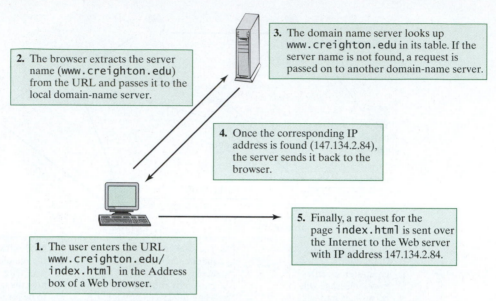

2. The browser extracts the server name (`www.creighton.edu`) from the URL and passes it to the local domain-name server.

3. The domain name server looks up `www.creighton.edu` in its table. If the server name is not found, a request is passed on to another domain-name server.

4. Once the corresponding IP address is found (147.134.2.84), the server sends it back to the browser.

1. The user enters the URL `www.creighton.edu/index.html` in the Address box of a Web browser.

5. Finally, a request for the page `index.html` is sent over the Internet to the Web server with IP address 147.134.2.84.

Figure 3.12 Domain-name servers translate domain names into IP addresses.

takes place over the Internet requires the IP addresses of the source and destination computers. Special-purpose computers called ***domain-name servers*** are used to store mappings between domain names and their corresponding IP addresses. When a computer sends a message to a destination such as `www.creighton.edu`, the sending computer first transmits a request to a domain-name server, which matches the recipient's domain name to an IP address. After looking up the domain name in a table, the domain-name server returns the associated IP address (here, 147.134.2.84) to the sender's computer. This enables the sender to transmit the message to the correct destination. If a particular domain-name server does not have the requested domain name stored locally, it forwards the request to another domain-name server on the Internet; this process continues until the corresponding IP address is found (see Figure 3.12).

History of the Web

Although Internet communications among universities and government organizations were common in the 1980s, the Internet did not achieve mainstream popularity until the early 1990s, when the World Wide Web was developed. The Web, a multimedia environment in which documents can be seamlessly linked over the Internet, was the brainchild of Tim Berners-Lee (1955–), pictured in Figure 3.13. During the 1980s, Berners-Lee was a researcher at the European Laboratory for Particle Physics (CERN). Because CERN researchers were located all across Europe and used different types of computers and software, they found it difficult to share information effectively. To address this problem, Berners-Lee envisioned a system in which researchers could freely exchange data, regardless of their locations and the types of computers they used. In 1989, he proposed the basic idea for the Web, suggesting that documents could be stored on Internet-linked computers such that an authorized individual on one computer could have access to files stored on another.

Hypertext and the Web

Although Berners-Lee's vision for the Web was revolutionary, his idea was built upon a long-standing practice of linking related documents to enable easy access. Books containing ***hypertext***, or documents with interlinked text and media, have existed for millennia. This hypertext might tie a portion of a document to related annotations, as in the Jewish Talmud (first century B.C.), or might provide links to nonsequential alternate story lines, as in the Indian epic Ramayana (third century B.C.). The concept of an electronic hypertext system was first conceived in 1945, when presidential science

Figure 3.13   Tim Berners-Lee.

advisor Vannevar Bush (1890–1974) outlined designs for a machine that would store textual and graphical information in such a way that any piece of information could be arbitrarily linked to any other piece. The first small-scale computer hypertext systems were developed in the 1960s and culminated in the popular HyperCard system that shipped with Apple Macintosh computers in the late 1980s.

Berners-Lee was innovative, however, in that he combined the key ideas of hypertext with the distributed nature of the Internet. His design for the Web relied on two different types of software running on Internet-enabled computers. The first kind of software executes on a ***Web server***, a computer that stores documents and "serves" them to other computers that want access. The second kind, called a ***Web browser***, allows users to request and view the documents stored on servers. Using Berners-Lee's system, a person running a Web browser could quickly access and jump between documents, even if the servers storing those documents were thousands of miles apart.

Mainstream Adoption of the Web

In 1990, Berners-Lee produced working prototypes of a Web server and browser. His browser was limited by today's standards, in that it was text based and offered only limited support for images and other media. This early version of the Web acquired a small but enthusiastic following when Berners-Lee made it available over the Internet in 1991. However, the Web might have remained an obscure research tool if others had not expanded on Berners-Lee's creation, developing browsers designed to accommodate the average computer user. In 1993, Marc Andreesen (1971–) and Eric Bina (1964–), of the University of Illinois's National Center for Supercomputing Association (NCSA), wrote the first graphical browser, which they called Mosaic (Figure 3.14). Mosaic employed buttons and clickable links as navigational aids, making the Web easier to traverse. The browser also supported the integration of images and media within pages, which enabled developers to create more visually appealing Web documents. The response to Mosaic's release in 1993 was overwhelming. As more and more people learned how easy it was to store and access information using the Web, the number of Web servers on the Internet grew from 50 in 1992 to 3,000 in 1994.[2] In 1994, Andreesen left NCSA to found the Netscape Communications Corporation, which marketed an extension of the Mosaic browser called Netscape Navigator. Originally, Netscape charged a small fee for its browser, although students and educators were exempt from this cost. However, when Microsoft introduced its Internet Explorer browser as free software in 1995, Netscape was eventually forced to follow suit. The availability of free, easy-to-use browsers certainly contributed to the astounding growth of the Web in the mid 1990s.

Figure 3.14 Marc Andreesen

The late 1990s were a dynamic time for the Web, during which Netscape and Microsoft released enhanced versions of their browsers and battled for market share. Initially, Netscape was successful in capitalizing on its first-mover advantage—in 1996, approximately 75% of all operational browsers were Netscape products. By 1999, however, Internet Explorer had surpassed Navigator as the most commonly used browser.[3] Finding it difficult to compete with Microsoft, Andreesen relinquished control of Netscape in 1999, selling the company to AOL for $10 billion in stock. Since then, Internet Explorer has dominated the browser market, accounting for more than 90% of all browsers by 2002. In recent years, Mozilla Firefox, a descendant of the Netscape browser, has grown in popularity, but Internet Explorer still held more than 62% of the market in 2009.[4]

The reasons behind Internet Explorer's ultimate dominance of the browser market are a topic of some debate. Certainly, Microsoft's financial position was much stronger than Netscape's. Owing to its success with other software products, Microsoft possessed vast resources with which to develop and market its browsers. Netscape's income, on the other hand, was derived solely from browser-based technology, and the company suffered financially when Microsoft's marketing strategy forced it to release its browser for free. More significantly, though, Microsoft was able to leverage its dominance in operating systems by packaging Internet Explorer as part of Windows. Any customer who purchased a computer with a Windows operating system automatically received a copy of Internet Explorer. This strategy did prove highly successful, but it also led to legal problems for Microsoft, which was found guilty of several antitrust charges in the late 1990s.

Although Internet Explorer and Mozilla Firefox are the most popular browsers on the market, new browsers such as Apple's Safari and Google's Chrome have small but devoted followings. In addition, the software industry offers numerous others to satisfy niche markets. These include text-based browsers for environments that don't support graphics, text-to-speech browsers for vision-impaired users, and browsers designed to run on new technologies such as cell phones and personal digital assistants (PDAs).

Web Growth

Figure 3.15 documents the growth of the World Wide Web over the past two decades as estimated by the 2010 Netcraft Web Server Survey. It is interesting to note the dramatic increases in the Web's size after advances in browser technology: the release of Mosaic in 1993, Netscape in 1995, and Internet Explorer in 1996. The number of Web sites has also grown considerably during the past ten years—according to the latest estimates, there is roughly one Web site for every four computers on the Internet. Of course, each Web site can store a large number of pages, so the size of the Web in terms of pages is even more impressive. In 2005, the Google search engine (`google.com`) claimed to have

Year	Computers on the Internet[5]	Web Servers on on the Internet[6]
2010	758,081,484	205,368,103
2008	570,937,778	175,480,931
2006	439,286,364	88,166,395
2004	285,139,107	52,131,889
2002	162,128,493	33,082,657
2000	93,047,785	18,169,498
1998	36,739,000	4,279,000
1996	12,881,000	300,000
1994	3,212,000	3,000
1992	992,000	50

Figure 3.15 Internet and Web growth

more than 8 billion Web pages indexed. By 2009, various sources have estimated as many as 50 billion Web pages.

The Web's development is now guided by a nonprofit organization called the World Wide Web Consortium (W3C), which was founded by Berners-Lee in 1994. The W3C maintains and regulates Web-related standards and oversees the design of Web-based technologies. Similar to the Internet Society, the W3C relies mainly on volunteer labor from technically qualified and interested individuals.

How the Web Works

Like Internet communications, the World Wide Web relies on protocols to ensure that Web pages are accessible to any computer, regardless of the machine's hardware, operating system, browser, or location. The standards most central to the Web interactions are HTML and the HyperText Transfer Protocol (HTTP), which work in combination with TCP/IP to enable the exchange of Web pages over the Internet.

HTML

As we saw in Chapters 1 and 2, authors define the content of Web pages using HTML, the HyperText Markup Language. By placing tags and special symbols within text documents, designers can create pages; format the included text; and incorporate links, images, and other media. Part of a Web browser's job is to read HTML tags and render pages accordingly. For example, when a browser encounters text enclosed in tags <b><b>, it interprets those tags as specifying bold text and displays the characters in a heavier font.

HTML is an evolving standard, which means that new features are added to the language in response to changes in technology and user needs. The latest proposed standard for HTML, as defined by the World Wide Web Consortium, is HTML5. Although the HTML5 standard is not expected to be finalized until 2010, it is already supported by the latest releases of Web browsers. There are subtle differences among browsers, but all Web browsers understand the same basic set of tags and display text and formatting similarly. Thus, when an author places an HTML document on a Web server, all users who view the page should see the same formatting, regardless of their machines or browser software.

Web Protocol: HTTP

To a person "surfing" the Web, the process of locating, accessing, and displaying Web pages is transparent. When the person requests a particular page, either by entering its location into the browser's Address box or by clicking a link, the new page is displayed in the browser window as if by magic. In

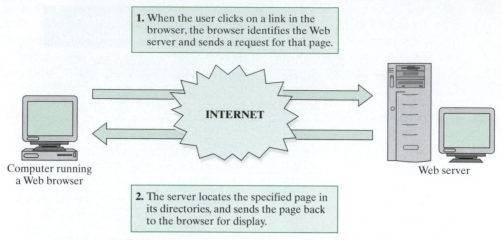

1. When the user clicks on a link in the browser, the browser identifies the Web server and sends a request for that page.

INTERNET

Computer running
a Web browser

Web server

2. The server locates the specified page in its directories, and sends the page back to the browser for display.

Figure 3.16 Web browser and server communications.

reality, complex communications are taking place between the computer running the browser and the Web server that stores the desired page. When the person requests the page, the browser must first identify the Web server on which that page resides. Recall from Chapter 1 that the Web address, or URL, for a page includes the name of the server, as well as the document name. Once the server name has been extracted from the URL, the browser sends a message to that server over the Internet and requests the page (following the steps depicted in Figure 3.10). The Web server receives the request, locates the page within its directories, and sends the page's text back in a message. When the message is received, the browser interprets the HTML formatting information embedded in the page and displays the page accordingly in the browser window (Figure 3.16). The protocol that determines how messages exchanged between browsers and servers are formatted is known as the ***HyperText Transfer Protocol (HTTP)***.

Caching

It is interesting to note that accessing a single page might involve several rounds of communication between the browser and server. If the Web page contains embedded elements, such as images or sound clips, the browser will not recognize this until it begins displaying the page. When the browser encounters an HTML tag that specifies an embedded element, the browser must then send a separate message to the server requesting the item. Thus, loading a page that contains 10 images will require 11 interactions between the browser and server—one for the page itself and one for each of the 10 images. To avoid redundant and excessive downloading, most browsers use a technique called ***caching***. When a page or image is first downloaded, it is stored in a temporary directory on the user's computer. The next time the page or image is requested, the browser first checks to see if it has a copy stored locally in the cache, and, if so, whether the copy is up to date (this is accomplished by contacting the server and asking how recently the page was changed). If an up-to-date copy is stored locally, then the browser can display this copy, instead of downloading the original. Note that it is still necessary for the browser to contact the Web server, as the document on the server might have been modified since it was last cached. However, caching can still save time, because the browser avoids downloading redundant copies.

Looking Ahead...

In the short time since their inception, the Internet and World Wide Web have revolutionized the way in which people use computers. As recently as 20 years ago, most computers were stand-alone devices, not connected to any other computers. With the popularization of the Internet, however, computers have progressed from computation devices into sophisticated communications vehicles. Through electronic mail, instant messaging, and social networking sites, people from around the world can communicate, sharing ideas and computing resources. The World Wide Web, an even more recent invention, has also greatly affected the role of computers in our society. By offering instant access to massive amounts of data, the Web has changed the way in which we communicate, learn, research, shop, and entertain ourselves. Furthermore, because almost anyone can create a Web page, the Web allows us to share information about ourselves and our work—from family photos to unpublished novels—with the world.

In Chapter 2, you were introduced to the basics of Web design and created your own Web page using HTML. Now that you are familiar with the history and architecture of the Internet and Web, the next chapter will teach you how to extend your pages to make them interactive. In Chapter 4, we will present the fundamentals of the JavaScript programming language, which you will be working with throughout the programming portion of this book. Instead of just displaying text and images, JavaScript-enabled pages react to actions taken by the user and process information that they can use to control the contents of the page. Once you become skilled at developing pages that respond and react to user input, you will be able to contribute even more engaging and useful documents to the Web.

Chapter Summary

- The Internet traces its roots back to the ARPANet, which was funded by the U.S. Department of Defense's Advanced Research Project Agency (ARPA). In 1969, the ARPANet linked four computers at UCLA, UCSB, SRI, and Utah.

- The growth of the ARPANet in the 1970s greatly exceeded expectations, prompting the National Science Foundation (NSF) to become involved in the upgrading and maintenance of the ARPANet in 1984.

- In the mid-1980s, the ARPANet became known as the Internet, acknowledging its structural similarities with the nation's interstate highway system.

- Recognizing that continued growth would require an influx of funding and research, the government decided in the mid-1990s to privatize the Internet.

- In 2010, there were an estimated 758 million computers connected to the Internet.

- The design of the ARPANet—and hence of today's Internet—was strongly influenced by the ideas of Paul Baran, who proposed that it be distributed and packet-switching.

- In a distributed network, control is distributed across a large number of machines, allowing for messages to be rerouted along alternate connections when a particular computer or connection fails.

- In a packet-switching network, messages are broken into smaller packets and sent independently. Advantages of this approach include a more efficient use of the connections, the ability to react to failures and congestion, and improved reliability.

- The Internet Society maintains and enforces standards and protocols concerning the Internet, and also organizes committees that propose new Internet-related technologies and software.

- The Transmission Control Protocol (TCP) controls the method by which messages are broken down into packets and then reassembled when they reach their final destination. The Internet Protocol (IP) is concerned with labeling the packets for delivery and controlling the packets' paths from sender to recipient.

- Each computer on the Internet is assigned an IP address (e.g., 147.134.2.84) that uniquely identifies it. Domain names (e.g., `www.creighton.edu`) can alternatively be used and then mapped to IP addresses by domain name servers.

- First proposed by Tim Berners-Lee in 1989, the World Wide Web is a multimedia environment in which documents can be seamlessly linked over the Internet.

- The Web relies on two different types of software running on Internet-enabled computers: a Web server stores documents and "serves" them to computers that want access; a Web browser, allows users to request and view the documents stored on servers.

- Although working prototypes of the Web were available in 1990, the growth of the Web was slow until the introduction of graphical browsers (NCSA Mosaic in 1993, Netscape Navigator in 1995, and Microsoft Internet Explorer in 1996), which better integrated multimedia elements and made navigation simpler.

- In 2010, there were an estimated 205 million Web sites worldwide, providing access to as many as 50 billion Web pages.

- The Web's development is now guided by a nonprofit organization called the World Wide Web Consortium (W3C), which was founded by Berners-Lee in 1994.

- The standards most central to the Web interations are HTML and HTTP. The Hypertext Markup Language (HTML) defines the content of Web pages, whereas the HyperText Transfer Protocol (HTTP) determines how messages exchanged between browsers and servers are formatted.

Review Questions

1. TRUE or FALSE? The ARPANet, the precursor to today's Internet, was funded primarily by the U.S. Department of Defense.

2. TRUE or FALSE? Because the ARPANet used ordinary phone lines to connect computers over large distances, it was slow compared to existing technologies of the time.

3. TRUE or FALSE? In a centralized computer network, the failure of a single machine or connection can isolate large portions of the network.

4. TRUE or FALSE? A router is a special-purpose computer on the Internet that receives message packets, accesses routing information, and passes the packets on toward their destination.

5. TRUE or FALSE? When a message is broken into packets for transmission over the Internet, it is guaranteed that all packets will take the same route from source to destination.

6. TRUE or FALSE? 147.134.2.84 is an example of an IP address.

7. TRUE or FALSE? The Internet Society, an international nonprofit organization, maintains and enforces standards for the hardware and software of the Internet.

8. TRUE or FALSE? The World Wide Web was developed in the early 1970s, shortly after the development of the Internet.

9. TRUE or FALSE? Microsoft marketed the first commercial Web browser.

10. TRUE or FALSE? In the URL http://balance3e.com/index.html, the part balance3e.com identifies the Web server where the page is stored.

11. The Internet of today evolved from the ARPANet of the 1960s and 70s. In what ways is the Internet similar to the old ARPANet? In what ways is it different?

12. The Internet is often described as the "Information Superhighway." Describe how the analogy of a highway system fits the structure of the Internet.

13. Paul Baran proposed two groundbreaking design ideas for the structure and behavior of the ARPANet. Describe these design ideas and the benefits they provide.

14. Describe how packet switching can increase the reliability of a network.

15. Internet communications are defined by a set of protocols called TCP/IP. What do TCP and IP stand for, and what is the role of each protocol in transmitting and receiving information?

16. What is an IP address? What steps are involved in mapping a computer's domain name (e.g., `www.creighton.edu`) to its IP address?

17. Which has grown at a faster rate, the Internet or the Web? Justify your answer.

18. What is hypertext? How are the key ideas of hypertext incorporated into the Web?

19. What specific features did the Mosaic browser include that were not available in earlier browsers? How did these features help make the Web accessible to a larger audience?

20. Describe two factors that contributed to Microsoft's dominance of the browser market.

21. What does HTTP stand for, and what is its role in facilitating Web communications?

22. The World Wide Web Consortium maintains and regulates Web-related standards and oversees the design of Web-based technologies. Visit its Web site (`www.w3.org`) to review the organization's goals and list of technologies under active development. Describe three technologies (other than HTML, HTTP, and XML) whose development is managed by the World Wide Web Consortium.

23. How does caching improve the performance of a Web browser? Does caching reduce the number of interactions that take place between the browser and the Web server?

Endnotes

1. "Internet Domain Survey." *Internet Software Consortium*, April 2010. Online at `http://www.isc.org/solutions/survey`.

2. "Netcraft Web Server Survey." *Netcraft*, April 2010. Online at `http://www.netcraft.com/survey/`.

3. Borland, John. "Browser Wars: High Price, Huge Rewards." *CNETNews.com*, April 2003. Online at `http://zdnet.com.com/2100-1104-996866.html`.

4. "Market Share by Net Applications." *Net Applications*, December 2009. Online at `http://marketshare.hitslink.com/`.

5. "Internet Domain Survey." *Internet Software Consortium*, April 2010. Online at `http://www.isc.org/solutions/survey`.

6. "Netcraft Web Server Survey." *Netcraft*, April 2010. Online at `http://www.netcraft.com/survey/`.

References

"About the Internet Society." *Internet Society*, December 2009. Online at `http://www.isoc.org/isoc/`.

Berners-Lee, Tim, Mark Fischetti, and Michael L. Derouzos. *Weaving the Web: The original design and ultimate destiny of the World Wide Web.* New York: HarperBusiness, 2000.

Bush, Vannevar. "As We May Think." *Atlantic Monthly*, July 1945. Online at `http://www.theatlantic.com/unbound/flashbks/computer/bushf.htm`.

Comer, Douglas E. *The Internet Book: Everything you need to know about computer networking and how the Internet works*, 4th ed. Upper Saddle River, NJ: Prentice Hall, 2006.

Deitel, H.M., P.J. Deitel, and A.B. Goldberg. *Internet and World Wide Web: How to Program 4th ed.* Upper Saddle River, NJ: Prentice Hall, 2007.

Griffin, Scott. "Internet Pioneers." December 2009. Online at `http://www.ibiblio.org/pioneers/index.html`.

Hafner, Katie, and Matthew Lyon. *Where Wizards Stay Up Late: The Origins of the Internet.* New York: Touchstone Books, 1998.

"HTML & CSS", World Wide Web Consortium, January 2009. Online at `http://www.w3.org/standards/webdesign/htmlcss/`.

Leiner, Barry M., et al. "A Brief History of the Internet." *Internet Society*, December 2009. Online at `http://www.isoc.org/internet/history/brief.shtml`.

JavaScript and Dynamic Web Pages

This chapter uses narrative, examples, and hands-on exercises to introduce programming concepts and Web development skills.

That which is static and repetitive is boring. That which is dynamic and random is confusing. In between lies art.

John A. Locke

Calling JavaScript "the glue that holds Web pages together" is short and easy to use but doesn't do justice to what's going on. Glue sets and hardens, but JavaScript is more dynamic than glue. It can create a reaction and make things keep going, like a catalyst.

Brendan Eich
Innovators of the Net: Brendan Eich and JavaScript, 1998

A s you learned in Chapters 2 and 3, the World Wide Web is a vast, interconnected network of documents that effectively integrates text and media such as images, movies, and sounds. HTML consists of tags that identify the contents of a page and provide formatting information for the Web browser. Using HTML tags, it is possible to develop attractive, information-rich pages that can be displayed on the Web. However, when used alone, HTML can produce only ***static pages***. This means that HTML pages look the same and behave in the same manner each time they are loaded into a browser.

In 1995, Brendan Eich and his research team at Netscape Communications Corporation developed a simple programming language, JavaScript, for augmenting Web pages and making them ***dynamic***—that is, capable of changing their appearance over time or in response to a user's actions. JavaScript statements are commands that instruct the browser to perform some action within the page, such as changing an image when the mouse moves over it or submitting credit card information to an online retailer when a button is clicked. In this chapter, you will begin augmenting your own Web pages with JavaScript, focusing on simple techniques for enabling user interaction. You will learn to write JavaScript statements that are associated with images and buttons, allowing them to change and update the page when the user moves the mouse over them or clicks on them. In subsequent chapters, you will build upon these basic skills, mastering the fundamentals of programming through the development of dynamic Web pages.

Dynamic Web Pages

If you have spent any time surfing the Web, you have no doubt encountered pages that change while you are looking at them, varying their contents and responding to your actions. At commercial sites, banner ads may cycle as you view the site or may react when you place the mouse pointer over them. Similarly, search engines prompt you to enter specific topics on which you want information and then retrieve lists of Web pages related to those topics. These are examples of *dynamic* pages, in that their behavior changes each time they are loaded or as events occur. Although HTML is sufficient for creating *static* pages—pages in which the content doesn't change—it does not provide capabilities for specifying dynamic behavior. In order for page designers to indicate actions that are to occur within the page, a programming language is needed.

A ***programming language*** is a language for specifying instructions that a computer can execute. Each ***statement*** in a programming language specifies a particular action that the computer is to carry out, such as changing an image or opening a new window when the user clicks a button. As you will see in Chapters 6 and 8, general-purpose programming languages such as C++ and Java allow the programmer to write applications that solve a variety of problems. JavaScript, which was derived from Java, is a simple programming language designed for a very specific task: adding dynamic features to Web pages. By associating JavaScript statements with HTML elements in a page, that page can be transformed from a static document to a dynamic presentation that acts and reacts to the user.

HTML Event Handlers

In Chapter 2, we learned that HTML elements have attributes that control the way they look in a page. For example, an IMG element has a SRC attribute that specifies the source file for the image and an ALT attribute that provides alternate text to display if the image fails to load. In addition to static attributes such as these, HTML elements may have dynamic attributes that specify how the element is to react to certain events. For this reason, these dynamic attributes are known as ***event handlers***.

Two commonly used event handler attributes are ONMOUSEOVER and ONMOUSEOUT. The ONMOUSEOVER attribute for an HTML element specifies the action that the browser is to carry out when the user moves the mouse over that element. Similarly, the ONMOUSEOUT attribute specifies the action that the browser is to carry out when the mouse is subsequently moved off of the element. The actions are encoded as statements in the JavaScript language. For example, below is the general form of an IMG element that is able to react to mouse events.

```
<img src="ADDRESS_OF_IMAGE" alt="ALT_TEXT"
     onmouseover="CODE_TO_EXECUTE_WHEN_MOUSE_GOES_OVER_IMAGE"
     onmouseout="CODE_TO_EXECUTE_WHEN_MOUSE_LEAVES_IMAGE">
```

The simplest type of action that can be specified by a JavaScript statement is changing the value of one of the element's other attributes. This is accomplished via a JavaScript ***assignment statement*** of the form:

```
this.ATTRIBUTE_NAME=NEW_ATTRIBUTE_VALUE;
```

where ATTRIBUTE_NAME is an attribute (such as SRC), and NEW_ATTRIBUTE_VALUE is the new value that is to be assigned to that attribute (such as the URL of an image). For example, the dynamic IMG element in Figure 4.1 includes event handlers for both the ONMOUSEOVER and ONMOUSEOUT events. When rendered (Figure 4.2), the image initially displays a question mark (as the SRC attribute is assigned to be the URL http://balance3e.com/Images/mystery. gif). When the mouse is moved over the image, however, the browser executes the JavaScript assignment statement associated with the ONMOUSEOVER event handler. This statement reassigns the SRC attribute to a new URL, http://balance3e.com/Images/happy.gif, resulting in a happy face being displayed (Figure 4.3). When the mouse is moved off of the image, the browser

```
1.  <!doctype html>
2.  <!-- mystery1.html                              Dave Reed -->
3.  <!-- This page changes an image source on mouseover. -->
4.  <!-- ============================================= -->
5.
6.  <html>
7.    <head>
8.      <title> Mystery Image </title>
9.    </head>
10.
11.   <body>
12.     <div style="text-align:center">
13.       <img src="http://balance3e.com/Images/mystery.gif" alt="Mystery image"
14.            onmouseover="this.src='http://balance3e.com/Images/happy.gif';"
15.            onmouseout="this.src=''http://balance3e.com/Images/mystery.gif';">
16.       <p>
17.         Move the mouse over the question mark to reveal the image.
18.       </p>
19.     </div>
20.   </body>
21. </html>
```

Figure 4.1 Web page that changes an image when the mouse moves over it.

executes the JavaScript assignment statement associated with the ONMOUSEOUT event handler, resulting in the SRC attribute being reassigned back to `http://balance3e.com/Images/mystery.gif`.

Note that in this and subsequent figures, JavaScript statements are highlighted in gray to differentiate them from HTML elements (blue) and text (black) within the page.

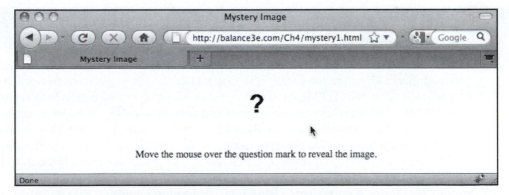

Figure 4.2 `mystery1.html` rendered in a Web browser.

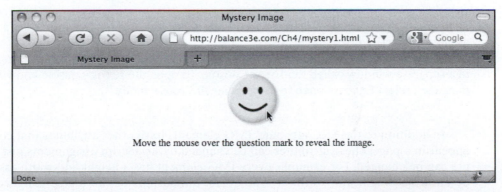

Figure 4.3 `mystery1.html` rendered in a Web browser, with mouse over the image.

EXERCISE 4.1

Enter the `mystery1.html` text from Figure 4.1 into a new Web page, then load the page in the browser to verify that it behaves as described.

Modify the page so that it uses any two images that you choose. These may be images located on the Web (specified by an absolute URL starting with `http://`) or local images that you have downloaded to your own machine (specified by a relative URL without `http://`).

Designer Secrets

You may note that JavaScript assignment statements and HTML attribute assignments have the same basic form. Both utilize the = symbol to denote the assignment of a value (on the right-hand side) to an attribute (on the left-hand side). The value on the right-hand side of an assignment can be a number (such as the width of a table border) or text enclosed in quotes (such as a URL). In programming language terminology, a sequence of characters enclosed in quotes is known as a *string literal*, or *string* for short. Technically, strings in HTML and JavaScript assignments can be enclosed in either single quotes (' ') or double quotes (" "). However, to avoid confusion, we will follow the convention that strings on the right-hand side of HTML assignments are enclosed in double quotes, while strings in JavaScript assignments utilize single quotes.

Technically, every JavaScript statement must end with a semicolon, although browsers tend to be forgiving if you occasionally omit the semicolons. As there are instances in which missing semicolons can cause confusion or even errors, you should always include semicolons at the end of your statements.

Common errors to avoid...

While you were working on Exercise 4.1, perhaps you made a mistake at some point. For example, you might have forgotten the closing quote on a URL, or you might have misspelled `this.src.` Such errors in the format of HTML or JavaScript statements are known as *syntax errors*. For the most part, HTML syntax errors are easy to spot and correct; usually, the browser ignores malformed tags and continues on with the page. By contrast, when a syntax error occurs in JavaScript code, the page may fail to load. As the designer cannot look at the rendered page to determine the exact nature and location of the problem, JavaScript syntax errors are more difficult to handle.

Fortunately, modern Web browsers provide features that help programmers identify and correct JavaScript syntax errors. Using Internet Explorer, you can set your preferences so that, when the browser encounters a JavaScript syntax error, a window appears with an error message specifying the cause of the error. To change your settings, select `Internet Options` under the Tools menu and click the `Advanced` tab. Then, make sure the box labeled "Display a notification about every script error" is checked.

Using Firefox, an error message will not automatically appear. Instead, messages can be seen in a separate window called the Error Console. To open the Error Console and view the error messages, select `Error Console` from under the `Tools` menu.

In addition to the SRC attribute, IMG elements have other attributes that control the way they appear in a page. These attributes can be changed by JavaScript assignments just as the SRC attribute can be changed. For example, every IMG element has a height and width associated with it. By default, the height and width are the actual dimensions of the image assigned to that element. However, using the HEIGHT and WIDTH attributes, the dimensions of the image can be reset, essentially shrinking or expanding the image. In the IMG element below, the HEIGHT and WIDTH attributes are set to 85 pixels each. If the actual image (here, `mystery.gif`) is smaller than 85 × 85, then the image is expanded when it is rendered in the page. Likewise, if it is larger than 85 × 85, it will be shrunken down to those dimensions when rendered.

```
<img src="mystery.gif" alt="Mystery image" height=85 width=85
     onmouseover="this.height=200; this.width=200;"
     onmouseout="this.height=85; this.width=85;">
```

The ONMOUSEOVER and ONMOUSEOUT attributes of this element are each assigned two JavaScript statements (separated by a semicolon). When the mouse moves over the image, the two JavaScript assignments are executed in order to expand the image (by setting the HEIGHT and WIDTH attributes to 200). When the mouse subsequently moves off the image, the image dimensions are restored (by setting the HEIGHT and WIDTH attributes back to 85).

EXERCISE 4.2

Similar to the `mystery1.html` page, create a Web page named `resize1.html` that contains a dynamic, resizable image. The ONMOUSEOVER attribute of that image should contain JavaScript assignments that set the height and width to twice that of the original dimensions. That is, if the image dimensions are 71 × 55 pixels, then moving the mouse over the image should result in the image expanding to 142 × 110. Conversely, the ONMOUSEOUT attribute should contain JavaScript assignments that reset the height and width back to the original dimensions of the image.

The `onclick` Event Handler

Another common event handler for HTML elements is the ONCLICK attribute. This event handler is triggered whenever the user clicks the mouse on that element. For example, below is the general form of an IMG element that is able to react to a mouse click.

```
<img src="ADDRESS_OF_IMAGE" alt="ALT_TEXT"
     onclick="CODE_TO_EXECUTE_WHEN_MOUSE_CLICKS_ON_IMAGE">
```

The Web page in Figure 4.4 is a variant of the `mystery1.html` page from Figure 4.1. This variant uses the ONCLICK event handler attribute to reveal the mystery image. When the user clicks on the

```
1.  <!doctype html>
2.  <!-- mystery2.html                          Dave Reed -->
3.  <!-- This page changes an image source on a click. -->
4.  <!-- ============================================ -->
5.
6.  <html>
7.   <head>
8.     <title> Mystery Image </title>
9.   </head>
10.
11.  <body>
12.    <div style="text-align:center">
13.      <img src="http://balance3e.com/Images/mystery.gif" alt="Mystery image"
14.           onclick="this.src='http://balance3e.com/Images/happy.gif';">
15.      <p>
16.        Click on the question mark to reveal the image.
17.      </p>
18.    </div>
19.  </body>
20. </html>
```

Figure 4.4 Web page that changes an image when the mouse clicks on it.

image, the JavaScript statement assigned to the ONCLICK attribute is executed, resulting in the happy face image being displayed.

EXERCISE 4.3

Enter the mystery2.html text from Figure 4.4 into a new Web page, then load the page in the browser to verify that it behaves as described.

Modify the page so that it uses the same two images that you chose for your mystery1.html page (from Exercise 4.1).

Interaction via Buttons

When applied to an image, the ONCLICK event handler provides only limited control. The JavaScript statement assigned to the ONCLICK attribute can specify one action that is to take place when the image is clicked (e.g., revealing a mystery image). However, if you wanted several different actions to be associated with an image, such as switching back and forth between different images, a single ONCLICK event handler will not suffice. Fortunately, HTML buttons provide a natural way to associate several different actions with a single element.

Input Buttons

If you have spent any time surfing the Web, you have no doubt run across buttons like the one shown in Figure 4.5. A **button** is an HTML element that you can embed in a Web page, just as you would an image or a table. Buttons are used to initiate actions within the page, using the ONCLICK event handler. The general form of a button element is as follows:

```
<input type="button" value="BUTTON_LABEL"
       onclick="CODE_TO_EXECUTE_WHEN_MOUSE_CLICKS_ON_BUTTON">
```

The structure of this tag emphasizes that a button is an INPUT element, since the input provided by the user in the form of a mouse click controls the behavior of the page. We will see in Chapter 5 that there are other types of INPUT elements, each with a different TYPE attribute. A button's VALUE attribute specifies the text label that appears on the button. For example, the button in Figure 4.5 would have the attribute assignment value="Click for free money!". As with other elements we have seen, the ONCLICK attribute specifies the action that occurs when a user clicks that button. The button in Figure 4.5 might have JavaScript code assigned to the ONCLICK attribute that takes you to a Web site advertising a product or service.

When defining the JavaScript statements that controlled dynamic images, we used the notation this.ATTRIBUTE_NAME to refer to a particular attribute of that image. For example, the image in Figure 4.1 changed its source when the mouse moved over it, by assigning a new URL to this.src. Similarly, the clickable image in Figure 4.4 assigned new dimensions to the image using this.height and this.width. In all of these examples, the prefix this. specifies that the attribute being changed belongs to the same element that contains the event handler. Since buttons are generally used to control the appearance of other elements in the page, however, there must be a more general way to identify the target of the particular action.

To access or change the attributes of another element in a Web page, that element must first be assigned a unique identifier (using the ID attribute). Once an element has an identifier, that identifier can be used to access that element using an expression of the form:

```
document.getElementById('ELEMENT_ID')
```

Figure 4.5 An HTML button.

```
 1. <!doctype html>
 2. <!-- mystery3.html                              Dave Reed -->
 3. <!-- This page changes an image source on button clicks. -->
 4. <!-- ====================================================== -->
 5.
 6. <html>
 7.   <head>
 8.     <title> Mystery Image </title>
 9.   </head>
10.
11.   <body>
12.     <div style="text-align:center">
13.       <img id="mysteryImg" src="mystery.gif">
14.       <p>
15.         <input type="button" value="Show Image"
16.                onclick="document.getElementById('mysteryImg').src=
17.                           'http://balance3e.com/Images/happy.gif';">
18.         <input type="button" value="Hide Image"
19.                onclick="document.getElementById('mysteryImg').src=
20.                           'http://balance3e.com/Images/mystery.gif';">
21.       </p>
22.     </div>
23.   </body>
24. </html>
```

Figure 4.6 Web page that changes an image by clicking on buttons.

For example, the IMG element in Figure 4.6 is given the identifier `mysteryImg` (line 13). Subsequently, the `Show Image` button accesses the `mysteryImg` element and changes its SRC attribute to the URL `'http://balance3e.com/Images/happy.gif'` (lines 16–17). Similarly, the `Hide Image` button accesses the `mysteryImg` element and changes its SRC attribute to the URL `'http://balance3e.com/Images/mystery.gif'` (lines 19–20). As a result, clicking on either of these buttons changes the image's source to the desired URL (Figures 4.7 and 4.8).

You may have noticed that the JavaScript assignment statements in Figure 4.6 (lines 16–17 and 18–19) were each broken across two lines. In general, a JavaScript statement can have spaces or even line breaks between the individual components of the statement—for example, before or after the = in an assignment statement. However, the components themselves must not be broken apart. For example, the expression on the left-hand side of an assignment statement cannot contain any spaces or line breaks. Similarly, the URL on the right-hand side cannot contain any spaces or line breaks.

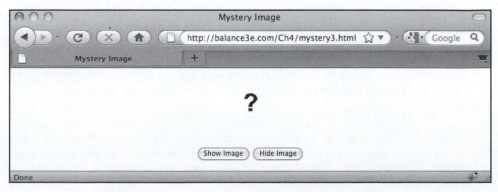

Figure 4.7 mystery3.html rendered in a Web browser.

Figure 4.8 `mystery3.html` rendered in a Web browser, after clicking the left button.

EXERCISE 4.4

Enter the `mystery3.html` text from Figure 4.6 into a new Web page, then load the page in the browser to verify that it behaves as described.

Modify the page so that it uses the same two images that you chose for your `mystery1.html` page (from Exercise 4.1).

Designer Secrets

When choosing the identifier name for a particular element in a page, you as the designer have considerable freedom. Most HTML identifiers start with a letter, followed by a sequence of letters and digits (although some special characters such as hyphens and underscores are allowed). Spaces are not allowed as part of an identifier.

You may have noted that standard identifiers in JavaScript follow a convention: they start with a lowercase letter and mix uppercase letters to highlight multiple words in the identifier. For example, `getElementById` is a readable combination of the phrase "get element by id." This is a useful convention to follow when you choose identifiers for your page elements. You should also choose identifiers that are descriptive in nature, providing a reader with a hint as to what that element represents. For example, the identifier `mysteryImg` implies both purpose (the contents are a mystery) and type (it is an image).

Common errors to avoid...

Unlike HTML tags, where you can enter the name of a tag in either uppercase or lowercase, the capitalization of names in JavaScript is important. You can use both lowercase and uppercase characters when specifying the identifier of an element, but you must be sure to recreate that name exactly when referring to it later in the page. For example, note that the `mysteryImage` identifier assigned to the image in Figure 4.6 contains a capital *I*. If you subsequently tried to access the image in Figure 4.6 using the following expression (note the lowercase *i*):

```
document.getElementById('mysteryimg')
```

the browser would not recognize the element since the capitalization does not match exactly.

A related and very common error that beginners make is to incorrectly type `getElementByID` (with a capital *D*). This will produce an error message since the browser will not recognize this as being the same as `getElementById`.

EXERCISE 4.5

Modify the `mystery3.html` page so that it acts as a simple slide show. You should add at least three more buttons, each associated with a different image. As before, these may be images located on the Web (specified by an absolute URL starting with `http://`) or local images that you have downloaded to your own machine (specified by a relative URL without `http://`). Be sure that the label on each button clearly identifies the image that is displayed at the click of that button.

EXERCISE 4.6

Create a variant of the `resize1.html` page from Exercise 4.2 named `resize2.html`. This page should contain an image and two buttons, labeled `Expand Image` and `Restore Image`. When the `Expand Image` button is clicked, the height and width of the image should be set to large values (e.g., 200 × 200). Likewise, when the `Restore Image` button is clicked, the height and width should be reset to their original values (e.g., 85 × 85).

Dynamic Text within a Page

All of the examples we have seen so far have involved changing the attributes of existing images in a page, in response to a user action (e.g., moving or clicking the mouse). It is also possible to generate new text within a page and thus customize a page in response to the user's behavior. This section will explore two techniques for generating dynamic page content: alert windows (which are sufficient for short messages) and the INNERHTML attribute (which easily integrates large amounts of text in the page).

Alert Windows

An *alert statement* is a JavaScript statement with the following general form:

```
alert('ALERT MESSAGE');
```

When executed by the browser, an alert statement causes a new window to appear and display the specified message. For example, the following button element, when clicked, would cause the *alert window* in Figure 4.9 to appear. This window will remain on the screen until the user clicks the OK button to close it.

```
<input type="button" value="Click for free money!"
       onclick="alert('Yeah, right.');">
```

When a JavaScript string is too long to fit on a single line in the text editor, you can break that string into pieces and concatenate (append end-to-end) the pieces using the + symbol. For example, the button below would display a two-sentence message when clicked. Note that each piece of the message has its own opening and closing single quotes and that the two pieces are connected using the + symbol. Also note that spaces are placed at the end of the first sentence in order to separate the two sentences in the alert window.

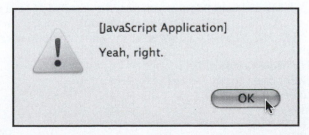

Figure 4.9 `alert` window generated by the "free money" button (using Firefox 3).

```
<input type="button" value="Click for free money!"
       onclick="alert('Did you really think it would work?  ' +
                'Nice try.');">
```

EXERCISE 4.7

Create a Web page named `alert.html` that contains a button. When clicked, the button should pop up an alert window that displays some message. The content of the message is entirely up to you.

The `innerHTML` Attribute

Although an alert statement is sufficient for displaying a brief message in a window, it has several shortcomings that limit its usefulness. The small size of an alert window makes it impractical to display long messages. In addition, the developer has very little control over the appearance of the text in the window, since the message cannot contain any HTML formatting (such as line breaks or bold font). Finally, the fact that the message appears in a separate window forces the user to shift attention to that window and then click on the OK button to close the window after reading the message.

Fortunately, HTML and JavaScript provide an alternative to alert statements that addresses these limitations. Instead of opening a separate alert window, it is possible to embed the text message within the existing page, using HTML formatting to control the appearance of the text as desired. This is accomplished using the INNERHTML attribute of a span, paragraph, or page division. When a JavaScript statement assigns text to the INNERHTML attribute of a SPAN, P, or DIV element, the text is inserted into that element and displayed within the page.

For example, the Web page in Figure 4.10 contains a page division with identifier `outputDiv`. Initially, the `outputDiv` division contains the text "Welcome to my site!" (as rendered in Figure 4.11). When the button labeled `Click for Help` is clicked, however, the JavaScript assignment statement associated with the ONCLICK attribute is executed. This statement assigns a message to the INNERHTML attribute of `outputDiv`, resulting in that message being displayed in the page (Figure 4.12).

```
1.  <!doctype html>
2.  <!-- help.html                                                  Dave Reed -->
3.  <!-- Web page that displays a help message when a button is clicked. -->
4.  <!-- ============================================================ -->
5.
6.  <html>
7.   <head>
8.    <title> Button Help </title>
9.   </head>
10.
11.  <body>
12.    <p>
13.      Contents of the page.
14.    </p>
15.    <input type="button" value="Click for Help"
16.           onclick="document.getElementById('outputDiv').innerHTML=
17.                    'If you have any trouble with this site, ' +
18.                    'contact <i>admin@foo.bar</i>.';">
19.    <hr>
20.    <div id="outputDiv">
21.      Welcome to my site!
22.    </div>
23.  </body>
24. </html>
```

Figure 4.10   Web page that displays text when a button is clicked.

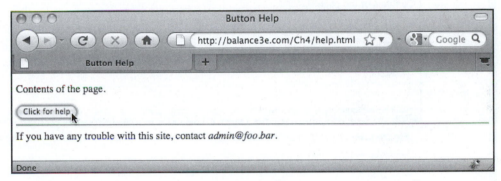

Figure 4.11 help.html rendered in a Web browser.

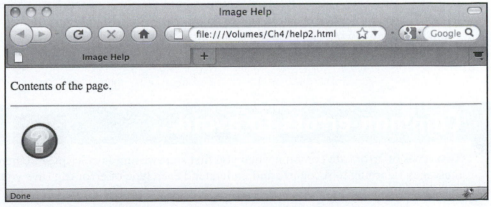

Figure 4.12 help.html rendered in a Web browser, after clicking the Help button.

EXERCISE 4.8

Enter the help.html text from Figure 4.10 into a new Web page, then load the page in the browser to verify that it behaves as described.

Modify the page so that it has an additional button labeled Clear Help. When clicked, the INNER-HTML attribute of the outputDiv page division should be reassigned so that the original text ("Welcome to my site!") is displayed.

EXERCISE 4.9

An alternative to using buttons to display and hide help messages in a page would be to have dynamic help icons within the page. By moving the mouse over a help icon, the user could see the message associated with that icon.

Figure 4.13 help2.html rendered in a Web browser.

Create a page named `help2.html` that contains a help icon at the bottom left (as in Figure 4.13). You may use the `http://balance3e.com/Images/help.jpg` image for your icon, or use your own image if you prefer. When the mouse moves over the icon, a help message should be displayed in a page division to the right of the icon (Figure 4.14). When the mouse moves off the icon, the page division should be cleared.

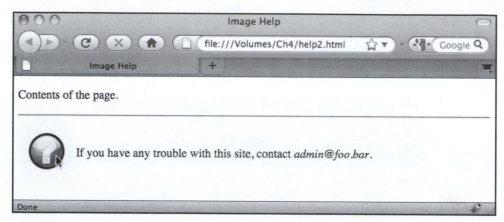

Figure 4.14 `help2.html` rendered in a Web browser, with the mouse over the help icon.

Hint: To position the text to the right of the image, consider embedding the image and page division in a table (similar to the `demo11.html` page from Figure 2.21).

Designer Secrets

As we saw in Chapter 2, a DIV element can group static elements within a page division, such as an image and button that are to be centered together in the page. Another common use for DIV elements is to provide a page division where dynamic text can be displayed. For example, Figure 4.10 contains a DIV element that displays a dynamic welcome message within the page. By convention, the generic name `outputDiv` is used throughout the text for a page division that displays dynamic text, although the name given to the DIV element can vary as desired.

While DIV elements are typically used for displaying dynamic text, there are occasions where other text elements, such as P and SPAN, may be more appropriate. For example, if a single dynamic word or phrase appeared within an otherwise static paragraph, then that word or phrase could be embedded in a SPAN element and changed via its INNERHTML attribute.

Common errors to avoid...

Two types of errors are common when you first start writing JavaScript statements with complex messages. Learning to recognize and understand each type of error can save you considerable amounts of time and frustration.

1) Error: unterminated string literal

This error message appears when the browser encounters the beginning of a JavaScript string but fails to find the closing quote on the same line. When breaking a long JavaScript string across lines (as in lines 17 and 18 of Figure 4.10), you must be very careful that each line contains only complete pieces, connected with the + symbol. In particular, you cannot start a string on one line and continue it on the next. For example,

```
alert('This example is illegal because the
       string is broken across lines');

alert('This example is OK because the message ' +
      'is broken into two distinct strings');
```

2) Error: missing) after argument list
  OR
  Error: missing ; after statement

One of these error messages will appear when the components of a string are not connected correctly, such as when the + is missing between two pieces of a string. When a string is not followed by a +, the browser expects to encounter either a right parenthesis or a semicolon to complete the statement (depending upon the context). For example,

```
alert('This example is illegal because '
      'there is not a + connecting the pieces');

alert('This example is OK because the ' +
      'pieces are properly connected');
```

Example: Quotations Page

Consider the task of designing a Web page for displaying quotations. Given a collection of quotations, we want the user to be able to select a quotation and see it displayed in the page. The material introduced in this chapter suggests two possibilities. First, we could utilize buttons, labeling each button in the page with the author of a quotation. When the user clicks on one of these buttons, the associated quotation would be displayed in the page (Figure 4.15). Alternatively, we could utilize dynamic images of the authors. When the user moves the mouse over an image, the quotation associated

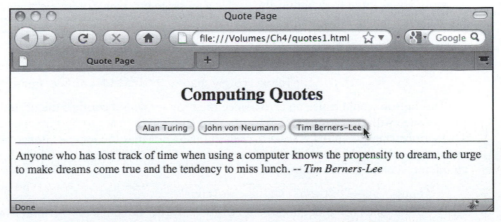

Figure 4.15 Button version of quotes.html rendered in a Web browser.

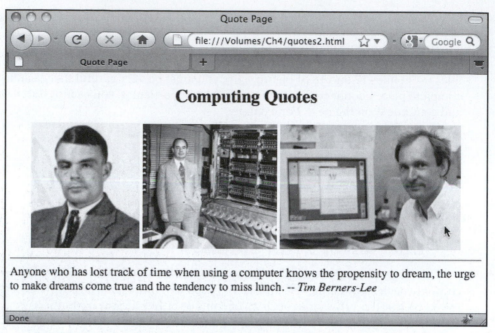

Figure 4.16 Dynamic image version of `quotes.html` rendered in a Web browser.

with that author would be displayed in the page and then erased when the mouse moves off that image (Figure 4.16).

EXERCISE 4.10

Create a Web page named `quotes.html` that can be used to select and display at least three of your favorite quotations. The layout of this page is up to you. In particular, you may choose to use buttons or dynamic images, as shown in Figures 4.15 and 4.16, respectively. The button or image should clearly identify the author of the quotation, and the author's name should appear in italics at the end of the quotation.

Designer Secrets

Suppose you wanted to dynamically display a message in a page (or an alert window) that contained apostrophes. For example,

```
<input type="button" value="Welcome"
        onclick="document.getElementById('outputDiv').innerHTML=
                'Welcome to my page. I'm glad you're here.';">
```

This button would cause an error, since the browser would confuse the nested apostrophe in the message with the closing quote for the string literal. In order to nest an apostrophe inside a JavaScript string, you must place a backslash (also known as the *escape character*) before the apostrophe. When the browser encounters a backslash inside a string, it knows to treat the next character as plain text. For example,

```
<input type="button" value="Welcome"
        onclick="document.getElementById('outputDiv').innerHTML=
                'Welcome to my page. I\'m glad you\'re here.';">
```

Looking Ahead...

In this chapter, you learned to create interactive Web pages using the JavaScript programming language. HTML event handlers such as ONMOUSEOVER and ONCLICK enable elements to react to events initiated by the user. By associating JavaScript statements with these event handlers, you were able to instruct the browser to dynamically alter the contents of the page, either by changing the attributes of an image or by displaying messages within the page.

While buttons and dynamic images provide a degree of user interactivity in a Web page, there are many applications where greater user control is required. For example, you might want to allow the user to enter her name when a page loads and then have personalized messages integrated into the page. Or, you might want to create a Web page that allows the user to enter his homework and test grades for a course and then have the page calculate and display the overall course average. Chapter 5 will focus on a new HTML element that enables the user to enter information and corresponding JavaScript statements that access, store, and perform calculations on that information.

Chapter Summary

- JavaScript is a simple programming language for making dynamic Web pages. Using JavaScript, Web designers can create pages that interact with the user and vary their contents each time they are loaded.

- A JavaScript statement is an instruction that tells the browser to perform some specific action, such changing another element's attributes or opening an alert window.

- An event handler is an HTML attribute that specifies how the element is to react to certain events. JavaScript statements are assigned to an event handler to define the specific action to be carried out.

- The ONMOUSEOVER event handler specifies how an element is to react when the user moves the mouse over the element. Similarly, the ONMOUSEOUT event handler specifies how the element reacts when the mouse is subsequently moved off the element. The general form for an image that reacts to mouse movement is:

```
<img src="ADDRESS_OF_IMAGE" alt="ALTERNATE_TEXT"
     onmouseover="CODE_TO_EXECUTE_WHEN_MOUSE_GOES_OVER_IMAGE"
     onmouseout="CODE_TO_EXECUTE_WHEN_MOUSE_LEAVES_IMAGE">
```

- A JavaScript assignment statement is used to assign a new value to an attribute of an element. The general form of a JavaScript assignment is:

```
 this.ATTRIBUTE_NAME=NEW_ATTRIBUTE_VALUE;
```

- A sequence of characters enclosed in quotes is known as a string literal, or string for short. By convention, HTML strings use double quotes while JavaScript strings use single quotes.

- An error in the format of HTML or JavaScript statement (e.g., a misspelled identifier name) is known as a syntax error. Syntax errors in HTML tags are typically ignored by the browser; syntax errors in JavaScript statements will typically cause the page to fail to load.

- IMG elements have optional HEIGHT and WIDTH attributes, which can be dynamically adjusted to expand and shrink the image.

- The ONCLICK event handler specifies how an element is to react when the user clicks the mouse on the element. The general form for an image that reacts to a mouse click is:

```
<img src="ADDRESS_OF_IMAGE" alt="ALT_TEXT"
     onclick="CODE_TO_EXECUTE_WHEN_MOUSE_CLICKS_ON_THE_IMAGE">
```

- A button is an HTML element that initiates actions in the page when clicked. The general form for a button is:

```
<input type="button" value="BUTTON_LABEL"
       onclick="CODE_TO_EXECUTE_WHEN_MOUSE_CLICKS_ON_BUTTON">
```

- In order for a button to change the attributes of another element, that element must first be assigned a unique identifier using the ID attribute. Capitalization matters, so `outputDiv` and `outputdiv` are considered two distinct identifiers by the browser.

- Within a JavaScript statement, an element can be accessed (and modified) using an expression of the form:

```
document.getElementById('ELEMENT_ID')
```

- When executed, an alert statement causes a new window to appear and display the specified message. The general form of an alert statement is:

```
alert('ALERT_MESSAGE');
```

- Text-based elements such as SPAN, P, and DIV have an attribute named INNERHTML that defines their contents. By assigning a new string to the INNERHTML attribute of an element, that text message can be dynamically inserted into the page. The string assigned to an INNERHTML attribute can contain HTML tags for formatting the text.

- To embed an apostrophe inside a JavaScript string, precede the apostrophe with a backslash (also known as an escape character).

Supplemental Material and Exercises

Changing an Image's Border

Whether or not an image appears with a border around the edge is controlled by the BORDER attribute. By default, the BORDER attribute is assigned to 0, meaning that no border will appear around the image. However, a border can be added to the image by assigning the BORDER attribute a positive integer value. For example, assigning `border=1` will put a border one pixel thick around the image. Assigning a higher number yields a thicker border, such as `border=3` (three pixels thick).

EXERCISE 4.11

Similar to the `mystery1.html` and `resize1.html` pages from Exercises 4.1 and 4.2, create a Web page named `border1.html` that contains a dynamic image without a border. When the mouse goes over the image, the border attribute for that image should be set to 1, which causes a line to appear around the edges of the image. When the mouse leaves the image, the border attribute should be reassigned back to 0.

EXERCISE 4.12

Create a variant of the `border1.html` page from Exercise 4.11 named `border2.html`. This page should contain an image and two buttons, labeled `Show Border` and `Hide Border`. When the `Show Border` button is clicked, the border on the image should be displayed. Likewise, when the `Hide Border` button is clicked, the border should be hidden.

Relative Resizing

In Exercise 4.6, you created a Web page with buttons and a resizable image. When the `Expand Image` button was clicked, the HEIGHT and WIDTH attributes of the image were assigned new values that were double their original values. Similarly, when the `Restore Image` button was clicked, the HEIGHT and WIDTH attributes were reset to their original values. While this approach worked, it was somewhat tedious in that you had to enter the specific dimensions of the image and ensure that the expansion maintained the correct height-to-width ratio.

An alternative approach to expanding an image in the page is to use relative values for the new height and width. That is, instead of specifying absolute numbers of pixels in the JavaScript assignments, you can define the new height and width relative to their old values. Expanding a 100×75 pixel image would double its size to 200×150 pixels; expanding again would double that size to 400×300 pixels. In Chapter 5, you will learn the general form of mathematical expression in JavaScript statements. For now, it suffices to know that you can multiply values on the right-hand side of a JavaScript assignment using the * operator. For example, the following button will double the HEIGHT and WIDTH attributes of the mysteryImg image when clicked:

```
<input type="button" value="Expand Image"
       onclick="document.getElementById('mysteryImg').height=
                2*document.getElementById('mysteryImg').height;
              document.getElementById('mysteryImg').width=
                2*document.getElementById('mysteryImg').width;">
```

EXERCISE 4.13

Create a variant of the resize2.html page from Exercise 4.6 named resize3.html. Modify the Expand Image button so that it doubles the dimensions of the image each time it is clicked. Conversely, modify the other button so that it halves the height and width when clicked.

EXERCISE 4.14

Similarly, create a variant of the border2.html page from Exercise 4.12 named border3.html. The page should have an image with a one-pixel border. When the button labeled Expand Border is clicked, the thickness of the border should double. Conversely, when the button labeled Shrink Border is clicked, the border thickness should be halved.

Changing an Element's Color

While the ONMOUSEOVER and ONMOUSEOUT event handlers are most commonly associated with images, they can be applied to any HTML element in a Web page. In particular, it is possible to apply these event handlers to paragraphs of text within the page, changing the style of the text when the mouse moves over it. For example, the color of the text in the following paragraph will change to red when the mouse is moved over any part of the paragraph, then back to black when the mouse is moved off:

```
<p onmouseover="this.style.color='red';"
   onmouseout="this.style.color='black';">
   This text will turn red when the mouse moves over it.
</p>
```

Other style attributes of an element can similarly be changed using the ONMOUSEOVER and ONMOUSEOUT event handlers. For example, the word *important* in the following paragraph will be highlighted with a yellow background when the mouse is moved over the word:

```
<p>
This is a really
<span onmouseover="this.style.backgroundColor='yellow';"
      onmouseout="this.style.backgroundColor='white';">important</span>
  point to note.
</p>
```

EXERCISE 4.15

Utilize the ONMOUSEOVER and ONMOUSEOUT event handlers to dynamically change the color of text or other elements within a page. Note that it is even possible to change the background color of a button when the mouse moves over it, making it appear dynamic to the user.

Nested Quotes

Technically, JavaScript string can use either single quotes (' ') or double quotes (" ") to enclose characters. This book uses the convention that JavaScript strings will always be enclosed in single quotes to avoid confusion between HTML strings (which are always written using double quotes). For example, in the following button element, the JavaScript statement assigned to the ONCLICK attribute itself contains a JavaScript string, so one type of string is nested inside the other.

```
<input type="button" value="Click here for free money!"
       onclick="alert('Yeah, right.');">
```

EXERCISE 4.16

What error(s) occur when a JavaScript string contains incorrectly nested double quotation marks? For example, add the following button to a Web page and describe what happens when that button is clicked.

```
<input type="button" value="oops"
       onclick="document.getElementById('outputDiv').innerHTML=
                'Please enter "your name" in the box';">
```

How would you modify the element so that it correctly displays the double quotes in the message?

EXERCISE 4.17

On paper, specify JavaScript assignment statements that would embed the following lines of text in a page division named outputDiv. Then verify that your statements work, associating each statement with the ONCLICK attribute of a button.

```
The announcer screamed "Cubs win! Cubs win!"
The oath began as "I, 'state your name' swear to uphold..."
The oath began as "I, "state your name" swear to uphold..."
```

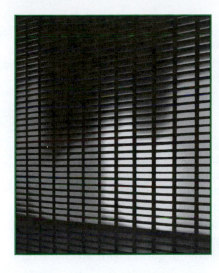

JavaScript and User Interaction

Chapter 5

This chapter uses narrative, examples, and hands-on exercises to introduce programming concepts and Web development skills.

The Internet already has too many static pages. Why add yours to the list? To get noticed, your page must be live, it must do something, or offer some service. What better way is there to liven pages up yourself than to use JavaScript, writing a short script that runs in the browser, right in front of the user? JavaScript puts all the elements in a web page—and the web page itself!—under your control.

Steven Holzner
Essential JavaScript

Debugging is twice as hard as writing the code in the first place. Therefore, if you write the code as cleverly as possible, you are, by definition, not smart enough to debug it.
Brian Kernighan

In Chapter 4, you began using JavaScript to develop interactive Web pages. By adding event handlers to HTML elements and associating JavaScript statements with those attributes, you enabled the elements to react to events within the page. For example, an image with ONMOUSEOVER and ONMOUSEOUT attributes could react to mouse movements and change its source or size in response. Similarly, a button with an ONCLICK attribute could display a help message in a page division when clicked. In this chapter, you will extend the interactivity of your pages using a new HTML element and JavaScript statements. In particular, a text box enables the user to enter information that can then be incorporated into the page. JavaScript variables will be used to simplify code and store values that can be used over and over. Finally, standard mathematical operators for addition, subtraction, multiplication, and division will enable pages to perform calculations and display numerical results within the page.

User Input via Text Boxes

While the Web pages in Chapter 4 allowed the user to interact with the page, the control provided by mouse movement and clicks is limited. If we want a page that can react in a variety of ways, we need additional mechanisms for providing richer input to the page. For example, to design a personalized page that integrates the user's name in the text, there must be a way for the user to first enter his or her name. A ***text box*** is an HTML element that provides a space within the page where the user can enter information.

The Text Box Element

Similar to the button element introduced in Chapter 4, a text box is a specific type of INPUT element. A page designer can embed a text box in a page just like a button or any other HTML element. When rendered, a text box appears as a rectangle in which the user can enter text. The general form of a text box element is shown below:

```
<input type="text" id="BOX_ID" size=NUM_CHARS
       value="INITIAL_CONTENTS_OF_BOX">
```

As we saw in Chapter 4, the ID attribute associates a unique identifier with the element, so that it can be referenced by other elements within the page. The SIZE attribute specifies the width of the text box, in terms of the number of characters that will fit within the box. The VALUE attribute specifies whatever text is to appear in that box when it is initially rendered in the page. For example, the Web page in Figure 5.1 contains a text box whose identifier is nameBox. It is wide enough to contain 12 characters (although the fit may not be exact, depending on browser default settings). And since the VALUE attribute for this text box is assigned the *empty string* (double quotes with no characters between them), the box is empty when rendered (Figure 5.2).

After a text box has been rendered in a page, the user can change its contents by typing text within the box. Then a JavaScript statement can access the contents of the box using the expression:

```
document.getElementById('BOX_ID').value
```

For example, the button in Figure 5.1 utilizes a JavaScript assignment statement that accesses the contents of nameBox. When the user clicks on that button, whatever name has been entered into the box will be integrated into the displayed message (Figure 5.3). Note that the message assigned to the INNERHTML attribute of the page division is broken across several lines (lines 18–20), with the individual pieces concatenated together using the + operator. The message integrates string literals (text enclosed in single quotes) with the expression representing the name entered in nameBox, which appears twice in the displayed message.

```
1.  <!doctype html>
2.  <!-- greet.html                                  Dave Reed -->
3.  <!-- Web page that displays a personalized greeting. -->
4.  <!-- ============================================== -->
5.
6.  <html>
7.   <head>
8.    <title> Greetings </title>
9.   </head>
10.
11.  <body>
12.    <h2>Greetings</h2>
13.    <p>
14.     Enter your name: <input type="text" id="nameBox" size=12 value="">
15.    </p>
16.    <input type="button" value="Click for Greeting"
17.          onclick="document.getElementById('outputDiv').innerHTML=
18.                   'Hello' + document.getElementById('nameBox').value +
19.                   ', welcome to my page.<br>Do you mind if I call you' +
20.                   document.getElementById('nameBox').value + '?';">
21.    <hr>
22.    <div id="outputDiv"></div>
23.   </body>
24.  </html>
```

Figure 5.1 Web page that displays a personalized greeting.

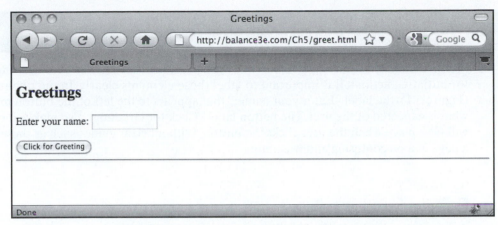

Figure 5.2 greet.html rendered in a Web browser.

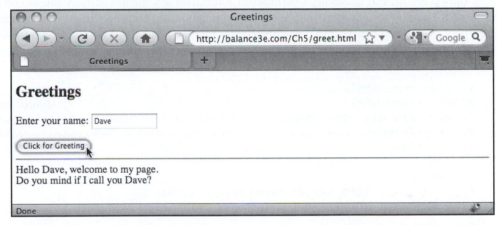

Figure 5.3 greet.html rendered in a Web browser, after entering "Dave" and clicking the button.

EXERCISE 5.1

Enter the greet.html text from Figure 5.1 into a new Web page, then load the page in the browser to verify that it behaves as described.

Modify the page so that both occurrences of the user's name appear in italics. *Hint:* to do this, you will need to add <i> and </i> tags to the text of the message, before and after each occurrence of the name. Since these tags are part of the plain text that is to be inserted into the page division (not JavaScript expressions to be evaluated), they will need to be placed within string literals in the message.

Common errors to avoid...

Consider a courtroom scene in which the bailiff instructs a witness to "Repeat after me: I, state your name, promise to tell the truth, the whole truth, and nothing but the truth." The intent is for the witness to not repeat this phrase exactly but instead to substitute his or her name in place of "state your name." The equivalent intention is involved when you integrate the contents of a text box into a message.

For example, the expression document.getElementById(nameBox).value appears twice in the text message in Figure 5.1 (lines 18 and 20). For each occurrence, the intention is that the value this expression represents—that is, the contents of the nameBox text box—should be inserted into the message. It is important to note that the expression is *not* enclosed in quotes. If it were, it would be treated as a string literal and the text "document.getElementById(nameBox).value" would be displayed (similar to the witness blindly repeating "state your name" in the oath).

Designer Secrets

When including interactive elements in a Web page, such as text boxes for user input and buttons for initiating actions, it is important to label those elements clearly. In the `greet.html` page (Figure 5.1), the label "Enter your name:" that appears to the left of the button makes it clear what is expected of the user. The button label "Click for Greeting" also makes it clear what action will take place when the user clicks the button. Without clear guides such as these, interacting with a page can be confusing and frustrating.

Example: Form Letter Page

A form letter is piece of mail (either electronic or paper) that is mass produced yet personalized to the recipient. For example, a form letter announcing a special activity might contain mostly generic information but then personalize the announcement by incorporating the recipient's name, a description of the activity, and the activity's date. The Web page in Figure 5.4 can be used to generate an online form letter. It contains three text boxes where the user can enter the recipient's name (line 15),

```
1.  <!doctype html>
2.  <!-- form.html                                        Dave Reed -->
3.  <!-- Web page that generates a form letter based on user inputs. -->
4.  <!-- ======================================================== -->
5.
6.  <html>
7.   <head>
8.     <title> Form Letter Generator </title>
9.   </head>
10.
11.  <body>
12.    <h2>Form Letter Generator</h2>
13.    <p>
14.      Enter recipient's name:
15.        <input type="text" id="recipientBox" size=20 value="Buddy"> <br>
16.      Enter activity:
17.        <input type="text" id="activityBox" size=20 value="my birthday"> <br>
18.      Enter date: <input type="text" id="dateBox" size=20 value="February 29">
19.    </p>
20.    <input type="button" value="Click for Form Letter"
21.          onclick="document.getElementById('outputDiv').innerHTML=
22.                '<p>Dear ' + document.getElementById('recipientBox').value +
23.                ',</p> <p>Have you heard about ' +
24.                document.getElementById('activityBox').value +
25.                ', which is coming up on ' +
26.                document.getElementById('dateBox').value +
27.                '? It would mean a lot to me if you could make it to ' +
28.                document.getElementById('activityBox').value +
29.                '. Hopefully, I\'ll see you ' +
30.                document.getElementById('dateBox').value + '.</p>' +
31.                '<p style=\'text-align:right\'>Your friend,<br> Dave</p>';">
32.    <hr>
33.    <div id="outputDiv"></div>
34.  </body>
35. </html>
```

Figure 5.4   Web page that generates a form letter at the click of a button.

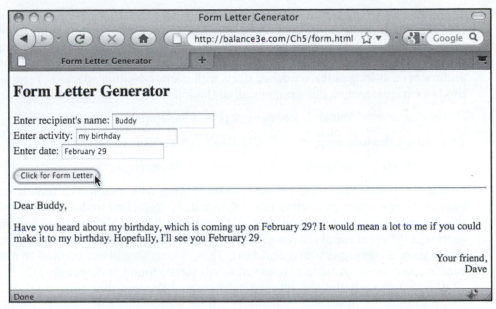

Figure 5.5 form.html rendered in a Web browser, after user input.

a description of the activity (line 17), and its date (line 18). After entering appropriate text in these boxes, the user can click the button to generate the form letter. The ONCLICK attribute of the button (lines 21–31) contains the JavaScript statement that combines the text from the boxes with string literals to produce the letter (Figure 5.5).

Since the text that makes up the form letter is long, the right-hand side of the JavaScript assignment in the ONCLICK attribute must be broken across several lines. Recall that a JavaScript string literal cannot span lines—that is, the closing quote for a JavaScript string literal must appear on the same line as the opening quote. A long message, such as this one, can be broken into many pieces, which are then concatenated together using the + operator. Also recall that apostrophes (single quotes) are embedded within a JavaScript string by placing a backslash before the apostrophe. The backslash instructs the browser that the apostrophe that follows is to be treated as a plain character and not the closing quote of the string.

EXERCISE 5.2

Enter the form.html text from Figure 5.4 into a new Web page, then load the page in the browser to verify that it behaves as described.

Modify the page so that there is an additional text box where the user can enter the time for the activity. Then modify the JavaScript button associated with the button so that the activity's time is incorporated into the form letter.

JavaScript Variables

The examples we have considered so far have utilized JavaScript assignment statements to directly change the attributes of HTML elements in the page. The left-hand side of the assignment specified the element and attribute to be changed, and the right-hand side specified the new value. For example, the following assignment changes the width attribute of the image with identifier mysteryImg, reassigning it to be 100 pixels.

```
document.getElementById('mysteryImg').width = 100;
```

In addition to these types of direct actions, JavaScript assignments can also be used for indirect actions, assigning values to temporary variables for subsequent use within the page.

In programming terminology, a ***variable*** is a name used to symbolize a dynamic value—that is, one that might change over time. More specifically, a variable stores a value in memory, making that value accessible via the variable's name. With a few exceptions, you can choose any name you wish for a JavaScript variable. Technically, a variable name can be any sequence of letters, digits, and underscores, as long as the sequence starts with a letter. Neither spaces nor special characters can be used in variable names. For example, all of the following are valid JavaScript variable names:

```
recipient    SUM    current_age    Sum2Date    x
```

By contrast, the following are not valid JavaScript variable names:

```
2hotforU    salary$    two words    "sum_to_date"
```

The first name, `2hotforU`, is invalid because it starts with a digit. The remaining names are invalid because they contain characters other than letters, digits, and underscores. JavaScript is case sensitive, meaning that capitalization matters. Consequently, variable names such as `sum`, `Sum`, and `SUM` all represent different variables. Also, JavaScript and Web browsers reserve certain words for other purposes, such as `name`, `password`, and `text`. These words should not be used to represent variables, as conflicts may occur. A table of reserved words can be found in Appendix D.

JavaScript variables are automatically created the first time they are used. When the browser first encounters a new variable name, it will set aside a piece of memory for that variable (known as its ***memory cell***). Any assignment to that variable directs the browser to store the specified value in that variable's memory cell. We can visualize assignments to variables by drawing a box to symbolize the memory cell and labeling the box with the variable name. When an assignment is made, the assigned value is written in the box to represent its storage in the corresponding memory cell. For example:

```
userName = 'Dave';
```
'Dave'
userName

After a value has been assigned to a particular variable, any reference to the variable name evaluates to the value stored in its associated memory cell. This means that the value stored in the memory cell is substituted for the variable name wherever that name appears. For example, after assigning the value `'Dave'` to the variable `userName`, the following two JavaScript statements are equivalent:

```
document.getElementById('outputDiv').innerHTML = 'Hi Dave';

document.getElementById('outputDiv').innerHTML = 'Hi ' + userName;
```

If you are familiar with algebra, the concept of a variable is not new to you. For example, the equation $y = x^2 + 1$ refers to an abstract relationship between variables x and y. By substituting the desired value of x into the equation, we can determine the corresponding value of y. Similarly, a JavaScript variable represents a value, and that value is substituted for the variable name each time it appears in an expression.

Variables for Reusing Values

One of the most common uses of variables in JavaScript is to temporarily store values that are used over and over again. Consider the `greet.html` page from Figure 5.1, for example. The expression

```
document.getElementById('nameBox').value
```

appears twice on the right-hand side of the JavaScript assignment. Since this expression is long, its duplication produces an assignment statement that is complex and spans several lines. Having to type in this complex expression multiple times also increases the likelihood of an error on the part of the developer.

An alternative to duplication would be to utilize a JavaScript variable, as in the following modified button:

```
<input type="button" value="Click for Greeting"
       onclick="userName=document.getElementById('nameBox').value;
                document.getElementById('outputDiv').innerHTML=
                  'Hello ' + userName + ', welcome to my page.<br>' +
                  'Do you mind if I call you ' + userName + '?';">
```

The first JavaScript statement in the ONCLICK attribute assigns the contents of the `nameBox` to a variable named `userName`. This variable is then used in both places in the message, making the message text simpler and shorter.

EXERCISE 5.3

Modify your `greet.html` page from Exercise 5.1 to similarly use a variable to simplify the displayed message. That is, the first JavaScript statement associated with the button's ONCLICK attribute should be an assignment that stores the contents of `nameBox` in a variable. Then that variable should be integrated into the message being displayed (as opposed to the full `getElementById` expression).

EXERCISE 5.4

Similarly, modify your `form.html` page from Exercise 5.2 to use variables. This will require a separate variable for each of the text boxes in the page. Once the contents of each of the boxes are assigned to variables, the variables should be integrated into the message being displayed.

Designer Secrets

You may have noticed that the pages you are writing are falling into a common pattern. There is a text box for each piece of information that is required of the user. Then a button (or buttons) has an ONCLICK attribute containing JavaScript statements that access the contents of the text boxes and integrate those values into a message. The general pattern for the button's ONCLICK code can be written as follows:

```
VAR1 = document.getElementById('BOX_ID1').value;
VAR2 = document.getElementById('BOX_ID2').value;
...
VARn = document.getElementById('BOX_IDn').value;

document.getElementById('outputDiv').innerHTML =
   MESSAGE_INTEGRATING_STRING_LITERALS_AND_VARIABLES;">
```

As a beginner programmer, recognizing general patterns such as this can be very useful. When given a new problem to solve, identifying a previously solved problem that is similar and then using its code as a template for solving the new problem is both smart and efficient.

Example: Fill-in-the-Blank Story

A variant of the form letter is the fill-in-the-blank story, where a potentially humorous story is written down with blanks inserted in place of some of the key words. Before reading the story, the storyteller asks others present to fill in the blanks. Those selecting the words are told only the type of word required and have no other knowledge of the story. This lack of context in selecting words can result in an entertaining story when the words are plugged into the appropriate places. For example, consider the following beginning to a story:

```
It was a adjective kind of day when person's name walked out into the
street. The sky was a deep color, and same name was walking his new pet
animal...
```

Then, imagine that the participants make the following substitutions:

```
adjective = smarmy
person's name = Chris
color = mauve
animal = gnu
```

If the blanks are replaced with these words, then the story will read,

```
It was a smarmy kind of day when Chris walked out into the street.
The sky was a deep mauve, and Chris was walking his new pet gnu ...
```

EXERCISE 5.5

Create a Web page named story.html that serves as an interactive fill-in-the-blank story program. Your page should contain text boxes where the user can enter words to fill in the blanks in a story. It should also contain a button that, when clicked, causes the story to be displayed with the user's words entered in the appropriate places. The content of the story can be anything that you like—be creative!—but your story must meet the following conditions:

1. It must be at least two paragraphs long.
2. It must have at least six missing words.
3. At least one of the missing words must be used multiple times in the story. For example, the person's name was used twice in the sample story above.
4. The page should have a title, centered at the top, which includes your name.

Variables for Temporary Values

The examples in the previous section demonstrated how variables can simplify JavaScript code. By replacing repeated copies of a complex expression with a single variable name, the resulting code is shorter and simpler. There are times, however, when using a variable is not just a matter of convenience but is necessary to perform the required logic in a page. Consider the task of swapping two images in a page. At the click of a button, we want the source files for two image elements in a page to be swapped. That is, if the left image portrays a happy face and the right a sad face (Figure 5.6), then clicking the mouse would cause the left image to display the sad face and the right image the happy face (Figure 5.7). Clicking the button again would swap the images back into their original positions. The following sequence of JavaScript statements *attempts* to carry out this swap:

```
document.getElementById('leftImg').src =
  document.getElementById('rightImg').src;

document.getElementById('rightImg').src =
  document.getElementById('leftImg').src;
```

Unfortunately, the destructive nature of assignments prevents these statements from performing the desired swap. When the first assignment is executed, the SRC attribute of rightImg (e.g., 'sad.gif') is assigned to leftImg's SRC attribute, overwriting its old value. When the second assignment is executed, it is this new value that is assigned back to the SRC attribute of rightImg, resulting in both images display 'sad.gif'. Changing the order of the assignments just means that the SRC attribute of rightImg is overwritten first.

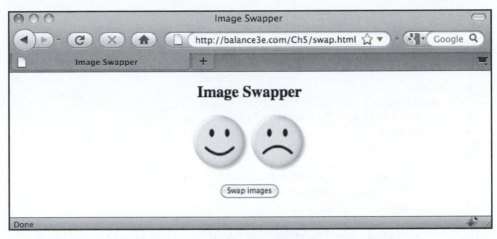

Figure 5.6 Web page with two images.

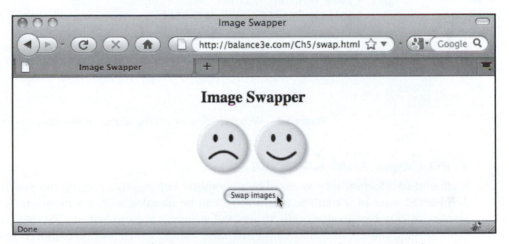

Figure 5.7 Web page with the source for the two images swapped.

While this task cannot be accomplished with two direct assignments, it can be accomplished using a third, indirect assignment. Before overwriting the SRC attribute of the leftImg, its initial value can be saved by assigning it to a variable (line 19 in Figure 5.8). Then, the SRC attribute of leftImg can be safely overwritten (lines 20–21 in Figure 5.8). The original SRC value for the leftImg, now safely stored in the variable, can finally be assigned to the SRC of the rightImg (line 22 in Figure 5.8).

EXERCISE 5.6

Enter the swap.html text from Figure 5.8 into a new Web page, then load the page in the browser to verify that it behaves as described.

Modify the page so that it has a third image to the right of the existing images. In place of the single button labeled Swap Images, there should be two buttons on the page labeled Rotate Left and Rotate Right. When the user clicks on the Rotate Left button, the SRC attributes of the images should be changed so that each image is shifted to the left (and the image originally at the far left is rotated around to the right). For example, if the three images were initially the three faces—sequenced happy-sad-surprised (from left to right)—clicking the Rotate Left button would result in the sequence sad-surprised-happy. Conversely, clicking on the Rotate Right button should shift the images to the right (with the rightmost image rotating around to the left).

```
1.  <!doctype html>
2.  <!-- swap.html                                      Dave Reed  -->
3.  <!-- Web page that swaps two images at the click of a button. -->
4.  <!-- ============================================================ -->
5.
6.  <html>
7.    <head>
8.      <title>Image Swapper</title>
9.    </head>
10.
11.   <body>
12.     <div style="text-align:center">
13.       <h2>Image Swapper</h2>
14.       <p>
15.         <img id="leftImg" src="http://balance3e.com/Images/happy.gif">
16.         <img id="rightImg" src="http://balance3e.com/Images/sad.gif">
17.       </p>
18.       <input type="button" value="Swap images"
19.              onclick="saved=document.getElementById('leftImg').src;
20.                    document.getElementById('leftImg').src=
21.                       document.getElementById('rightImg').src;
22.                    document.getElementById('rightImg').src=saved;">
23.     </div>
24.   </body>
25. </html>
```

Figure 5.8 Web page that swaps the source of two images.

Web Pages That Compute

Each unit of information processed by a computer belongs to a general category, or ***data type***, which defines the ways in which the information can be handled within a program. So far, we have used JavaScript variables to store only strings, but strings represent just one JavaScript data type—values can also be numbers and Booleans (true/false values, which will be explored in Chapter 11). Each JavaScript data type is associated with a specific set of predefined operators, which are part of the JavaScript language and may be used by programmers to manipulate values of that type. For example, we have already seen that strings can be concatenated (joined end to end) using the + operator. Similarly, JavaScript predefines the standard arithmetic operators + (addition), – (subtraction), * (multiplication), and / (division) for use with numbers.

JavaScript Numbers and Expressions

JavaScript variables can be assigned various kinds of numerical values, including numbers and mathematical expressions formed by applying operators to numbers. When an expression appears on the right-hand side of an assignment statement, that expression is evaluated and the resulting value is assigned to the variable on the left-hand side. For example, Figure 5.9 traces a sequence of assignments,

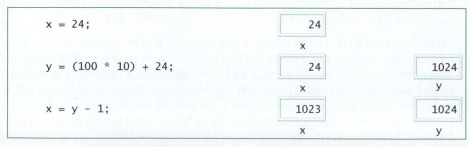

Figure 5.9 Tracing a sequence of assignment statements.

in which the result of each assignment is represented by the memory cell(s) to the right. In the first assignment, the variable x is assigned the number 24, which is then stored in the memory cell corresponding to x. In the second assignment, the expression on the right-hand side evaluates to 1024, resulting in 1024 being assigned to y's memory cell while x remains unchanged. In the third assignment, the expression on the right-hand side evaluates to 1023 (this computation is performed using the current value of y). Therefore, 1023 is assigned to x's memory cell, overwriting the cell's previous contents.

In mathematics, the symbol = is used to indicate equality—thus, a statement such as x = x + 1; wouldn't make much sense in an algebraic context. However, you must remind yourself that JavaScript uses = to assign values to variables, rather than to test equality. The expression on the right-hand side of an assignment is evaluated using the current values of variables. Then the value of that expression is assigned to the variable on the left-hand side of the assignment. In the example x = x + 1, the current value of x is increased by 1, and the result is assigned back to x.

Common errors to avoid...

Try to refrain from using the word *equals* when referring to the = operator. Instead, say "gets" to emphasize the fact that an assignment statement gives the variable on the left-hand side a value. Thus, you should refer to the assignment "x = x + 1;" as "x *gets* x + 1;". This reading will reinforce your knowledge of the operator's purpose and will prevent confusion later, when the equality operator (==) is introduced (Chapter 11).

Designer Secrets

According to mathematical convention, multiplication and division have "higher precedence" in expressions than addition and subtraction do. This means that in an expression containing both a multiplication/division and an addition/subtraction operation, the multiplication/division operator is applied first. Thus, the expression (2 + 4 * 5) will evaluate to (2 + (4 * 5)) = 22. If more than one operator of the same precedence appears in an expression (such as a series of divisions), the operators are applied from left to right. Thus, (8 / 4 / 2) will evaluate to ((8 / 4) / 2) = 1.

Although JavaScript adheres strictly to these **precedence rules**, it can be risky to rely on your own knowledge of the rules when creating complex mathematical expressions. For example, a programmer might write (x+1 * z), intending that the value of x be increased by 1 before the multiplication occurs. However, the browser would ignore the spacing and perform the higher-precedence multiplication first. To avoid this kind of mistake, use parentheses to group subexpressions. This will make your expressions easier to read and will ensure that the operators are evaluated in the desired order. Using this technique, the expression above would be written as ((x+1) * z).

EXERCISE 5.7

Trace the execution of the following sequence of JavaScript assignments. For each assignment, fill in the values of the variables in their corresponding boxes—even those values that aren't changed.

```
num1 = 14;

num2 = 8 - (3 + 2);

num3 = 99;

num1 = 99 / 2;

num2 = 2 * num1;

num3 = num2 - (num1 + 45.5);

num1 = num1 + 1;

num1 = num1 + 1;
```

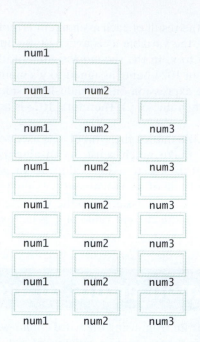

Number Representation

As we have seen in this chapter's examples, JavaScript can store numbers in variables and use numbers to perform computations. The following list provides several useful facts regarding how JavaScript stores and manipulates numbers:

- To improve readability, JavaScript automatically displays very large or very small values using **scientific notation**. In this format, values are written as numbers between 1 and 10 multiplied by 10 to a particular power. For example, if you attempted to display the number 1000000000000000000000000 in a page, the number would be displayed as 1e24, symbolizing 1 times 10 to the 24th power. In general, JavaScript displays a value $(X * 10^Y)$ as XeY, where the e stands for exponent, the power to which 10 is raised.

- Like most programming languages, JavaScript stores all numbers in memory cells of a fixed size (64 bits, to be exact). As a result, only a finite range of numbers can be represented in JavaScript. For example, 1e308 (which represents a 1 followed by 308 zeros!) can be represented in JavaScript, but 1e309 cannot. If you try to evaluate 1e309, the value will be treated as "Infinity." Similarly, 1e-323 is representable, but 1e-324 is rounded down to 0.

- Even within this range of numbers, JavaScript cannot represent all possible values. Between any two numbers lie infinitely more numbers, so representing all of them on a computer is impossible. Instead, JavaScript can represent approximately 17 significant digits (ignoring leading and trailing zeros). For example, JavaScript represents the number 0.9999999999999999 (with sixteen 9s to the right of the decimal) exactly, but 0.99999999999999999 (with seventeen 9s) is rounded up to the value 1.

EXERCISE 5.8

Consider the following button element, which executes a computation and displays the result when clicked:

```
<input type="button" value="Click for Result"
       onclick="x = 3333333333;
                y = x * (1/x);
                alert('The value is ' + y);">
```

Create a Web page named `number.html` that contains the above button. Mathematically speaking, multiplying x * (1/x) should yield 1, regardless of the particular value of x. Click the button and report the value that is displayed in the alert window. If it is not 1, can you explain why not?

Text Boxes and `parseFloat`

When a user enters a sequence of digits into a text box, it is impossible to know whether he intended it to be treated as a string (e.g., '123') or as a number (e.g., 123). By default, JavaScript statements will always assume that the contents of a text box are intended to be a string. If you want to treat the contents of a text box as a number, there is a predefined JavaScript function, `parseFloat`, that performs the appropriate conversion. A general definition of functions and their behavior will be provided in Chapter 7. For now, it suffices to know that the `parseFloat` function, when applied to the contents of a text box, converts a string of digits into a number. This is accomplished by placing the expression representing the contents of the box in parentheses, preceded by `parseFloat`.

For example, Figure 5.10 shows two different JavaScript statements for accessing the contents of a text box named `userBox`. Assume that the user has entered the characters '123' into that box. The first statement accesses that text and stores it as a string literal in the variable `contents1`. In the second statement, the `parseFloat` function is applied to the contents of the box, converting it to the number 123, which is then assigned and stored in `contents2`.

Whenever you access the contents of a text box and want to treat the value as a number, you should always apply the `parseFloat` function to the box contents. This will avoid subtle errors that can occur and will also provide a simple form of error checking within the page. If the `parseFloat` function is applied to a string that does not represent a number, it will produce the special symbol NaN, which is short for Not a Number. Any subsequent mathematical operations you try to perform on a NaN value will also evaluate to NaN. Thus, if the user erroneously enters a word in a text box where a number is expected, the results displayed in the page will contain NaN, making it clear that an error has occurred.

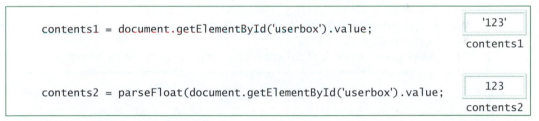

Figure 5.10   Accessing the contents of a text box, with and without `parseFloat`.

Common errors to avoid...

It turns out that many Web pages involving text boxes and numbers will work just fine without `parseFloat`. If you apply a purely mathematical operator (–, *, or /) to the contents of a text box, the browser will automatically convert the contents to a number value before applying the operator. The only time problems will occur is when the + operator is applied, since it has dual meaning as addition (for numbers) and concatenation (for strings).

When the + operator is applied to mixed values—that is, a string and a number—the browser will first convert the number value to a string and then perform concatenation. This can produce unexpected results if the `parseFloat` function is not used consistently. For example, consider the following JavaScript statements:

```
myNumber = document.getElementById('numBox').value;
oneMore = myNumber + 1;
document.getElementById('outputDiv').innerHTML='One more is ' + oneMore;
```

If the user entered 123 in the text box with identifier numBox, you would expect for the message 'One more is 124' to be displayed. Instead, the bizarre message 'One more is 1231' appears. To see why, consider the behavior of each statement in sequence. Since the first statement does not utilize parseFloat, it would access the text box and store its contents as the string literal '123'. The second statement would then attempt to add the string '123' to the number 1. The browser would handle this mismatch by converting the number 1 to the string '1' and concatenating, yielding the string '1231'. As a result, the third statement would display the message 'One more is 1231' in the page division.

To avoid errors such as this, you should always apply the parseFloat function to the contents of a text box when accessing a number. This ensures that the value is stored as a number and that subsequent expressions involving that number will utilize addition instead of string concatenation.

The Web page in Figure 5.11 serves as a simple tip calculator. If you enter the dollar amount of a restaurant check in the text box and click the button, it will display the tip amount, assuming a 15% tip (Figure 5.12). Note that the JavaScript assignment utilizes the parseFloat function to access and store the dollar amount (line 19).

EXERCISE 5.9

Enter the tip.html text from Figure 5.11 into a new Web page, then load the page in the browser to verify that it behaves as described.

Modify your page so that it contains a second text box, where the user can enter the tip percentage. For example, if the user entered 15 in the percentage box, the page would produce the same calculations as in Figure 5.12. If the user entered 20 in the percentage box, however, the tip amount would be 20% of the check amount.

```
1.  <!doctype html>
2.  <!-- tip.html                                    Dave Reed -->
3.  <!-- Web page that calculates the tip amount on a check. -->
4.  <!-- =================================================== -->
5.
6.  <html>
7.   <head>
8.     <title> Tip Calculator </title>
9.   </head>
10.
11.  <body>
12.     <h2>Tip Calculator</h2>
13.     <p>
14.       Enter the check amount: $<input type="text" id="amountBox" size=10 value="">
15.       <br>
16.       Tip percentage: 15%
17.     </p>
18.     <input type="button" value="Calculate Tip"
19.         onclick="amount=parseFloat(document.getElementById('amountBox').value);
20.                  tip = amount * (15/100);
21.                  document.getElementById('outputDiv').innerHTML=
22.                    'You should tip $' + tip;">
23.     <hr>
24.     <div id="outputDiv"></div>
25.  </body>
26. </html>
```

Figure 5.11 Web page that calculates the tip amount for a check.

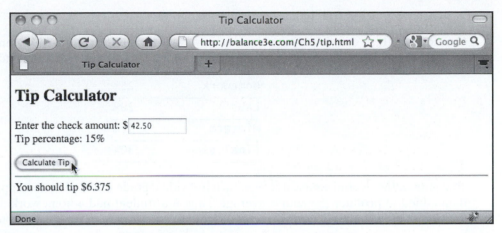

Figure 5.12 `tip.html` rendered in a Web browser.

EXERCISE 5.10

Computer science often deals with extremes when it comes to time. Even though modern computers can perform billions of operations per second, some tasks—such as decoding an encrypted message—still might require decades of computation.

Create a Web page named `years.html` that prompts the user to enter a specific number of years and then displays the corresponding time in seconds. To simplify this task, ignore leap years and assume that all years consist of exactly 365 days. For example, given an input value of 2.5, your page should display the message:

```
That's 78840000 seconds!
```

Once you complete your page, use it to approximate the number of seconds left in the current school semester. How many seconds remain in your college career? Report your results.

Designer Secrets

Just as we saw with text-oriented interactive pages, Web pages that process numbers often fall into a basic pattern. As before, there are text boxes where the user can enter numeric values and a button (or buttons) for initiating the computation. Accessing each of the number values in the text boxes requires calling `parseFloat` on the box contents before assigning to a variable. After accessing and storing the input numbers, a JavaScript assignment statement (or statements) can perform mathematical operations on the inputs and store the results in a new variable. The general pattern for the button's ONCLICK code can be written as follows:

```
VAR1 = parseFloat(document.getElementById('BOX_ID1').value);
VAR2 = parseFloat(document.getElementById('BOX_ID2').value);
...
VARn = parseFloat(document.getElementById('BOX_IDn').value);

RESULT = EXPRESSION_INVOLVING_VARIABLES;

document.getElementById('outputDiv').innerHTML =
   MESSAGE_INTEGRATING_STRING_LITERALS_AND_RESULT;
```

Example: Grade Calculation

Consider the task of calculating a student's overall average for a course. Assume the course has a grading scheme with weighted averages for homework, labs, a midterm exam, and a final exam:

Homework	25%
Labs	20%
Midterm	25%
Final exam	30%

To compute the overall course average, each individual grade is scaled by the appropriate factor and then added to produce the course average. Thus, if a student had a homework average of 90, a lab average of 86, a midterm exam score of 93, and a final exam score of 88, her course average would be:

```
average = 92*0.25 + 86*0.20 + 95*0.25 + 88*0.30 = 90.35
```

EXERCISE 5.11

Create a Web page named `grades.html` that can be used to compute a student's overall average for a course. Your page should contain text boxes where the user can enter his or her homework average, lab average, midterm exam score, and final exam score. The page should store each value as a number in a separate variable and then use the four numbers to calculate the overall course average. Once the average has been calculated, a message containing the course average should be displayed in a page division.

Programming Errors and Debugging

In computer jargon, the term *bug* refers to an error in a program. Although computer historians debate the origin of this word, we know that it was used as early as 1945, when an error generated by the Harvard Mark II computer was eventually traced to a moth that had flown into the machine and shorted out one of its relays. In any case, *debugging* is the process of systematically locating and fixing errors in a program.

Although rarely fun, debugging is a fact of life for programmers. It is uncommon for a program of any complexity to work perfectly the first time it is executed. Instead, programming is a continual cycle of designing, testing, debugging, redesigning, testing, debugging, and so on. Errors that you find when testing and debugging your program often lead you to other errors and can even force you to redesign entire sections of code. Three types of errors can occur in a program:

1. *Syntax errors* are simply typographic errors, such as omitting a quote or misspelling a function name. Because the browser catches these types of errors, they are usually easy to identify and fix.
2. *Run-time errors* occur when operations are applied to illegal values—for example, dividing by zero or attempting to multiply a string would generate a run-time error. These errors are also caught by the browser, which either produces an error message or—in the case of number values—continues execution using the NaN value.
3. *Logic errors* represent flaws in the design or implementation of a program. If your program runs but produces the wrong answer, the problem can be traced to a logic error (or, more often, to numerous logic errors). Unlike syntax and run-time errors, logic errors are not caught by the browser. The code is legal—it's just not what you intended! Logic errors are the most difficult type to address, because it is your responsibility to determine where the program went wrong.

Because the programs you've written so far have been relatively short and uncomplicated, errors have probably been easy to spot and correct. However, debugging more complex programs—such as those you will implement in future chapters—can be a daunting task. A simple but effective way of identifying logic errors is to utilize **diagnostic alerts**. These are nothing more than alert windows that display the values of variables at certain points in the program's execution. Diagnostic alerts allow you to discern the exact location of an error. For example, if you see that a certain variable has the correct value at one point in the code but an incorrect value at a later point, then you know that an error occurred somewhere in between.

In practice, it is much more efficient to avoid bugs than to waste effort fixing them. This might seem obvious, but it is a profound lesson to learn. A little extra time spent reviewing your program design at the beginning of a project can save you lots of debugging time later on. As a rule, students tend to rush into coding without thinking through their ideas and then become frustrated when they spend the majority of their time trying to debug ill-conceived code. As the noted computer science professor and software developer Henry Ledgard once quipped, "The sooner you start coding your program, the longer it's going to take." We will discuss the tenets of effective program design in Chapter 8, once your programming skills have advanced further.

Another important fact to recognize is that bugs are rarely unique. As you program, you will likely make the same mistakes over and over until you learn from them. Be sure to approach debugging as an instructive exercise. When you identify a bug, make a mental note of the error and how it manifested itself, so that you can locate (or avoid) similar bugs more easily in the future.

Looking Ahead...

In this chapter, you were introduced to new HTML and JavaScript features that allowed for more interactivity in Web pages. By incorporating text boxes into Web pages, the user can enter information, either text or numbers, directly into the page. JavaScript statements associated with event handlers can then access that information, perform computations, and display the results in the page. This chapter also introduced numbers as a JavaScript data type—including how numbers are represented, stored, displayed, and processed using mathematical operators. Since your pages are becoming increasingly more complex, the final section of this chapter considered the types of errors that can occur when programming and approaches to avoiding and responding to errors.

Now that you have been exposed to many basic programming concepts—such as how various data types are stored, manipulated, and displayed—the next chapter will provide perspective on how the machines that run programs were developed and evolved over time. Chapter 6 traces the history of computer technology, emphasizing the technological advances that led to modern computers and the impact of those advances on our society. This information should help you understand computers in a broader context as you continue to develop your programming skills.

Chapter Summary

- A text box is an HTML element included in Web pages for accepting user input. The following represents a generalized text-box element:

  ```
  <input type="text" id="BOX_ID" size=NUM_CHARS value="INITIAL_TEXT">
  ```

- You can access the contents of a text box using an expression of the form:

  ```
  document.getElementById('BOX_ID').value
  ```

- A variable is a name that is given to a dynamic value so that the value can be remembered and referred to later.

- In JavaScript, a variable name can be any sequence of letters, digits, and underscores that starts with a letter. Because JavaScript is case sensitive, capitalization matters.

- Each JavaScript variable is associated with a corresponding memory cell that stores the variable's value. A value is assigned to a variable (and thus stored in the corresponding memory cell) via an assignment statement (using =).

- JavaScript has three basic data types: strings, numbers, and Booleans. The basic arithmetic operators + (addition), – (subtraction), * (multiplication), and / (division) are provided for numbers.

- JavaScript variables can be assigned values of any type, including numbers and mathematical expressions formed by applying operators to numbers.

- When an assignment statement is executed, the expression on the right-hand side is evaluated first, and then the resulting value is assigned to the variable on the left-hand side.

- For readability, JavaScript uses scientific notation to display very small and very large numbers.

- As numbers are stored in memory cells of fixed size, JavaScript can represent only a limited range of numbers. If numbers exceed a certain number of significant digits, the numbers may be rounded off.

- In JavaScript, multiplication and division have higher precedence than addition and subtraction do. When an expression contains operators of equal precedence, the expression is evaluated in left-to-right order.

- The contents of a text box are always assumed to be a string, even when the user enters a number. A string can be converted to its corresponding numeric value by applying the predefined `parseFloat` function.

- Debugging is the process of systematically locating and fixing errors (also known as bugs) in a program. Three types of errors can occur in a program: (1) syntax errors are typographic errors, such as omitting a quote; (2) run-time errors occur when operations are applied to illegal values, such as multiplying string values; and (3) logic errors occur when the program runs but produces unintended results.

Supplemental Material and Exercises

Aligning Elements with Tables

Chapter 2 described how tables could be used to align text within a page. Web developers often employ tables in conjunction with text boxes to align the boxes and their associated labels. For example, suppose that you wanted a page to include two text boxes, each accompanied by a label to its left. By default, the text boxes would immediately follow the labels, leading to a ragged appearance (Figure 5.13).

```
First name: <input type="text" id="firstBox" size=12 value="">
<br>
Age: <input type="text" id="ageBox" size=3 value="">
```

By placing the elements in a table and designating one column for labels and another for text boxes, you can align the elements and improve their appearance (Figure 5.14).

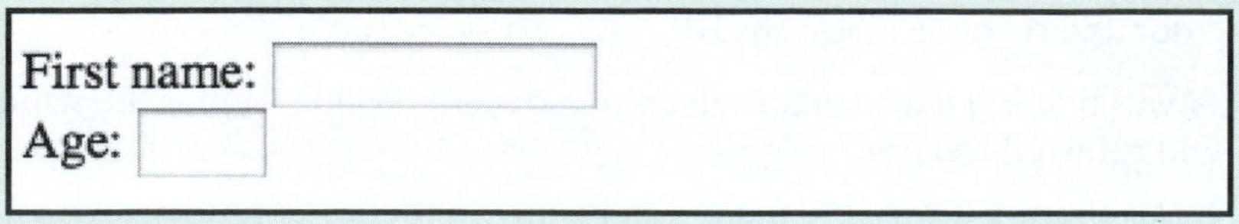

Figure 5.13 Default alignment of text boxes with labels.

Figure 5.14 Aligning the text boxes with a table.

```
<table>
  <tr><td>First name:</td>
      <td><input type="text" id="firstBox" size=12 value=""></td>
  </tr>
  <tr><td>Age: </td>
      <td><input type="text" id="ageBox" size=3 value=""></td>
  </tr>
</table>
```

EXERCISE 5.12

Modify your `form.html` page (Exercise 5.4) so that the labels and text boxes for the words/phrases align in columns.

EXERCISE 5.13

Modify your `story.html` page (Exercise 5.5) so that the labels and text boxes for the words/phrases align in columns.

EXERCISE 5.14

Modify your `grades.html` page (Exercise 5.11) so that the labels and text boxes for the student's grades align in columns.

More on Expressions and Assignments

Exercise 5.7 asked you to trace the execution of assignment statements. Tracing code is an excellent way to make sure that you understand exactly what is going on as expressions are evaluated and values are assigned to variables.

EXERCISE 5.15

Trace the execution of the following JavaScript statements and try to predict their behavior. For each assignment, fill in the values of the variables in their corresponding boxes—even those values that aren't changed.

`word1 = 'foo';`	word1		
`word2 = 'foo' + 'bar';`	word1	word2	
`word3 = 'biz';`	word1	word2	word3
`word1 = word2 + word3;`	word1	word2	word3
`word2 = word2 + word2;`	word1	word2	word3

EXERCISE 5.16

Trace the execution of the following JavaScript statements and try to predict their behavior. For each assignment, fill in the values of the variables in their corresponding boxes—even those values that aren't changed.

```
num = 1024;
```
num

```
msg1 = 'x = 0';
```
num   msg1

```
msg2 = 'num = '+num;
```
num   msg1   msg2

```
num = num / 2;
```
num   msg1   msg2

```
msg1 = msg2;
```
num   msg1   msg2

In addition to the standard operators for addition, subtraction, multiplication, and division, JavaScript provides a fifth mathematical operator. The remainder operator, %, returns the remainder after dividing one number by another. For example, the expression (5 % 2) would evaluate to 1, since 2 goes into 5 twice, with a remainder of 1. Similarly, (10 % 2) would evaluate to 0, since 2 goes into 10 five times, with no remainder. Note that the remainder operator provides a simple means of determining whether a number is even or odd: if X is even, then (X % 2) will evaluate to 0; if X is odd, then (X % 2) will evaluate to 1.

EXERCISE 5.17

Create a Web page named `remainder.html` that contains a text box and a button. When the button is clicked, JavaScript statements should (1) access the number entered in the text box, (2) calculate the remainder after dividing that number by 2, and (3) display that remainder in the page. Use your page to verify that the remainder is always 0 for an even number and 1 for an odd number.

More on Mixed Expressions

We have seen that the + operator has two meanings in JavaScript, depending on the types of values on which it is operating. When applied to two numbers, it represents addition, so 3 + 2 evaluates to 5. When applied to two strings, it represents concatenation, so 'foo' + 'bar' evaluates to 'foobar'. When applied to mixed values—that is, a string and a number—it converts the number to a string (by putting quotes around it) and then concatenates the two string literals. Thus, 'foo' + 3 is converted to 'foo' + '3', which evaluates to 'foo3'. Consider a more complex expression, involving more than one + operator:

```
'foo' + 3 + 4
```

Following the precedence rules of JavaScript, the leftmost + operator is evaluated first. Since the values 'foo' and 3 are of mixed types, the 3 is converted to '3', and then concatenation produces 'foo3'. Then, the rightmost + operator is applied to the result 'foo3' and 4, producing 'foo34'. These steps can be broken down as follows:

```
'foo' + 3 + 4  →  ('foo' + 3) + 4
               →  ('foo' + '3') + 4
               →  'foo3' + 4
               →  'foo3' + '4'
               →  'foo34'
```

Using parentheses, you can force the order of evaluation in a complex expression. For example, parentheses can force the rightmost operator to be evaluated first and produce a very different result:

```
'foo' + (3 + 4)  ➜  'foo' + 7
                 ➜  'foo' + '7'
                 ➜  'foo7'
```

EXERCISE 5.18

Similar to the examples above, show the steps involved in evaluating each of the following mixed expressions:

```
'The sum is' + 12 + 20
12 + 20 + ' is the sum'
12 + (20 + ' is the sum')
```

Text Boxes for Output

Throughout this chapter, we have used text boxes solely as input elements in the page, in which the user could enter information (text or numbers) for subsequent use within the page. In fact, text boxes are general-purpose elements that can be used for outputting results as well. Like other elements, the attributes of a text box can be changed via JavaScript assignment statements. In particular, the VALUE attribute of a text box can be reassigned to change its contents dynamically.

Consider the following button, which assumes there is a text box named numberBox in the page:

```
<input type="button" value="Click to Double"
       onclick="number=document.getElementById('numberBox').value;
                doubled=2*number;
                document.getElementById('numberBox').value=doubled;">
```

The statements in the ONCLICK attribute access the number in the text box, multiply that number by 2, and assign the result back to the box. Thus, every time the button is clicked, the current value of the text box will be doubled. A user can enter any number in the text box and then click the button repeatedly to update the value displayed in the box.

EXERCISE 5.19

Create a Web page named double.html that contains this button and a text box named numberBox, which has an initial value of 1.

If you start with a value of 1 in the text box, how many times must you click the button before the displayed value exceeds 500? How many times to exceed 1,000?

EXERCISE 5.20

Add a second button to your double.html page from Exercise 5.19. Each time this new button is clicked, the value in the text box named numberBox should be halved. For example, if the box contains the number 1,024, clicking the button should reduce the number to 512.

If you start with a value of 1,024 in the text box, how many times must you click the halving button before the displayed value is reduced to 1? How many times if you start with 2,048?

Chapter 6

The History of Computers

This chapter uses narrative, illustrations, and review questions to introduce computer science and technology concepts.

Where a calculator on the ENIAC is equipped with 18,000 vacuum tubes and weighs 30 tons, computers in the future may have only 1,000 vacuum tubes and weigh only 1½ tons.

Popular Mechanics, 1949

Never trust a computer you can't lift.

Stan Mazor, 1970

If the automobile had followed the same development cycle as the computer, a Rolls Royce would today cost $100, get one million miles to the gallon, and explode once a year, killing everyone inside.

Robert X. Cringely

Computers are such an integral part of our society that it is sometimes difficult to imagine life without them. However, computers as we know them are relatively new devices—the first electronic computers date back only to the 1940s. Over the past 70 years, technology has advanced at an astounding rate, with the capacity and speed of computers doubling every 12 to 18 months. Today, pocket calculators contain many times more memory capacity and processing power than did the mammoth computers of the 1950s and 1960s.

This chapter provides an overview of the history of computers and computer technology, tracing the progression from primitive mechanical calculators to modern PCs and mobile devices. As you will see, the development of computers has been rapid, but far from steady. Several key inventions have completely revolutionized computing technology, prompting drastic improvements in computer design, efficiency, and ease of use. Owing to this punctuated evolution, the history of computers is commonly divided into generations, each with its own defining technology (Figure 6.1). Although later chapters will revisit some of the more technical material, this chapter explores history's most significant computer-related inventions, why and how they came about, and their eventual impact on society.

	Time Period	Defining Technology
Generation 0	1642–1945	Mechanical devices (e.g., gears, relays)
Generation 1	1945–1954	Vacuum tubes
Generation 2	1954–1963	Transistors
Generation 3	1963–1973	Integrated circuits
Generation 4	1973–1985	Very large scale integration (VLSI)
Generation 5	1985–????	Parallel processing and networking

Figure 6.1   Generations of computer technology.

Generation 0: Mechanical Computers (1642–1945)

The 17th century was a period of great scientific achievement, sometimes referred to as "the century of genius."[1] Scientific pioneers such as astronomers Galileo (1564–1642) and Kepler (1570–1630), mathematicians Fermat (1601–1665) and Leibniz (1646–1716), and physicists Boyle (1627–1691) and Newton (1643–1727) laid the foundation for modern science by defining a rigorous, methodical approach to technical investigation based on a belief in unalterable natural laws. The universe, it was believed, was a complex machine that could be understood through careful observation and experimentation. Owing to this increased interest in complex science and mathematics, as well as contemporary advancements in mechanics, the first computing devices were invented during this period.

The German inventor Wilhelm Schickard (1592–1635) is credited with building the first working calculator in 1623. However, the details of Schickard's design were lost in a fire soon after the calculator's construction, and historians know little about the workings of this machine. The earliest prototype that has survived is that of the French scientist Blaise Pascal (1623–1662), who built a mechanical calculator in 1642, when he was only 19. His machine used mechanical gears and was powered by hand—a person could enter numbers up to eight digits long using dials and then turn a crank to either add or subtract (Figure 6.2). Thirty years later, the German mathematician Gottfried Wilhelm von Leibniz (1646–1716) expanded on Pascal's designs to build a mechanical calculator that could also multiply and divide.

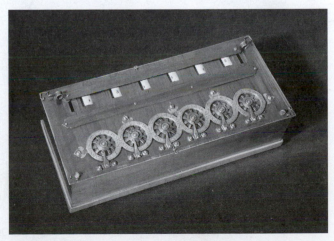

Figure 6.2   Pascal's calculator. A person entered digits by turning the wheels along the bottom, turned a crank, and viewed the results of calculations in the windows along the top.

Although inventors such as Pascal and Leibniz were able to demonstrate the design principles of mechanical calculators, constructing working models was difficult, owing to the precision required in making and assembling all the interlocking pieces. It wasn't until the early 1800s, when manufacturing methods improved to the point where mass production was possible, that mechanical calculators became commonplace in businesses and laboratories. A variation of Leibniz's calculator, built by Thomas de Colmar (1785–1870) in 1820, was widely used throughout the 19th century.

Programmable Devices

Although mechanical calculators grew in popularity during the 1800s, the first programmable machine was not a calculator at all, but a loom. Around 1801, Frenchman Joseph-Marie Jacquard (1752–1834) invented a programmable loom in which removable punch cards were used to represent patterns (Figure 6.3). Before Jacquard designed this loom, producing tapestries and patterned fabric was complex and tedious work. To generate a pattern, loom operators had to manually weave different colored threads (called wefts) over and under the cross-threads (called warps), producing the desired effect. Jacquard devised a way of encoding the thread patterns using metal cards with holes punched in them. When a card was fed through the machine, hooks passed through the holes to raise selected warp threads and create a specific over-and-under pattern.

Figure 6.3 Jacquard's loom. A string of punch cards for controlling the weave pattern is shown to the left, feeding into the top of the loom.

Figure 6.4   Babbage's Difference Engine, with interlocking gears and numbered wheels visible.

Using Jacquard's invention, complex brocades could be symbolized on the cards and reproduced exactly. Furthermore, weavers could program the same loom to generate different patterns simply by switching the cards. In addition to laying the foundation for later programmable devices, Jacquard's loom had a significant impact on the economy and culture of 19th-century Europe. Elaborate fabrics, which were once considered a symbol of wealth and prestige, could now be mass produced, and therefore became affordable to the masses.

Approximately twenty years later, Jacquard's idea of storing information as holes punched into cards resurfaced in the work of English mathematician Charles Babbage (1791–1871). Babbage incorporated punch cards in the 1821 design of his Difference Engine, a steam-powered mechanical calculator for solving mathematical equations (Figure 6.4). Because of limitations in manufacturing technology, Babbage was never able to construct a fully functional model of the Difference Engine. However, a prototype that punched output onto copper plates was built and used to compute data for naval navigation. In 1833, Babbage expanded on his plans for the Difference Engine to design a more powerful machine that included many of the features of modern computers. Babbage envisioned this machine, which he called the Analytical Engine, as a general-purpose, programmable computer that accepted input via punched cards and printed output on paper. Like modern computers, the Analytical Engine was to encompass various integrated components, including a readable/writable memory (which Babbage called the *store*) for holding data and programs and a control unit (which he called the *mill*) for fetching and executing instructions. Although a working model of the Analytical Engine was never completed, its innovative and visionary design was popularized by the writings and patronage of Augusta Ada Byron, Countess of Lovelace (1815–1852). Ada Byron's extensive notes on the Analytical Engine included step-by-step instructions to be carried out by the machine; this contribution has since led the computing industry to recognize her as the world's first programmer.

Figure 6.5 Electromagnetic relay. When an electrical current is applied to the wire at the bottom, the metal coil to the left generates a magnetic field. The magnetic attraction pulls the armature on the right, closing the switch and allowing electricity to flow through the relay. *(Photograph by Grant Braught, 2003.)*

Electromagnetic Relays

Despite the progression of mechanical calculators and programmable machines, computer technology as we think of it today did not really begin to develop until the 1930s, when electromagnetic relays were used. An ***electromagnetic relay***, a mechanical switch that can be used to control the flow of electricity through a wire, consists of a magnet attached to a metal arm (Figure 6.5). By default, the metal arm is in an open position, disconnected from the other metal components of the relay, and thus interrupting the flow of electricity. However, if current is applied to a control wire, the magnetic field generated by the magnet pulls the arm so that it closes, allowing electricity to flow through the relay.

Electromagnetic relays were used extensively in early telephone exchanges to control the connections between phones. In the 1930s, researchers began to utilize these simple electrical switches to define the complex logic that controls a computer. The German engineer Konrad Zuse (1910–1995) is credited with building the first relay-powered computer in the late 1930s. However, his work was classified by the German government and eventually destroyed during World War II; thus, it did not influence other researchers. During the same time period, John Atanasoff (1903–1995) at Iowa State and George Stibitz (1904–1995) at Bell Labs independently designed and built computers using electromagnetic relays. In the early 1940s, Harvard University's Howard Aiken (1900–1973) rediscovered Babbage's designs and applied some of Babbage's ideas to modern technology; Aiken's work culminated in the construction of the Mark I computer in 1944.

When compared to that of modern computers, the speed and computational power of these early machines might seem primitive. For example, the Mark I computer could perform a series of mathematical operations, but its computational capabilities were limited to addition, subtraction, multiplication, division, and various trigonometric functions. It could store only 72 numbers in memory and required roughly one-tenth of a second to perform an addition, 6 seconds to perform a multiplication, and 12 seconds to perform a division. Nevertheless, the Mark I represented a major advance in that it could complete complex calculations approximately 100 times faster than could existing technology of the time.

Generation 1: Vacuum Tubes (1945–1954)

Although electromagnetic relays certainly function much faster than wheels and gears can, relay-based computing still required the opening and closing of mechanical switches. Thus, maximum computing speeds were limited by the inertia of moving parts. Relays also posed reliability problems, as they had a tendency to jam. A classic example is an incident involving the Harvard Mark II (1947), in which a computer failure was eventually traced to a moth that had become wedged between relay contacts. Grace Murray Hopper (1906–1992), who was on Aiken's staff at the time, taped the moth into the computer logbook and facetiously noted the "First actual case of bug being found."[2]

During the mid-1940s, computer designers began to replace electromagnetic relays with *vacuum tubes*, small glass tubes from which all or most of the gas has been removed, permitting electrons to move with minimal interference from gas molecules (Figure 6.6). Although vacuum tubes had been invented in 1906 by Lee de Forest (1873–1961), they did not represent an affordable alternative to relays until the 1940s, when improvements in manufacturing reduced their cost significantly. Vacuum tubes are similar in function to electromagnetic relays, in that they are capable of controlling the flow of electricity, dependent on whether they are "on" or "off". However, because vacuum tubes have no moving parts (only the electrons move), they enable the switching of electrical signals at speeds far exceeding those of relays. The ability to modify electrical signals up to 1,000 times faster allowed vacuum tube powered machines to perform complex calculations more quickly, thus drastically enhancing the capabilities of computers.

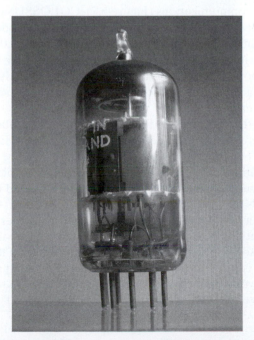

Figure 6.6   Vacuum tube. A filament inside the tube controls the flow of electricity—when a current is applied to the filament, electrons are released to bridge the vacuum and allow electrical current to flow through the tube.

Figure 6.7 The COLOSSUS at Bletchley Park, England. The messages to be decoded were fed into the machine on paper tape, as shown on the right. The panels show some of the more than 2,300 vacuum tubes that comprised the logic for breaking German codes. Courtesy of the Computer History Museum.

Computing and World War II

The development of the electronic (vacuum tube) computer, like many other technological inventions, was hastened by World War II. Building upon the ideas of computer pioneer Alan Turing (1912–1954), the British government built the first electronic computer, COLOSSUS, to decode encrypted Nazi communications (Figure 6.7). COLOSSUS contained more than 2,300 vacuum tubes and was uniquely adapted to its intended purpose as a code breaker. It included five different processing units, each of which could read in and interpret 5,000 characters of code per second. Using COLOSSUS, British Intelligence was able to decode many Nazi military communications, providing invaluable support to Allied operations during the war. Although COLOSSUS became operational in 1943, its design did not significantly influence other researchers, because its existence remained classified for over 30 years.

At roughly the same time in the United States, John Mauchly (1907–1980) and J. Presper Eckert (1919–1995) were building an electronic computer called ENIAC (Electronic Numerical Integrator And Computer) at the University of Pennsylvania (Figure 6.8). The ENIAC was designed to compute ballistics tables for the U.S. Army, but it was not completed until 1946. The machine consisted of 18,000 vacuum tubes and 1,500 relays, weighed 30 tons, and required 140 kilowatts of power. In some respects, the ENIAC was less advanced than its predecessors—it could store only 20 numbers in memory, whereas the Mark I could store 72. On the other hand, the ENIAC could perform more complex calculations than the Mark I could and operated up to 500 times faster (the ENIAC could complete 5,000 additions per second). Another advantage of the ENIAC was that it was programmable, meaning that it could be reconfigured to perform different computations. However, reprogramming the machine involved manually setting as many as 6,000 multiposition switches and reconnecting cables. In essence, the ENIAC's operators "reprogrammed" the computer by rewiring it to carry out each new task.

The von Neumann Architecture

Among the scientists involved in the ENIAC project was John von Neumann (1903–1957), who, along with Turing, is considered one of computer science's founding fathers (Figure 6.9). Von

Figure 6.8   ENIAC, with some of its 18,000 vacuum tubes visible. (U.S. Army photo.)

Neumann recognized that programming via switches and cables was tedious and error prone. To address this problem, he designed an alternative computer architecture in which programs could be stored in memory along with data. Although Babbage initially proposed this idea in his plans for the Analytical Engine, von Neumann is credited with formalizing it in accordance with modern designs (see Chapter 1 for more details on the von Neumann architecture). Von Neumann also introduced the use of binary (base 2) representation in memory, which provided many advantages over decimal (base 10) representation, which had been employed previously (see Chapter 12 for more on binary numbers). The von Neumann architecture was first used in vacuum tube computers such as EDVAC (Eckert and Mauchly at Penn, 1952) and IAS (von Neumann at Princeton, 1952), and it continues to form the basis for nearly all modern computers.

Once computer designers adopted von Neumann's "stored-program" architecture, the process of programming computers became even more important than designing them. Before von Neumann, computers were not so much programmed as they were wired to perform a particular task. However, through the von Neumann architecture, a program could be read in (via cards or tapes) and stored in the computer's memory. At first, programs were written in *machine language*, sequences of 0s and 1s that corresponded to instructions executed by the hardware. This was an improvement over rewiring, but it still required programmers to write and manipulate pages of binary numbers—a formidable and error-prone task. In the early 1950s, computer designers introduced *assembly languages*, which simplified the act of programming somewhat by substituting mnemonic names for binary numbers. (See Chapter 8 for more details regarding machine and assembly languages.)

The early 1950s also marked the emergence of the commercial computer industry. Eckert and Mauchly left the University of Pennsylvania to form their own company and, in 1951, the

Figure 6.9 John von Neumann with the IAS computer (Princeton University).

Eckert-Mauchly Computer Corporation (later a part of Remington-Rand, then Sperry-Rand) began selling the UNIVAC I computer. The first UNIVAC I was purchased by the U.S. Census Bureau, and a subsequent UNIVAC I captured the public imagination when CBS used it to predict the 1952 presidential election. Several other companies soon joined Eckert-Mauchly and began to market computers commercially. It is interesting to note that, at this time, IBM was a small company producing card punches and mechanical card-sorting machines. IBM entered the computer industry in 1953 but did not begin its rise to prominence until the early 1960s.

Generation 2: Transistors (1954–1963)

As computing technology evolved throughout the early 1950s, the disadvantages of vacuum tubes became more apparent. In addition to being relatively large (several inches long), vacuum tubes dissipated an enormous amount of heat, which meant that they required lots of space for cooling and tended to burn out frequently. The next major advance in computer technology was the replacement of vacuum tubes with ***transistors*** (Figure 6.10). Invented by John Bardeen (1908–1991), Walter Brattain (1902–1987), and William Shockley (1910–1989) in 1948, a transistor is a piece of silicon whose conductivity can be turned on and off using an electric current (see Chapter 16 for more details). Transistors were much smaller, cheaper, more reliable, and more energy efficient than vacuum tubes were. Thus, transistors' introduction allowed computer designers to produce smaller, faster machines at a drastically lower cost.

Many experts consider transistors to be the most important technological development of the 20th century. Transistors spurred the proliferation of countless small and affordable electronic devices—including radios, televisions, phones, and computers—as well as the information-based, media-reliant economy that accompanied these inventions. The scientific community recognized the potential impact of transistors almost immediately, awarding Bardeen, Brattain, and Shockley the 1956 Nobel Prize in Physics. The first transistorized computers, Sperry-Rand's LARC and IBM's STRETCH, were supercomputers commissioned in 1956 by the Atomic Energy Commission to assist in nuclear research. By the early 1960s, companies such as IBM, Sperry-Rand, and Digital Equipment Corporation (DEC) began marketing transistor-based computers to private businesses.

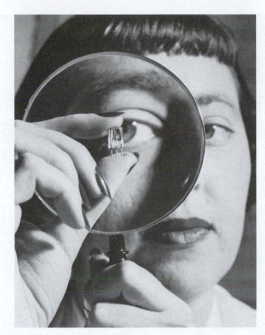

Figure 6.10   A laboratory technician inspects a 1952 RCA transistor.

High-Level Programming Languages

As transistors enabled the creation of more affordable computers, even more emphasis was placed on programming. If people other than engineering experts were going to use computers, interacting with the computer would have to become simpler. In 1957, John Backus (1924–2007) and his group at IBM introduced the first ***high-level programming language***, FORTRAN (FORmula TRANslator). This language allowed programmers to work at a higher level of abstraction, specifying computer tasks via mathematical formulas instead of assembly-level instructions. High-level languages like FORTRAN greatly simplified the task of programming, although IBM's original claims that FORTRAN would "eliminate coding errors and the debugging process"[3] were overly optimistic. FORTRAN was soon followed by other high-level languages, including LISP (John McCarthy at MIT, 1959), BASIC (John Kemeny at Dartmouth, 1959), and COBOL (Grace Murray Hopper at the Department of Defense, 1960). (Again, see Chapter 8 for more details.)

Generation 3: Integrated Circuits (1963–1973)

Transistors represented a major improvement over the vacuum tubes they replaced: they were smaller, cheaper to mass produce, and more energy efficient. By wiring transistors together, a computer designer could build circuits to perform particular computations. However, even simple calculations, such as adding two numbers, could require complex circuitry involving hundreds or even thousands of transistors. Linking transistors together via wires was tedious and limited the reduction of transistor size (because a person had to be able to physically connect wires between transistors). In 1958, Jack Kilby (1923–2005) at Texas Instruments and Robert Noyce (1927–1990) at Fairchild Semiconductor Corporation independently developed techniques for mass producing much smaller, interconnected transistors. Instead of building individual transistors and connecting wires, Kilby and Noyce proposed manufacturing the transistors and their connections together as metallic patterns on a silicon disc. As both researchers demonstrated, transistors could be formed out of layers of conductive and nonconductive metals, while their connections could be made as lines of conductive metal (Figure 6.11).

As building this type of circuitry involved layering the transistors and their connections together during a circuit's construction, the transistors could be made much smaller and also placed much closer together than before. Initially, tens or even hundreds of transistors could be layered onto the

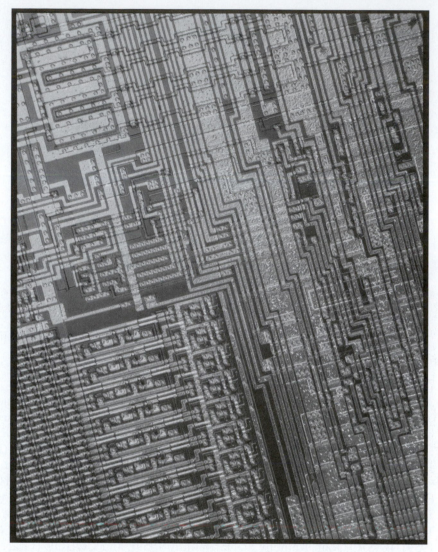

Figure 6.11 Microscopic photograph of electronic circuitry. Transistors (seen as small rectangles) and connecting wires (seen as lines) are constructed out of layers of metal on a silicon chip.

same disc and connected to form simple circuits. This type of disc, known as an ***integrated circuit*** or ***IC chip***, is packaged in metal or plastic and accompanied by external pins that connect to other components (Figure 6.12). The ability to package transistors and related circuitry on mass-produced ICs made it possible to build computers that were smaller, faster, and cheaper. Instead of starting with transistors, an engineer could build computers out of prepackaged IC chips, which simplified design and construction tasks. In recognition of his work in developing the integrated circuit, Jack Kilby was awarded the 2000 Nobel Prize in Physics.

Large Scale Integration

As manufacturing technology improved, the number of transistors that could be mounted on a single chip increased. In 1965, Gordon Moore (1929–) of Intel Corporation noticed that the number of transistors that could fit on a chip doubled every 12 to 18 months. This trend, which became known as Moore's Law, has continued to be an accurate predictor of technological advancements. By the 1970s, the ***large scale integration*** (*LSI*) of thousands of transistors on a single IC chip became possible. In 1971, Intel took the logical step of combining all the control circuitry for a calculator into a single chip called a ***microprocessor***. This first microprocessor, the Intel 4004, contained more than 2,300 transistors

Figure 6.12   Early integrated circuits, packaged in plastic with metal pins as connectors.

(Figure 6.13). Three years later, Intel released the 8080, which contained 6,000 transistors and could be programmed to perform a wide variety of computational tasks. The Intel 8080 and its successors, the 8086 and 8088 chips, served as central processing units for numerous personal computers in the 1970s. Other chip vendors, including Texas Instruments, National Semiconductors, Fairchild Semiconductors, and Motorola, also began producing microprocessors during this period.

Computing for Businesses

The development of integrated circuits facilitated the construction of even faster and cheaper computers. Whereas only large corporations could afford computers in the early 1960s, IC technology allowed manufacturers to lower computer prices significantly, enabling small businesses to purchase their own

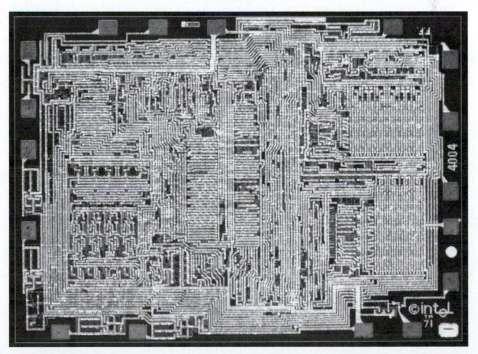

Figure 6.13   Microscopic image of the Intel 4044 microprocessor, with the connections between transistors dyed to appear white. The rectangles around the outside represent the pins, which connected the circuitry of the chip to the other computer components.

machines. This meant that more and more people needed to be able to interact with computers. A key to making computers accessible to nontechnical users was the development of operating systems, master control programs that oversee the computer's operation, manage peripheral devices (such as keyboards, monitors, and printers), and schedule the execution of tasks. Specialized programming languages were also developed to fill the needs of computers' new, broader base of users. In 1971, Niklaus Wirth (1934–) developed Pascal, a simple language designed primarily for teaching programming skills, but that has dedicated users to this day. In 1972, Dennis Ritchie (1941–) developed C, a programming language used in the development of UNIX and numerous other operating systems in the 1970s and 80s.

Generation 4: VLSI (1973–1985)

So far, each computer generation we have discussed was defined by the introduction of a new technology. By contrast, the jump from generation 3 to generation 4 is based largely upon scale. By the mid-1970s, advances in manufacturing technology led to the *very large scale integration* (VLSI) of hundreds of thousands and eventually millions of transistors on an IC chip. To understand the speed of this evolution, consider Figure 6.14, which lists chips in the Intel family, the year they were released, and the number of transistors they contained. It is interesting to note that the first microprocessor, the 4004, had approximately the same number of switching devices (transistors) as did the 1943 COLOSSUS, which used vacuum tubes. Throughout the 1970s and 1980s, successive generations of IC chips held more and more transistors, thus providing more complex functionality in the same amount of space. It is astounding to consider that the Intel Quad Core Itanium, which was released in 2009, contains more than 2 billion transistors, with individual transistors as small as 65 nanometers (0.000000065 meters).

The Personal Computer Revolution

Once VLSI enabled the mass production of microprocessors (entire processing units on individual chips), the cost of computers dropped to the point where individuals could afford them. The first personal computer (PC), the MITS Altair 8800, was marketed in 1975 for less than $500. In reality, the Altair was a computer kit consisting of all the necessary electronic components, including the Intel 8080 microprocessor that served as the machine's central processing unit. Customers were responsible for wiring and soldering these components together to assemble the computer. Once constructed, the Altair had no keyboard, no monitor, and no permanent storage—the user entered instructions directly by flipping switches on the console and viewed output as blinking lights. However, despite these limitations, demand for the Altair was overwhelming.

Year	Intel Processor	Number of Transistors[4]
2009	Quad Core Itanium	2,000,000,000
2006	Core 2 Duo	291,000,000
2000	Pentium 4	42,000,000
1999	Pentium III	9,500,000
1997	Pentium II	7,500,000
1993	Pentium	3,100,000
1989	80486	1,200,000
1985	80386	275,000
1982	80286	134,000
1978	8088	29,000
1974	8080	6,000
1972	8008	3,500
1971	4004	2,300

Figure 6.14 Numbers of transistors in Intel processors.

Figure 6.15 Steven Jobs, John Sculley, and Stephen Wozniak introduce the Apple IIc (1984).

Although the company that sold the Altair, MITS, folded within a few years, other small computer companies were able to successfully navigate the PC market during the late 1970s. In 1976, Steven Jobs (1955–) and Stephen Wozniak (1950–) started selling a computer kit similar to the Altair, which they called the Apple. In 1977, the two men founded Apple Computers and began marketing the Apple II, the first preassembled personal computer that included a keyboard, color monitor, sound, and graphics (Figure 6.15). By 1980, Apple's annual sales of personal computers reached nearly $200 million.[5] Other companies such as Tandy, Amiga, and Commodore soon began promoting their own versions of the personal computer. IBM, which was a dominant force in the world of business computing but had been slow to enter the personal computer market, introduced the IBM PC in 1980 and immediately became a key player. In 1984, Apple countered with the Macintosh, which introduced the now familiar graphical user interface of windows, icons, pull-down menus, and a mouse pointer.

Throughout the early years of computing, the software industry was dominated by a few large companies, such as IBM and Hewlett-Packard, which developed specialized programs and marketed them in combination with hardware systems. As more and more people began using computers for business and pleasure, the software industry grew and adapted. Bill Gates (1955–) and Paul Allen (1953–) are credited with writing the first commercial software for personal computers, an interpreter for the BASIC programming language that ran on the Altair (Figure 6.16). The two founded Microsoft in 1975, while Gates was a freshman at Harvard, and have built the company into the software giant it is today. Much of Microsoft's initial success can be attributed to its marketing of the MS-DOS operating system for PCs, as well as popular applications programs such as word processors and spreadsheets. By the mid-1990s, Microsoft Windows (the successor to MS-DOS) had become the dominant operating system for desktop computers, and Bill Gates had become the richest person in the world.

Object-Oriented Programming

The past thirty years have also produced a proliferation of new programming languages, including those with an emphasis on object-oriented programming methodologies. Object orientation is an approach to software development in which the programmer models software components after real-world objects. In 1980, Alan Kay (1940–) developed Smalltalk, the first object-oriented language. Ada, a programming language developed for the Department of Defense to be used in government

Figure 6.16 Paul Allen and Bill Gates (1981).

contracts, was also introduced in 1980. In 1985, Bjarne Stroustrup (1950–) developed C++, an object-oriented extension of the C language. C++ and its offshoot Java (developed in 1995 at Sun Microsystems) have become the dominant languages in commercial software development today. Modern high-level programming languages are discussed in Chapter 8, and Chapter 15 covers object-oriented programming techniques in greater detail.

Generation 5: Parallel Processing & Networking (1985–????)

The scope of computer technology's fifth generation remains a debated issue among computer science historians. Unlike previous generations, which were punctuated by monolithic shifts in technology or scale, modern computer history has been defined by advances in **parallel processing** and **networking**. Parallel processing refers to the integration of multiple (sometimes hundreds or thousands of) processors in a single computer. By sharing the computational load across multiple processors, a parallel computer is able to execute programs in a fraction of the time required by a single-processor computer. For example, high-end Web servers commonly use multiple processors. Recall that a Web server receives requests for Web pages, looks up those pages in its own local storage, and then sends the pages back to the requesting computers. Because each request is independent, multiple processors can be used to service requests simultaneously, thus improving overall performance. With the introduction of the Intel Core 2 Duo processor in 2006, parallel processing has finally reached the casual PC user. Two separate processors, or cores, packaged on the same chip allow for the simultaneous execution of two tasks, such as playing music and browsing the Web. Multiple tasks can be spread across the two processors to balance the computational load and thus improve overall performance. More details on parallel processing are provided in Chapter 10.

Networking advancements have had an even more significant impact on recent computing history. Until the 1990s, most computers were **stand-alone** devices, not connected to other computers. Small-scale networks of computers were common in large businesses, but communication between networks was rare. The first large-scale computer network, the ARPANet, was created in 1969, but its use was initially limited to government and academic researchers. The ARPANet—or Internet, as it would later be called—grew at a slow but steady pace during the 1970s and 1980s. However, the Internet's scope and popularity increased dramatically in the 1990s with the development of the World Wide Web, a multimedia environment in which documents can be seamlessly linked together and accessed remotely. As of 2010, it was estimated that more than 758 million computers are connected to the Internet,[6] with 205 million Web sites that distribute up to 50 billion individual Web pages.[7] For more details on the development of the Internet and Web, refer back to Chapter 3.

The latest trend in networking is the explosive growth of wireless computing. Using **WiFi (Wireless Fidelity)** networks at work or home, users are freed from the desktop and able to access the Internet through mobile laptops. In addition, wireless broadband service provided by telephone companies enable users to access the Internet and email accounts via cellular phones and other smart devices. In 2009, it was estimated that 55% of American adults connect to the Internet wirelessly, with as many as 30% doing so using a phone.[8] More details on networking are provided in Chapter 10.

Looking Ahead...

The evolutionary pace of computing technology has been nothing short of astounding. Fueled by key inventions (vacuum tubes, transistors, integrated circuits, VLSI, and networking), each generation of computers represented a dramatic improvement over its predecessors, both in computational power and affordability. It is interesting to note, however, that progress has not been without its price. Modern computer systems, both hardware and software, often exceed our capacity to fully understand them. When the number of components reaches into the thousands or even millions, it becomes infeasible to predict all possible interactions and, by extension, all potential problems. Therefore, users of computer technology have become accustomed to occasional errors or system failures. Although the industry has devised techniques for developing more robust systems, consumer demands have tended to place a higher priority on improving performance, rather than providing greater reliability.

Now that you are equipped with a better understanding of computer technology and its history, you are prepared to tackle more complex programming tasks. The next chapter, Chapter 7, introduces functions as units of computational abstraction. Using predefined JavaScript mathematical functions, you will be able to develop interactive Web pages that perform complex calculations. Several real-world applications will be explored that utilize random elements, including a random slide show and rotating banner ads. In addition, you will learn to create your own simple functions in order to simplify your pages.

Chapter Summary

- The history of computers is commonly divided into generations, each with its own defining technology that prompted drastic improvements in computer design, efficiency, and ease of use.

- Generation 0 (1642–1945) is defined by mechanical computing devices, such as Pascal's calculator (1642), Babbage's Difference Engine (1821), and Aiken's Mark I (1944).

- The first programmable device was Jacquard's loom (1801), which used metal cards with holes punched into them to specify the pattern to be woven into a tapestry. Punch cards were subsequently used in Babbage's Analytical Engine (1833).

- An electromagnetic relay is a mechanical switch that can be used to control the flow of electricity through a wire. Relays were used to construct mechanical computers in the 1930s and 1940s.

- Generation 1 (1945–1954) is defined by vacuum tubes–small glass tubes from which all or most of the gas has been removed. As vacuum tubes have no moving parts, they enable the switching of electrical signals at speeds far exceeding those of relays.

- The first electronic (vacuum tube) computer was COLOSSUS (1943), built by the British government to decode encrypted Nazi communications. Since COLOSSUS was classified, the first publicly known electronic computer was ENIAC (1946), developed at the University of Pennsylvania.

- In the early 1950s, John von Neumann introduced the design of a stored-program computer–one in which programs could be stored in memory along with data. The von Neumann architecture continues to form the basis for nearly all modern computers.

- Generation 2 (1954–1963) is defined by transistors–pieces of silicon whose conductivity can be turned on and off using an electric current. Since transistors were smaller, cheaper, more reliable, and more energy-efficient than vacuum tubes, they allowed for the production of more powerful yet inexpensive computers.

- As computers became more affordable, high-level programming languages such as FORTRAN (1957), LISP (1959), and COBOL (1960) made it easier for non-technical users to program and interact with computers.

- Generation 3 (1963–1973) is defined by integrated circuits (ICs)–electronic circuitry that is layered onto silicon chips and packaged in metal or plastic. The ability to package transistors and related circuitry on mass-produced ICs made it possible to build computers that were smaller, faster, and cheaper.

- Moore's Law predicts that the number of transistors that can fit on a chip will double every 12 to 18 months.

- A microprocessor is a single chip that contains all of the circuitry for a computing device, such as a calculator or computer. The first microprocessor was the Intel 4004 (1971).

- Generation 4 (1973–1985) is defined by very large scale integration (VLSI)–the ability to manufacture hundreds of thousands or even millions of transistors on an IC chip.

- The personal computer revolution occurred when technological advances allowed for the production of affordable, desktop computers, such as the MITS Altair 8800 (1975), Apple II (1977), and IBM PC (1980). The development of graphical user interfaces (GUIs) and the growth of the software industry, led by Microsoft, also made computers more accessible to non-technical users.

- The scope of Generation 5 (1985–????) remains a debated issue, but advances in parallel processing and networking have had significant impacts on modern computing.

Review Questions

1. TRUE or FALSE? The first programmable machine was a mechanical calculator designed by Charles Babbage.

2. TRUE or FALSE? Ada Byron is generally acknowledged as the world's first programmer, because of her work on Babbage's Analytical Engine.

3. TRUE or FALSE? An electromagnetic relay is a mechanical switch that can be used to control the flow of electricity through a wire.

4. TRUE or FALSE? Vacuum tubes, as they have no moving parts, enable the switching of electrical signals at speeds far exceeding those of relays.

5. TRUE or FALSE? Although they were large and expensive by today's standards, early computers such as the MARK I and ENIAC were comparable in performance (memory capacity and processing speed) to modern desktop computers.

6. TRUE or FALSE? Because transistors were smaller and produced less heat than vacuum tubes, they allowed for the design of smaller and faster computers.

7. TRUE or FALSE? A microprocessor is a special-purpose computer that is used to control scientific machinery.

8. TRUE or FALSE? Moore's Law states that the number of transistors that can be manufactured on a computer chip doubles every 12 to 18 months.

9. TRUE or FALSE? The first personal computer was the IBM PC, which first hit the market in 1980.

10. TRUE or FALSE? Many Web servers improve performance by uses parallel processing, in which multiple processors run simultaneously to handle page requests.

11. Mechanical calculators, such as those designed by Pascal and Leibniz, were first developed in the 1600s. However, they were not widely used in businesses and laboratories until the 1800s. Why was this the case?

12. Jacquard's loom, although unrelated to computing, influenced the development of modern computing devices. What design features of that machine are relevant to modern computer architectures?

13. What advantages did vacuum tubes provide over electromagnetic relays? What were the disadvantages of vacuum tubes?

14. As it did with many technologies, World War II greatly influenced the development of computers. In what ways did the war effort contribute to the evolution of computer technology? In what ways did the need for secrecy during the war hinder computer development?

15. What features of Babbage's Analytical Engine did von Neumann incorporate into his architecture? Why did it take over a century for Babbage's vision of a general-purpose, programmable computer to be realized?

16. It was claimed that the ENIAC was but programmable, but programming it to perform a different task required rewiring and reconfiguring the physical components of the machine. Describe how the adoption of the von Neumann architecture allowed subsequent machines to be more easily programmed to perform different tasks.

17. What is a transistor, and how did the introduction of transistors lead to faster and cheaper computers? What other effects did transistors have on modern technology and society?

18. What does the acronym VLSI stand for? How did the development of VLSI technology contribute to the personal computer revolution of the late 1970s?

19. What was the first personal computer and when was it first marketed? How was this product different from today's PCs?

20. Describe two innovations introduced by Apple Computer in the late 1970s and early 1980s.

21. Each generation of computers resulted in machines that were cheaper, faster, and thus accessible to more people. How did this trend affect the development of programming languages?

22. Two of the technological advances described in this chapter were so influential that they earned their inventors a Nobel Prize in Physics. Identify the inventions and inventors.

Endnotes

1. Huggins, James A. "The 17th Century: The Coming of Science." October 2002. Online at `http://www.uu.edu/centers/science/voice/`.

2. U.S. Naval Historical Center Photograph #: NH 96566-KN, Department of the Navy—Navy Historical Center. September 1999. Online at `http://www.history.navy.mil/photos/pers-us/uspers-h/g-hoppr.htm`.

3. IBM Programming Research Group. `Preliminary Report, Specifications for the IBM Mathematical FORmula TRANslating System, FORTRAN`. New York: IBM Corp., 1954.

4. Intel Research. "Silicon—Moore's Law." December 2009. Online at `http://www.intel.com/technology/mooreslaw/index.htm`.

5. Metz, Robert. "I.B.M. Threat to Apple." *New York Times*, September 2, 1981.

6. "Internet Domain Survey." `Internet Software Consortium`, April 2010. Online at `http://www.isc.org/solutions/survey`.

7. "Netcraft Web Server Survey." `Netcraft`, April 2010. Online at `http://www.netcraft.com/survey/`.

8. Rainie, Lee. "Internet, broadband, and cell phone statistics." Pew Internet and American Life Project, January 2010.

References

Abelson, Hal, Ken Ledeen and Harry Ellis. *Blown to Bits: Your Life, Liberty, and Happiness After the Digital Explosion.* Addison-Wesley, 2008.

Computer History Museum. "Timeline of Computer History." October 2006. Online at `http://www.computerhistory.org/timeline/`.

Goldstine, Herman H. *The Computer from Pascal to von Neumann.* Princeton, NJ: Princeton University Press, 1972.

Intel Museum. "Online Exhibits." December 2009. Online at `http://www.intel.com/museum/onlineexhibits.htm`.

LaMorte, Christopher, and John Lilly. "Computers: History and Development." *Jones Telecommunications and Multimedia Encyclopedia*, 1999.

Levy, Steven. *Hackers: Heroes of the Computer Revolution.* New York: Penguin Putnam, 1994.

Long, Larry, and Nancy Long. *Computers*, 12th ed. Upper Saddle River, NJ: Prentice Hall, 2004.

Malone, Michael. *The Microprocessor: A Biography.* New York: Springer-Verlag, 1995.

Stern, Nancy. *From ENIAC to UNIVAC: An Appraisal of the Eckert-Mauchly Computers.* Burlington, MA: Digital Press, 1981.

Stranahan, Paul. "Personal Computers: History and Development." *Jones Telecommunications and Multimedia Encyclopedia*, 1999.

Winegrad, Dilys, and Atsushi Akera. "A Short History of the Second American Revolution." *Penn Almanac*, 42(18), 1996. Online at `http://www.upenn.edu/almanac/v42/n18/eniac.html`.

Functions and Randomness

This chapter uses narrative, examples, and hands-on exercises to introduce programming concepts and Web development skills.

7 Chapter

You can increase your brain power three- to fivefold simply by laughing and having fun before working on a problem.

Doug Hall

We've heard that a million monkeys at a million keyboards could produce the complete works of Shakespeare; now, thanks to the Internet, we know that is not true.

Robert Wilensky

In Chapter 5, you learned to create interactive Web pages using JavaScript. These pages contained text boxes where the user could enter information, which could then be accessed and processed by JavaScript statements at the click of a button. Some of those pages involved entering numbers and performing calculations using the basic mathematical operators. In this chapter, you will be introduced to functions as units of computational abstraction, and you will become familiar with some of JavaScript's predefined mathematical functions. These functions will enable you to perform more complex calculations within pages. In particular, the Math.random function will enable you to add random elements to your pages and explore real-world applications such as random slide shows and rotating banner ads. In addition, you will learn to create your own simple functions in order to simplify your pages.

Predefined JavaScript Functions

In mathematical terms, a ***function*** is a mapping from some number of inputs to a single output. For example, the mathematical function for calculating the square root of a number takes that number as input and produces the square root as output. In mathematics, functions are often given special symbols to denote their application, such as:

$$\sqrt{9} \rightarrow 3$$

In most programming languages, functions are identified by name with the inputs to the function placed in parentheses. For example, in Chapter 5 you were introduced to the

JavaScript `parseFloat` function, which takes a single string as input (such as `'500'`) and produces as output the corresponding number value (here, 500). In short:

```
parseFloat('500') → 500
```

From a programming point of view, a function can be seen as a unit of ***computational abstraction***. To convert a string into its corresponding number, you do not need to know the computational steps involved in the conversion. You simply apply the predefined `parseFloat` function and obtain the desired value. With this computational perspective in mind, we will often refer to applying a function to inputs as ***calling*** that function, and we will refer to the output of the function as its ***return value***. Thus, the expression `parseFloat('500')` *calls* the `parseFloat` function with input string `'500'` and *returns* the number 500. The alert statement, introduced in Chapter 4, calls the JavaScript `alert` function with a message string as input. While a call to the `alert` function does not return an explicit value, the result is an alert window that appears on the screen.

A function call can appear anywhere in a JavaScript expression. When an expression containing a function call is evaluated, the return value for that call is substituted into the expression. For example, the following JavaScript assignment (taken from the `tip.html` page in Figure 5.11) contains a call to the `parseFloat` function on the right-hand side. This function call returns the numeric equivalent of the box contents, which is then assigned to the `amount` variable.

```
amount = parseFloat(document.getElementById('amountBox').value);
```

Math Functions

In addition to `parseFloat`, JavaScript provides an extensive library of predefined mathematical functions, including a function that calculates the square root of an input (`Math.sqrt`) and a function that returns the larger of two inputs (`Math.max`). These functions have names beginning with the prefix `Math.`, signifying that they are part of a library of mathematical routines. (Technically speaking, `Math` is the name of a JavaScript object that contains these functions—objects are introduced in Chapter 15.)

The `functest.html` page (accessible as `http://balance3e.com/Ch7/functest.html`) is provided to enable you to explore the behavior of predefined JavaScript functions such as these. Using the pull-down menus, you can select a method and enter input values in the text boxes. Then, click the button next to the function call to see the output value displayed below (Figure 7.1).

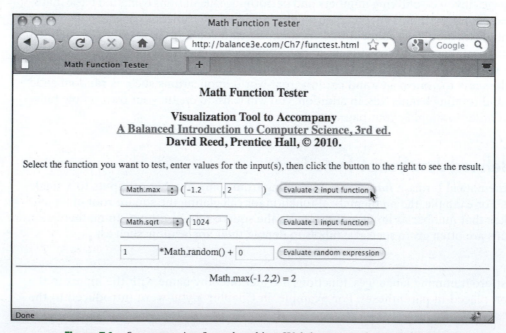

Figure 7.1 `functest.html` rendered in a Web browser, after user input.

EXERCISE 7.1

Use the `functest.html` page to determine the purpose of each of the following mathematical functions. Be sure to test each function using a variety of numerical inputs, including negative numbers and fractions. Descriptions of the `Math.sqrt` and `Math.max` functions are already provided for you.

Function	Inputs	Description
Math.sqrt	one number	*returns the square root of the input*
Math.max	two numbers	*returns the greater of the two inputs*
Math.min	two numbers	
Math.abs	one number	
Math.floor	one number	
Math.ceil	one number	
Math.round	one number	

The Web page in Figure 7.2 demonstrates a useful application of the `Math.round` function. The page contains a text box where the user enters a number. When a button is clicked, the value in the box is accessed and then rounded to one decimal place (Figure 7.3). This is accomplished in line 18 by multiplying the number by 10, rounding to the nearest integer, and then dividing by 10. For example, 3.14159 would be multiplied by 10 to yield 31.4159, rounded to 31, and then divided by 10 to yield 3.1. Similarly, 5.986 would be multiplied by 10 to yield 59.86, rounded to 60, and then divided by 10 to yield 6.0.

EXERCISE 7.2

Enter the `round.html` text from Figure 7.2 into a new Web page, then load the page in the browser to verify that it behaves as described.

Modify the page so that instead of rounding the number to one decimal place, it rounds to two decimal places. For example, the number 3.14159 would be rounded down to 3.14, whereas the number 5.986 would be rounded up to 5.99.

```
1.  <!doctype html>
2.  <!-- round.html                                    Dave Reed -->
3.  <!-- Web page that rounds a number to one decimal place. -->
4.  <!-- =============================================== -->
5.
6.  <html>
7.   <head>
8.    <title> Number Rounder </title>
9.   </head>
10.
11.  <body>
12.   <h2>Number Rounder</h2>
13.   <p>
14.    Enter a number: <input type="text" id="numberBox" size=12 value=3.14159>
15.   </p>
16.   <input type="button" value="Round It"
17.       onclick="number=parseFloat(document.getElementById('numberBox').value);
18.              rounded=Math.round(number*10)/10;
19.              document.getElementById('outputDiv').innerHTML=
20.                number + ' rounded to one decimal place is ' + rounded;">
21.      <hr>
22.   <div id="outputDiv"></div>
23.  </body>
24. </html>
```

Figure 7.2 Web page that rounds a number to one decimal place.

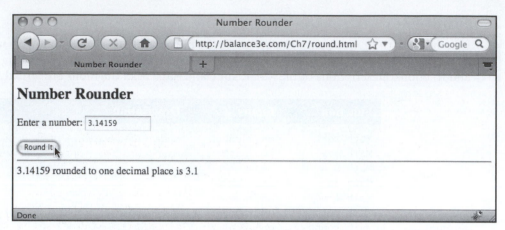

Figure 7.3 round.html rendered in a Web browser, after user input.

EXERCISE 7.3

Consider your tip.html page from Exercise 5.9. If you enter a check amount of $17.73 and select a 15% tip, the page will report "You should tip $2.6595." While mathematically accurate, this amount of precision is overkill. When dealing with dollars and cents, you really want the answer rounded up to two decimal places. In this case, $2.66.

Modify your tip.html page so that the tip amount is rounded up to two decimal places. Note that to round up, you will need to use the Math.ceil function instead of Math.round (which can round either up or down, depending on which integer value is closer).

Common errors to avoid...

Inexperienced programmers commonly make two types of errors when attempting to call functions. The ability to recognize and correct these errors will save you a lot of time as you start incorporating functions in your pages.

1. If you mistype the name of a function, then an error will occur when the browser attempts to execute the function call. The browser will attempt to identify the error by displaying a descriptive error message. If you are using Firefox, the error message will read, "Error: XXX is not a function" or "Error: XXX is not defined," where XXX represents the mistyped name. If you are using Internet Explorer, the error message is more cryptic—it states, "Error: Object Expected." This message refers to the fact that the browser expected to locate an object with that name (i.e., the function) but could not find its definition.

2. If you specify a function call with the wrong number of inputs, the browser does not generate an error, but the call might produce unexpected results. Inputs are automatically matched with function parameters in left-to-right order. If too many inputs are provided in the function call, the extra input values are simply ignored. If too few inputs are provided, the remaining parameters are assigned the special symbol undefined.

Similarly, unexpected results may be produced if you specify a function call with the wrong type of inputs. Whenever possible, the browser automatically converts between numbers and strings so that inputs match the specified type. Thus, the call Math.ceil('3.2') will return the value 4. However, imagine that a function requires a number, but the specified input is a string that cannot be converted to a number. In such a case, the function would return the value NaN (a special symbol that stands for "Not a Number"). Any mathematical operations performed on NaN will likewise yield NaN. Thus, the call Math.ceil('xyz') will produce NaN, as will the expression Math.ceil('xyz')+1.

Raising Numbers to a Power

The predefined function `Math.pow` can be called to raise a number to a power. For example, the call `Math.pow(2, 3)` returns $2^3 = 8$. The inputs to `Math.pow` can be any number values, including negative numbers and fractions. For example, `Math.pow(2, -1)` returns `0.5`, and `Math.pow(9, 0.5)` returns `3`.

EXERCISE 7.4

Recall from Chapter 1 that computer memory comprises individual bits of data. A bit (short for binary digit) can store one of only two values, commonly referred to as 0 and 1. However, using two bits, you can represent four different values through the bit patterns 00, 01, 10, and 11. With three bits, you can represent eight different values—via 000, 001, 010, 011, 100, 101, 110, and 111. In general, N bits of memory enable you to represent 2^N different values.

Create a Web page named `bits.html` that contains a text box where the user can enter a number, call it N. At the click of a button, your page should compute and display 2^N, the number of values that can be represented using the specified quantity of bits. For example, if the user entered 10 in the text box, the page would display the message:

```
With 10 bits, you can represent 1024 different values.
```

Once you have created your page, use it to determine the number of values that each of the following can represent:

```
 8 bits (1 byte)
16 bits (2 byte)
32 bits (4 bytes)
64 bits (8 bytes)
```

Generating Random Numbers

Recall that a function is a mapping from some number of inputs to a single output. According to this definition, a function can require zero inputs. At first, you might not see the purpose of a function without inputs, but there is a predefined function named `Math.random` that takes no inputs and returns a useful result. Every time `Math.random()` is called, a different pseudorandom number between 0 (inclusive) and 1 (exclusive) is returned. That is, the smallest value that may be returned is 0, and the largest value is very close to but not quite 1. We use the term *pseudorandom* to describe the results of `Math.random` because the function actually uses a complex algorithm to generate random-seeming values from within that range. As you will see throughout this book, `Math.random` is useful whenever random chance is involved in the behavior of a page, such as selecting a random image each time the page is loaded or simulating the rolls of dice.

 # Common errors to avoid...

Because the `Math.random` function does not require any inputs, you might be tempted to leave off the parentheses when attempting to call it. Although such an omission does not generate an error, the resulting behavior is far from that of the intended call. Like variable names, function names represent values, but instead of representing a number or string, a function name represents a collection of JavaScript statements that define a computation. If you specify the name of a function and do not include parentheses, you are accessing the value associated with that function name. Thus, `alert(Math.random)` would actually display the value (underlying code) of the `Math.random` function in an alert window, not the result of a call. In this case, the browser would identify the random function as predefined, displaying:

```
function random() { [native code] }
```

By itself, the `Math.random` function is not incredibly useful. There are not very many applications that require a random number between 0 and 1, but a call to `Math.random` can be placed in an expression to adjust the range of the numbers. For example, the expression 2*`Math.random()` would evaluate to a random number in the range 0 (inclusive) to 2 (exclusive). One way to see this is to consider the extreme values obtainable from `Math.random()`. The smallest value that `Math.random()` can return is 0—if that number is doubled, you still have 0. The largest value that `Math.random()` can return is 0.999999...—if that number is doubled, you get 1.999999... Any values between 0 and 1 would yield a number between 0 and 2 when doubled. Similarly, `Math.random()+1` would evaluate to a random number between 1 (inclusive) and 2 (exclusive).

EXERCISE 7.5

The `functest.html` page (Figure 7.1) contains text boxes and a button that can be used to evaluate expressions of the form X*`Math.random()`+Y, where X and Y are values entered by the user. Use the page to determine the range of random numbers generated by each of the following expressions. You will need to evaluate each expression multiple times to be assured of obtaining the full range of values. Descriptions of the first two expressions are already provided for you.

Expression	Range
2*Math.random()	0 (inclusive) to 2 (exclusive)
Math.random()+1	1 (inclusive) to 2 (exclusive)
2*Math.random()+1	
10*Math.random()+5	
5*Math.random()+10	

The Web page in Figure 7.4 uses an expression involving `Math.random` to generate a lucky number from a specified range. The low and high values of the range are entered by the user in text boxes. When the button is clicked, a random integer value from within that range is generated (line 20) and displayed in a page division (Figure 7.5).

EXERCISE 7.6

Enter the `lucky1.html` text from Figure 7.4 into a new Web page, then load the page in the browser to verify that it behaves as described.

Most lotteries select winning numbers by drawing numbered balls out of bins. For example, a typical Pick-4 lottery will utilize four bins, each containing balls with numbers starting at 0. If there are 10 balls to choose from in each of four bins, labeled 0 to 9, then $10^4 = 10,000$ different number sequences can potentially be picked. Increasing the number of balls significantly increases the number of possible sequences, which significantly decreases a person's odds of winning. For example, if there are 20 balls to choose from in each bin, labeled from 0 to 19, then $20^4 = 160,000$ different number sequences could be selected.

Make a copy of the `lucky1.html` page from Figure 7.2 and name it `pick4.html`. Then modify this new page so that it simulates a Pick-4 lottery. Your page should have one text box, where the user can enter the highest ball number (it is assumed that the lowest ball number is always 0). When a button is clicked, four random ball numbers should be selected and displayed in a message such as the following:

```
The Pick-4 winners are: 5-0-8-2
```

```
 1. <!doctype html>
 2. <!-- lucky1.html                                         Dave Reed -->
 3. <!-- Web page that generates a lucky number from a range.        -->
 4. <!-- ======================================================== -->
 5.
 6. <html>
 7.  <head>
 8.    <title> Lucky Number </title>
 9.  </head>
10.
11.  <body>
12.    <h2>Lucky Number</h2>
13.    <p>
14.      Numbers are selected between <input type="text" id="minBox"
                                      size=3 value=0>
15.      and <input type="text" id="maxBox" size=3 value=9>.
16.    </p>
17.    <input type="button" value="Generate Lucky Number"
18.         onclick="min=parseFloat(document.getElementById('minBox').value);
19.                 max=parseFloat(document.getElementById('maxBox').value);
20.                 number=Math.floor(Math.random()*(max-min+1))+min;
21.                 document.getElementById('outputDiv').innerHTML=
22.                   'Your lucky number is ' + number;">
23.    <hr>
24.    <div id="outputDiv"></div>
25.  </body>
26. </html>
```

Figure 7.4 Web page that generates a random lucky number.

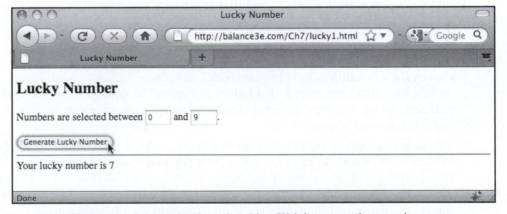

Figure 7.5 lucky1.html rendered in a Web browser, after user input.

Simple User-Defined Functions

Functions simplify the programmer's task in two important ways. First, functions help minimize the amount of detail that a programmer must keep track of. Because the Math.sqrt function is available, the programmer does not need to remember the sequence of steps involved in computing a square root. Instead, he or she only needs to remember how to call the Math.sqrt function. Second, functions help minimize the length and complexity of code. Given that the Math.sqrt function has been defined, the square root of a value can be obtained via a single call to this function. This can significantly reduce code complexity, because the number of steps otherwise required to compute the square root would be considerable.

```
function FUNCTION_NAME()
// Assumes: DESCRIPTION OF ANY ASSUMPTIONS ABOUT THE PAGE
// Results: DESCRIPTION OF THE ACTION PERFORMED BY THE FUNCTION
{
    STATEMENTS_TO_BE_EXECUTED
}
```

Figure 7.6 General form of a simple, user-defined function.

JavaScript's predefined functions represent a collection of useful, general-purpose abstractions. Since computations such as square root and absolute value are common in many applications, JavaScript's designers provided these abstractions for you in the form of predefined functions. Individual programmers can construct new abstractions by defining functions of their own design. Such functions are typically referred to as ***user-defined functions***. You can encapsulate any computation that you find especially useful as a user-defined function. Once you write a function definition and include it in a Web page, your function can be called just like any predefined function. In this way, user-defined functions can be viewed as extending the capabilities of the JavaScript language.

Chapter 9 will explore user-defined functions at length, but we can start seeing the benefit of simple functions right away. Consider the lucky1.html page from Figure 7.4. Since numerous JavaScript statements are required to access the text boxes, construct the message, and display it in a text area, the ONCLICK attribute of the button element is fairly complicated. In addition, the fact that the ONCLICK attribute encloses those statements in double quotes means that the programmer must be careful when nesting quotes inside a string. Both of these complexities can be avoided by defining a new function that encapsulates the statements to be carried out by the button. Then the button merely needs to call that function when clicked in order to achieve the desired behavior.

The general form of a simple, user-defined function is given in Figure 7.6.

- The first line begins with the keyword function, followed by the name of the function. The name chosen for a function follows the same rules as variable names (a word made of letters, digits, and underscores that must start with a letter) and should be descriptive of the task that it is meant to perform. As we will only consider simple functions with no inputs in this chapter, the function name is followed by parentheses.

- The next two lines in the function definition are comments that describe the function's behavior. Within JavaScript code, the browser ignores anything that appears to the right of a double slash (the purpose and treatment of JavaScript comments are similar to those of HTML comments, which are delimited by <!-- and -->). Although JavaScript does not require programmers to insert comments, you should always include them in your functions to improve the readability of your code. Code that is easier to read and understand is also easier to modify and reuse, which can help you avoid writing entirely new code to perform similar tasks.

- Finally, the statements to be executed when the function is called are enclosed in curly braces ({}). Although not required by the browser, you should always indent the code inside the curly braces to improve readability, making it easier to spot where the function definition begins and ends.

By convention, JavaScript function definitions are placed in the HEAD of the page, enclosed in tags of the form <script type="text/javascript">...</script>. These SCRIPT tags instruct the browser that their contents are JavaScript statements (in this case, a function definition) and so should be interpreted. Since the HEAD of a Web page is processed before the BODY, placing the function definition in the HEAD ensures that the function will be defined and callable by any JavaScript statements in the BODY of the page.

```
1.  <!doctype html>
2.  <!-- lucky2.html                                          Dave Reed -->
3.  <!-- Web page that generates a lucky number from a range.     -->
4.  <!-- ====================================================== -->
5.
6.  <html>
7.   <head>
8.    <title> Lucky Number </title>
9.    <script type="text/javascript">
10.      function GenerateNumber()
11.      // Assumes: minBox and maxBox define the range for the value
12.      // Results: picks a random number and displays it in outputDiv
13.      {
14.         min=parseFloat(document.getElementById('minBox').value);
15.         max=parseFloat(document.getElementById('maxBox').value);
16.         number=Math.floor(Math.random()*(max-min+1))+min;
17.         document.getElementById('outputDiv').innerHTML=
18.           'Your lucky number is ' + number;
19.      }
20.    </script>
21.   </head>
22.
23.   <body>
24.    <h2>Lucky Number</h2>
25.    <p>
26.       Numbers are selected between
27.       <input type="text" id="minBox" size=3 value=0>
28.       and <input type="text" id="maxBox" size=3 value=9>.
29.    </p>
30.    <input type="button" value="Generate Lucky Number"
31.           onclick="GenerateNumber();">
32.    <hr>
33.    <div id="outputDiv"></div>
34.   </body>
35.  </html>
```

Figure 7.7 Variant of `lucky1.html` that utilizes a user-defined function.

Figure 7.7 shows the `lucky1.html` page from Figure 7.4, rewritten to utilize a user-defined function named `GenerateNumber`. Note that the statements inside the curly braces of the function are precisely those statements that were assigned to the ONCLICK attribute in Figure 7.4. The function does not change the behavior of the page; it simply restructures it to simplify the button element. With those statements moved to the function definition, the only code that must be specified in the ONCLICK attribute is a call to that function.

EXERCISE 7.7

Enter the `lucky2.html` text from Figure 7.7 into a new Web page, then load the page in the browser to verify that it behaves as described.

Once you have done this, modify your `pick4.html` page from Exercise 7.6 so that it similarly makes use of a function in the HEAD. Your function should contain the code previously assigned to the button and have a name descriptive of the task it performs, such as `GeneratePicks` or `PickNumbers`. You should then modify the button's ONCLICK attribute to call that function.

EXERCISE 7.8

Modify your `tip.html` page from Exercise 7.3 so that it similarly uses a function in the HEAD. When the button is clicked, the function should be called to perform the tip calculation and display the result in the page division.

Designer Secrets

In Chapter 5, we described the rules for creating valid variable names. Function names must adhere to these same rules—the name must begin with a letter and consist of letters, digits, and/or underscores. Just as it was with variable names, it is important to select names for functions that indicate their purpose. Doing so makes it easier to read the code and quickly understand the purpose of functions. Throughout this book, function names will always start with capital letters, to easily distinguish them from variable names (which always start with a lowercase letter).

Common errors to avoid...

Sometimes, beginning programmers accidentally give a variable the same name as a function. For example, in the `lucky2.html` page just described, it is conceivable (although unlikely) that a programmer might reuse the name `GenerateNumber` for a variable in the BODY of the page. This would not generate an immediate error, but any subsequent attempt to call the function would cause the browser to display the error message "Error: Object does not support this property or method" (using Internet Explorer) or "Error: GenerateNumber is not a function" (using Firefox). To prevent this problem, take care to select unique function and variable names, thus avoiding conflicts. Following the convention of always starting function names with capital letters and variable names with lowercase letters also helps to avoid confusion.

Functions That Simplify

When designing a page with a button, the choice of whether to define a separate function should be determined based on complexity. If multiple statements are to be executed when the button is clicked, then the overhead of encapsulating those statements in a separate function and calling that function from the ONCLICK attribute is worthwhile. For example, the button element in Figure 7.7 is shorter and much simpler to read than the button in Figure 7.4, and it avoids the potential confusion regarding nested quotes. If, however, there is only a single statement to be executed when the button is clicked, then writing that statement directly in the ONCLICK attribute suffices. For example, most of the Web pages in Chapter 4 had simple, one-statement actions associated with buttons. Adding a function to one of these pages would only lengthen the page without simplifying the buttons.

EXERCISE 7.9

Modify your `story.html` page from Chapter 5 (Exercise 5.5) so that it uses a function to encapsulate the statements for accessing the words and phrases entered by the user and then displaying the story. The button in the page should call this function when clicked.

EXERCISE 7.10

Similarly, modify your `grades.html` page from Chapter 5 (Exercise 5.11) so that it uses a function to encapsulate the statements for accessing individual grades, calculating their average, and displaying that average in the page. The button in the page should call this function when clicked.

Randomness in a Page

The predefined math functions introduced in this chapter, when combined with simple user-defined functions, provide a powerful collection of abstractions for creating interactive Web pages. For example, the `Math.random` function can be used in a variety of applications where randomness is required. This section considers three real-world examples that demonstrate the power of the `Math.random` function for controlling random elements in a page.

Example: Simulated Dice

The Web page in Figure 7.8 demonstrates the use of the `Math.random` function in simulating the roll of a six-sided die. The page assumes that there are six die images stored online at `http://balance3e.com/Images`. The file `die1.gif` at that location contains an image of a die with one dot. Similarly, the files `die2.gif` through `die6.gif` contain the other die images, with two through six dots, respectively. Initially, the image in the page displays the die image with one dot (Figure 7.9). When the button is clicked, however, the `SelectImage` function (lines 10–17) is called to pick a new die image at random. This function carries out this task by first picking a random number between one and six using an expression involving `Math.random` (line 14), constructing the full URL of the die image corresponding to that roll (line 15), and then assigning that URL to the SRC attribute of the image (line 16). The result is that a new, randomly selected die image is displayed in the page each time the button is clicked.

```
1.  <!doctype html>
2.  <!-- dice.html                                        Dave Reed -->
3.  <!-- This page simulates and displays the roll of a die. -->
4.  <!-- =============================================== -->
5.
6.  <html>
7.   <head>
8.    <title> Die Rolls </title>
9.    <script type="text/javascript">
10.     function SelectImage()
11.     // Assumes: die images are in balance3e.com/Images
12.     // Results: displays a randomly selected image of a 6-sided die
13.     {
14.         roll=Math.floor(Math.random()*6) + 1;
15.         imgName='http://balance3e.com/Images/die' + roll + '.gif';
16.         document.getElementById('dieImg').src = imgName;
17.     }
18.    </script>
19.   </head>
20.
21.   <body>
22.     <div style="text-align:center">
23.       <p>
24.         <img id="dieImg" alt="die image"
25.              src="http://balance3e.com/Images/die1.gif">
26.       </p>
27.       <input type="button" value="Click to Roll" onclick="SelectImage();">
28.     </div>
29.   </body>
30.  </html>
```

Figure 7.8 Web page that displays a random die face at the click of a button.

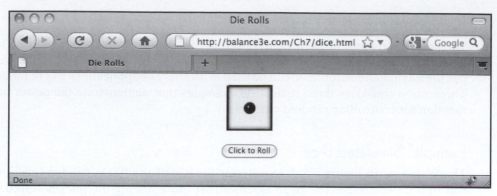

Figure 7.9 dice.html rendered in a Web browser.

EXERCISE 7.11

Enter the dice.html text from Figure 7.8 into a new Web page, then load the page in the browser to verify that it behaves as described.

Once you have done this, modify the page so that it contains two die images, side by side above the button. When the button is clicked, both die images should be assigned to random die faces. This will require adding code to the SelectImage function so that it selects two random numbers and changes both images accordingly.

Example: Random Slide Show

In Chapter 4 (Exercise 4.5), you developed a Web page that served as a simple slide show. A single IMG element was at the top of the page, with numerous buttons below. Each button was associated with an image file, so that when the button was clicked, that image file was assigned to the SRC attribute of the IMG element. Thus, the user could select the image she wanted to view simply by clicking on the appropriate button.

An alternative approach to a slide show might involve randomness. Instead of having one button for each possible image, the page might have only a single button. When that button is clicked, one of the possible images is selected at random and displayed in the page.

EXERCISE 7.12

Make a copy of the dice.html page from Figure 7.8 and name it slides.html. Then modify this new page to serve as random slide show. You will need to store the image files for your slide show in the same folder as your Web page and use a consistent naming scheme for the image files (similar to the die image files). For example, if you have four image files, you might name them slide1.jpg, slide2.jpg, slide3.jpg, and slide4.jpg. Then, modify the SelectImage function so that it selects from among these image files. You will also need to alter the IMG element so that it initially displays the image of your choice.

The slide show you created in slides.html is able to select a random image each time the button is clicked, but it always starts with the same image in the page: the image specified in the SRC attribute of the IMG element. To make a completely random slide show, we would also need the initial image to be selected at random.

The BODY element has an optional event-handler attribute named ONLOAD, which specifies JavaScript code that is to be executed when the page is done loading. Thus, the opening tag of the BODY of a Web page can be of the general form:

```
<body onload="CODE_TO_EXECUTE_AFTER_PAGE_LOADS">
```

In the case of our random slide show, we would like the page to call the `SelectImage` function automatically once the page is loaded. By doing so, a random image would be selected and displayed immediately after the page loads.

EXERCISE 7.13

Add the attribute `onload="SelectImage();"` to the BODY element of your `slides.html` page, so that it randomly selects from the images and displays that image when the page loads. Verify that your page behaves as desired.

Example: Random Banner Ads

Many commercial Web sites make money by selling ads on their pages. These so-called ***banner ads*** are images that appear in the page and react to actions taken by the user. For example, a banner ad might change if the user moves the mouse over the ad, perhaps displaying more information to an interested consumer. Or the banner ad might react to a click of the mouse by opening the Web page for the product being advertised. Because advertising space is limited within a Web page, many Web sites sell the same space to multiple advertisers, rotating between the different ads at random or at the initiative of the user.

The Web page in Figure 7.10 implements a simple version of rotating banner ads. It utilizes the predefined JavaScript function `setInterval`, which takes two arguments: a JavaScript string containing a function call and a number of milliseconds. The general form of a call to `setInterval` looks like the following:

```
setInterval('JAVASCRIPT_FUNCTION_CALL', INTERVAL_IN_MSEC)
```

```
1.  <!doctype html>
2.  <!-- bannerads.html                                          Dave Reed  -->
3.  <!-- This page displays banner ads that change at regular intervals. -->
4.  <!-- ============================================================== -->
5.
6.  <html>
7.   <head>
8.    <title> Random Banner Ads </title>
9.    <script type="text/javascript">
10.     function SelectAd()
11.     // Assumes: the banners ad0.gif, ad1.gif, ad2.gif, and ad3.gif are
12.     //          stored in http://balance3e.com/Images
13.     // Results: displays the next banner ad image in the page
14.     {
15.         adNum = Math.floor(4*Math.random());
16.         document.getElementById('adImg').src=
17.             'http://balance3e.com/Images/ad' + adNum + '.gif';
18.     }
19.    </script>
20.   </head>
21.
22.   <body onload="setInterval('SelectAd()', 5000);">
23.    <div style="text-align:center">
24.      <img id="adImg" alt="banner ad"
25.           src="http://balance3e.com/Images/ad0.gif">
26.    </div>
27.    <p>
28.      Contents of the page.
29.    </p>
30.   </body>
31.  </html>
```

Figure 7.10 Web page that displays rotating banner ads.

Figure 7.11 bannerads.html rendered in a Web browser.

The setInterval function causes its first argument (the function call) to be executed repeatedly at regular intervals (as specified by the second argument). For example, in Figure 7.10 the function call setInterval('SelectAd()', 5000) is assigned to the ONLOAD attribute of the BODY (line 22). Thus, when the page loads, the SelectAd function is scheduled to be executed every five seconds (5,000 milliseconds). The result is that every five seconds, a new banner ad is selected at random and displayed in the page (Figure 7.11).

EXERCISE 7.14

Enter the bannerads.html text from Figure 7.10 into a new Web page, then load the page in the browser to verify that it behaves as described.

Modify the second argument in the setInterval function call so that the banner ad changes every ten seconds instead of every five seconds.

In a commercial Web site, having banner ads selected at random would not be acceptable. A client who paid for advertising space on the page would want to know exactly what they were paying for. Being assured that their ad might or might not show up at random intervals would hardly reassure them. A more equitable approach would be to have the ads rotate in a set pattern. If four ads shared the same space, the client could be assured that their ad would appear every fourth interval.

EXERCISE 7.15

Make the following modifications to your bannerads.html page so that it rotates the banner ads as opposed to selecting them at random. First, modify the opening BODY tag (line 22) so that it appears as follows:

```
<body onload="adNum=0; setInterval('SelectAd()', 5000);">
```

The new statement added to the ONLOAD attribute initializes the variable adNum to have the value 0. Next, change the assignment to adNum in the SelectAd function (line 15) to the following:

```
adNum = (adNum + 1) % 4;
```

This statement utilizes the JavaScript remainder operator, %, to calculate a new banner ad number based on the old one. The remainder operator returns the remainder after dividing one number by another. In this case, the value (adNum + 1) is divided by 4 and the resulting remainder is assigned back to adNum. The result is that the variable adNum rotates from 0, to 1, to 2, to 3, and then back to 0 each time the SelectAd function is called:

if adNum=0, (adNum + 1) % 4 → (1 % 4) → 1   *since 4 goes into 1 zero times with a remainder of 1*

if adNum=1, (adNum + 1) % 4 → (2 % 4) → 2   *since 4 goes into 2 zero times with a remainder of 2*

if adNum=2, (adNum + 1) % 4 → (3 % 4) → 3   *since 4 goes into 3 zero times with a remainder of 3*

if adNum=3, (adNum + 1) % 4 → (4 % 4) → 0   *since 4 goes into 4 one time with*
                                                 a remainder of 0

Thus, the page rotates between the banner ads named `ad0.gif`, `ad1.gif`, `ad2.gif`, and `ad3.gif`. Make these two changes to your `bannerads.html` page and verify that it rotates the banner ads as described.

Looking Ahead ...

In this chapter, you learned to make use of the mathematical functions provided by JavaScript. Using predefined functions such as `Math.sqrt` and `Math.pow`, you were able to create Web pages that performed complex calculations on numbers entered by the user. Similarly, the `Math.random` function enabled you to integrate random elements in the page, such as simulated dice or a random slide show. The introduction of simple, user-defined functions allowed for the easier development of pages, as complex sequences of JavaScript code could be moved to the HEAD of the page and out of the button elements. In subsequent chapters, you will learn to write more general-purpose functions and package them into libraries for repeated use.

At this point in the text, you have developed an impressive set of programming skills, including the ability to use variables, assignments, expressions, event handlers, and functions. The next chapter, Chapter 8, attempts to generalize some of these skills, focusing on the concept of an algorithm and its connection to programming. As you will learn, an algorithm is a step-by-step sequence of instructions for carrying out some task. A program is a special kind of algorithm, in which the instructions specify actions to be carried out by the computer (such as prompting the user for his name or displaying a message in a page). In Chapter 8, several examples of complex algorithms are studied, as are techniques for implementing and executing algorithms as programs.

Chapter Summary

- Mathematically speaking, a function is a mapping from some number of inputs to a single output. From a programming perspective, a function is a unit of computational abstraction. When calling a function, you do not need to understand the steps the function uses; you simply apply the desired function and obtain the result.

- JavaScript provides an extensive library of predefined mathematical functions, including square root (`Math.sqrt`), absolute value (`Math.abs`), maximum (`Math.max`), minimum (`Math.min`), round down (`Math.floor`), round up (`Math.ceil`), round to the nearest integer (`Math.round`), and raise to a power (`Math.pow`).

- The random-number function (`Math.random`) is an example of a function requiring no inputs. Each call to `Math.random` returns a pseudorandom number between 0 (inclusive) and 1 (exclusive).

- Functions simplify the programmer's task by (1) minimizing the amount of detail that the programmer must keep track of and (2) minimizing the size and complexity of code.

- Programmers insert comments in JavaScript programs by placing a double slash (`//`) at the beginning of a line.

- The general form for simple, user-defined functions is as follows:

```
function FUNCTION_NAME()
// Assumes: DESCRIPTION OF ANY ASSUMPTIONS ABOUT THE PAGE
// Results: DESCRIPTION OF THE ACTION PERFORMED BY THE FUNCTION
{
    STATEMENTS_TO_BE_EXECUTED
}
```

- By convention, user-defined functions are placed in the HEAD of the page, between the tags `<script type="text/javascript">` and `</script>`.
- The ONLOAD event handler attribute can be added to the BODY of a Web page to specify JavaScript code that is to be executed when the page loads.
- The `setInterval` function can be used to repeatedly execute a JavaScript statement (e.g., a function call) at regular intervals.
- The remainder operator, `%`, is applied to two numbers and produces the remainder after dividing the first number by the second.

Supplemental Material and Exercises

Revising Pages with Functions

EXERCISE 7.16

Modify your `round.html` page from Exercise 7.2 so that it uses a function to encapsulate the statements for accessing the number, rounding it, and displaying it in the page. The button in the page should call this function when clicked.

EXERCISE 7.17

Modify your `bits.html` page from Exercise 7.4 so that it uses a function to encapsulate the statements for accessing the number of bits, calculating the number of values, and displaying it in the page. The button in the page should call this function when clicked.

EXERCISE 7.18

Modify your `form.html` page from Chapter 5 (Exercise 5.4) so that it uses a function to encapsulate the statements for accessing the words or phrases and displaying the form letter in the page. The button in the page should call this function when clicked.

EXERCISE 7.19

Modify your `swap.html` page from Chapter 5 (Exercise 5.6) so that it uses a function to encapsulate the statements for swapping the source files for the two image elements. The button in the page should call this function when clicked.

EXERCISE 7.20

Modify your `years.html` page from Chapter 5 (Exercise 5.10) so that it uses a function to encapsulate the statements for accessing the number of years, calculating the corresponding number of seconds, and displaying the seconds in the page. The button in the page should call this function when clicked.

More on Math Functions

EXERCISE 7.21

Many applications in computer graphics involve determining the relative positions of pixels in the plane. The following formula computes the distance between two points (x_1, y_1) and (x_2, y_2).

$$\sqrt{(x_1 - x_2)^2 + (y_1 - y_2)^2}$$

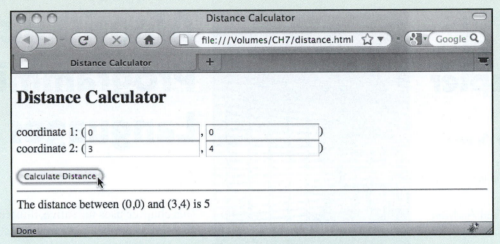

Figure 7.12 Sample appearance of `distance.html`.

Create a Web page named `distance.html` that computes the distance between two arbitrary points. Your page should have text boxes where the user can enter the coordinates and then display the distance between those points at the click of a button. Figure 7.12 shows a screen shot of what your page might look like.

EXERCISE 7.22

In Exercise 7.2, you modified the `round.html` page so that it rounded the number to two decimal places instead of one. This involved multiplying the number by 100 (instead of 10), rounding to the nearest integer, then dividing by 100 (instead of 10). This process can be generalized to any number of decimal places, by using the appropriate power of 10. To round a number to N digits, you multiply that number by 10^N, round to the nearest integer, then divide by 10^N.

Modify your `round.html` page so that it has an additional text box where the user can specify the number of digits. When the button is clicked, the number in the original text box will be rounded to the specified number of digits and displayed in the page.

ONLOAD and ONUNLOAD Attributes

EXERCISE 7.23

Add an ONLOAD attribute to your home page from Chapter 2. Within that attribute, place a call to the `alert` function so that a greeting is displayed when the page loads. For example, the alert window might display the message "Hello and welcome to my page!"

Complementary to the ONLOAD attribute is the ONUNLOAD attribute. When placed in the opening BODY tag of a Web page, the ONUNLOAD attribute specifies code to be executed when the user leaves the page (by clicking on a link, entering a new address, or closing the browser).

EXERCISE 7.24

Add an ONUNLOAD attribute to your home page from Chapter 2. Within that attribute, place a call to the `alert` function so that a farewell is displayed when the page unloads. For example, the alert window might display the message "Thanks for visiting my page. Come back soon!"

Chapter 8

Algorithms and Programming Languages

This chapter uses narrative, illustrations, hands-on experimentation, and review questions to introduce computer science and technology concepts.

> *When I am working on a problem, I never think about beauty. I think only of how to solve the problem. But when I have finished, if the solution is not beautiful, I know it is wrong.*
>
> R. Buckminster Fuller

> *If you cannot describe what you are doing as a process, you don't know what you're doing.*
>
> W. Edwards Deming

> *A programming language is a system of notation for describing computations. A useful programming language must therefore be suited for both description (i.e., for human writers and readers of programs) and for computation (i.e., for efficient implementation on computers). But human beings and computers are so different that it is difficult to find notational devices that are well suited to the capabilities of both.*
>
> R.D. Tennant
> *Principles of Programming Languages*

The central concept underlying all computation is that of the ***algorithm***, a step-by-step sequence of instructions for carrying out some task. When you interact with a computer, you provide instructions in the form of mouse clicks, menu selections, or command sequences. These instructions tell the computer to execute particular tasks, such as copying a piece of text or saving an image. At a more detailed level, when you write JavaScript statements, you are specifying instructions that the browser must follow to perform actions, such as prompting the user for input or displaying a message in the page.

This chapter presents an overview of algorithms, their design and analysis, and their connection to computer science. After introducing techniques for solving problems, we provide several example algorithms for you to study, accompanying each with an interactive Web page that will help you visualize and experiment with the algorithms. We also discuss the evolution of programming languages and the advantage of using advanced languages to write computer algorithms at a high level of abstraction. After completing this chapter, you will be familiar with the steps involved in designing an algorithm, coding it in a programming language, and executing the resulting program.

Algorithms

Programming may be viewed as the process of designing and implementing algorithms that a computer (or a program executing on that computer) can carry out. The programmer's job is to create an algorithm for accomplishing a given objective and then to translate the individual steps of the algorithm into a programming language that the computer understands. For example, the JavaScript programs you have written have contained statements that instruct the browser to carry out particular tasks, such as displaying a message or updating an image in the page. The browser understands these statements and is therefore able to carry them out, producing the desired results.

Algorithms in the Real World

The use of algorithms is not limited to the domain of computing. For example, a recipe for baking chocolate chip cookies is an algorithm. By following the instructions carefully, anyone familiar with cooking should be able to bake a perfect batch of cookies. Similarly, when you give someone directions to your house, you are defining an algorithm that the person can follow to reach that specific destination. Algorithms are prevalent in modern society, because we are constantly faced with unfamiliar tasks that we could not complete without instructions. You probably don't know exactly how long to cook macaroni or how to assemble a bicycle, so algorithms are provided (e.g., cooking instructions on the macaroni box, or printed assembly instructions accompanying the bike) to guide you through these activities.

Of course, we have all had experiences with vague or misleading instructions, such as recipes that assume the knowledge of a master chef or directions to a house that rely on obscure landmarks. For an algorithm to be effective, it must be stated in a manner that its intended executor can understand. If you buy an expensive cookbook, it will probably assume that you are experienced in the kitchen. Instructions such as "create a white sauce" or "fold in egg whites until desired consistency" are probably clear to a chef. On the other hand, the instructions on the side of a typical macaroni and cheese box do not assume much culinary expertise. They tend to be simple and precise, like those in Figure 8.1. As you have no

Figure 8.1 Cooking instructions on a box of KRAFT® Macaroni and Cheese. (KRAFT is a registered trademark used with the permission of Kraft Foods.)

Figure 8.2 Ancient Babylonians used cuneiform writing to record mathematical formulas and then carved them into clay tablets. Such tablets represent the first historical examples of written algorithms. (British Museum, London, UK/Bridgeman Art Library)

doubt experienced in developing interactive Web pages, computers are more demanding with regard to algorithm specificity than any human audience could be. Computers require that the steps in an algorithm be stated in an extremely precise form. Even simple mistakes in a program, such as misspelling a variable name or forgetting a comma, can confuse the computer and render it unable to execute the program.

Specifying the solution to a problem in precise steps can be difficult, and the process often requires experience, creativity, and deep thought. However, once the problem's solution is designed and written down in the form of an algorithm, that particular problem can be solved by anyone capable of following the algorithm steps. The earliest surviving examples of written algorithms date back some four thousand years to the Babylonian civilization that inhabited present-day Iraq. Archeologists have discovered numerous examples of Babylonian clay tablets containing step-by-step instructions for solving mathematical and geometric problems (Figure 8.2).

Designing and Analyzing Algorithms

Life is full of problems whose solutions require a careful, step-by-step approach. Designing solutions to those problems involves both logical reasoning and creativity. In his classic book, *How to Solve It*, the mathematician George Polya (1887–1985) outlined four steps that can be applied to solving most problems:

1. Understand the problem.
2. Devise a plan.
3. Carry out your plan.
4. Examine the solution.

Polya's first step, understanding the problem, involves identifying exactly what is required (What are the initial conditions? What is the overall goal?) and what constraints are involved

(What properties must the solution have?). For example, suppose that you are presented with the following task:

Problem Statement: Find the oldest person in a room full of people.

At first glance, this problem seems relatively straightforward to comprehend. The initial condition is a room full of people. The goal is to identify the oldest person. However, deeper issues have to be explored before a solution can be proposed. For example, how do you determine how old a person is? Can you tell someone's age just by looking at her? If you ask someone his age, will he tell the truth? What if there is more than one oldest person (i.e., if two individuals were born on the same day at the same time)?

For simplicity, let us assume that, when asked, a person will give his or her real birthday. Also, let us further assume that we don't care about the time of day at which a person was born—if two people were born on the same day, they are considered the same age. If there is more than one oldest person, finding any one of them is acceptable.

Equipped with our new understanding of the problem, we are prepared to devise a solution:

Finding the oldest person in a room (Algorithm 1):

1. Line up all the people along one wall.
2. Ask the first person to state his or her name and birthday, then write this information down on a piece of paper.
3. For each successive person in line:
   a. Ask the person his or her name and birthday.
   b. If the stated birthday is earlier than the date written on the paper, cross out the old information and write down the name and birthday of this person.
4. When you have reached the end of the line, the name and birthday of the oldest person will be written on the paper.

To see how this algorithm works, we can carry out the steps on a fictitious group of people (Figure 8.3). Initially, you write down the name and birthday of the first person (Chris, 8/4/92). Working your way down the line, you ask each person's birthday and update the page when an earlier birthday is encountered (first Pat, 10/7/90; then Joan, 2/6/90). When you reach the end of the line, the name and birthday of the oldest person (Joan, 2/6/90) is written on the paper.

This algorithm is simple, and it's easy to see that it would work on any group of people. Because you go through the entire line, every person is eventually asked his or her birthday. When you reach the oldest person, his or her birthday will be earlier than the birthday currently on the paper. And once you write the oldest person's information down, that name will stay on the paper, as no one older will be found.

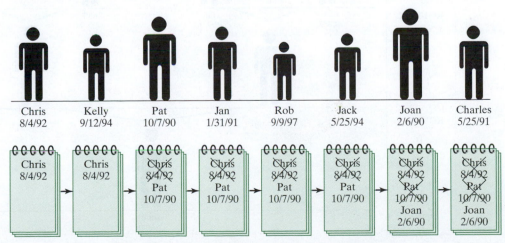

Figure 8.3 Algorithm 1 for finding the oldest person.

An Alternative Algorithm

Algorithm 1, as demonstrated in Figure 8.3, effectively locates the oldest person in a room. However, this problem—like most—can be solved many different ways. Once alternative algorithms for the same task have been proposed, you can analyze each option to determine which is simpler, more efficient, or better serves your particular objectives. As an example, consider the following alternative algorithm for finding the oldest person:

Finding the oldest person in a room (Algorithm 2):

1. Line up all the people along one wall.
2. As long as there is more than one person in the line, repeatedly:
   a. Have the people pair up (1st and 2nd in line, 3rd and 4th in line, and so on). If there is an odd number of people, the last person will remain without a partner.
   b. Ask each pair of people to compare their birthdays.
   c. Request that the younger of the two leave the line.
3. When there is only one person left in the line, that person is the oldest.

Algorithm 2 is slightly more complex than Algorithm 1, but has the same end result—the oldest person in the room is located. In the first round, each pair compare their birthdays, and the younger of the two partners subsequently leaves the line. Thus, the number of people in line is cut roughly in half (if there is an odd number of people, the extra person will remain). The older members of the original pairs then repeat this process, reducing the size of the line each time. Eventually, the number of people in line drops to one. Clearly, the oldest person cannot have left, because he or she would have been older than any potential partner in the line. Therefore, the last person remaining is the oldest. Figure 8.4

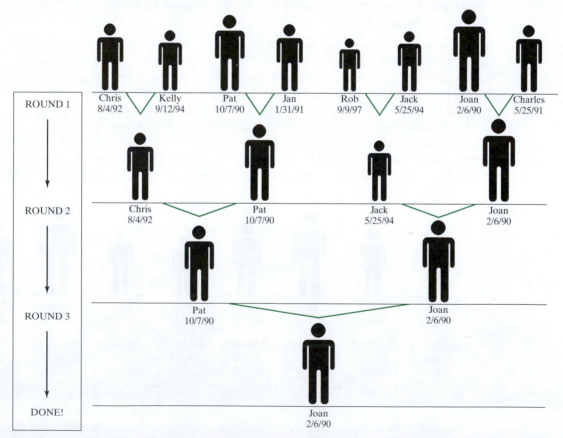

Figure 8.4 Algorithm 2 for finding the oldest person.

demonstrates performing this algorithm on the same eight people used in Figure 8.3. In three rounds, the line of people shrinks until it contains only the oldest person.

Algorithm Analysis

When more than one algorithm has been established to solve a problem, it is necessary to determine which is better. Often, there is not a single correct answer: your choice for the "better" algorithm depends on what features matter to you. If you don't care how long it takes to solve a problem but want to be sure of the answer, it makes sense for you to favor the simplest, most easily understood algorithm. However, if you are concerned about the time or effort required to solve the problem, you will want to analyze your alternatives more carefully before making a decision.

For example, consider the two algorithms that we have developed for finding the oldest person in a room. As Figure 8.3 demonstrates, Algorithm 1 involves asking each person's birthday and then comparing it with the birthday written on the page. Thus, the amount of time needed to find the oldest person using Algorithm 1 will be directly proportional to the number of people. If there are 100 people in line and it takes 5 seconds to compare birthdays, then executing Algorithm 1 will require 5 * 100 = 500 seconds. Likewise, if there are 200 people in line, then executing Algorithm 1 will require 5 * 200 = 1,000 seconds. In general, if you double the number of people, the time necessary to complete Algorithm 1 will also double.

By contrast, Algorithm 2 allows you to perform multiple comparisons simultaneously, which saves time. While the first pair of people compares their ages, all other pairs are doing the same. Thus, you can eliminate half the people in line in the time it takes to perform one comparison. This implies that the total time involved in executing Algorithm 2 will be proportional to the number of rounds needed to shrink the line down to one person. In Figure 8.4, we reduced a group of eight people to the single oldest person in three rounds: $8 \rightarrow 4 \rightarrow 2 \rightarrow 1$. If there were twice as many people in the room, it would still require only four rounds to eliminate all but the single oldest person: $16 \rightarrow 8 \rightarrow 4 \rightarrow 2 \rightarrow 1$. In mathematics, the notion of a logarithm captures this halving effect: $\lceil \log_2(N) \rceil$ represents the number of times a value N can be halved before it reaches 1, where $\lceil \ \rceil$ denotes rounding up to the next integer if necessary (Figure 8.5). Therefore, Algorithm 2 will find the oldest person in an amount of time proportional to the logarithm of the number of people. For example, if there are 100 people in line and it takes 5 seconds to compare birthdays, completing Algorithm 2 will require $5 * \lceil \log_2(100) \rceil = 5*7 = 35$ seconds. If there are 200 people in line, then completing Algorithm 2 will require $5 * \lceil \log_2(200) \rceil = 5*8 = 40$ seconds. In general, if you double the number of people, the time required to execute Algorithm 2 will increase by the duration of one additional comparison.

An algorithm's performance can be measured by the speed at which the algorithm (or program designed to carry out that algorithm) accomplishes its task. It should be noted that the relative performance of these algorithms remains the same, regardless of how long it takes to complete an individual comparison. In the timings we have considered so far, we assumed that birthdays

N	$\lceil \log_2(N) \rceil$
100	7
200	8
400	9
800	10
1,600	11
...	...
10,000	14
20,000	15
40,000	16
...	...
1,000,000	20

Figure 8.5 Table of logarithms (where $\lceil \ \rceil$ denotes rounding up to the next integer).

could be compared in 5 seconds. If a comparison instead took 10 seconds, you would still find that doubling the number of people doubles the time needed to perform Algorithm 1: 100 people would require 10 * 100 = 1,000 seconds, and 200 people would require 10 * 200 = 2,000 seconds. Likewise, doubling the number of people increases Algorithm 2's execution time by the duration of one additional comparison: 100 people would require $10 * \lceil \log_2(100) \rceil = 10 * 7 = 70$ seconds, and 200 people would require $10 * \lceil \log_2(200) \rceil = 10 * 8 = 80$ seconds.

Big-Oh Notation

To represent an algorithm's performance in relation to the size of the problem, computer scientists use what is known as the *Big-Oh* notation. Executing an $O(N)$ algorithm requires time proportional to the size of the problem. That is, if the problem size doubles, the time needed to solve that problem using the algorithm will also double. By contrast, executing an $O(\log N)$ algorithm requires time proportional to the logarithm of the problem size. That is, if the problem size doubles, the time needed to solve that problem increases by a constant amount. Based on our previous analysis, we can classify Algorithm 1 for finding the oldest person as an $O(N)$ algorithm, where problem size N is defined as the number of people in the room. Algorithm 2, on the other hand, is classified as an $O(\log N)$ algorithm. The performance difference between an $O(N)$ algorithm and an $O(\log N)$ algorithm can be quite dramatic, especially when you are contemplating extremely large problems. As we demonstrated above, Algorithm 1 would need 1,000 seconds to handle 200 people (assuming 5 seconds per comparison), whereas Algorithm 2 would need only 40. As the number of people increases, the performance benefit offered by Algorithm 2 increases as well. If the room in question contained 1,000 people, completing Algorithm 1 would require 5,000 seconds, whereas Algorithm 2 could be executed in only 50 seconds.

Algorithm Example: Searching a List

The problem of finding the oldest person in a room is similar to a more general problem that occurs frequently in computer science. Computers are often required to store and maintain large amounts of information and then search through data for particular values. For example, commercial databases typically contain large numbers of records, such as product inventories or payroll receipts, and allow the user to search for information on particular entries. Similarly, a Web browser that executes a JavaScript program must keep track of all the variables used throughout the program, as well as their corresponding values. Each time a variable appears in an expression, the browser must access the list of variables to obtain the associated value.

If a computer attempted to locate information in an arbitrary manner, pinpointing a particular entry in a list would be time-consuming and tedious. For example, consider the task of searching a large payroll database for a particular record. If the computer simply selected entries at random and compared them with the desired record, there would be no guarantee that the computer would eventually find the correct entry. A systematic approach (i.e., an algorithm) is needed to ensure that the desired entry is found, no matter where it appears in the database.

Sequential Search

The simplest algorithm for searching a list is *sequential search*, an approach that involves examining each list item in sequential order until the desired item is found.

Sequential search for finding an item in a list:

1. Start at the beginning of the list.
2. For each item in the list:
    a. Examine the item. If that item is the one you are seeking, then you are done.
    b. If it is not the item you are seeking, then go on to the next item in the list.

If you reach the end of the list and have not found the item, then it was not in the list. This algorithm is simple and guaranteed to find the item if it is in the list, but its execution can take a very long time. If the desired item is at the end of the list or not in the list at all, then the algorithm will have to look at every entry before returning a result. Although sequentially searching a list of 10 or 100 items might be feasible, this approach becomes impractical when a list contains thousands or tens of thousands of entries. Just imagine how tedious searching a phone book in this manner would be!

Binary Search

Fortunately, there is a more efficient algorithm for searching a list, as long as the list adheres to some organizational structure. For example, entries in the phone book are alphabetized to help people find numbers quickly. If you were looking for "Dave Reed" in the phone book, you might guess that it would appear toward the back of the book, because 'R' is late in the alphabet. However, if you opened the book to a page near the end and found "Joan Smith" at the top, you would know that you had gone too far and would back up some number of pages. In most cases, your knowledge of the alphabet and the phone book's alphabetical ordering system should enable you to hone in on an entry after a few page flips.

By generalizing this approach, we can create an algorithm for searching any ordered list. The first step is to inspect the entry at the middle position of the list (rounding down this position number if the list contains an even number of items). If this middle entry is the one you are looking for, then you are done. If, in the list's ordering scheme, the middle entry comes after the item you are seeking (e.g., "Joan Smith" comes after "Dave Reed" alphabetically), then you know that the desired item appears in the first half of the list (unless the item is not in the list at all). However, if the middle entry comes before the desired item in sequence (e.g., "Adam Miller" comes before "Dave Reed"), then the desired item must appear in the second half of the list. Once you have determined the half in which the item must appear, you can search that half via the same technique. Because each check cuts the list that must be searched in half, this algorithm is known as *binary search*.

Binary search for finding an item in an ordered list:

1. Initially, the potential range in which the item could occur is the entire list.
2. As long as items remain in the potential range and the desired item has not been found, repeatedly:
   a. Examine at the middle entry in the potential range.
   b. If the middle entry is the item you are looking for, then you are done.
   c. If the middle entry is greater than the desired item, then reduce the potential range to those entries left of the middle.
   d. If the middle entry is less than the desired item, then reduce the potential range to those entries right of the middle.

As step 2 consistently reduces the range in which the item could occur, repeating this step will eventually converge on the item (or reduce the potential range down to nothing, indicating that the item is not in the list). Figure 8.6 depicts a binary search that locates "MD" in an alphabetical list of state abbreviations. Because "MD" could conceivably appear anywhere in the list, the initial range that must be searched is the entire list (positions 1 through 31). Thus, you begin by checking the midpoint of this range, which is located by averaging the left and right boundaries of the range: position $(1 + 31)/2 = 16$. As the entry at position 16, "ND", comes after "MD" in the alphabet, you know that "MD" must appear in the left half of the list. Note that, in the second step, we have crossed out the entries at position 16 and beyond to highlight the fact that they are no longer under consideration. After eliminating part of the list, you repeat the process, checking the midpoint of the new potential range, position $(1 + 15)/2 = 8$. Because the entry at position 8, "IA", comes before "MD" in the alphabet, you know that "MD" must occupy a position to the right of position 8. The potential

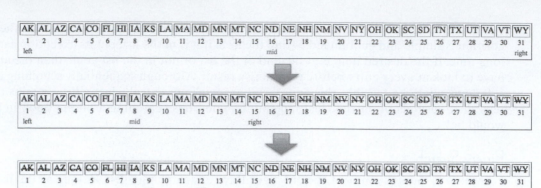

Figure 8.6 Steps in a binary search for "MD". The labels "left" and "right" denote the range in which the desired item can appear. With each step, the middle item in the range is checked and half the range is eliminated.

range in which "MD" can appear is now limited to positions 9 through 15. As before, you check the midpoint of the new potential range, position $(9 + 15)/2 = 12$. Because the entry at that position is indeed "MD", the search concludes successfully.

The Web page `search.html` (accessible at `http://balance3e.com/Ch8/search.html`) provides an interactive tool for studying the behavior of the binary search algorithm. Included with the page is a list of state abbreviations similar to the one used in Figure 8.6. The user can enter a desired state abbreviation in a text box, then click a button to see the steps required to locate that state in the list.

Algorithm Analysis

Recall that, in the worst case, sequential search involves checking every single entry in a list. This implies that the time required to locate a list item using sequential search is proportional to the size of the list. Thus, sequential search is an $O(N)$ algorithm, where problem size N is defined as the number of items in the list.

By contrast, when you perform a binary search, each examination of an entry enables you to rule out an entire range of entries. For example, in Figure 8.6, checking the midpoint of the list and finding that "Missouri" comes after "Illinois" allowed for the elimination of eight entries (positions 8 through 15). Subsequently checking the midpoint of the list's first half and finding that "Florida" comes before "Illinois" eliminated an additional four entries (positions 1 through 4). In general, each time you look at an entry, you can rule out roughly half the remaining entries. This halving effect yields the same logarithmic behavior that we noted in Algorithm 2 for finding the oldest person in a room. Thus, the time required to find a list item using binary search is proportional to the logarithm of the size of the list, making binary search an $O(\log N)$ algorithm. This makes binary search a much more efficient technique for searching large amounts of information. Using binary search, a phone book for a small town (10,000 people) could be searched in at most $\lceil \log_2(10{,}000) \rceil = 14$ checks, a large city (1 million people) in at most $\lceil \log_2(1{,}000{,}000) \rceil = 20$ checks, and the entire United States (310 million people) in at most $\lceil \log_2(310{,}000{,}000) \rceil = 29$ checks.

Algorithm Example: Approximating a Square Root

Recall that, in Chapter 7, we introduced the `Math.sqrt` function as an example of computational abstraction. As JavaScript predefines this function, it was not necessary for you to understand how the function works—you just needed to know how to use it. In this section, however, we are going to examine the actual steps required to calculate the square root of a number. Several different algorithms can be used to perform this computation; one in particular, devised by Sir Isaac Newton (1643–1727) in the late 17th century (Figure 8.7), is simple to describe and is discussed next.

Figure 8.7 Sir Isaac Newton.

Newton's algorithm for finding the square root of N:

1. Start with the initial approximation 1.
2. As long as the approximation isn't close enough, repeatedly:
   a. Refine the approximation using the formula
      `newApproximation = (oldApproximation + N/oldApproximation)/2.`

While reading Newton's algorithm, you might have noticed that the stopping condition is somewhat vague. Because some numbers' square roots (such as the square root of 2) cannot be represented as finite fractions, Newton's algorithm will not always be able to find the exact square root. However, each successive approximation is guaranteed to be closer to the square root. Thus, the person using the algorithm can determine exactly how close the approximation needs to be in order to suffice.

For example, suppose that we wanted to find the square root of 1,024. Newton's algorithm starts with the initial approximation 1. The next approximation is obtained by plugging 1 into Newton's formula; we therefore evaluate the expression (1 + 1,024/1)/2, which yields 512.5. The next approximation is (512.5 + 1,024/512.5)/2 = 257.2, followed by (257.2 + 1,024/257.2)/2 = 130.6, and so on. After only 10 refinements, the approximation is so close to the actual square root, 32, that a computer will round the value to 32 (see Figure 8.8).

```
Initial approximation = 1
Next approximation = 512.5
Next approximation = 257.2490243902439
Next approximation = 130.61480157022683
Next approximation = 69.22732405448894
Next approximation = 42.00958563100827
Next approximation = 33.19248741685438
Next approximation = 32.02142090500024
Next approximation = 32.0000071648159
Next approximation = 32.0000000000008
Next approximation = 32
```

Figure 8.8 Using Newton's algorithm to calculate the square root of 1,024.

The Web page `Newton.html` (accessible at `http://balance3e.com/Ch8/Newton.html`) provides an interactive tool for studying the behavior of Newton's algorithm. The user can enter a desired number *N* in a text box, then click a button to see the first approximation of *N*'s square root as calculated using Newton's algorithm. Each time the user clicks the button, the program displays a successive approximation. The user can continue clicking until the desired level of accuracy is reached.

Algorithm Analysis

Analyzing the performance of Newton's algorithm is trickier than in previous examples, and a detailed investigation of this topic is beyond the scope of this book. The algorithm does converge on the square root in the sense that each successive approximation is closer to the square root than the previous one was. However, the fact that the square root might be a nonterminating fraction makes it difficult to define the exact number of steps required for convergence. In general, the algorithm does tend to demonstrate logarithmic behavior, as the difference between a given approximation and the actual square root is cut roughly in half by each successive refinement.

Algorithms and Programming

Programming is all about designing and coding algorithms for solving problems. The intended executor of those algorithms is the computer or a program executing on that computer, which must be able to understand the instructions and then carry them out in order. Because computers are not very intelligent, the instructions they receive must be extraordinarily specific. Unfortunately, human languages such as English are notoriously ambiguous, and the technology for programming computers in a human language is still many years away. Instead, we write computer instructions in programming languages, which are more constrained and exact than human languages are.

The level of precision necessary to write a successful program often frustrates beginning programmers. However, it is much easier to program today's computers than those of fifty years ago. As we explained in Chapter 6, the first electronic computers were not programmable at all—machines such as the ENIAC were wired to perform a certain computation. Although users could enter inputs via switches, the computational steps that the computer performed could be changed only by rewiring the physical components into a different configuration. Clearly, this arrangement made specifying an algorithm tedious and time-consuming. With the advent of von Neumann's stored-program architecture, computers could be programmed instead of rewired. For the first time, computing engineers were able to write algorithms as sequences of instructions in a language understood by the computer, and these instructions could be loaded into memory and executed.

Machine Languages

Programming languages introduce a level of abstraction that insulates the programmer from the computer's low-level, mechanical details. Instead of having to worry about which wires should connect which components, the programmer must instead learn to speak the language that controls the machinery. However, the first programming languages, which were developed in the late 1940s, provided a very low level of abstraction. Instructions written in these languages correspond directly to the hardware operations of a particular machine. As such, these languages are called ***machine languages***. Machine-language instructions deal directly with the computer's physical components, including main memory locations and registers, memory cells located inside the CPU and used for storing values as computations take place. (Chapter 14 discusses the role of registers in greater detail.) Examples of these primitive instructions might include:

- Move the value at main memory address 100 to register 3.
- Add 1 to the value in register 3.
- Jump to the instruction at main memory address 1024.

Of course, machine-language instructions aren't represented as statements in English. As we learned in Chapter 1, computers store and manipulate data in the form of binary values (i.e., patterns

```
0000000000000001101000011001010110110001101100011011110010111001100011011100000
1110000000000001100111011100011011100011001100100101111101100011011011110110110
1011100000110100101101100011001010110100000101110000000001011111010100001010011
1110111000101110100011011111011001000000000010111110101111101101100011110011010
1111101011111001101110110111101110011011101000110010011001010110000101101110101010
1010000010001100101001000110111011011110111001101110100011100100110010101100000
1011011010101111010100100011011101101111011100110111101000111001001100101011010000
0010110110100000000010111110101011111010110110001101001101101011111010111110011101101
0111101110010111010001101010110000101010110001101011110011010000100110110111110001101110001011
0000000011001010110110011001000110110001011111010111110100011001010010001100110110010110001011010
1011011110111001101110100011100100110010101100001011011010000000001101101010101100
0010110100101101110000000000011000110110111101110101010110100000000000000000000000000
```

Figure 8.9 Excerpt from a machine-language program.

of 0s and 1s). It is not surprising, then, that machine-language instructions are also represented in binary. For example, these instructions might be written as:

- 0110011001000011
- 1100000000010011
- 0101010000000000

Thus, machine-language programs are comprised of binary-number sequences corresponding to primitive machine operations. Although writing such a program and storing it in memory is certainly preferable to rewiring the machine, machine languages do not facilitate easy, intuitive programming. Programmers have to memorize the binary codes that correspond to machine instructions, which is extremely tedious. Entering in long sequences of zeros and ones is error prone, to say the least. And, if errors do occur, trying to debug a sheet full of zeros and ones is next to impossible. To make matters worse, each type of computer has its own machine language that correlates directly to the machine's underlying hardware. Machine-language programs written for one type of computer can be executed only on identical machines.

To provide a taste of what these earlier programmers went through, Figure 8.9 depicts an excerpt from an actual machine-language program. How easy do you think it would be to look at this program and determine what it does? If you ran this program and it did not behave as desired, how easy would it be to work through the code and determine where it went wrong?

High-Level Languages

Although machine languages enable computers to be reprogrammed without being rewired, these languages introduce only a low level of abstraction. As each binary instruction corresponds to a physical operation, programmers must still specify algorithms at the level of the machinery. Furthermore, the programmer has to represent all instructions and data as binary-number sequences.

In the early 1950s, programming capabilities evolved through the introduction of **assembly languages**. Assembly languages provide a slightly higher level of abstraction by allowing programmers to specify instructions using words, rather than binary-number sequences. However, these words still correspond to operations performed by the computer's physical components, so assembly-language programming still involves thinking at a low level of abstraction.

To solve complex problems quickly and reliably, programmers must be able to write instructions at a higher level of abstraction that more closely relates to the way humans think. When we solve problems, we make use of high-level abstractions and constructs, such as variables, conditional choices, repetition, and functions. A language that includes such abstractions provides a more natural framework through which to solve problems. Starting in the late 1950s, computer scientists began developing **high-level languages** to address this need. The first such language was FORTRAN, written by John Backus (1924–2007) at IBM in 1957. Two years later, John McCarthy (1927–) invented LISP at MIT, and a multitude of high-level languages soon followed. JavaScript, the high-level language that you have been using throughout this text, was invented in 1995 by Brendan Eich (1964–) and his research team at Netscape Communications Corporation.

```
<!doctype html>
<!-- hello.html      Simple demo page. -->

<html>
 <head>
   <title> Greetings </title>
 </head>
 <body>
   <p>Your name: <input type="text" id="nameBox" value=""></p>
   <input type="button" value="Click for Greeting"
          onclick="document.getElementById('outputDiv').innerHTML=
                'Hello '+document.getElementById('nameBox').value+
                '!';">

   <hr>
   <div id="outputDiv"></div>
 </body>
</html>
```

```cpp
// hello.cpp                    Dave Reed
// This program displays a greeting.
/////////////////////////////////////////
#include <iostream>
#include <string>
using namespace std;

int main()

{
   string userName;
   cout << "Enter your name" << endl;
   cin >> userName;

   cout << "Hello " << userName << "!";

   return 0;
}
```

Figure 8.10 High-level language programs (JavaScript and C++).

Figure 8.10 depicts two different high-level language programs that perform the same task: each asks the user to enter a name and then displays a customized greeting. The program on the left is written in JavaScript, and the one on the right is written in C++. As you can see, high-level programming languages are much closer to human languages than machine languages are. With only a little knowledge of each language, anyone could detect and fix errors in these programs.

Another advantage of high-level languages is that the resulting programs are machine independent. Because high-level instructions are not specific to the underlying computer's hardware configuration, programs written in high-level languages are theoretically portable across computers. Such portability is essential, because it enables programmers to market their software to a wide variety of users. If a different version of the same program were required for each brand of computer, software development would be both inefficient and prohibitively expensive.

Not surprisingly, almost all software development today uses high-level programming languages, such as C++ and Java. However, it should be noted that low-level languages have not gone away. As you will see in the next section, programs written in a high-level language must still be translated into the machine language of a particular computer before they can be executed. And in application areas where execution time is critical, say in controllers for jet stabilizers, modern programmers may still use assembly and machine languages to optimize the use of memory and the sequencing of instructions.

Program Translation

Although it is desirable for programmers to be able to reason at a high level of abstraction, we cannot forget that programs are written to be executed. At some point, a high-level program must be translated to machine instructions that computer hardware can implement. Two basic techniques, known as interpretation and compilation, are employed to perform these translations. However, before we formally define these approaches, let us examine the following analogies.

Consider the task of translating a speech from one language to another. Usually, this is accomplished by having an interpreter listen to the speech as it is being given, translating it a phrase or sentence at a time (Figure 8.11). In effect, the interpreter becomes a substitute for the original speaker, repeating the speaker's words in a different language after a slight delay to perform the translation (Figure 8.12). One advantage of this approach is that it provides a real-time translation: an observer can see the speaker and hear the translated words in the same approximate time frame. The immediacy of the translation also enables the observer to give feedback to the interpreter. For example, if the interpreter were using the wrong dialect of a language, the observer could correct this early in the speech.

1. A speech is delivered in Chinese.

2. An interpreter listens, translates each sentence, and speaks in English.

3. The listener hears each sentence in English (with some delay).

Figure 8.11 Using an interpreter to translate a speech.

Figure 8.12 Chinese Premier Deng Xiaoping with interpreter (1975).

If there is no need for the translation to be provided in real time, the interpreter could instead translate the speech in its entirety after the fact. Given a recording (or transcript), a translator could take the time to convert the entire speech to the desired language and then produce a recording (or transcript) of the translation (Figure 8.13). Although this approach is less immediate and more time-consuming than real-time interpretation is, there are several advantages. A key benefit is that, once the speech has been translated, multiple people can listen to it as many times as desired, without the need for retranslation. Furthermore, after the initial translation process, listeners do not have to suffer through additional delays when hearing the content of the speech. This approach is clearly required for translating books, because it is impractical to translate the book phrase by phrase every time someone wants to read it.

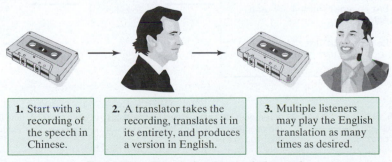

1. Start with a recording of the speech in Chinese.

2. A translator takes the recording, translates it in its entirety, and produces a version in English.

3. Multiple listeners may play the English translation as many times as desired.

Figure 8.13 Translating a recorded speech.

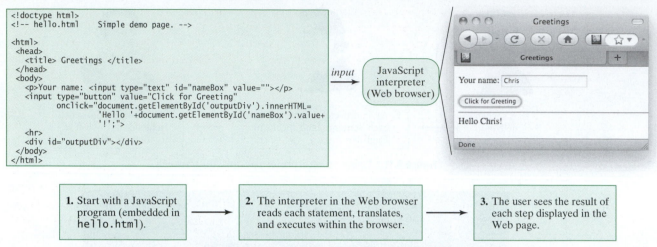

1. Start with a JavaScript program (embedded in `hello.html`).

2. The interpreter in the Web browser reads each statement, translates, and executes within the browser.

3. The user sees the result of each step displayed in the Web page.

Figure 8.14 Interpreting a JavaScript program.

Interpreters and Compilers

Translating a high-level language program into machine language is not unlike translating spoken languages. The two techniques we have described are analogous to the two approaches used in programming-language translation: *interpretation* and *compilation*. The interpretation approach relies on a program known as an *interpreter* to translate and execute the statements in a high-level language program. An interpreter reads the statements one at a time, immediately translating and executing each statement before processing the next one. This is, in fact, what happens when JavaScript programs are executed. A JavaScript interpreter is embedded in every modern Web browser; when the browser loads a page containing JavaScript code, the interpreter executes the code one statement at a time, displaying the corresponding output in the page (Figure 8.14).

By contrast, the compilation approach relies on a program known as a *compiler* to translate the entire high-level language program into its equivalent machine-language instructions. The resulting machine-language program can then be executed directly on the computer (Figure 8.15). Most programming languages used in the development of commercial software, such as C and C++, employ the compilation technique.

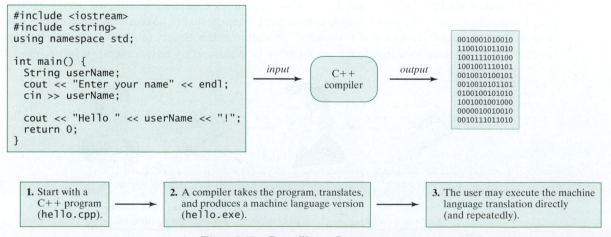

1. Start with a C++ program (`hello.cpp`).

2. A compiler takes the program, translates, and produces a machine language version (`hello.exe`).

3. The user may execute the machine language translation directly (and repeatedly).

Figure 8.15 Compiling a C++ program.

As with the human-language translation options, there are trade-offs between the interpretation and compilation approaches. An interpreter starts producing results almost immediately, as it reads in and executes each instruction before moving on to the next. This immediacy is particularly desirable for languages used in highly interactive applications. For example, JavaScript was designed specifically for adding dynamic, interactive features to Web pages. If the first statement in a JavaScript program involves prompting the user for a value, then you would like this to happen as soon as the page loads, rather than waiting for the rest of the program to be translated. The disadvantage of interpretation, however, is that the program executes more slowly. The interpreter must take the time to translate each statement as it executes, so there will be a slight delay between each statement's execution. A compiler, on the other hand, produces a machine-language program that can be run directly on the underlying hardware. Once compiled, the program will run very quickly. If a language is intended for developing large software applications, execution speed is of the utmost importance; thus, languages such as C++ are translated using compilers. The drawback to compilation, however, is that the programmer must take the time to compile the entire program before executing it.

Looking Ahead...

In this chapter, you looked at programming from an algorithmic perspective. You learned that programming, in essence, is the process of designing algorithms for solving problems and then implementing those algorithms so that a computer can understand them. After introducing the basics of algorithm design, we explored several example problems: finding the oldest person in a room, finding a particular entry in a list, and computing the square root of a number. In addition, we described methods for translating programs from a high-level language such as JavaScript to the underlying, low-level language of the computer.

Now that you are equipped with a more general understanding of algorithms, you can move on to solving more complex problems. In the next chapter, you will return to the concept of user-defined functions. Recall that in Chapter 7, you wrote simple JavaScript functions that encapsulated the statements to be executed when a button was clicked or a text box was changed. Chapter 9 introduces the more general form of user-defined functions. With the addition of parameters and return statements, functions can provide an even greater level of computational abstraction and aid the programmer in solving complex tasks.

Chapter Summary

- The central concept underlying all computation is that of the algorithm, a step-by-step sequence of instructions for carrying out some task.

- Programming may be viewed as the process of designing and implementing algorithms that a computer (or a program executing on that computer) can carry out.

- Algorithms are prevalent in modern society (e.g., cooking instructions, directions for assembling a bike), because we are constantly faced with unfamiliar tasks that we could not complete without instructions.

- George Polya outlined four steps that can be applied to solving most problems: (1) understand the problem, (2) devise a plan, (3) carry out your plan, and (4) examine the solution.

- Performance measures the speed at which a particular algorithm (or program designed to carry out that algorithm) accomplishes its task. Performance may be characterized by the number of steps involved or the time it takes to complete the task.

- Big-Oh notation is used to represent an algorithm's performance in relation to the size of the problem. An $O(N)$ algorithm requires time proportional to the size of the problem, so doubling the problem size will roughly double the time required. An $O(\log N)$ algorithm requires time proportional to the logarithm of the size of the problem, so doubling the problem size only increases the time required by a constant amount.

- The sequential search algorithm, which can be used to find a particular item in a list, is an example of an $O(N)$ algorithm, where N is the number of items in the list. Binary search, which can be used when the list is ordered, is an example of an $O(\log N)$ algorithm.

- Newton's algorithm is a simple, yet efficient, algorithm for approximating the square root of a number.

- Machine languages are low-level programming languages in which each instruction is a binary number sequence that corresponds directly to a hardware operation of the machine. Assembly languages provide a slightly higher level of abstraction by allowing programmers to specify instructions using words, rather than binary-number sequences.

- High-level programming languages provide abstractions and problem-solving constructs that make problem solving simpler and more intuitive for the programmer.

- Before it can be executed on a computer, a program written in a high-level language must be translated into the machine language for that particular computer. This can be accomplished via an interpreter (which translates and executes each statement in the program in sequence) or a compiler (which translates the entire program into an equivalent machine-language program).

Review Questions

1. TRUE or FALSE? An algorithm is a step-by-step sequence of instructions for carrying out some task.

2. TRUE or FALSE? A sequence of instructions for assembling a bookcase does not qualify as an "algorithm," as the instructions are not written in formal, mathematical notation.

3. TRUE or FALSE? For a precise, clearly stated problem, there can be only one algorithm that provides a solution.

4. TRUE or FALSE? Big-Oh notation is used to measure the exact number of seconds required by a particular algorithm when executing on a particular computer.

5. TRUE or FALSE? Suppose you have been given a sorted list of 100 names and need to find a particular name in that list. Using sequential search, it is possible that you might have to look at every location in the list before finding the desired name.

6. TRUE or FALSE? Suppose you have been given a sorted list of 100 names and need to find a particular name in that list. Using binary search, it is possible that you might have to look at every location in the list before finding the desired name.

7. TRUE or FALSE? Binary search is an example of an $O(\log N)$ algorithm, where the number of items in the list to be searched is N.

8. TRUE or FALSE? One advantage of assembly languages over machine languages is that they enable the programmer to use words to identify instructions instead of using binary-number sequences.

9. TRUE or FALSE? JavaScript, C++, and Java are all examples of high-level programming languages.

10. TRUE or FALSE? When a Web page is loaded into a Web browser, JavaScript code in that page is executed by a JavaScript interpreter that is embedded in the browser.

11. An algorithm must be clear to its intended executor in order to be effective. Give an example of a real-world algorithm that you have encountered and felt was *not* clear. Do you think that the algorithm writer did a poor job, or do you think that the algorithm was formalized with a different audience in mind? Explain your answer. Then, give an example of a real-world algorithm that you felt was clearly stated. What features of this algorithm allow you to understand it more easily?

12. Write an algorithm for directing a person to your house, apartment, or dorm from a central location. For example, if you live on campus, the directions might originate at a campus landmark. Assume that the person following the directions is familiar with the neighborhood or campus.

13. Write an alternative algorithm for directing a person to your residence, but this time, assume that the person is unfamiliar with the area. How does this condition affect the way you describe the algorithm?

14. Suppose that you were asked to arrange a group of people in sequence from oldest to youngest. You must organize a line that begins with the oldest person and continues in descending order according to age. Describe an algorithm for completing this task.

15. Suppose that you have been given an $O(N)$ algorithm that averages student grades, where N is the number of grades. If it takes 1 minute to average 100 grades using the algorithm, how long would you expect it to take to average 200 grades? 400 grades? Justify your answer.

16. Suppose you needed to look up a number in your local phone book. Roughly, what is the population of your city? How many checks would be required, in the worst case, to find the phone number using sequential search? How many checks would be required, in the worst case, to find the phone number using binary search?

17. Consider the list of states from Figure 8.5. Which state in the list is the "easiest" to find using binary search? That is, which state could be located in the fewest number of checks? Generalize your answer so that it applies to any sorted list of items.

18. Again, consider the list of states from Figure 8.5. Which state in the list is the "hardest" to find using binary search? That is, which state would require the largest number of checks to be located? Generalize your answer so that it applies to any sorted list of items.

19. Refer to the `Newton.html` page. How many refinements does Newton's algorithm require to compute the square root of 900? 10,000? 152,399,025?

20. Imagine that, while you are using Newton's algorithm, the approximations converge on the actual square root of the number. What would happen if you tried to further refine the square root? Would the value change? Why or why not?

21. A disadvantage of machine languages is that they are machine dependent. That is, each machine language is specific to a particular computer, and different computers require different machine languages. Describe why this is the case.

22. Describe two advantages of high-level language programming over machine-language programming.

23. What is the difference between a compiler and an interpreter? What characteristics of an interpreter make it better suited for executing JavaScript programs?

References

Ben-Ari, Mordechai. *Principles of Concurrent and Distributed Programming,* 2nd ed. Reading, MA: Addison-Wesley, 2006.

Brassard, Gilles, and Paul Bratley. *Fundamentals of Algorithmics.* Upper Saddle River, NJ: Prentice Hall, 1996.

Cormen, Thomas H., Ronald L. Rivest, Charles E. Leiserson, and Clifford Stein. *Introduction to Algorithms*, 3rd ed. Boston, MA: MIT Press, 2009.

Knuth, Donald E. "Algorithms in Modern Mathematics and Computer Science." *Lecture Notes in Computer Science 122*, 1981. Also appears in *Selected Papers in Computer Science*. Cambridge, MA: Cambridge University Press, 1996.

Knuth, Donald E. "Ancient Babylonian Algorithms." *Communications of the ACM*, 15(7), 1972. Also appears in *Selected Papers in Computer Science*. Cambridge, MA: Cambridge University Press, 1996.

Knuth, Donald E. *The Art of Computer Programming*, Vol. 3, *Sorting and Searching*, 2d ed. Reading, MA: Addison-Wesley, 1998.

Polya, George. *How to Solve It: A New Aspect of Mathematical Method*, 2d ed. Princeton, NJ: Princeton University Press, 1945.

Sedgewick, Robert. *Algorithms in* C++, Parts 1–4, *Fundamentals, Data Structures, Sorting, Searching*, 3d ed. Reading, MA: Addison-Wesley, 1998.

Sedgewick, Robert. *Algorithms in Java*, Parts 1–4, *Fundamentals, Data Structures, Sorting, Searching*, 3d ed. Reading, MA: Addison-Wesley, 2002.

Skiena, Steven S. *The Algorithm Design Manual.* New York: Springer-Verlag, 1998.

Abstraction and Libraries

Chapter 9

This chapter uses narrative, examples, and hands-on exercises to introduce programming concepts and Web development skills.

In the development of the understanding of complex phenomena, the most powerful tool available to the human intellect is abstraction. Abstraction arises from the recognition of similarities between certain objects, situations, or processes in the real world and the decision to concentrate on these similarities and to ignore, for the time being, their differences.

C.A.R. Hoare
Structured Programming

Civilization advances by extending the number of important operations which we can perform without thinking.

Alfred Lord Whitehead
An Introduction to Mathematics

Abstraction is the process of ignoring minutiae and focusing on the big picture. In modern life, we are constantly confronted with objects much too complex to be understood by the average person. For example, to really grasp how a television works, one must have extensive knowledge of electrical engineering, electronics, and physics, but most of us watch and operate television sets every day. This is possible because we abstract away unnecessary details and focus on the features relevant to our needs. At the level of abstraction through which most people view a television, it is a box with several inputs (power cord, on/off button, channel selector, and volume control) and two outputs (picture and sound). This degree of understanding enables us to watch and have control over the television set without knowing the specifics of television's functionality.

You have already been introduced to the idea of abstraction in programming through the use of functions. In a programming language, a function represents a unit of computation from which the details are abstracted away. For example, the computation involved in finding the square root of a number is certainly not trivial, but the `Math.sqrt` function encapsulates this multistep process in a single function call. Without worrying about how this function computes the square root, the programmer is able to call the function and use it to obtain a result. Chapter 7 demonstrated how the user could define simple functions that augmented the predefined functions already provided. By encapsulating all of the JavaScript statements to be executed when a button is clicked, a user-defined function (such as the GenerateNumber function in the lucky1.html page) simplifies the button and makes the page body easier to read. In this chapter, you will learn how to design and write more powerful user-defined functions, with features including parameters, local variables, and return statements. You will even learn how to create libraries of useful functions, which can then be used as computational abstractions in solving a variety of problems.

The Structure of Functions

Recall from Chapter 7 that, mathematically speaking, a function is a mapping from some number of inputs to a single output. For example, the Math.sqrt function maps a single input—say, the number 9, to its square root: 3. Likewise, the Math.max function maps two inputs—say, the numbers 7 and 3, to the maximum of the two: 7. Using programming terminology, we say that the function call Math.sqrt(9) returns 3, while the function call Math.max(7, 3) returns 7.

The functions that you defined in Chapter 7 were of the simplest possible form. They did not require any inputs; instead, they accessed text boxes directly to obtain values for their computation. Likewise, they did not return any values; instead, they displayed their results directly in the page. To write general-purpose functions that take inputs, perform computations, and return a value, we must extend the general form of user-defined functions to include parameters, local variables, and return statements (Figure 9.1).

- *Parameters* are variables that appear in the parentheses (separated by commas) following the function name. They correspond to the function's inputs, so a function that requires one input value (such as Math.sqrt) would have one parameter inside the parentheses, while a function that requires two input values (such as Math.max) would have two parameters. When the function is called, the input values specified in the call are assigned to the parameter variables, which can then be used in performing the computation. If the function has no inputs, as was the case with the user-defined functions from Chapter 7, then there will be no parameters listed inside the parentheses.

- The first statement inside the general form is a *local variable declaration*. This statement declares all of the variables that will be used by the function to carry out its computation. As a result of the declaration, these variables are treated as local to the function, meaning that they exist only inside that function while it is executing. Without this declaration, the variables are considered *global* and thus accessible and changeable from anywhere in the page. To avoid unintended changes, all variables used for storing temporary values in a function should be declared as local, separated by commas and following the keyword var.

- A *return statement* is an optional statement that can appear at the end of a function definition. A return statement consists of the word return, followed by a variable or expression. When the statement is executed, the variable or expression is evaluated and the resulting value is returned as the output of this function.

```
function FUNCTION_NAME(PARAMETER1, PARAMETER2, ..., PARAMETERn)
// Assumes: DESCRIPTION OF ASSUMPTIONS MADE ABOUT PARAMETERS
// Returns: DESCRIPTION OF VALUE RETURNED BY FUNCTION
{
    var LOCAL1, LOCAL2, ..., LOCALn;

    STATEMENTS_TO_PERFORM_THE_DESIRED_COMPUTATION

    return OUTPUT_VALUE;                                // optional
}
```

Figure 9.1 General form of a user-defined function.

The rest of this chapter will provide further details and examples demonstrating these new function features.

Local Variables

Despite no scientific evidence to support its existence, some people continue to believe in extrasensory perception (ESP). The traditional test for determining whether someone has ESP involves asking the person to guess randomly selected values. For example, you might generate random integers in some range—such as 1 to 4—and then have the person try to guess each number. Given four possible values, you would expect random guessing to be correct approximately one-fourth of the time. If a person were correct significantly more often, you might be tempted to say that the subject has ESP (rather than being just lucky).

The Web page in Figure 9.2 implements a simple ESP test. When the user clicks on the button, the PickNumber function is called to pick a random number between 1 and 4 and display that number in a page division (Figure 9.3). Note that the variable number, which is used to store the randomly generated number, is declared to be a local variable in line 13.

```
1.  <!doctype html>
2.  <!-- esp1.html                                              Dave Reed   -->
3.  <!-- This page performs an ESP test by displaying a random number. -->
4.  <!-- ============================================================ -->
5.
6.  <html>
7.   <head>
8.     <title> ESP Test </title>
9.     <script type="text/javascript">
10.       function PickNumber()
11.       // Results: displays a random number between 1 and 4 in outputDiv
12.       {
13.         var number;
14.
15.         number = Math.floor(Math.random()*4) + 1;
16.         document.getElementById('outputDiv').innerHTML =
17.           'My number was ' + number + '. Were you correct?';
18.       }
19.     </script>
20.   </head>
21.
22.   <body>
23.     <div style="text-align:center">
24.       <h2>ESP Test</h2>
25.       <p>
26.         Think of a number between 1 and 4, then click the button to see
27.         if you were right.
28.       </p>
29.       <input type="button" value="Click to see the number"
30.               onclick="PickNumber();">
31.       <hr>
32.       <div id="outputDiv"></div>
33.     </div>
34.   </body>
35. </html>
```

Figure 9.2 Web page for performing a simple ESP test.

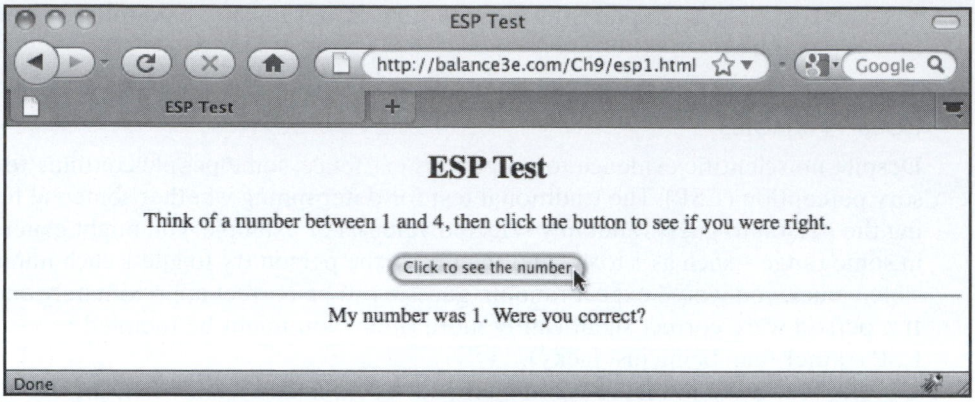

Figure 9.3 `esp1.html` rendered in a Web browser.

When the browser encounters a local variable declaration, it allocates memory cells for each of the local variables. These memory cells are then used to store the values associated with the local variables within the function. When the function terminates, these values "go away," and the memory cells are freed. As a result, local variables only exist while the function they belong to is executing. In contrast, the memory cell associated with a global variable persists as long as the page exists. This can result in conflicts if multiple functions utilize and modify the same global variable.

For example, suppose we extended the `esp1.html` page to include a `GetInfo` function that obtained information about the user, including his or her student ID number. If the `GetInfo` function used a variable named `number` to store the ID number and neither function declared the variable to be local, then the two functions would both be assigning values to the same global variable. When one function changed the value of the global variable, that change would affect the other function as well. If the variables are declared to be local in each of the functions, however, no conflict occurs. Instead, the browser recognizes two distinct variables that appear in different environments (much the same way that Paris, France, and Paris, Texas, are recognizable as different cities). If it helps, you can think of each variable as having an implicit subscript that identifies its environment, such as $number_{PickNumber}$ and $number_{GetInfo}$. Within the `PickNumber` function, any reference to the local variable number is actually $number_{PickNumber}$, whereas any reference to a number in `GetInfo` is actually $number_{GetInfo}$. This representation makes it clear that the local variables are treated as two distinct variables within the page.

EXERCISE 9.1

Enter the `esp1.html` text from Figure 9.2 into a new Web page, then load the page in the browser to verify that it behaves as described.

Test your ESP potential by repeatedly loading the page and trying to guess a number between 1 and 4. Out of 20 tests, how many times did you guess correctly? Do you think you have ESP?

Common errors to avoid...

When you develop a Web page, you should always think to the future. That is, develop the page using good style so that the page can easily be extended or modified in the future. When defining a function, this means always declaring temporary variables in the function to be local. Otherwise, global variables can lead to errors, as statements in one function can affect values used in another function.

Functions with Inputs

While the `esp1.html` page suffices as a rudimentary ESP test, its design is far from ideal. The page simply asks the user to think of a number and then relies on him to be honest as to whether the guess was correct. A better design would require the user to commit to a guess before seeing the selected number in the page. This could be accomplished by having four buttons, each with its own version of the `PickNumber` function. Clicking on the button labeled Guess 1 would call a version named `PickNumber1`, which is identical to the `PickNumber` function from Figure 9.2 except that it also displays the user's guess of 1. Similarly, clicking on the Guess 2 button would call a version named `PickNumber2`, and so on, with each version of the function displaying the user's guess and the selected number.

Fortunately, a more elegant solution is possible. Instead of having four functions that behave identically (except for displaying a different user guess), the Web page in Figure 9.4 utilizes a single function with a parameter. If the user clicks on the Guess 1 button, the `PickNumber` function is

```
1.  <!doctype html>
2.  <!-- esp2.html                                              Dave Reed   -->
3.  <!-- This page performs an ESP test by displaying a random number. -->
4.  <!-- ======================================================= -->
5.
6.  <html>
7.   <head>
8.     <title> ESP Test </title>
9.     <script type="text/javascript">
10.      function PickNumber(guess)
11.      // Assumes: guess is the user's guess (between 1 and 4)
12.      // Results: displays a random number between 1 and 4 in outputDiv
13.      {
14.        var number;
15.
16.        number = Math.floor(Math.random()*4) + 1;
17.        document.getElementById('outputDiv').innerHTML =
18.          'You guessed ' + guess + '. My number was ' + number +
19.          '. Were you correct?';
20.      }
21.     </script>
22.   </head>
23.
24.   <body>
25.     <div style="text-align:center">
26.       <h2>ESP Test</h2>
27.       <p>
28.         Think of a number between 1 and 4, then click the button to see
29.         if you were right.
30.       </p>
31.       <input type="button" value="Guess 1" onclick="PickNumber(1);">
32.       <input type="button" value="Guess 2" onclick="PickNumber(2);">
33.       <input type="button" value="Guess 3" onclick="PickNumber(3);">
34.       <input type="button" value="Guess 4" onclick="PickNumber(4);">
35.       <hr>
36.       <div id="outputDiv"></div>
37.     </div>
38.   </body>
39.  </html>
```

Figure 9.4 Generalized Web page for performing a simple ESP test.

Figure 9.5 esp2.html rendered in a Web browser.

called with input value 1. This input value is assigned to the guess parameter in the function, and subsequently any reference to the variable name guess evaluates to 1. Similarly, clicking on the Guess 2 button would call the PickNumber function with input value 2, and so on for each button. The end result is that the single PickNumber function serves to handle any of the four guesses, displaying the guess along with the randomly selected value (Figure 9.5).

In general, a function encapsulates a computation and allows the programmer to perform that computation simply by calling the function. Parameters play an important role in functions, because they facilitate the creation of generalized computations. For example, the PickNumber function isn't limited to handling only one particular user guess; it can be called to process any guess by providing that guess as input.

Technically, a parameter is a local variable, meaning it exists only inside its particular function. When the function is called, the program allocates a memory cell for each parameter and then assigns each input from the call to its corresponding parameter. For example, the call PickNumber(3) would allocate a memory cell for the parameter guess and store the value 3 in that cell. Once a parameter has been assigned a value, you can refer to that parameter within the function just as you would any other local variable. When the function terminates, the parameter "goes away," and the associated memory cells is freed.

EXERCISE 9.2

Enter the esp2.html text from Figure 9.4 into a new Web page, then load the page in the browser to verify that it behaves as described.

Add a fifth button to the page so that the user can select a number between 1 and 5. How does adding the extra button affect the likelihood of guessing correctly? Test your ESP potential by repeatedly loading the page and trying to guess a number between 1 and 5. Out of 20 tests, how many times did you guess correctly? Do you think you have ESP?

Designer Secrets

The same rules apply for parameter names as other variables: a parameter name must start with a letter and consist of letters and digits (and possibly underscores). You should choose parameter names that are descriptive in nature, providing a reader with a hint as to what that parameter represents. The convention used throughout this text is that variables, including parameters, will always start with a lowercase letter.

```
function OldMacVerse(animal, sound)
// Assumes: animal is the name of an animal, sound is the sound it makes
// Results: displays a verse of the song "Old MacDonald Had a Farm" in outputDiv
{
  document.getElementById('outputDiv').innerHTML =
      '<p>Old MacDonald had a farm, E-I-E-I-O.<br>' +
      'And on that farm he had a ' + animal + ', E-I-E-I-O.<br>' +
      'With a ' + sound + '-' + sound + ' here, and a ' + sound + '-' + sound +
      ' there,<br>' + ' here a ' + sound + ', there a ' + sound +
      ', everywhere a ' + sound + '-' + sound + '.<br>' +
      'Old MacDonald had a farm, E-I-E-I-O.</p>';
}
```

Figure 9.6   Function for displaying a verse from "Old MacDonald Had a Farm."

Multiple Inputs

If a function has multiple inputs, then each input must have a corresponding parameter in the function definition. For example, consider the OldMacVerse function in Figure 9.6, which can be called to display a verse of the children's song "Old MacDonald Had a Farm." The OldMacVerse function has two parameters, corresponding to the animal name and sound.

When calling a function with multiple inputs, the inputs must be specified in the order in which the parameters appear in the function definition. This is because the first input in the function call is assigned to the first parameter in the function, the second input is assigned to the second parameter, and so on. For example, in the function call OldMacVerse("cow", "moo"), the input value "cow" is assigned to the parameter animal, whereas "moo" is assigned to sound. The result is that the verse with a mooing cow is displayed in the page. A call with different input values, say OldMacVerse("pig", "oink"), would assign different values to the parameters and result in a different verse.

EXERCISE 9.3

Create a Web page named oldmac.html that defines the OldMacVerse function within SCRIPT tags in the HEAD. Your page should have a page division named outputDiv and at least three buttons, each of which calls the OldMacVerse function with appropriate inputs. For example, a button labeled Pig Verse should call OldMacVerse('pig', 'oink') when clicked, whereas a button labeled Cow Verse should call OldMacVerse('cow', 'moo') when clicked.

EXERCISE 9.4

What would you expect to happen as a result of the following call?

```
OldMacVerse('baa', 'sheep')
```

Modify your oldmac.html page to include a button with this call, then load the page and verify your prediction.

EXERCISE 9.5

As it is currently written, each call to the OldMacVerse function displays a new verse in the page division, overwriting any previous verse that may have been displayed. If we instead wanted each new verse to be appended to the previous verses, only a small change is necessary. In general, an assignment of the following form will append 'NEW TEXT' to the end of the contents of a page division with identifier DIV_ID.

```
document.getElementById('DIV_ID').innerHTML =
    document.getElementById('DIV_ID').innerHTML + 'NEW TEXT';
```

The assignment works by taking the current value of the page division, appending 'NEW TEXT' to the end of that text, and then assigning the updated text back to the page division.

Modify the assignment in the OldMacVerse function in your oldmac.html page so that each verse is appended to the page division.

Functions That Return Values

The user-defined functions we have seen so far all displayed the results of their computations directly in the page, such as assigning text to a page division or changing the source of an image. To be applicable in a variety of settings, however, a function must not be tied to a particular page element. For example, the predefined Math.sqrt function does not refer to any elements in the page—it is passed an input value and returns the square root of that input. As a result, a call to Math.sqrt can be used to perform a calculation in any page.

Using a return statement, it is possible to define general-purpose functions that calculate and return values. For example, Figure 9.7 shows the definition of two functions, which may be used to convert between inches and centimeters. The InchesToCentimeters function takes a number of inches as input. That number, which is stored in the parameter inches, is multiplied by 2.54 to obtain the corresponding number of centimeters. That number is then returned by the function. The CentimetersToInches function performs the opposite conversion, taking a number of centimeters as input and returning the corresponding number of inches.

These functions could be placed in the HEAD of any Web page that needed to convert between inches and centimeters. If a Web site had many pages that needed to perform the same conversions, however, this could result in massive duplication. To avoid duplicating the same functions across multiple pages, a better alternative exists in the form of function libraries.

```
function InchesToCentimeters(inches)
// Assumes: inches is a distance, measured in inches
// Returns: the corresponding distance in centimeters
{
    var cm;

    cm = inches * 2.54;
    return cm;
}

function CentimetersToInches(cm)
// Assumes: cm is a distance, measured in centimeters
// Returns: the corresponding distance in inches
{
    var inches;

    inches = cm / 2.54;
    return inches;
}
```

Figure 9.7 Functions for converting between inches and centimeters.

Function Libraries

A ***function library*** is nothing more than a text file that contains the definition of one or more functions. The advantage of placing general-purpose functions in library files is that those files can easily be loaded into any Web page that wishes to use them. The functions are only defined once in the library file and then loaded whenever they are needed. To load a function library into a Web page, a SCRIPT tag with a SRC attribute is added to the HEAD of the page:

```
<script type="text/javascript" src="LIBRARY_FILENAME"></script>
```

As was the case with the SRC attribute of IMG elements, the address assigned to SRC attribute can be relative (specifying a file that is stored in the same location as the page) or absolute (representing a file stored on a remote Web server). Note that no code is placed between the opening and closing SCRIPT tags—instead, the code from the library file is inserted into the page when the browser encounters the SCRIPT tags.

For example, suppose the two functions from Figure 9.7 have been entered into a local file named `convert.js` (by convention, function library files are given the extension `.js` to designate that they contain JavaScript code). The Web page in Figure 9.8 loads the library file (line 9) and then calls the `InchesToCentimeters` function when the button is clicked (line 18). The converted value returned by this function is displayed within the page (Figure 9.9).

```
1.  <!doctype html>
2.  <!-- metric.html                                          Dave Reed -->
3.  <!-- This page converts between English and metric measurements.   -->
4.  <!-- ============================================================= -->
5.
6.  <html>
7.   <head>
8.    <title>Metric Conversion</title>
9.    <script type="text/javascript" src="convert.js"></script>
10.   <script type="text/javascript">
11.     function ConvertToCm()
12.     // Assumes: inchBox contains a distance in inches
13.     // Results: displays the distance in centimeters in outputDiv
14.     {
15.        var inches, cm;
16.
17.        inches = parseFloat(document.getElementById('inchBox').value);
18.        cm = InchesToCentimeters(inches);
19.        document.getElementById('outputDiv').innerHTML =
20.          'That is ' + cm + ' centimeters.';
21.     }
22.   </script>
23.  </head>
24.
25.  <body>
26.    <p>Length in inches:
27.      <input type="text" id="inchBox" size=6 value=1>
28.      <input type="button" value="Convert to Centimeters"
29.             onclick="ConvertToCm();">
30.    </p>
31.    <hr>
32.    <div id="outputDiv"></div>
33.  </body>
34.  </html>
```

Figure 9.8 Web page that uses `convert.js` to convert from inches to centimeters.

Metric Conversion

http://balance3e.com/Ch9/metric.html

Metric Conversion

Length in inches: 10 [Convert to Centimeters]

That is 25.4 centimeters.

Done

Figure 9.9 `metric.html` rendered in a Web browser.

EXERCISE 9.6

Enter the `InchesToCentimeters` and `CentimetersToInches` functions from Figure 9.7 in a text file named `convert.js`. Then enter the text from Figure 9.8 into a new Web page named `metric.html` (in the same location) and verify that it behaves as described.

Once you have done this, modify the page so that it can also perform the opposite conversion, from centimeters to inches. You will need to add a new text box, where the user can enter a number of centimeters and a button for carrying out the conversion. The converted value should be displayed in the same page division, `outputDiv`, as before.

Common errors to avoid...

When beginning programmers attempt to load a JavaScript function library, errors of two types commonly occur.

1. If the SCRIPT tags are malformed or the name/address of the library is incorrect, the library will fail to load. This will not cause an error in itself, but any subsequent attempt to call a function from the library will produce "Error: Object Expected" (using Internet Explorer) or "Error: XXX is not defined" (using Firefox), where XXX represents the typed function name.

2. When you use the SRC attribute in a pair of SCRIPT tags to load a code library, you cannot place additional JavaScript code between the tags. You can think of the SRC attribute as causing the contents of the library to be inserted between the tags, overwriting any other code that was erroneously placed there. Thus, if a given page incorporates both a function loaded from a library and a function defined directly in the HEAD, two pairs of SCRIPT tags are required. Similarly, if a page utilizes functions from multiple library files, each library requires its own pair of SCRIPT tags.

Also note that a library file should only contain JavaScript code. If you place non-code elements in the file, including HTML tags, an error will occur when the browser loads the library and tries to interpret the contents.

EXERCISE 9.7

Add four new functions to your `convert.js` library file that convert between pounds and kilograms and also between square feet and square meters. Note that:

1 kilogram = 2.205 pounds
1 square meter = 10.764 square feet

Once you have done this, modify your `metric.html` page so that the user can convert values using each of these functions.

EXERCISE 9.8

The Mosteller Formula is often used by doctors and dieticians to estimate the surface area of a person's body given height and weight. The formula is as follows, where height is assumed to be in centimeters, weight is in kilograms, and surface area is in square meters:

$$\text{surface area} = \sqrt{\frac{\text{height} \times \text{weight}}{3600}}$$

Create a Web page named `surface.html` that calculates a person's body surface area using this formula. The page should have text boxes where the user can enter the person's weight (in pounds) and height (in inches). At the click of a button, a function should be called to calculate and display the surface area (in square feet) in a page division.

Since the Mosteller Formula is defined using metric values, you will need to load the `convert.js` library in the HEAD of the page to perform the required conversions. In particular, you will need to convert the user inputs from pounds to kilograms and from inches to centimeters before calculating the surface area using the Mosteller Formula. Once you have the area in square meters, you will need to convert it to square feet before displaying the result in the page.

The random.js Library

Many of the example Web pages in Chapter 7 involved randomness. For example, the `dice.html` page (Exercise 7.11) used `Math.random` to generate a random dice roll, whereas `slides.html` (Exercise 7.12) used `Math.random` to select a random image in a slide show. Earlier in this chapter, the pages `esp1.html` and `esp2.html` used `Math.random` to generate a random value for an ESP test. To simplify the development of pages such as these, a library of functions for generating random values has been provided for you (accessible as `http://balance3e.com/random.js`). The functions in the `random.js` library build upon `Math.random`, offering additional flexibility and power (Figure 9.10).

EXERCISE 9.9

Modify your `esp2.html` page from Figure 9.4 so that it utilizes the `random.js` library. You will need to add SCRIPT tags to the HEAD of your page so that it loads the library:

```
<script type="text/javascript" src="http://balance3e.com/random.js"></script>
```

Then, modify line 16 so that it calls the `RandomInt` function to pick the random number for the ESP test. Verify that your modified page behaves as before.

Function	Inputs	Output
RandomNum	Two numbers (low and high limits of a range); e.g., RandomNum(2, 4.5)	A random number from the range low (inclusive) to high (exclusive)
RandomInt	Two integers (low and high limits of a range); e.g., RandomInt(1, 10)	A random integer from the range low to high (both inclusive)
RandomChar	A nonempty string; e.g., RandomChar('abcd')	A random character taken from the string
RandomOneOf	A list of options in square brackets, separated by commas; e.g., RandomOneOf(['yes', 'no'])	A random value taken from the list of options

Figure 9.10 Functions defined in the `random.js` library.

EXERCISE 9.10

Similarly, modify your `dice.html` page from Exercise 7.11 so that it utilizes the `random.js` library. Again, you will need to load the `random.js` library using SCRIPT tags and then call the `RandomInt` function to generate a random die roll. Verify that your modified page behaves as before.

Many secure computer systems require the use of complex passwords that are difficult to guess. One way to create secure passwords is to generate them as random sequences of characters. While a hacker might be able to predict your password if it is the name of your pet dog, it is unlikely that they would be able to guess a random password such as d6CW4!m.

EXERCISE 9.11

Create a Web page named `randSeq.html` that generates a random three-letter sequence. When the user clicks on a button, a function named `GenerateSequence` should be called to generate and display a sequence of three randomly chosen letters. The function should contain the following statement, which calls the `RandomChar` function from the `random.js` library to select the random letters and concatenate them.

```
sequence = RandomChar('abcdefghijklmnopqrstuvwxyz') +
           RandomChar('abcdefghijklmnopqrstuvwxyz') +
           RandomChar('abcdefghijklmnopqrstuvwxyz');
```

There are approximately 550 different three-letter words in the English language and $26^3 = 17,576$ possible three-letter sequences. As a result, the likelihood of obtaining a word at random is 550/17,576, or close to 1/32. Use your Web page to generate 32 random three-letter sequences. Did you obtain any words? Would it surprise you if you didn't obtain any words, or obtained more than one? Explain.

EXERCISE 9.12

Modify your `randSeq.html` function so that the possible characters that make up the random sequence are specified by the user. Your modified page should have a text box where the user can enter the possible characters. The `GenerateSequence` function should access the text box and use its contents as input to the `RandomChar` function calls. For example, if the user enters "abcdefghijklmnopqrstuvwxyz" in the text box, then the function should generate and display a random three-letter sequence, as before. If the user enters "0123456789" in the text box, however, then the function should generate and display a random three-digit sequence.

The ten most frequently used letters in the English language, ordered by frequency, are *e, t, a, o, i, n, s, h, r,* and *d*. As a result, if you generated random letter sequences using only these ten letters, you might expect to have a greater likelihood of obtaining words. Use your modified `randseq.html` page to generate random three-letter sequences using "etaionshrd" as the alphabet. Do you obtain more words than you did with the complete alphabet?

In Exercises 7.12 and 7.13, you developed a Web page for displaying a random slide show. Each image that could appear in the show was given a similar name, such as `slide1.jpg` and `slide2.jpg`. Then, each time the button was clicked, a random slide number was generated and the corresponding image name constructed.

Using `RandomOneOf`, it is no longer necessary for the slide show images to have similar names. In fact, a slide show can now be constructed out of images that are stored locally, stored on the Web, or even a mixture of the two. For example, the following assignment would randomly select from three image files, two of which are stored locally (`family.jpg` and `pets.jpg`) and the third stored on the Web (`http://balance3e.com/Images/reed.jpg`):

```
imgName = RandomOneOf(['family.jpg', 'pets.jpg',
                       'http://balance3e.com/Images/reed.jpg']);
```

EXERCISE 9.13

Modify your `slides.html` page so that it uses the `RandomOneOf` function to select from a list of files, at least some of which are stored remotely on the Web.

A popular children's toy is the Magic 8 Ball, an oversized, plastic billiard ball that yields answers to simple questions. (Magic 8 Ball is a trademark owned by Mattel, Inc. © 2003 Mattel, Inc. All Rights Reserved.) To receive its wisdom, you ask the Magic 8 Ball a question, shake it vigorously, and then read the response that appears in a window on the bottom. Functionally speaking, the Magic 8 Ball determines its answer by randomly selecting from a list of predetermined responses, such as "yes," "no," and "reply hazy—try again."

EXERCISE 9.14

Create a Web page named `magic.html` that simulates the functionality of a Magic 8 Ball. Your page should look similar to the one in Figure 9.11, with a text box for entering a yes/no question and a clickable 8-ball image (a simple one is provided in `http://balance3e.com/Images/8ball.gif`). When the button is clicked, a function should be called to select a random response from a list of at least five possible responses (using the `RandomOneOf` function) and display the response in a page division.

Test your page to make sure that it operates correctly, providing a (potentially) different answer on each click.

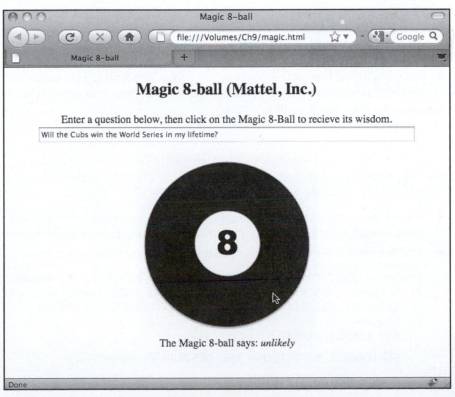

Figure 9.11 Sample appearance of `magic.html` page. (Magic 8 Ball® is a registered trademark of Mattel, Inc. All Rights Reserved.)

Common errors to avoid...

The `RandomOneOf` function in the `random.js` library requires a list of options, enclosed in square brackets and separated by commas. For example, the call

```
RandomOneOf(['yes', 'no', 'maybe'])
```

would randomly choose between the three string options and return either `'yes'`, `'no'`, or `'maybe'`. A common error when calling `RandomOneOf` is to forget the square brackets—for example,

```
RandomOneOf('yes', 'no', 'maybe')
```

This mistake will not cause an error in the page, but it will produce unintended results. If the first input to `RandomOneOf` is a string (as is the case here), the function will actually select a random character from that string and return the character. Thus, the above call would return either `'y'`, `'e'`, or `'s'`. If the first input is a number, the function call will returned the special value `undefined`.

Looking Ahead ...

In this chapter, you learned to extend the expressive power of JavaScript by defining your own general-purpose functions. A user-defined function introduces a unit of computational abstraction because it encapsulates a computation or sequence of statements under a single name. Once a function has been defined, the programmer no longer needs to know the details of how it works—she simply needs to know how to call that function. As you saw in this chapter, JavaScript functions can be defined in the HEAD of a Web page, or they can be collected in a library file and loaded into pages when needed.

Before we move on to more advanced programming skills, Chapter 10 pauses at the text's mid-way point to reflect upon computer science as a discipline. In earlier chapters, you learned about the hardware and software components of computer systems, the history of computers and the Internet, and the role of algorithms in solving problems. You also learned fundamental programming concepts as you developed interactive Web pages using JavaScript. The next chapter provides a general overview of computer science, including the basic themes and approaches that unite such disparate topics into a cohesive discipline.

Chapter Summary

- Functions simplify the programmer's task by (1) minimizing the amount of detail that the programmer must keep track of and (2) minimizing the size and complexity of code.
- The general form in which programmers define functions is as follows:

```
function FUNCTION_NAME(PARAMETER1, PARAMETER2,..., PARAMETERn)
// Assumes: DESCRIPTION OF ASSUMPTIONS MADE ABOUT PARAMETERS
// Returns: DESCRIPTION OF VALUE RETURNED BY FUNCTION
{
    var LOCAL1, LOCAL2, ..., LOCALn;

    STATEMENTS_TO_PERFORM_THE DESIRED_COMPUTATION;

    return OUTPUT_VALUE;
}
```

- A parameter is a function-specific variable. When a function is called, its parameters are automatically assigned values corresponding to the input values in the call. If a function has multiple parameters, they are matched with the input values in sequential order: the first parameter is assigned the first input value, the second parameter is assigned the second input value, and so on.

- Parameters are considered local variables, meaning they exist and can be accessed only from within the function.

- Variables that are used to provide temporary storage within a function should be declared as local using the keyword var. When a function definition declares certain variables as local, the variables exist only while the function executes (similar to parameters), and their values will not alter other variables that might share their names.

- In a function definition, a return statement specifies the value that should be returned by the function. Return statements are optional, because some functions are designed to display text in a page division or text box, rather than to compute a value.

- Special-purpose functions can be defined directly in the HEAD of a Web page, enclosed in SCRIPT tags. General-purpose function definitions should be placed in separate library files and then loaded into Web pages as needed. To load a library file, use SCRIPT tags of the form:

```
<script type="text/javascript" src="LIBRARY_FILENAME"></script>
```

- The random.js library defines functions for generating random numbers in a specified range (RandomNum), random integers in a specified range (RandomInt), random characters from a string (RandomChar), and random items from a list of options (RandomOneOf).

Supplemental Material and Exercises

More User-Defined Functions

"The Wheels on the Bus" is another a highly repetitive children's song. The first verse of the song is:

> The wheels on the bus go round and round, round and round, round and round.
>
> The wheels on the bus go round and round, all through the town.

Subsequent verses have the same form but with a different bus part and action. For example, the wipers on the bus go swish-swish-swish, and the brakes on the bus go screech-screech-screech.

EXERCISE 9.15

Create a Web page named bus.html can be used to display verses of "The Wheels on the Bus." Similar to the oldmac.html page from Exercise 9.3, your page should define a function named BusVerse that has two parameters, representing the bus part and action. The page should contain a page division and multiple buttons, each of which calls the BusVerse function when clicked to display a verse.

Another example of a function that computes and returns a value is shown in Figure 9.12. The IncomeTax function has two parameters: income (representing the individual's gross income) and itemized (representing the individual's itemized deduction). It uses those values to calculate a person's income tax payment according to the following system:

- The taxpayer's deduction is the larger of two numbers: the standard deduction ($4,150) or the itemized deduction (computed using some complicated form).

```
function IncomeTax(income, itemized)
// Assumes: income >= 0, itemized >= 0
// Returns: flat tax (13%) due after deductions
{

        var deduction, taxableIncome, totalTax;

        deduction = Math.max(itemized, 4150);
        taxableIncome = Math.max(income - deduction, 0);
        totalTax = 0.13*taxableIncome

        return totalTax;
}
```

Figure 9.12 Function that uses multiple steps in computing income tax.

- Taxable income is determined by subtracting the deduction from the taxpayer's gross income (or 0, whichever is larger).

- Total tax owed is determined by multiplying the taxable income by the tax rate (13%).

EXERCISE 9.16

Create a library file named `income.js` that contains the definition of the `IncomeTax` function from Figure 9.12. Then, create a Web page named `taxes.html` that loads the `income.js` library and uses the `IncomeTax` function to calculate and display a person's income tax. The page should have text boxes where the person's income and itemized deductions are entered and a button for initiating the calculation. When the button is clicked, a function should be called to access the income and itemized deduction amounts, call the `IncomeTax` function, and display the calculated tax in a page division.

Use your page to determine the amount a person would owe with:

```
income = 100000.00    itemized = 12017.50
income = 42500.00     itemized = 8900.99
income = 13267.45     itemized = 14000.00
```

Suppose you have been hired by a weather service to develop Web pages for displaying local weather conditions. Two measures you may consider are dew point and wind chill. The dew point identifies the temperature at which water vapor condenses into dew. It can be calculated using the following formula, where `temp` is the current temperature (in Fahrenheit) and `humidity` is the relative humidity (between 0% and 100%):

$$\text{dew point} = \text{temp} - \left(\frac{100 - \text{humidity}}{2.778} \right)$$

The wind chill index is a measurement that combines actual temperature and wind speed to estimate the temperature experienced by an exposed human being. The wind chill index can be calculated using the following (somewhat simplified) formula, where `temp` is the current temperature (in Fahrenheit) and `wind` is the wind speed (in miles per hour):

$$\text{wind chill} = 35.74 + 0.6215*\text{temp} + (0.4275*\text{temp} - 35.75)*\text{wind}^{0.16}$$

EXERCISE 9.17

Create a library file named `weather.js` that contains the definitions of your dew point and wind chill functions. Then create a Web page named `indexes.html` that has text boxes where the user can enter the temperature, humidity, and wind speed. The page should load the `weather.js` library and call the appropriate functions to display the dew point or wind chill at the click of a button.

Use your page to determine the dew point under the following conditions:

```
temperature = 85° F     humidity = 60%
temperature = 95° F     humidity = 75%
temperature = 100° F    humidity = 90%
```

Use your page to determine the wind chill under the following conditions:

```
temperature = 20° F     wind speed = 10 mph
temperature = 10° F     wind speed = 20 mph
temperature = 0° F      wind speed = 30 mph
```

More with `random.js`

EXERCISE 9.18

Modify your `pick4.html` page (from Exercise 7.7) to utilize the `RandomInt` function from the `random.js` library. That is, each random lottery number should be simulated by an appropriate call to the `RandomInt` function. Verify that your modified page behaves as before.

EXERCISE 9.19

Modify your `randSeq.html` page (from Exercise 9.12) so that it instead generates random four-letter sequences. When the user clicks on a button, the `GenerateSequence` function should be called to generate and display a sequence of four randomly chosen letters.

Use your modified page to generate four-letter sequences using the entire alphabet. How many sequences do you have to generate before you obtain an English word? Would you expect it to be more or less likely to obtain a four-letter word at random when compared to three-letter words? Explain your answer.

The `time.js` Library

JavaScript provides basic features for manipulating dates and times. Building upon these features, the `time.js` library (available as `http://balance3e.com/time.js`) contains the definitions of several functions that can be useful within a variety of pages (Figure 9.13).

The Web page in Figure 9.14 uses the `CurrentTime` function from `time.js` to timestamp the page as it loads. The `showClock` function, which is defined in the HEAD of the page, is automatically called when the page is finished loading (line 24). That function calls `CurrentTime` to get the current time and displays that time in the `outputDiv` page division (lines 18–19). The rendered page is shown in Figure 9.15.

Function	Inputs	Output
CurrentTime	none; e.g., CurrentTime()	A string representing the current time in hours, minutes, and seconds. *Note:* times are represented in military format; e.g., 22:00:00 for 10 p.m.
SecondsUntil	A string representing a date and time; e.g., SecondsUntil ('Jan 1, 2012 10:30:00')	The number of seconds from the current time to the specified date and time.
TimeUntil	A string representing a date and time; e.g., TimeUntil ('Dec 31, 2011 23:59:59')	A string specifying the number of days, hours, minutes, and seconds to the specified date and time.

Figure 9.13 Functions defined in the `time.js` library.

```
1.  <!doctype html>
2.  <!-- clock.html                                              Dave Reed   -->
3.  <!-- This page displays the current time in a division when loaded. -->
4.  <!-- ============================================================ -->
5.
6.  <html>
7.   <head>
8.    <title>Current Time</title>
9.    <script type="text/javascript" src="http://balance3e.com/time.js">
10.   </script>
11.   <script type="text/javascript">
12.    function showClock()
13.    // Assumes: the time.js library has been loaded
14.    // Results: displays the current time in outputDiv
15.    {
16.      var current;
17.
18.      current = CurrentTime();
19.      document.getElementById('outputDiv').innerHTML =
20.        'The current time is: ' + current;
21.    }
22.   </script>
23.  </head>
24.
25.  <body onload="showClock();">
26.    <h2>Current Time</h2>
27.    <div id="outputDiv"></div>
28.  </body>
29. </html>
```

Figure 9.14 Web page that displays the current time when loaded.

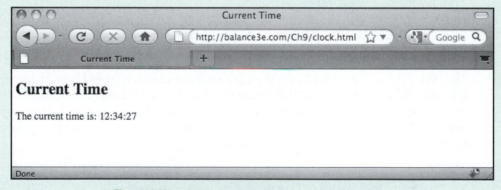

Figure 9.15 clock.html rendered in a Web browser.

EXERCISE 9.20

Enter the clock.html text from Figure 9.14 into a new Web page, then load the page in the browser to verify that it behaves as described.

As is, your clock.html page displays a single time—the clock time when the page was loaded. Modifying this page so that it displays a dynamic, running clock is surprisingly simple. Recall from Chapter 7 that the predefined setInterval function schedules the repeated execution of a function call at regular intervals. In particular, the call

```
setInterval('showClock()', 1000)
```

will schedule the showClock function to be called every second (1,000 milliseconds). The result is that the current time is repeatedly updated in place on the screen, in effect turning the page division into a digital clock.

Modify the ONLOAD attribute of the BODY so that it executes this call to setInterval when the page loads (instead of the single call to showClock). Verify that the resulting clock "runs" in the page.

While embedded clocks are common on many Web pages, an even more common and useful tool is a countdown clock. For example, a commercial Web site might have a countdown in the corner, counting down the days, hours, and minutes remaining in a sale. Or, a student Web page might contain a countdown clock, counting down the time until graduation or the next vacation.

EXERCISE 9.21

Create a Web page named until.html that calculates and displays the amount of time remaining until a specified date and time. The page should have a text box where the user can enter a date and time in the format "Month Day, Year hour:minutes:seconds". For example, noon on January 1, 2020, would be represented by the string "Jan 1, 2020 12:00:00". Note that times are represented using a 24-hour clock, so one second before midnight would be "Dec 31, 2019 23:59:59". When a button is subsequently clicked, a function should be called to determine the amount of time remaining until the user's date and time. The function will have to perform the following steps:

1. Access the date entered in the text box.
2. Call the TimeUntil function (from time.js) with that date as input.
3. Display the resulting time interval in a page division.

Figure 9.16 shows an example of what your page might look like.

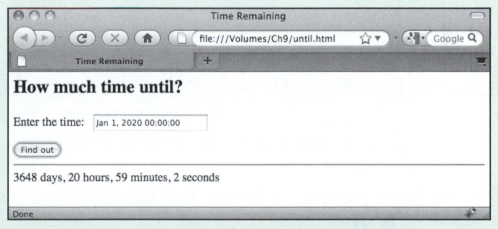

Figure 9.16 Sample appearance of until.html page.

EXERCISE 9.22

Modify your until.html page so that it serves as a countdown clock, regularly updating the time interval in the page. Instead of a button, the BODY of the page should have an ONLOAD attribute to initiate the countdown clock. Similar to the modified clock.html page from Exercise 9.20, the ONLOAD attribute should call setInterval to schedule the repeated execution of your function so that the time is updated every second.

10 Chapter

Computer Science as a Discipline

This chapter uses narrative, illustrations, and review questions to introduce computer science and technology concepts.

Having surveyed the relationships of computer science with other disciplines, it remains to answer the basic questions: What is the central core of the subject? What is it that distinguishes it from the separate subjects with which it is related? What is the linking thread which gathers these disparate branches into a single discipline? My answer to these questions is simple—it is the art of programming a computer. It is the art of designing efficient and elegant methods of getting a computer to solve problems, theoretical or practical, small or large, simple or complex. It is the art of translating this design into an effective and accurate computer program.

C.A.R. Hoare
Essays in Computing Science

Computer Science is the first engineering discipline in which the complexity of the objects created is limited solely by the skill of the creator, and not by the strength of raw materials.

Brian K. Reid
Communications of the ACM, October 1987

In theory, there is no difference between theory and practice. But, in practice, there is.
Jan van de Snepscheut

Most traditional sciences, such as biology and chemistry, trace their origins back hundreds or even thousands of years. As electronic computers were not introduced until the 1940s, computer science is clearly a much newer field of study. Nonetheless, computers and related technology have made an astounding impact on our society in this short period of time.

This chapter presents an overview of computer science as a discipline, emphasizing its common themes (hardware, software, and theory) as well as its diversity. As you will learn, computer science comprises much more than just the study of computers. It encompasses all aspects of computation, from the design and analysis of algorithms to the construction of computers for carrying out those algorithms. The jobs performed by computer scientists are as varied as computer science itself, and this chapter examines the roles played by computational theorists, programmers, systems architects, and microchip designers, among others. To further your understanding of this diverse field, we delve into specific computer science subfields, providing details on topics such as systems architecture, operating systems, networks, and artificial intelligence. We conclude with a discussion of ethical conduct within the computing profession.

Computer "Science"

Although government and industry began embracing computer technology as early as the 1940s, the scientific community was slower to acknowledge computer science's importance. Most colleges and universities did not even recognize computer science as a separate field of study until the 1970s or 1980s. Many people still argue that computer science is not a science in the same sense that biology and chemistry are. In fact, computer science has a lot in common with the natural sciences, but it is also closely related to other fields, such as engineering and mathematics. This interdisciplinary nature has made computer science a difficult field to classify. Biology can be neatly described as the study of life, whereas chemistry can be defined as the study of chemicals and their interactions. Is computer science, as its name suggests, simply the study of computers?

Although computers are the most visible feature of computer science, it would be inaccurate to characterize the field as dealing only with machinery. A more inclusive definition would be that computer science is the study of *computation*. The term "computation" denotes more than just machinery—it encompasses all aspects of problem solving. This includes the design and analysis algorithms, the formalization of algorithms as programs, and the development of computational devices for executing those programs. The computer science field also addresses more theoretical questions, such as those surrounding the power and limitations of algorithms and computational models.

Whether this combination of problem solving, engineering, and theory constitutes a "science" is a matter of interpretation. Some define "science" as a rigorous approach to understanding complex phenomena and solving problems. The process developed by the scientific community for examining observations and events, commonly referred to as the *scientific method*, can be summarized as an algorithm (Figure 10.1).

Using this definition, we can classify many activities performed by computer scientists as "science." The design and analysis of algorithms for solving problems involves a rigorous approach that is based on the scientific method. In particular, verifying the behavior of an algorithm requires forming hypotheses, testing those hypotheses (either through experimentation or mathematical analysis), and then revising the algorithm in response to the results. For example, to design an effective algorithm for accessing records in a large database, you would need to form hypotheses regarding the database's behavior under various conditions. Then, you would test those hypotheses, either by implementing the algorithm as a computer program and executing it on actual data or by performing rigorous mathematical analysis. Finally, if the result failed to validate your hypotheses, you would modify the algorithm and retest. The development of complex hardware and software systems adheres to this same rigorous, experimental approach—when applied to projects involving millions of transistors or thousands of lines of code, the scientific method is merely implemented on a much larger scale.

The Scientific Method:

1. Formulate a hypothesis that explains an observed behavior.
2. Design an experiment to test your hypothesis.
3. Conduct the experiment.
4. Analyze the results of the experiment — if the results do not support the hypothesis, revise and repeat.

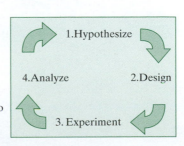

Figure 10.1   The scientific method for understanding phenomena.

Artificial Science

What sets computer science apart from the natural sciences is the type of items being studied. All natural sciences, as well as many social sciences, are concerned with examining complex, naturally occurring phenomena. These sciences work within the confines of innate laws that define the way matter behaves, the way chemicals react, the way life evolves, and even the way people interact. Experiments in physics, chemistry, biology, and psychology strive to understand natural occurrences and extract the underlying laws that control behavior. By contrast, the systems that computer scientists investigate are largely artificial. Programs, computers, and computational models are designed and constructed by people. When a computer scientist analyzes the behavior of a program executing on a particular computer, the phenomena being studied are defined within the artificial world of that machine. Likewise, by devising new computers or other computational models, computer scientists can create their own artificial laws to govern how systems behave. This distinction was effectively summarized by artificial intelligence pioneer Herbert Simon (1916–2001), who coined the phrase "artificial science" to distinguish computer science from the "natural sciences."

European institutions often bypass the question of whether computer science is a science by calling the field "Informatics" or "Information Systems." However, these names are limiting in that they denote an emphasis on information processing, rather than on the machinery used to process that information. Donald Knuth (1938–), a noted computer scientist and author of *The Art of Computer Programming*, has proposed the alternative name "Algorithmics," which highlights the central role of algorithms in computation. The name "Algorithmics" also suggests a mathematical approach to computing, reflecting the fact that many early researchers in what would eventually be called computer science were mathematicians.

It should be noted that computer science is linked to several other disciplines, each of which approaches computing from a slightly different perspective. For instance, computer engineering is an offshoot of electrical engineering focused on applying scientific theory and engineering principles to the development of new computing technology. The fields of information technology and information systems management approach computing from a business perspective, concentrating on the effective use of information and computer technology in supporting government and commercial organizations. Although the historical backgrounds of these fields are very different, the divisions between the disciplines are not always distinct. A computer scientist conducting research in circuit design might use methods similar to those of a computer engineer, and an information technology manager organizing a network might use methods similar to those of a computer scientist.

Computer Science Themes

Because computation encompasses so many different types of activities, the research conducted by computer scientists is often difficult to classify. However, there are three recurring themes that define the discipline: hardware, software, and theory (Figure 10.2). Some computer scientists focus on hardware,

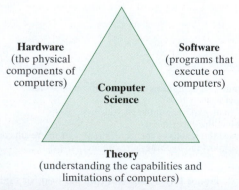

Figure 10.2 Main themes of computer science.

designing and building computers and related infrastructure. Others concern themselves with the process of composing software and encoding algorithms that can be executed on computers. Still others attack computation from a theoretical standpoint, striving to understand the foundations of the discipline. Although it is possible to find computer scientists whose expertise is exclusive to one of these areas, most activities involve a combination of all three.

Hardware

As we saw in Chapter 1, the term "hardware" refers to the physical components of a computer and its supporting devices. The design of most modern computers is based on the von Neumann architecture, which consists of a CPU, memory, and input/output devices (see Chapter 6 for additional information regarding the von Neumann architecture). In combination, these three components form a general-purpose machine that can store and execute programs for accomplishing various tasks.

Although most computers are built according to this basic architecture, ongoing research and development projects aim to improve the design and organization of hardware. For example, computer scientists involved in circuit design and microchip manufacturing must draw on expertise from chemistry, particle physics, and mechanical engineering to squeeze millions of transistors onto dime-sized microchips. Systems architects, on the other hand, study different ways of connecting components to increase computational *throughput* (i.e., the amount of work that can be completed in a given time). One subfield of systems architecture is *parallel processing*, in which a computer's computational burden is split across multiple CPUs. As the Internet has grown in popularity, many hardware specialists have turned their attention to networking, creating new ways for separate computers to share information and work together.

Software

Whereas hardware consists of machinery for performing computations, "software" refers to the programs that execute on computers. Most people in the computer industry work on the software side, holding positions such as programmer, systems analyst, software engineer, or Web developer. In fact, despite the recent economic recession, the software industry remains one of the fastest-growing facets of the U.S. economy.

Software can be divided into three basic categories according to each application's purpose and intended audience. *Systems software* includes programs that directly control the execution of hardware components. For example, an operating system includes systems software for managing files and directories, linking programs with hardware devices such as printers and scanners, and processing user inputs such as keystrokes and mouse clicks. The term *development software* refers to programs that are used as tools in the development of other programs. Microsoft .NET and Oracle's Java Development Kit are examples of development environments for creating, testing, and executing programs using a variety of languages (such as C++ and Java). The *applications software* category encompasses all other programs, which perform a wide variety of complex tasks. Examples include Web browsers such as Internet Explorer and Mozilla Firefox, word processors such as Word and WordPerfect, presentation tools such as PowerPoint and FrameMaker, editors such as NotePad and emacs, and games such as Solitaire and Halo.

Many diverse jobs in computer science are related to the design, development, testing, and maintenance of software. Some software experts' work is more theoretical, focusing on the formulation and analysis of algorithms. While examining general approaches to problems, these computer scientists strive to understand the complexity of those problems and their solutions. Such "software people" may never write a program in their lives! Another subcategory of the software industry involves developing and extending programming languages so that problems can be solved more easily and efficiently. But perhaps the most common type of software expert is the programmer, who designs algorithms and encodes them into a particular programming language for execution on a computer.

Figure 10.3 Alan Turing.

Theory

Just as certain computer scientists study algorithms but never write a program, other experts may never even touch a computer. This is because computer science is concerned with the study of computational methods, in addition to the more practical fields of hardware and software. Theoretical computer scientists, whose work is closely related to mathematics and formal logic, examine different models of computation and strive to understand the capabilities of algorithms and computers. It may surprise you to learn that some of computer science's key theories were formulated years before the development of electronic computers. For example, in 1930, Alan Turing (1912–1954) (Figure 10.3) designed an abstract computational machine now known as a ***Turing machine***.

A Turing machine is a very simple processing unit that can read and write data on a potentially infinite tape. The tape, which we can think of as being divided into cells, serves as the Turing machine's memory. The processor has the ability to read the data at a particular cell on the tape, write new data to that cell, move in either direction, and distinguish between a finite number of states (distinct situations that alter the behavior of the machine). A Turing machine is programmable in that you can specify a finite set of rules describing the processor's behavior. However, these rules are limited by the machine's capabilities (reading, writing, and moving right or left) and are specific to the data stored on the tape. For instance, the example Turing machine in Figure 10.4 is programmed to recognize an even number of "a"s written on the tape. If the tape contains an even number of "a"s, the machine writes the value "Y" to the final cell, but if the tape contains an odd number of "a"s, the machine writes "N" to that cell.

1. Initially, the processor is positioned at the left end of the sequence in state 0.
2. Following the processor instructions, the processor moves right, alternating between state 0 (on odd-numbered cells) and state 1 (on even-numbered cells).
3. If the processor reaches the end of the sequence (marked by a space) in state 0, then there was an even number of a's — write "Y" in the cell and HALT.
4. If the processor reaches the end of the sequence (marked by a space) in state 1, then there was an odd number of a's — write "N" in the cell and HALT.

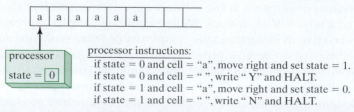

Figure 10.4 Turing machine to recognize an even number of a's on the tape.

Although Turing machines might seem simplistic, analysis has proven them to be as powerful as today's computers. That is, any computation that can be programmed and performed using a modern computer can also be programmed and performed using a Turing machine. Of course, the equivalent Turing machine program might be much more complex and involve a much larger number of steps; however, the Turing machine would eventually complete the task. The advantage of a simple model such as the Turing machine is that it provides a manageable tool for studying computation. In fact, Turing was able to use the Turing machine model of computation to prove a rather astounding result: there exist problems whose solutions cannot be computed. In other words, he was able to verify that certain problems are not solvable using algorithms or any computing device. The most famous example is referred to as the Halting Problem, which Turing demonstrated to be noncomputable in 1930. In programming terminology, the Halting Problem states that you can't write a program that determines in all cases whether another program will terminate. As you will see in Chapter 13, the introduction of loops in a programming language raises the possibility of endless cycles, where the same statements are executed over and over.

Using the Turing machine as his model of computation, Turing was able to prove the impossibility of writing a program (algorithm) that is guaranteed to recognize every program (algorithm) containing a nonterminating loop. In general, theoretical computer science attempts to understand computation at a level that is independent of any particular machine architecture. This enables the discipline to provide a strong foundation for developing new algorithms and computers.

Subfields of Computer Science

In his classic description of the field, *Computer Science: The Discipline*, Peter J. Denning identifies 12 major subfields of computer science (Figure 10.5). Each subfield constitutes a unique viewpoint and approach to computation, many of which have close ties to other disciplines, such as physics, psychology, and biology. However, the common themes of computer science—hardware, software, and theory—influence every subfield.

The following sections examine computer science's six most visible subfields: algorithms and data structures, architecture, operating systems and networks, software engineering, artificial intelligence and robotics, and bioinformatics. Although it is impossible to include a complete description of these subfields in such a short space, these sections summarize the key ideas that define the disciplines and provide representative examples from each.

Algorithms and Data Structures

The subfield of algorithms and data structures involves developing, analyzing, and implementing algorithms for solving problems. As algorithms are fundamental to all computer science (see Chapter 8), researchers in this subfield can approach the topic from various perspectives. A theoretical computer scientist might be concerned with analyzing the characteristics, efficiency, and limitations of various algorithms. This type of work is relevant, because examining which types of algorithms are best suited to certain tasks can lead to more effective problem solving. As programs are simply implementations of algorithms, software development is driven by an understanding and mastery of algorithms. To develop software, a programmer must be familiar with common algorithmic approaches and the data structures they manipulate. And because programs must ultimately be executed by computers, the connection between algorithms and underlying hardware must also be understood.

One application area in which the design of new algorithms has had great impact is encryption. **Encryption** is the process of encoding a message so that it is decipherable only by its intended recipient—i.e., anyone intercepting the message would be unable to interpret its contents. Since the time of Julius Caesar (100–44 B.C.), people have developed various algorithms for encoding secret messages to ensure military, political, and even commercial security. For example, Caesar is known to have used an algorithm that involved replacing each letter in a message with the letter three positions later in the alphabet. Thus, the Latin phrase "ET TU BRUTE" would be encoded as "HW WX EUXWH", as "H" is three positions after "E", "W" is three positions after "T", and so on. Of course, in order for the message to be decoded, the recipient must understand the encoding method and perform the reverse translation.

Subfields of Computer Science[1]	
Algorithms and Data Structures	The study of methods for solving problems, designing and analyzing algorithms, and effectively using data structures in software systems.
Architecture	The design and implementation of computing technology, including the integration of effective hardware systems and the development of new manufacturing methods.
Operating Systems and Networks	The design and development of software and hardware systems for managing the components of a computer or network of communicating computers.
Software Engineering	The development and application of methodologies for designing, implementing, testing, and maintaining software systems.
Artificial Intelligence and Robotics	The study and development of software and hardware systems that solve complex problems through seemingly "intelligent" behavior.
Bioinformatics	The application of computing methodologies and information structures to biological research, such as the characterization and analysis of the human genome.
Programming Languages	The design and implementation of languages that allow programmers to express algorithms so that they are executable on computers.
Databases and Information Retrieval	The organization and efficient management of large collections of data, including the development of methods for searching and recognizing patterns in the data.
Graphics	The design of software and hardware systems for representing physical and conceptual objects visually, such as with images, video, or three-dimensional holograms.
Human–Computer Interaction	The design, implementation, and testing of interfaces that allow users to interact more effectively with computing technology.
Computational Science	Explorations in science and engineering that utilize high-performance computing, such as modeling complex systems or simulating experimental conditions.
Organizational Informatics	The development and study of management processes and information systems that support technology workers and organizations.

Figure 10.5 Subfields of computer science.

Caesar's algorithm is categorized as a ***private-key encryption*** algorithm, because it relies on the sender and recipient sharing a secret key (in this case, the knowledge that letters are shifted three positions). Although Caesar's algorithm is not very secure by modern standards, we now possess more complex secret-key algorithms, enabling parties to transmit sensitive information across networks without fear that their data will be compromised. For example, in 2002 the U.S. government adopted the Advanced Encryption Standard (AES) for encrypting sensitive data. The strongest version of AES uses a 256-bit number as the key. Decoding an AES-encrypted message without knowing the key is virtually impossible, as this process would involve performing trial-and-error tests on $2^{256} \approx 10^{77}$ possible keys. To appreciate just how large this number is (a 1 followed by 77 zeros), note that it is roughly the same as the number of atoms in the entire universe.[2] The steps required to encode, send, and decode a message using private-key encryption are illustrated in Figure 10.6.

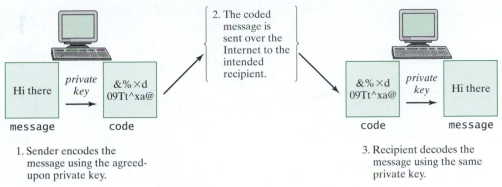

Figure 10.6 Private-key encryption.

Private-key encryption algorithms rely on the assumption that the sender and recipient have agreed upon the secret key ahead of time. However, the exchange of keys for private-key encryption introduces additional security concerns, because anyone who intercepts the key will be able to decode subsequent messages. In situations that require extreme security—for example, the transfer of sensitive government documents—the involved parties might go to great lengths to ensure a safe exchange of keys, such as by arranging a face-to-face meeting. Unfortunately, these sorts of measures are clearly not feasible for other types of communications, such as the exchange of messages or credit information over the Internet.

Secure online transactions use a different class of encryption algorithms, known as **public-key encryption**. Invented by Whitfield Diffie (1944–) and Martin Hellman (1946–) in 1976, public-key encryption uses not one key, but two, for encrypting and decrypting messages. A public key is used to encrypt the message, which can then only be decrypted using the corresponding private key. The advantage of this approach is that a secure message can be sent to someone without having to exchange a secret key—only the recipient's public key is needed to encrypt the message. The RSA algorithm, invented in 1977 by Ron Rivest (1947–), Adi Shamir (1952–), and Len Adleman (1945–) at MIT, was the first practical implementation of a public-key encryption algorithm and provides the basis for almost all secure communications occurring over the Internet.

For example, consider a typical online transaction. When a customer purchases an item on the Web from a reputable retailer, public-key encryption is automatically used to send his credit card information in a safe and secure manner. While the process may be transparent to the customer, the following steps occur to ensure that the customer's sensitive data cannot be intercepted.

1. When the customer submits his order, an initial request is sent to the retailer's server.
2. The retailer's server responds with the public key to be used for the transaction (and retains the corresponding private key).
3. The customer's browser uses the server's public key to encrypt sensitive customer data (e.g., credit card number) and sends that encrypted data to the server.
4. Upon receiving the encrypted data, the server uses its corresponding private key to decrypt it and process the transaction.
5. After processing the transaction, the server sends a confirmation message to the browser, which displays a message so that the user knows the transaction has been completed.

Note that the use of public-key encryption ensures the security of the sensitive data. Even if a thief intercepts the message, the encoded data cannot be extracted without the corresponding private key, which is known only to the retailer.

Many online transactions use two levels of public-key encryption not only to send secure data but also to verify the identity of the sender. Figure 10.7 shows how this can be accomplished using two pairs of public and private keys. The message is encrypted twice, first with the sender's private

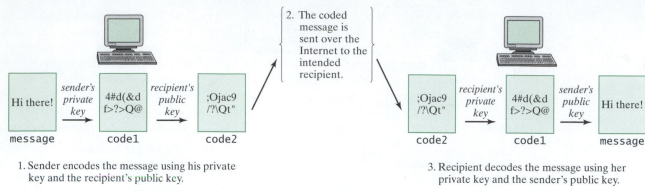

1. Sender encodes the message using his private
key and the recipient's public key.

3. Recipient decodes the message using her
private key and the sender's public key.

Figure 10.7 The use of public-key encryption for security and verification.

key and then with the recipient's public key. When this doubly encrypted message is received by the recipient, it is decrypted in the reverse sequence using the retailer's private key and the customer's public key. Using this approach, the sender is assured that only the intended recipient can access the encrypted data, since decoding the message requires the use of the recipient's private key. Likewise, the recipient is assured that the message came from the identified sender, since encoding the message requires the use of the sender's private key.

Architecture

The architecture subfield is concerned with methods of organizing hardware components into efficient, reliable systems. As we have discussed, the design of most computer systems is based on the von Neumann architecture. However, within this model, new technologies and techniques are constantly being developed to improve system performance and capabilities. For example, Chapter 6 outlined the historical evolution of computers, explaining how new technologies for switching electrical signals (e.g., relays, vacuum tubes, transistors, and finally integrated circuits) facilitated the introduction of smaller, cheaper, and more accessible computers. Other improvements in areas such as microchip manufacturing (see Chapter 16), memory storage and access, and input/output methods have also contributed to the construction of more powerful and usable systems (Figure 10.8).

Figure 10.8 Computer-controlled robots are used to manufacture microchips on a miniscule scale. Here, metal pins are being connected to the circuitry on the microchip by a robotic arm.

In recent years, computer architectures that deviate from the von Neumann model have been developed and used effectively in certain application areas. ***Parallel processing***, as its name suggests, is an approach that employs multiple processors working in parallel to share a computational load. Ideally, if you doubled the number of processors in a system, your program would accomplish its task in half the time, as the various processors can handle subtasks simultaneously. In practice, however, additional computation is required to divide up the work, and not all tasks are well suited for parallel processing. For example, if each step in an algorithm is dependent on the results from the previous step, then the steps must be executed one at a time in the specified order, and additional processors will be of little help. Even when a task can be broken up, there are costs associated with coordinating the processors and enabling them to share information.

Evaluating how and when parallel processing can be effectively applied to solve problems is a complex process. For example, an architect who works on parallel-computing systems must understand theory (in order to divide the algorithmic steps among the processors) and software methods (in order to specify control information within programs), as well as the design and implementation of hardware. As we discussed in Chapter 1, the new generation of multicore CPUs support simple parallel processing by packaging the circuitry for multiple processors on a single chip. For example, Intel's Core 2 Duo (introduced in 2006) and its successor, the Core i3 (2010), contain two processor cores that can execute programs independently. The Core 2 Quad (2006) and its successors, the Core i5 and Core i7 (2010), contain four processor cores. With a multicore CPU, the operating system will attempt to distribute programs so that both processing paths are used equally. Even a casual computer user can experience the benefits of this type of parallel processing. Suppose the user was listening to music on a computer while simultaneously surfing the Web or editing a document. With multiple cores, each program would be assigned to a separate core and so would execute independently. In contrast, with a single core CPU, the user might experience degradations in music quality due to the programs sharing the same CPU.

Web servers are another common application of parallel-computing technology. Recall that a Web server manages Web pages and other resources, such as images and sound files; when a computer communicates a request to a server, the server must respond by sending the appropriate resources back to that computer. Because a Web server may be called upon to service multiple independent requests during a short period of time, many Web servers distribute their computational loads among multiple processors. Thus, numerous page requests might be served simultaneously by different processors within the Web server.

A more extreme implementation of parallel processing can be seen in Deep Blue, the chess-playing computer developed at IBM in the mid 1990s. Deep Blue contains 32 general-purpose processors and 512 special-purpose chess processors, each of which can work in parallel to evaluate potential chess moves. Together, these processors can consider an average of 200 million possible chess moves per second! In 1997, Deep Blue became the first computer to beat a world champion in a chess tournament, defeating Gary Kasparov in six games (Figure 10.9).

Operating Systems and Networks

The subfield of operating systems and networks examines mechanisms that control the hardware and software components of computer systems. As we saw in Chapter 1, an operating system is the collection of programs that coordinates the hardware and software associated with a single computer. When operating systems were introduced in the 1950s, they were relatively simple, allowing other pieces of software to manage system resources such as printers or external memory devices. In the 1960s, operating systems with ***time-sharing*** capabilities were introduced, permitting multiple users to share one machine's computing power (Figure 10.10). Recall that, at this time, computers were still relatively expensive, so it was desirable for multiple users to employ the same computer. With a time-sharing computer, multiple users could interact with the same machine from separate physical locations. A portion of the computer's processor was allocated to each user, allowing the processor to rotate among tasks—this rotation occurred so rapidly that human observers could not tell that the applications were not executing simultaneously.

Figure 10.9 Gary Kasparov vs. Deep Blue (1997).

In the 1970s, the idea of time sharing was extended to ***multitasking***, through which a single user could have multiple programs executing simultaneously. For example, the user might have three different applications running, with each application allocated a portion of the processor. In addition to these features, modern operating systems such as Windows XP, Mac OS X, and Linux provide intuitive GUIs, enabling users to interact with programs and hardware devices through windows, icons, and menus.

Although an operating system is sufficient to control the software and hardware components of a single machine, today's computers are rarely isolated. Instead, computers are connected in networks, allowing them to communicate with each other and share resources. Every computer network is classified as either a ***wide area network (WAN)*** or ***local area network (LAN)***. A WAN connects computers

Figure 10.10 DEC PDP-1, the first commercial time-sharing computer. Note that there are different stations in the room where users can interact with the computer simultaneously.

Figure 10.11 A typical consumer-quality Wi-Fi router.

over long distances, so it must include built-in controls for routing messages and adapting to the failures that will inevitably occur. The most obvious example of a WAN is the Internet, which uses a distributed architecture and packet-switching technology to form an effective, robust network (see Chapter 3). By contrast, LANs are used to link computers over short distances, such as within the same room or building. In this type of network, the mechanisms for controlling messages can be much simpler.

The most popular family of technologies used to build LANs is known as **Ethernet**. Ethernet hubs or switches route messages between individual computers on the network based on their Media Access Control (MAC) addresses, unique numbers assigned to the hardware of each computer. Ethernet networks are able to provide impressive communication speeds over short distances—information can be transmitted at 100M bits per second, up to 1G bits per second (depending on the specific technology used).

In the past decade, computers have become increasingly mobile, with laptops and smart phones replacing desktop computers for many users. Using a **wireless**, or **Wi-Fi** (Wireless Fidelity), network, a user can connect a laptop to the Internet from coffee shops, campus lounges, hotel rooms, or even the living room couch. To connect to a Wi-Fi network, a computer must have a wireless adapter that translates data into a radio signal and broadcasts that signal using an antenna. A **wireless access point**, or **router** (Figure 10.11), receives that signal, decodes it, and passes it through to the Internet through a wired Ethernet connection. In the other direction, the router receives data from the Internet, translates it into a radio signal, and broadcasts the signal back to the computer. The convenience of wireless connectivity comes at a cost, however. Wi-Fi networks can transmit and receive data at maximum of 54 Mbits per second, significantly less than the 100 Mbits or 1 Gbits per second achievable with wired Ethernet. If the network is congested due to multiple computers broadcasting simultaneously, actual transmission rates may degrade considerably. In addition, users need to be concerned about privacy when using a public Wi-Fi network. Since data is broadcast as a radio signal, it can be easily intercepted by anyone within range. Fortunately, Wi-Fi networks can be configured to encrypt the data sent between the computer and the router, thus making the data transmissions secure.

The range of Wi-Fi networks can vary, depending on the power of the radio transmitter in the router. Typically, a consumer-quality router will broadcast 50–100 yards, enough to cover a house or building floor. A longer-range alternative to Wi-Fi is **3rd Generation**, or **3G**, broadcast via mobile telecommunications. Cellular providers such as AT&T, Verizon, and Sprint offer services in which they broadcast data as well as voice communications over long-range radio signals. Since most cities and population centers are covered by cellular towers, a user with a 3G-enabled phone or laptop can access the Internet from virtually anywhere. Transmission rates are considerably slower than Wi-Fi, however, typically 5.8 Mbits per second for uploading data and 14 Mbits per second for downloading.

Software Engineering

Software engineering is the subfield of computer science concerned with creating effective software systems. The development and support of computer software has become a major factor in the global, information-based economy of the 21st century. During the 1990s, the worldwide sales of packaged software grew by 10–12% per year. Although this growth tapered off during the subsequent economic downturn, market researcher Datamonitor estimated worldwide software sales in 2008 to be $303 billion, up 6.5% from 2007. Datamonitor further forecasts that software sales will reach $457 billion by 2013.[3]

Developing large, reliable, cost-effective software systems can be extremely difficult, as it presents both technical and management challenges. Large software projects can encompass millions of lines of code, requiring extensive teams of programmers and analysts. For example, the Windows XP operating system, released in 2001, contained over 45 million lines of code.[4] When teams of programmers are working together on the same project, software must be carefully designed so that components can be developed and tested independently, then integrated into the whole. A variety of tools are used to facilitate this, including design formalisms (such as the Unified Modeling Language, or UML) that clearly define the intended behavior of software components, and version control systems (such as the Concurrent Versions System, or CVS) that allow multiple programmers to share files and integrate changes. In addition, the efforts of the individual developer must be coordinated to ensure that work is not being duplicated and that the individual components being developed will fit together as a whole. As the software components are developed, they must be tested in isolation and again as part of the overall project to ensure that they are correct and reliable. Although different software companies might use different tools or personnel management policies, effective software engineering requires an overall development methodology that addresses all aspects of the software life cycle (Figure 10.12).

As the demand for software continues to grow, increases in programmer productivity threaten to lag behind. It would be nice if there were a software-related equivalent to Moore's Law, which states that the number of transistors that can be placed on a computer chip doubles every 18 months. However, it is not reasonable to expect programmers to double their output every year. In addition, increased productivity cannot always be obtained just by assigning more programmers to a project, because personnel management and coordination become increasingly complex as project size grows. Fortunately, new development tools and methodologies (such as those mentioned previously) are constantly being introduced and refined to assist the software developer in managing complexity. In recent years, object-oriented programming languages such as Java and C++ have been widely adopted because of their support for code reuse. These languages provide large libraries of software components and enable programmers to easily build upon existing components. Often it is possible to use code that has already been developed and tested, as opposed to developing new code from scratch. Thus, the overall complexity of the project can be reduced.

Stages in the Software Life Cycle

1. *Requirement analysis and specification:* Initially, the needs of the customer must be assessed and the intended behavior of the software specified in detail.

2. *Design:* Next, the software system must be designed, including its breakdown into manageable pieces, and the underlying algorithms and data structures to be used.

3. *Implementation:* After completion of the design documents, the code must be written. For large software projects, teams may work independently on separate modules and then integrate those modules to complete the system.

4. *Testing:* The software must be systematically tested, both as independent modules and as a whole. As testing reveals errors or unforeseen conditions, reimplementation and even redesign may need to take place.

5. *Operation and maintenance:* Once the software system is complete, it must be installed and supported. It is estimated that maintenance, which involves fixing errors and updating code to meet changing customer needs, accounts for as much as half of a software project's total development budget.

Figure 10.12   The software life cycle.

The Turing Test

In his 1950 paper, *Computing Machinery and Intelligence,* Alan Turing proposed what is still considered the ultimate test for artificial intelligence. The Turing Test is based on the observation that we, as humans, make assumptions about intelligence and self-awareness in other humans by monitoring and interacting with them. Turing proposed that if the behavior of a machine were indistinguishable from a human's behavior, then we ought to give the machine the same credit for being intelligent that we give people.

The Turing Test involves a human judge and two contestants, one being the computer to be tested and the second being a human control subject. The job of the judge is to converse with the two contestants via computer terminals, without knowing which contestant is which. If, after a sufficiently long period of conversation, the judge is unable to identify the computer, then the computer is said to have passed the test and must be considered to possess human-like intelligence.

Figure 10.13   The Turing Test for artificial intelligence.

Artificial Intelligence and Robotics

One of the best-known subfields of computer science is artificial intelligence, which aims to design computers that exhibit more humanlike characteristics—i.e., the ability to see, hear, speak, and even reason and think. In his 1950 paper, *Computing Machinery and Intelligence*, Alan Turing predicted that, by the end of the 20th century, the intelligence exhibited by programmed machines would rival that of humans (Figure 10.13).

Although we are still many years away from reaching Turing's goal of artificially intelligent machines, much progress has been made in areas such as robotics, machine vision, and speech recognition. Robots are used extensively in manufacturing (Figure 10.14), and some robotic products (such as the self-powered vacuum cleaner shown in Figure 10.15) are being introduced into private homes. *Expert systems*—programs that encapsulate the knowledge and reasoning of experts in specific domains, such as medical diagnosis and finance—have been implemented with impressive success. For example,

- Expert systems have been highly effective in medical diagnosis, where specialist expertise can be encoded in rule form. For example, the FocalPoint Primary Screening System from BD Diagnostics is an expert system that is commonly used by doctors to process Pap test slides and detect early signs of cervical cancer.

- Major credit card companies utilize expert systems (e.g., MasterCard's EMS and Visa's Intellilink) to monitor transactions and identify potential fraud. These systems use general-purpose rules and

Figure 10.14   Manufacturing robots welding automobile parts on an assembly line.

Figure 10.15 The Roomba intelligent floor vacuum from iRobot is able to sense obstacles and move freely around the floor as it vacuums.

specific information from the cardholder's history to decide between approving a purchase or flagging it for further investigation.

- A variety of commercial expert systems have been developed to provide expert guidance in specialized activities. For example, the help facilities provided by operating systems are expert systems that provide advice and solutions to common user problems.

Research on topics such as machine learning and knowledge representation has not only produced practical results but has also helped further our understanding of how humans reason and learn. *Neural computing*, the design of computer architectures that mimic the human brain, is an especially promising area of research, both for its technical applications and for its potential to help us understand our own physiology. Artificial neural networks made up of hundreds or thousands of computational units, each of which models a single brain cell or *neuron*, are used in a variety of commercial applications that involve complex pattern recognition. For example, neural networks are at the heart of digital scanners and handwriting recognition software. One of the most powerful supercomputers in the world, IBM's Dawn, was used in 2009 to build a cell-by-cell simulation of the human visual cortex consisting of 1.6 billion artificial neurons with more than 9 trillion connections.[5]

Bioinformatics

The newest and most dynamic subfield of computer science is *bioinformatics*. As the name suggests, this subfield bridges the gap between biology and computer science (or, as it is known internationally, informatics), focusing on the use of computers and computer science techniques in the solution of biological problems. Perhaps more than any other natural science, biology is becoming increasingly dependent on computers in order to conduct research and analyze biological data. One obvious aspect of this is the integration of computers with laboratory tools and equipment. For example, many of today's microscopes connect to computers and digital cameras, allowing the researcher to view the magnified image on a computer screen, manipulate that image using image-processing software, process image data using analytical tools, and save the image directly to a file. It is interesting to note that the confocal microscope, a common research tool used to generate three-dimensional images of samples, was invented by a computer scientist, artificial intelligence pioneer Marvin Minsky. Computers are also used extensively for modeling biological systems, such as the migration pattern of birds or the evolution of a virus. Pharmaceutical companies make extensive use of computer models in drug testing, as it is faster and safer to model drug interactions

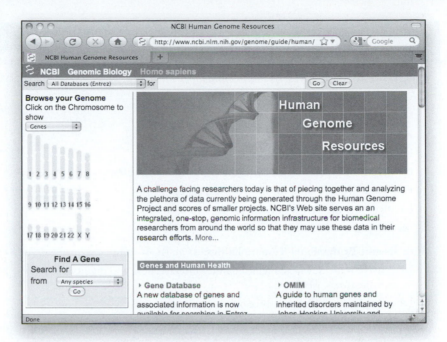

Figure 10.16 The NCBI Web site provides access to genetic databases and tools for searching and analyzing their contents.

and their predicted effect on cells, as opposed to the cost and risks of human testing. IBM's Blue Gene/P supercomputer was specifically designed for performing complex biological modeling including human genome mapping and drug interaction simulations. This computer has 294,912 processors working in parallel, and is capable of more than one quadrillion (10^{15}) operations per second.[6]

Although high-tech tools and computer-based models are important, the area of bioinformatics making the greatest impact involves the processing of vast databases of genetic data that have been collected over the last decade. Begun in 1990, the Human Genome Project was a collaborative government and private industry initiative, coordinated by the U.S. Department of Energy and the National Institutes of Health. The goals of this project included (1) identifying all of the approximately 20,000–25,000 genes in human DNA, (2) determining the sequences of the 3 billion chemical base pairs that make up human DNA, and (3) disseminating this information for scientific research in the form of Web-accessible databases. In 2003, two years ahead of schedule, the project announced that it had completed mapping the DNA in all 24 human chromosomes. This data is available in various online databases, most notably the National Center for Biological Information (NCBI), which is maintained by the National Institutes of Health and the National Library of Medicine. At the NCBI Web site, `http://www.ncbi.nlm.nih.gov`, researchers from around the world can access the human genetic database and use a variety of tools for analyzing DNA sequences (Figure 10.16).

The Ethics of Computing

Despite the diverse approaches taken by the various computer science subfields, computing professionals have much in common. All perform work relating to the three themes (theory, software, and hardware), and all contribute to computing's overall impact on society. Careers in this field continue to be attractive and challenging, with demand for computer professionals far exceeding supply and with salaries that are among the highest of any discipline.

In an effort to unite computing professionals into a cohesive community, professional organizations supervise the orchestration of industrywide resources. This includes publishing journals relevant to the field, organizing conferences, providing career resources, and representing technology workers' interests to government and society. The oldest and largest professional organization is the Association for Computing Machinery (ACM), founded in 1947. However, the industry supports

ACM Code of Ethics and Professional Conduct[7]
Copyright © 1997, Association for Computing Machinery, Inc.

General Moral Imperatives. *As an ACM member I will . . .*

1.1 Contribute to society and human well-being.

1.2 Avoid harm to others.

1.3 Be honest and trustworthy.

1.4 Be fair and take action not to discriminate.

1.5 Honor property rights including copyrights and patent.

1.6 Give proper credit for intellectual property.

1.7 Respect the privacy of others.

1.8 Honor confidentiality.

More Specific Professional Responsibilities. *As an ACM computing professional I will . . .*

2.1 Strive to achieve the highest quality, effectiveness and dignity in both the process and products of professional work.

2.2 Acquire and maintain professional competence.

2.3 Know and respect existing laws pertaining to professional work.

2.4 Accept and provide appropriate professional review.

2.5 Give comprehensive and thorough evaluations of computer systems and their impacts, including analysis of possible risks.

2.6 Honor contracts, agreements, and assigned responsibilities.

2.7 Improve public understanding of computing and its consequences.

2.8 Access computing and communication resources only when authorized to do so.

Figure 10.17 Excerpts from the ACM Code of Ethics. (© 1992 Association for Computing Machinery. All Rights Reserved.)

numerous similar groups, such as the IEEE Computer Society, which also originated in the 1940s and is especially popular among computing professionals with engineering backgrounds.

In 1992, the ACM responded to society's increasing reliance on technology and technology workers by adopting a Code of Ethics and Professional Conduct for computing professionals. This code outlines computer professionals' responsibilities for ensuring that hardware and software are used safely, fairly, and effectively. Excerpts from this code are listed in Figure 10.17. The moral imperatives provided in section 1 of the code represent general guidelines relevant to any professional field. For example, all ethical citizens are expected to behave fairly to all (imperative 1.4) and honor others' property and intellectual rights (imperatives 1.5 and 1.6). Section 2 of the code relates specifically to computing and the need to protect technology users from incompetence and unethical practices in the computing industry. For example, imperative 2.5 recognizes that computer technology plays a role in critical systems, such as those in which human life (e.g., medical monitoring systems) and wealth (e.g., banking systems) are at risk. This part of the code indicates that computer professionals must understand the potential impact of their work and strive to minimize risks. A related section, imperative 2.7, implies that computer professionals are obligated to publicize the societal impacts of computing, including the inherent risks associated with our technological dependence.

Looking Ahead...

In this chapter, you reviewed the fundamental concepts and research methods that define the computer science field. Computer science is the study of computation, which encompasses all aspects of problem solving. The three themes that span all computer-related research are hardware (the physical manifestation of computation), software (the logical manifestation of computation), and theory (an understanding of computation and its limits). Although these themes recur throughout the discipline, computer science has been divided into subfields that focus on particular aspects of computation, such as the design and analysis of algorithms, methods of engineering software, and the quest for artificial intelligence.

After reading this chapter, you should have greater insight into what computer science is and what computer scientists do. If you are considering a career in any computer-related field, the information that we have presented can help you determine where your particular interests fit in the range of computer science subfields and positions. However, even if you have no interest in continuing your computer science education beyond this course, your newly acquired understanding of the discipline will strengthen your problem-solving skills and will provide additional context for the more advanced programming topics covered in future chapters. The next chapter, Chapter 11, returns to programming by introducing the concept of conditional execution, a programming skill that can greatly expand the expressive power of your algorithms. Conditional execution refers to a program's ability to decide between alternative actions on the basis of some condition. For example, you might write a program that simulates a coin flip and then reacts differently depending on the result of the flip. In JavaScript, conditional execution is implemented using if statements, which will be fully explained in Chapter 11.

Chapter Summary

- Computer science is the study of computation, encompassing all facets of problem solving including the design and analysis algorithms, the formalization of algorithms as programs, and the development of computational devices for executing those programs.

- Computer science shares common elements with natural sciences, including a rigorous approach to understanding complex phenomena and solving problems. However, computer science has been classified by some as an "artificial science," because the systems studied by computer sciences are largely designed and constructed by people.

- The three recurring themes that define the discipline of computer science are hardware (the physical components of computers), software (the programs that execute on computers), and theory (an understanding of the capabilities and limitations of computers).

- A Turing machine is an abstract model of computation designed by Alan Turing in 1930. Using this model, Turing was able to demonstrate that there exist problems whose solutions cannot be computed.

- The discipline of computer science encompasses many subfields, including algorithms and data structures, architecture, operating systems and networks, software engineering, and artificial intelligence and robotics.

- The subfield of algorithms and data structures involves developing, analyzing, and implementing algorithms for solving problems. For example, the development of new algorithms for encrypting data and messages (e.g., public-key and private-key encryption) has had significant impact on electronic commerce and security.

- The architecture subfield of computer science is concerned with methods of organizing hardware components into efficient, reliable systems. For example, new architectures in which multiple processors work in parallel to share a computational load have produced powerful results (e.g., the Deep Blue computer that beat a world champion in chess).

- The subfield of operating systems and networks examines mechanisms that control the hardware and software components of computer systems. For example, Ethernet technology has been developed as a simple yet effective means of networking computers over short distances.

- Software engineering is the subfield of computer science concerned with creating effective software systems. Stages in the development and maintenance of software projects include requirement analysis and specification, design, implementation, testing, operation and maintenance.

- One of the most well-known subfields of computer science is artificial intelligence, which aims to design computers that exhibit more humanlike characteristics. Commercial successes in this area of research include expert systems and manufacturing robotics.

- The subfield of bioinformatics bridges biology and computer science, focusing on the use of computers and computer science techniques in solving biological problems. An example of a large-scale bioinformatics initiative was the Human Genome Project, which identified and catalogued the structure of human chromosomes.

- In 1992, the Association for Computing Machinery adopted a Code of Ethics and Professional Conduct for computing professionals that identifies general moral imperatives and specific responsibilities of professionals in information technology fields.

Review Questions

1. TRUE or FALSE? The discipline of computer science is concerned solely with the design and development of computational machines.

2. TRUE or FALSE? Unlike in the natural sciences (such as physics and biology), the systems that computer scientists investigate are largely artificial (e.g., programs, computers, computation models).

3. TRUE or FALSE? The three recurring themes that define the discipline of computer science are hardware, software, and theory.

4. TRUE or FALSE? Theoretical computer scientists have proven that any problem that can be stated clearly is solvable via an algorithm.

5. TRUE or FALSE? Private-key encryption algorithms require the sender and recipient of a message to agree upon a secret key (or password) for encoding and decoding the message.

6. TRUE or FALSE? In a time-sharing computer, the processor executes user programs in sequence, completing the execution of one program before beginning the next one.

7. TRUE or FALSE? On an Ethernet network, computer A can send a message directly to computer B, without any other computer on the network receiving that message.

8. TRUE or FALSE? When developing large software projects, it generally takes more time to develop the code than it does to test and maintain it.

9. TRUE or FALSE? The Turing Test was proposed by Alan Turing as a means of determining whether an artificially intelligent machine has been constructed.

10. TRUE or FALSE? According to the Code of Ethics proposed by the Association for Computing Machinery (ACM), a computer professional is responsible for understanding the potential impact of his or her work and for striving to minimize risks to the public.

11. Describe at least two similarities between computer science and natural sciences such as physics, biology, and chemistry. Describe at least two differences.

12. Alan Turing is considered one of computer science's founding fathers. Describe two of his contributions to the discipline, and explain the importance of those contributions.

13. Encrypt the message "Beware the Ides of March" using the Caesar encryption algorithm. Recall that the Caesar algorithm encodes each individual letter by replacing it with the letter three positions later in the alphabet.

14. The following encoded text was created using Caesar's encryption algorithm: "Brx jrw lw". Decode this message by performing the reverse translation, replacing each letter in the code with the letter three positions earlier.

15. Using public-key encryption, the sender and recipient of a message do not need to agree on a shared secret key before initiating secure communications. How is this possible? That is, how can the sender, using publicly available information, encode a message that can be decoded only by the intended recipient?

16. Describe the fundamentals of parallel processing and explain how they are implemented in Deep Blue, the first computer to defeat a world chess champion in a tournament setting.

17. What does it mean for an operating system to support multitasking? How is multitasking different from time sharing?

18. Describe one potential danger of accessing the Internet over a wireless connection, such as WiFi or 3G? How can this danger be reduced?

19. Describe the individual steps that make up the software life cycle. What is the life cycle's significance in relation to the software engineering process?

20. Imagine that you are serving as the judge in a Turing Test. Describe the strategy you would use to identify the computer. That is, what kinds of questions would you ask the contestants, and how would the answers you received help you differentiate between the computer and human?

21. Describe three different ways in which computer technology is contributing to research in the biological sciences.

22. Many diseases have genetic causes, which can be traced to mutations in a particular gene. Visit the NCBI Web site (`http://www.ncbi.nlm.nih.gov`) and search through the online resources to find two such diseases. Identify the diseases and the genetic mutations that have been associated with those diseases.

23. Software piracy, the unauthorized copying of software without payment to the legal owner, is a growing problem worldwide. Suppose that you were offered a chance to copy a friend's disk containing copyrighted software. What portions of the ACM Code of Ethics would address this situation? According to the code, how should a computer professional respond to such an offer?

24. Imagine that you are working for a software company, writing a program that will control air traffic at major airports. Management is pressuring you to complete the program on schedule, but you know that remaining bugs in the software might cause the program to fail under certain circumstances. What portions of the ACM Code of Ethics would address this situation? According to the code, how should you react to the situation?

Endnotes

1. Denning, Peter. "Computer Science: The Discipline." In *Encyclopedia of Computer Science*, 4th ed., A. Ralston, E. Reilly, and D. Hemmendinger, editors. New York: Nature Publishing Group, 2000. Online at `http://cs.gmu.edu/cne/pjd/PUBS/ENC/cs99.pdf`.

2. Sagan, Carl. "Can We Know the Universe?: Reflections on a Grain of Salt;" from Broca's Brain: Reflections on the Romance of Science, New York: Random House, 1979.

3. Software: Global Industry Guide, Datamonitor, 2009.

4. Salkever, Alex. "Windows XP: A Firewall for All." *BusinessWeek Online*, June 12, 2001. Online at `http://www.businessweek.com/bwdaily/dnflash/jun2001/nf20010612_227.htm`.

5. Fox, Douglas. "Virtual Smarts." *Popular Mechanics*, June 2010.

6. "Overview of the IBM Blue Gene/P Project." *IBM Journal of Research and Development*, 52(1), 2008.

7. ACM Ethics Task Force. "ACM Code of Ethics and Professional Conduct." *Communications of the ACM*, 35(5), 1992. Online at `http://www.acm.org/about/code-of-ethics`.

References

Bergeron, Bryan. *Bioinformatics Computing,* Upper Saddle River, NJ: Prentice Hall Professional Technical Reference, 2003.

Brain, Marshall, and Tracy V. Wilson. "How WiFi Works." 2001. HowStuffWorks.com. Online at `http://computer.howstuffworks.com/wireless-network.htm`.

Brooks, Frederick P., Jr. *The Mythical Man-Month: Essays on Software Engineering, Anniversary Edition.* Reading, MA: Addison-Wesley, 1995.

Hodges, Andrew. *Alan Turing: The Enigma.* New York: Walker and Company, 2000.

Joint IEEE Computer Society/ACM Task Force for CC2001. "Computing Curricula 2001 (Dec 15, 2001)." *ACM Journal of Educational Resources in Computing*, 1(3), 2001. Online at `http://www.acm.org/education/curric_vols/cc2001.pdf`.

Knuth, Donald. *The Art of Computer Programming*, Vol. 1, *Fundamental Algorithms*, 3d ed. Reading, MA: Addison-Wesley, 1997.

Simon, Herbert. *The Sciences of the Artificial*, 3d ed. Cambridge, MA: MIT Press, 1996.

Stallings, William. *Cryptography and Network Security: Principles and Practice*, 5th ed. Upper Saddle River, NJ: Prentice Hall, 2010.

Stewart, N.F. "Science and Computer Science." *ACM Computing Surveys*, 27(1), 1995. Extended version online at `http://www.iro.umontreal.ca/~stewart/science_computerscience.pdf`.

Turing, Alan. "Computing Machinery and Intelligence." *Mind*, LIX(236), 1950.

Conditional Execution

This chapter uses narrative, examples, and hands-on exercises to introduce programming concepts and Web development skills.

Destiny is no matter of chance. It is a matter of choice. It is not a thing to be waited for, it is a thing to be achieved.

William Jennings Bryan

"Contrariwise," continued Tweedledee, "if it was so, it might be; and if it were so, it would be; but as it isn't, it ain't. That's logic."

Lewis Carroll
Through the Looking Glass

So far, all the JavaScript code that you have written has been executed unconditionally. This means that the browser carried out statements in a set order, one after another. By entering different input values in text boxes, the user could affect the results, but the code always went through the same steps and produced output of the same form.

Many programming tasks, however, require code that reacts differently under varying circumstances or conditions. This capability is called *conditional execution*. For example, consider a program that converts a student's numerical course average to a letter grade. Depending on the particular student's average, the program would need to assign a different letter grade (90 to 100 would be an A, 80 to 89 a B, and so on). Similarly, you might want to design a page that simulates dice rolls and distinguishes between rolls that are doubles or not. In this chapter, you will be introduced to the *if statement*, which is used to incorporate conditional execution into JavaScript programs. After determining whether some condition is met, an if statement can choose among alternative sequences of code to execute—or can even choose to execute no code at all. This chapter describes the behavior of if statements, including the Boolean tests that control them.

If Statements

Conditional execution refers to a program's ability to execute a statement or sequence of statements only if some condition holds true. The simplest form of conditional statement involves only one possible action. For example, if your program employs a variable to represent a student's grade on a test, you might want to include code that recognizes a failing grade and warns the student. However, conditional execution can also involve alternative JavaScript sequences triggered by related conditions. That is, a program can take one action if some condition is true but take a different action if the condition is not true (the code that executes in the latter instance is called the *else case*). For example, you might want your program to display one message for a failing grade and another message for a passing grade. JavaScript if statements enable you to specify both these types of conditional execution.

The general form of an *if statement* is as follows, where the else case is optional:

```
if (BOOLEAN_TEST) {
    STATEMENTS_EXECUTED_IF_TRUE
}
else {
    STATEMENTS_EXECUTED_IF_FALSE
}
```

Boolean Tests

After encountering a JavaScript if statement, the browser's first action is to evaluate the test that appears in parentheses in the first line. The test can be any Boolean expression—that is, any expression that evaluates to either `true` or `false`. In JavaScript, Boolean tests are formed using *relational operators*, so named because they test the relationships between values (Figure 11.1). For example, the `==` operator tests for equality, so the Boolean expression (x `==` 5) would evaluate to `true` if the variable x stored the value 5. Similarly, the Boolean expression (y < 100) would evaluate to `true` if y stored a number less than 100.

The Boolean test at the beginning of an if statement determines which (if any) code will be executed. If the test succeeds (evaluates to `true`), then the code inside the subsequent curly braces is executed. If the test fails (evaluates to `false`) and there is an else case, then the code inside the curly braces following the else is executed. Note that if the test fails and there is no else case, then no statements are executed, and the program moves on to the statement directly after the if.

Figure 11.2 depicts three different if statements that print messages in response to student grades. When executing the first if statement, the browser evaluates the test to see whether the value of variable `grade` is less than 60. If so, the browser calls the `alert` function to display the warning "You failed! Time to hit the books." However, if `grade` is greater than or equal to 60, then the statement inside the curly braces is skipped over. The second example demonstrates that an if statement can control the execution of entire sequences of statements. If the test succeeds (`grade` is less than 60), then the statements inside the curly braces are executed in order. In this case, the statements compute the difference (stored in variable `diff`) between a passing grade (60) and the grade earned (`grade`) and then incorporate the value in an alert message. The third example adds an else case to the if statement, ensuring that a message is generated regardless of `grade`'s value. If the `grade` is less than 60, the browser will compute and display the difference between a passing grade and the earned grade, as before. If not, then the message "Congratulations, you passed." is displayed.

The Web page in Figure 11.3 contains a text box in which to enter a grade and a button for calling the function `ShowMessage.` `ShowMessage`, which opens an alert window if the user entered a grade

Relational Operator	Comparison Defined by the Operator
==	equal to
!=	not equal to
<	less than
<=	less than or equal to
>	greater than
>=	greater than or equal to

Figure 11.1 Relational operators in JavaScript.

```
if (grade < 60) {
    alert('You failed!  Time to hit the books.');
}
```
code executed if
grade < 60

```
if (grade < 60) {
    diff = 60 - grade;
    alert('You failed! If only you could have ' +
          'earned ' + diff + ' more points,');
}
```
code executed if
grade < 60

```
if (grade < 60) {
    diff = 60 - grade;
    alert('You failed! If only you could have ' +
          'earned ' + diff + ' more points.');
}
else {
    alert('Congratulations, you passed,');
}
```
code executed if
grade < 60

code executed otherwise
(grade >= 60)

Figure 11.2 Example if statements.

```
1.  <!doctype html>
2.  <!-- ifdemo.html                                    Dave Reed -->
3.  <!-- This program warns a student of a failing grade.        -->
4.  <!-- ======================================================= -->
5.
6.  <html>
7.   <head>
8.     <title> If Demo Page </title>
9.     <script type="text/javascript">
10.       function ShowMessage()
11.       // Assumes: gradeBox contains a grade (non-negative number)
12.       // Results: displays a warning in response to a failing grade
13.       {
14.           var grade;
15.
16.           grade = parseFloat(document.getElementById('gradeBox').value);
17.
18.           if (grade < 60) {
19.               alert('You failed! Time to hit the books.');
20.           }
21.       }
22.     </script>
23.   </head>
24.
25.   <body>
26.     <p>
27.       Your grade: <input type="text" id="gradeBox" size=6 value="">
28.     </p>
29.     <input type="button" value="Click for Message" onclick="ShowMessage();">
30.   </body>
31.  </html>
```

Figure 11.3 Web page that demonstrates an if statement.

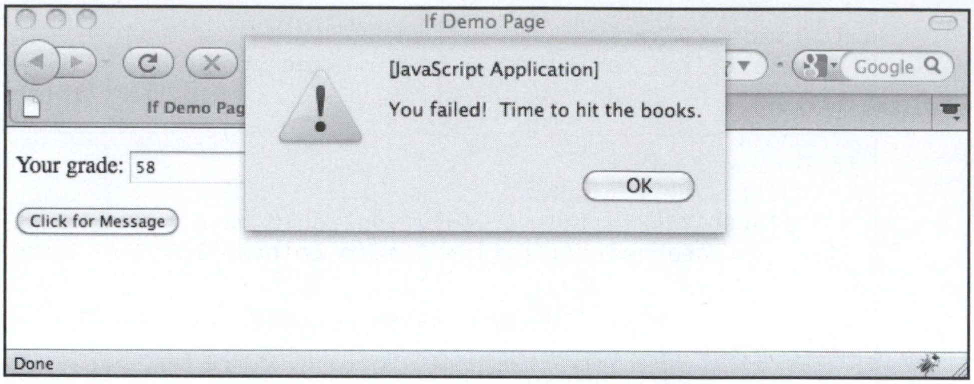

Figure 11.4 `ifdemo.html` rendered in a Web browser.

that is less than 60, incorporates the first if statement from Figure 11.2. The rendered Web page is shown in Figure 11.4.

EXERCISE 11.1

Enter the `ifdemo.html` text from Figure 11.3 into a new Web page. Load this page, then describe how it behaves when you enter various grades in the text box.

Once you have done this, modify the page by replacing the if statement in the `ShowMessage` function with the third if statement example from Figure 11.2. Load this modified page and describe how it behaves when you enter various grades.

Designer Secrets

Web browsers ignore indentation and spacing when executing JavaScript code, so such formatting is irrelevant from the browser's perspective. However, from the programmer's perspective, indentation and spacing are vitally important. When you write an if statement, it is important to lay out the code so that its structure is apparent. Otherwise, another programmer modifying your code might introduce errors by misinterpreting which statements are controlled by the if and which are not. For example, in Figure 11.2, the closing curly brace of each if statement is aligned with the beginning if, whereas all statements inside the curly braces are indented. This arrangement emphasizes where each if statement begins and ends, enabling others to read and understand the code more easily.

Technically speaking, the curly braces in an if statement are optional when there is only one statement to be executed conditionally, but you should always include curly braces in every if statement you write. When all if statements look the same, it is easier for you to code them correctly. The consistent use of curly braces also helps prevent subtle errors when code is modified.

EXERCISE 11.2

In Chapter 9, you created a `magic.html` page that simulated the behavior of a Magic 8 Ball. As written, your page completely ignores the user's question while randomly selecting from a list of possible responses. Modify your page so that it is less obvious that the entered questions are irrelevant to the page's execution. In particular, the function in the page should use an if statement to make sure the user entered a question. If not (i.e., the value accessed from the text box is the empty string), then the browser should open an alert window reminding the user to enter a question. However, if the user did enter a question (i.e., the text box is not empty), the page should proceed as before and display a randomly chosen answer. For example,

```
if (document.getElementById('questionBox').value == '') {
    alert('You need to enter a question first!');
}
else {
    // existing code for selecting and displaying an answer
}
```

EXERCISE 11.3

In Exercise 9.11, you wrote a Web page that selected a sequence of random letters from a string that was entered by the user. Similar to the modification in Exercise 11.2, modify your randSeq.html page so that it checks to make sure that the user has correctly entered characters to choose from. If not (i.e., if the text box is empty when the button is clicked), an alert window should appear to warn the user. Otherwise, the random sequence should be generated and displayed as before.

 ## Common errors to avoid...

Recall from Chapter 5 that values entered via text boxes are treated by default as strings. If you wish to treat a value obtained from a text box as a number, you must apply the parseFloat function to convert the string to its numeric equivalent. As we have established, forgetting to parseFloat such values can introduce subtle errors; this holds true when referencing the contents of text boxes in if statements. For example, consider the following if statement, which is intended to display a message indicating whether a person is old enough to vote (i.e., whether an age entered in a text box is greater than or equal to 18):

```
if (document.getElementById('ageBox').value >= 18) {
    alert('You are old enough to vote.');
}
else {
    alert('Sorry. You are too young to vote.');
}
```

When certain ages are entered in the text box, this code may appear to behave correctly, but if you test the code using numerous inputs, you can obtain surprising results. For example, a 9-year-old will be considered old enough to vote, but a 100-year-old will not!

The problem is that, without a call to parseFloat, the browser treats the contents of the text box as a string. Thus, when the if test is evaluated, the Boolean expression is comparing a string value (the age from the text box) with a number value (18). In situations where a test must compare values of mixed data types, the browser automatically converts the number value into a string and then performs string comparison. Because strings are compared character by character, '9' is considered to be greater than '18' ('9' > '1'), and '100' is considered to be less than '18' (the first characters are identical, so the comparison moves to the second character, where '0' < '8').

To avoid this type of error, always parseFloat the contents of a text box or text area if you intend to treat the value as a number.

Nested If Statements

Often, programming tasks require code that responds to more than one condition. If you want to attach multiple conditions to the same set of JavaScript statements, you can do so by nesting one if statement inside another. In fact, nesting if statements can be a highly effective way of structuring complex code.

```
if (grade < 60) {
  alert('You failed!  Time to hit the books.');     executed if
}                                                    grade < 60
else {
  if (grade < 90) {
    alert('You passed, but could do better.');     executed if
  }                                                 grade < 90      executed if
  else {                                                            grade >= 60
    alert('Congratulations!  You got an A.');      executed if
  }                                                 grade >= 90
}
```

Figure 11.5 Nested if statements for differentiating three classes of grades.

For example, the nested if statements in Figure 11.5 perform a three-way test on grades. The outer if statement differentiates between failing grades (grade < 60) and passing grades (grade > = 60). In the case of a passing grade, a nested if statement further differentiates between simply passing (grade < 90) and A-level (grade >= 90) grades.

Cascading If-Else Statements

Nested if-else structures such as the one in Figure 11.5 are known as ***cascading if-else statements***, because control cascades down the statement like water down a waterfall. The topmost test is evaluated first—in this case (grade < 60). If this test succeeds, then the corresponding statements are executed, and program control moves to the next statement following the cascading if-else. If the test fails, then control cascades down to the next if test—in this case (grade < 90). In general, control cascades down the statement from one test to another until one succeeds or the end of the statement is reached. If (as in Figure 11.5) the final case is an unconditional else, then this final case will execute if none of the preceding conditional tests succeed. However, if the final case is conditional (i.e., another if statement), it is possible that none of the conditions will be met and that no code controlled by the cascading if-else statements will be executed.

When it is necessary to handle a large number of alternatives, cascading if-else statements can become cumbersome and unwieldy. This is because each nested if-else statement introduces another level of indentation and curly braces, causing the code to look cluttered. Fortunately, programmers can write more concise, clearer cascading if-else statements by adopting a slightly different notation. The left-hand side of Figure 11.6 depicts a set of nested if-else statements that determine a student's letter grade using a traditional grading system. On the right is an equivalent section of code that is much more readable. This cleaner notation omits some redundant curly braces and indents each case an equal amount. Using this notation, it is easier to discern that there are five alternatives, each assigning a letter grade on the basis of grade's value.

EXERCISE 11.4

Augment your grades.html page from Exercise 7.10 by inserting a cascading if-else statement similar to the one on the right-hand side of Figure 11.6. In addition to displaying the student's class average, the associated letter grade should also be displayed. For example, if the student's average was calculated to be 85.5, then the message displayed in the page division should be:

```
Your overall course average is 85.5
Letter grade: B
```

EXERCISE 11.5

Modify your surface.html page from Exercise 9.8 so that it ensures that both the height and weight values entered by the user are positive values. If either of the values in the text boxes is less than or equal to 0 when the button is clicked, then the surface area should be displayed as NaN. Otherwise, the surface are should be calculated and displayed as before.

```
if (grade < 60) {                      if (grade < 60) {
   letterGrade = 'F';                     letterGrade = 'F';
}                                      }
else {                                 else if (grade < 70) {
   if (grade < 70) {                      letterGrade = 'D';
      letterGrade = 'D';              }
   }                                   else if (grade < 80) {
   else {                                 letterGrade = 'C';
      if (grade < 80) {               }
         letterGrade = 'C';           else if (grade < 90) {
      }                                  letterGrade = 'B';
      else {                           }
         if (grade < 90) {            else {
            letterGrade = 'B';            letterGrade = 'A';
         }                             }
         else {
            letterGrade = 'A';
         }
      }
   }
}
```

Figure 11.6 Examples of equivalent cascading if-else statements.

Designer Secrets

An if statement is different from other JavaScript statements we have studied in that it does not perform a particular task in and of itself. Instead, it is known as a ***control statement***, as its purpose is to control the execution of other statements. When solving problems, most programmers find it fairly easy to determine when an if statement is required. If the program needs to make any choices during execution—that is, the code should react differently under different circumstances—then you should include some version of an if statement.

- If the choice involves only one alternative—that is, the code should carry out some action if a condition holds and do nothing if the condition does not hold—then a simple if statement is needed.
- If the choice involves two alternatives—that is, the code should carry out some action if a condition holds and do something else if it does not hold—then an if statement with an else case is needed.
- If the choice involves more than two alternatives—that is, the code should carry out one of three or more actions on the basis of various conditions—then nested or cascading if-else statements are needed.

Example: Dice Simulations

In Chapter 7, you developed a Web page that simulated dice rolls (Exercise 7.11). Your page contained two die images and a button. When the user clicked on the button, random die faces were selected and displayed in the page. In this section, you will revisit the dice simulation, adding code to maintain statistics on the rolls obtained.

Counters

In software applications, if statements are often used to count occurrences of conditional or user-initiated events. To understand the relevance of recording such data, consider that many research experiments in the natural sciences involve observing phenomena and keeping track of how many times certain actions occur. For example, a particle physicist might want to count the number of atomic collisions that take place within a certain time period, whereas a biologist might want to count the number of encounters between animals at an oasis over the course of a day. Certain computer programs provide a similar ability to record the number of times a certain action is taken within an application. In computer science terminology, any variable that is used to record occurrences of an event is known as a ***counter***. Before a counter begins tallying, it must have an initial value of zero. Then, each time the specified event occurs, the value of the counter is incremented (increased by

```
1.  <!doctype html>
2.  <!-- stats.html                                    Dave Reed -->
3.  <!-- This page simulates dice rolls and keeps a roll count. -->
4.  <!-- ===================================================== -->
5.
6.  <html>
7.   <head>
8.    <title> Die Rolls </title>
9.    <script type="text/javascript" src="http://balance3e.com/random.js">
10.   </script>
11.   <script type="text/javascript">
12.     function RollDice()
13.     // Assumes: die images are in http://balance3e.com/Images
14.     // Results: displays 2 random die rolls & keeps a count in rollSpan
15.     {
16.        var roll1, roll2;
17.
18.        roll1 = RandomInt(1, 6);
19.        roll2 = RandomInt(1, 6);
20.
21.        document.getElementById('die1Img').src =
22.                'http://balance3e.com/Images/die' + roll1 + '.gif';
23.        document.getElementById('die2Img').src =
24.                'http://balance3e.com/Images/die' + roll2 + '.gif';
25.
26.        document.getElementById('rollSpan').innerHTML =
27.                parseFloat(document.getElementById('rollSpan').innerHTML) + 1;
28.     }
29.   </script>
30.  </head>
31.
32.  <body>
33.    <div style="text-align:center">
34.      <p>
35.        <img id="die1Img" alt="die image"
36.             src="http://balance3e.com/Images/die1.gif">
37.        <img id="die2Img" alt="die image"
38.             src="http://balance3e.com/Images/die1.gif">
39.      </p>
40.      <input type="button" value="Click to Roll" onclick="RollDice();">
41.      <hr>
42.      <p>
43.        Number of rolls: <span id="rollSpan">0</span>
44.      </p>
45.    </div>
46.  </body>
47.  </html>
```

Figure 11.7 Web page that uses a counter to keep track of dice rolls.

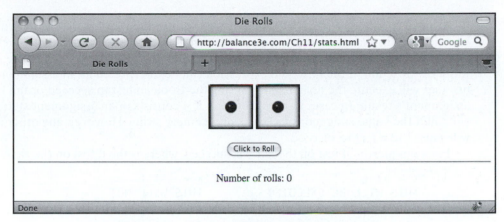

Figure 11.8 `stats.html` rendered in a Web browser.

one). At the end of the observation period, the value stored in the counter represents the number of times that the desired event took place.

The Web page in Figure 11.7 reimplements the `dice.html` page from Chapter 7, now utilizing the `random.js` library from Chapter 9. When the button is clicked, the `RollDice` function is called to select random die images (using the `RandomInt` function) and display them in the page (Figure 11.8). In addition, the page contains a text span (line 43) that keeps a counter of the number of rolls. Initially, this span contains a 0, since no rolls have taken place when the page first loads. Within the `RollDice` function, however, an assignment statement increments the roll counter by accessing the contents of the text span, adding one to that value, and then reassigning the new count back to the span (lines 26–27).

Counters can be combined with if statements to count conditional events, or events that occur only under certain circumstances. For example, in addition to counting the total number of dice rolls, you might also want your `stats.html` page to record how many times doubles occur (i.e., how many times two identical die faces are displayed concurrently in the page). This will require conditional execution, because the counter corresponding to doubles should be incremented only on the condition that the two dice rolls are the same.

EXERCISE 11.6

Enter the `stats.html` text from Figure 11.7 into a new Web page, then load the page in the browser to verify that it behaves as described.

Add an additional text span to your `stats.html` page that serves as a conditional counter, keeping track of the number of times the user rolls doubles. The new SPAN element should appear below the existing one that displays the number of rolls and should be preceded by an appropriate label. Within the `RollDice` function, add an if statement that checks whether the two rolls are identical and, if so, increments the doubles counter in the text span.

Note: Statistically speaking, users should obtain doubles on one-sixth their rolls. This is attributable to the fact that 6 out of the 36 possible dice combinations are doubles. After a reasonable number of rolls, is your doubles count roughly one-sixth of the total number of rolls?

Common errors to avoid...

Despite the apparent similarity of = and ==, it is important to distinguish between the two. As you saw in Chapter 4, = is the assignment operator that programmers use to assign values to variables, images, and text boxes. By contrast, == is a comparison operator for testing equality. When you write a Boolean expression that compares two values, always make sure that you type the proper operator (==).

Most of the time, if you accidentally type = rather than == in a Boolean expression, the browser will display an error message. Unfortunately, there are instances in which this mistake will not generate an immediate error but will instead cause your code to behave in unexpected ways. In particular, if the mistyped expression can be interpreted as an assignment, then the browser will execute the assignment, causing the Boolean test to succeed or fail based on the assignment's result. In cases where a Boolean test consists of an assignment statement, the test will fail if the value assigned is false, 0, or an empty string. However, any other assigned value will cause the if test to succeed.

For example, the if test on the left will succeed, whereas the if test on the right will fail.

```
if (x = 5) {                    if (x = '') {
    THIS WILL BE EXECUTED            THIS WILL NOT
}                               }
```

To avoid such odd behavior, always use the == operator when an equality test is intended.

EXERCISE 11.7

Imagine that users of your stats.html page would like to perform repeated experiments with the dice simulator. It would greatly help these users if they were able to reset the roll and doubles counts within the page. This can be accomplished by reloading the page—that is, by clicking on the browser's reload button or reentering the page's address—but a more elegant solution would be to add another button to the page labeled Reset counters. When the user clicks this button, the values in the two text spans should be reset to 0. Add such a button to your page and verify that it behaves appropriately.

EXERCISE 11.8

There are six different dice combinations that add up to 7: 6-1, 5-2, 4-3, 3-4, 2-5, and 1-6, making it the most common dice roll. Add an additional text span to your stats.html page that keeps track of the number of times the user rolls dice that total 7. The new SPAN element should appear below the existing ones and should be preceded by an appropriate label. Within the RollDice function, add an if statement that checks whether the two rolls add up to 7 and, if so, increments the sevens counter in the text span. This counter should also be reset to 0 when the user clicks on the reset button (from Exercise 11.7).

Once you have done this, use your page to simulate repeated dice rolls. After a reasonable number of rolls, is your sevens count roughly one-sixth of the total number of rolls?

Boolean Expressions

So far, all of the if statements you have written have involved simple tests. This means that each test contained a single comparison using one of the Boolean operators: == (equal to), ! = (not equal to), < (less than), > (greater than), <= (less than or equal to), and >= (greater than or equal to). For example, the simple test in the following if statement involves evaluating the sum of two variables, roll1 and roll2. If the sum is 8 then the Boolean expression (roll1 + roll2 == 8) will evaluate to true, and the code inside the if statement will be executed.

```
if (roll1 + roll2 == 8) {
    // code to be executed if sum is 8
}
```

In more complex applications, however, simple comparisons between two values may not be adequate to express the conditions under which code should execute. Suppose, for example, that you wanted to count the number of times that both die faces in `stats.html` display four dots (we call this a 4-4 combination). Simply testing the sum of the two die faces would not suffice, as this would not distinguish between 4-4 and other combinations that total 8, such as 3-5 and 2-6. Instead, the values of both die faces must be tested to determine that they are both 4s.

One option for creating this type of two-part test is to nest one if statement inside another. Because the browser evaluates the nested if statement only if the outer test succeeds, the code inside the nested if statement is executed on the condition that both tests succeed. The following example contains nested if statements that form a two-part test:

```
if (roll1 == 4) {
  if (roll2 == 4) {
    // code for incrementing the 4-4 counter
  }
}
```

Fortunately, JavaScript provides a more natural and compact alternative for expressing multipart tests. The `&&` operator, when placed between two Boolean tests, represents the conjunction of those tests. This operator is referred to as logical AND, because the Boolean expression (TEST1 `&&` TEST2) will evaluate to `true` if TEST1 is `true` and TEST2 is `true`. Consider the following example:

```
if (roll1 == 4 && roll2 == 4) {
    // code for incrementing the 4-4 counter
}
```

As `&&` represents conjunction, the Boolean expression (`roll1 == 4 && roll2 == 4`) will evaluate to `true` only if both (`roll1 == 4`) and (`roll2 == 4`) evaluate to `true`. That is, the test will succeed if both values are 4s.

Similarly, a disjunction of tests is accomplished in JavaScript using the `||` operator. This operator is referred to as logical OR, because the Boolean expression (TEST1 `||` TEST2) will evaluate to true if either TEST1 is `true` or TEST2 is `true`. For example, the Boolean expression (`roll1 == 4 || roll2 == 4`) will evaluate to `true` if either (`roll1 == 4`) or (`roll2 == 4`) evaluates to `true`. That is, the test will succeed if either of the rolls is a 4.

Finally, the negation of a test is accomplished in JavaScript using the `!` operator. This operator is referred to as logical NOT, because the Boolean expression (`!TEST`) will evaluate to `true` if TEST is not `true`. For example, the Boolean expression (`!(roll1 == 4 && roll2 == 4)`) will evaluate to `true` if (`roll1 == 4 && roll2 == 4`) is `false`. That is, the test will succeed as long as double 4s are not obtained.

The `&&`, `||`, and `!` operators are known as *logical connectives*, because programmers use them to build complex logical expressions by combining simpler logical expressions.

EXERCISE 11.9

In gambling circles, the combination of a 3 and 4 (in either order) is known as a *natural seven*. Add an additional text span to your `stats.html` page that keeps track of the number of natural sevens that are rolled. The new SPAN element should appear below the existing ones and should be preceded by an appropriate label. Within the `RollDice` function, add code that increments the natural sevens counter in the text span. This counter should also be reset to 0 when the user clicks on the reset button (from Exercise 11.7).

Once you have done this, use your page to simulate repeated dice rolls. How frequently would you expect to obtain a natural seven? Do the results of your repeated simulations match your expectations?

Common errors to avoid...

Note that logical connectives must be applied to complete Boolean expressions. For example, imagine that you want to test whether the first die in dice.html displays either a 3 or a 4. A common beginner's mistake would be to write partial expressions using the logical OR operator, such as:

```
(roll1 == 3 || 4)
```

However, to test this condition correctly, full comparisons must appear on each side of the logical connective:

```
(roll1 == 3 || roll1 == 4).
```

Example: Slot Machine

A rapidly growing sector of electronic commerce is in the area of online gambling. Since the Internet crosses international borders, online casinos are often able to circumvent federal gambling laws and provide unregulated gambling through the Internet. Whether for real money or just for entertainment, a multitude of online gambling sites are accessible via the Web.

A slot machine, also known as a one-armed bandit, is a gambling device that involves three or more random images called slots (Figure 11.9). When the user pulls a mechanical arm or pushes a button, these slot images rotate at random. If the slot images match at the end of the spin, the player wins; otherwise, the player loses.

The Web page in Figure 11.10 simulates a simple slot machine. It contains three images, initially displaying cherries, a lemon, and a bar (Figure 11.11). When the user clicks on the button, the SpinSlots function is called to randomly select a new image for each slot (using the RandomOneOf function from random.js).

In a real slot machine, the player must enter some number of credits in order to play the game. The player wins if the spin results in all three slots displaying the same image. While most slot machines differentiate between different matches (e.g., paying out more for matching bars as opposed to

Figure 11.9 Slot machine.

```
1.  <!doctype html>
2.  <!-- slots.html                                        Dave Reed -->
3.  <!-- This page simulates a simple slot machine with 3 slots. -->
4.  <!-- ===================================================== -->
5.
6.  <html>
7.   <head>
8.    <title> Slot Machine </title>
9.    <script type="text/javascript" src="http://balance3e.com/random.js">
10.   </script>
11.   <script type="text/javascript">
12.     function SpinSlots()
13.     // Assumes: slot images are in http://balance3e.com/Images
14.     // Results: displays 3 random slot images
15.     {
16.       var slot1, slot2, slot3;
17.
18.       slot1 = RandomOneOf(['lemon', 'cherry', 'bar', 'donut']);
19.       slot2 = RandomOneOf(['lemon', 'cherry', 'bar', 'donut']);
20.       slot3 = RandomOneOf(['lemon', 'cherry', 'bar', 'donut']);
21.
22.       document.getElementById('slot1Img').src =
23.           'http://balance3e.com/Images/' + slot1 + '.jpg';
24.       document.getElementById('slot2Img').src =
25.           'http://balance3e.com/Images/' + slot2 + '.jpg';
26.       document.getElementById('slot3Img').src =
27.           'http://balance3e.com/Images/' + slot3 + '.jpg';
28.     }
29.   </script>
30.  </head>
31.
32.  <body>
33.   <div style="text-align:center">
34.    <p>
35.      <img id="slot1Img" border=1 alt="slot image"
36.          src="http://balance3e.com/Images/cherry.jpg">
37.      <img id="slot2Img" border=1 alt="slot image"
38.          src="http://balance3e.com/Images/lemon.jpg">
39.      <img id="slot3Img" border=1 alt="slot image"
40.          src="http://balance3e.com/Images/bar.jpg">
41.    </p>
42.    <input type="button" value="Click to Spin" onclick="SpinSlots();">
43.   </div>
44.  </body>
45. </html>
```

Figure 11.10 Web page that simulates a simple slot machine.

matching lemons), we will not make this distinction. Any combination of three identical slots will be considered a winner.

EXERCISE 11.10

Enter the slots.html text from Figure 11.10 into a new Web page, then load the page in the browser to verify that it behaves as described.

Modify your page so that it simulates a slot machine, with the player's credits displayed in a text span in the page. When the game begins, the number of credits should start at 20. Each spin of the slots should cost the player one credit. If all three slot images match, however, the player wins and is

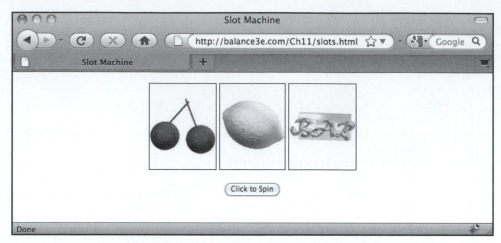

Figure 11.11 `slots.html` rendered in a Web browser.

credited with 13 credits (for a net gain of 12 credits). In addition, an alert window should appear to notify the player of the winning spin. Augment the `SpinSlots` function so that the number of credits is updated appropriately on each spin.

Note: As is the case with all organized gambling, the odds here favor the house. Since there are four different images that can appear in a slot, there is a 1 in 16 chance of all three slots coming up the same. Thus, you would expect (in the long run) for the player to win 1 out of every 16 spins. Consequently, the payoff of $13 does not quite offset the $16 cost of the spins. As a result, you are more likely to lose money (in the long run) than win money. Perform numerous simulations with your updated page to see if this pattern holds.

Designer Secrets

Most of the interactive Web pages we have considered so far have utilized page divisions for displaying dynamic text in the page. In this chapter, however, we have seen pages that utilize text spans (Figure 11.8) and alert windows (Figure 11.11) The following general guidelines can help to decide which type of display element is best suited to a Web page.

- DIV element: A page division is most appropriate when the Web page must display an entire message as a result of an action. For example, the grade calculator page (Chapter 5) calculated a student's course average given his individual grades, displaying the average in a page division. Since it doesn't make sense to display anything until the user has entered his grades, the page division is initially empty. Each time the user clicks the button, however, a complete message containing the calculated average is displayed in the division.
- SPAN element: A text span is most appropriate when the Web page must display a more constant message, with small parts that change as a result of actions. For example, the dice stats page (Figure 11.8) always displays the number of rolls at the bottom of the page. Initially, the text "Number of rolls: 0" is displayed, with the number part of that message enclosed in a SPAN element. Thus, the contents of that text span can be updated after each roll without altering the first part of the message.
- ALERT window: An alert window is most appropriate when the Web page must display a temporary message, such as a warning or notice of some special event. For example, the slot machine page (Exercise 11.10) uses an alert window to alert the user to a winning spin. Since this is a fairly uncommon and important event, the pop-up window draws the user's attention more effectively than a message embedded in the page.

EXERCISE 11.11

As is, your page does not recognize when a player has run out of money. It is possible for the user to play your slots game even after the number of credits becomes 0, and the credits can become negative as a result. Any smart casino owner would put a stop to this immediately. Add code to SpinSlots that disallows a spin if the player's credits have reached 0. In particular, the existing code for simulating the spin and displaying the results should only be executed if the player has money.

EXERCISE 11.12

In a real slot machine, the player always has the option of adding more credits to the machine and continuing play indefinitely (or until they go completely broke). Add an additional button to your page labeled Add 20 credits. When the user clicks this button, 20 credits should be added to the credit total on the page.

Looking Ahead...

In this chapter, you were introduced to the if statement, which specifies conditional execution in JavaScript code. An if statement is known as a control statement, because its purpose is to control the execution of other JavaScript statements. In it simplest form, an if statement allows the browser to skip over a section of code if some condition (expressed as a Boolean test) fails to hold. When an else case is included, an if statement can decide between two alternative sections of code, executing one or the other depending on the result of the Boolean test. If more than two alternatives must be considered, programmers can nest multiple if statements to create a cascading if-else structure. As the examples in the chapter demonstrated, the ability to write code that makes choices can greatly enhance a programmer's expressive power. Using if statements, you can write code that reacts to user input, displays different images on the basis of random dice rolls, and even maintains statistics concerning a series of repeated dice rolls.

Up to this point, you have used the data types provided by JavaScript (number, string, and Boolean) as abstractions. For example, you thought of a number as representing a value (in decimal notation) and a string as representing a sequence of characters (enclosed in quotes). You learned to store and manipulate such values without worrying about how the various data types were actually implemented. In the next chapter, Chapter 12, you will look more closely at the representation of data—including numbers, strings, and Booleans—inside computers. In particular, you will learn that computers store and process all data values as binary signals. When numbers are represented in binary, the mappings are relatively straightforward. By contrast, the mapping of string and Boolean values to their binary equivalents is a matter of convention, rather than inherent logic. To represent other kinds of data, such as sound and images, computers must apply complex algorithms that compress the data or make it easier to store in binary form. Understanding how data is represented inside the computer should prove useful in later programming chapters as you approach more complex tasks, including counter-controlled repetition and structured data (e.g., strings and arrays).

Chapter Summary

- Conditional execution refers to a program's ability to execute a statement or sequence of statements only if some condition holds. In JavaScript, conditional execution is performed using if statements.

- The general form of an if statement is as follows, where the else case is optional:

```
if (BOOLEAN_TEST) {
    STATEMENTS_EXECUTED_IF_TRUE
} else {
    STATEMENTS_EXECUTED_IF_FALSE
}
```

If the Boolean test succeeds (evaluates to `true`), then the browser executes the code inside the subsequent curly braces. If the test fails (evaluates to `false`) and there is an else case, then the code inside the curly braces following the else is executed.

- The following relational operators can be used to build simple Boolean expressions: `==` (equal to), `!=` (not equal to), `<` (less than), `<=` (less than or equal to), `>` (greater than), and `>=` (greater than or equal to).

- Programmers can write code that chooses among an arbitrary number of alternative cases by using a cascading if-else statement, which is really nothing more than a series of nested if statements. The general form of a cascading if-else statement is as follows:

```
if (TEST1) {
    STATEMENTS_EXECUTED_IF_TEST1_SUCCEEDS
}
else if (TEST_2) {
    STATEMENTS_EXECUTED_IF_TEST2_SUCCEEDS
}
else if (TEST_3) {
    STATEMENTS_EXECUTED_IF_TEST3_SUCCEEDS
}
    .
    .
    .
else {
    STATEMENTS_IF_ELSE
}
```

- A variable that records the number of occurrences of some event is known as a counter. To function properly, a counter must be initialized to 0, then incremented (increased by one) each time the desired event occurs.

- The conjunction (`&&`), disjunction (`||`), and negation (`!`) operators are known as logical connectives, as they are used to build complex logical expressions by combining simpler logical expressions.

- A Boolean expression involving conjunction (`&&`) will evaluate to true if all its components evaluate to true—for example, (`true && true`) evaluates to `true`.

- A Boolean expression involving disjunction (`||`) will evaluate to true if any of its components evaluate to true—for example, (`true || false`) evaluates to `true`.

- A Boolean expression involving negation (`!`) will evaluate to true if the expression following the negation operator is not true—for example, (`! false`) evaluates to `true`.

Supplemental Material and Exercises

More Practice with Nested Ifs

If statements, especially when they are nested or involve logical connectives, can be tricky to follow. Additional exercises may prove beneficial.

Consider the following code segment containing a nested if-else statement:

```
if (x >= y) {
    if (x*10 < 100) {
        alert('ONE');
    }
    else {
        alert('TWO');
    }
}
else {
    alert('THREE');
}
```

Given the following assignments, predict the behavior of the preceding code.

```
x=0;    y=5;
x=0;    y=-5;
x=9;    y=9;
x=22;   y=21;
```

Consider the following code segment containing an if-else statement:

```
if (x > y) {
    y = x;
}
else if (x == y) {
    x = 100;
}
alert('x = ' + x + ', y = ' + y);
```

Given the following assignments, predict the output that the preceding code would produce:

```
x=0;    y=5;
x=0;    y=-5;
x=9;    y=9;
x=22;   y=21;
```

Create a Web page named `classify.html` that reads in a number entered by the user and then determines whether that number is positive, negative, or zero. The page should contain a text box in which the user can enter the number and a button for initiating the analysis. When the user inputs the desired number and clicks the button, a function should be called to identify the number's type and display the result in a page division. Be sure to `parseFloat` the contents of the text box before testing the value. Load your page and verify that it correctly identifies positive, negative, and zero values.

Imagine that variables `roll1`, `roll2`, and `roll3` represent three die rolls (each storing a value between 1 and 6). Examine the following Boolean expressions, then describe in English the condition that each represents.

```
(roll1 == 1 && roll2 == 1)
((roll1 + roll2 == 11) || (roll1 + roll2 == 12))
(roll1 > 2 && roll1 < 5)
(roll3 < 3 || roll3 > 4)
(roll1 == roll2 && roll2 == roll3)
(roll1 == 1 && roll2 == 1 && roll3 == 1)
```

Does the following expression correctly represent the condition that all three die rolls are different? That is, does this expression evaluate to `true` if all three variables have unique values but evaluate to `false` in all other cases? If you believe that the expression accurately represents this condition, justify your claim. If not, provide a correct expression that performs the task.

```
(roll1 != roll2 && roll2 != roll3)
```

Extreme Weather

In the Supplemental Material section of Chapter 9, you wrote several weather-related functions and stored them in the library file `weather.js`. In particular, the `DewPoint` function calculated the dew point given a temperature and relative humidity. At the time, we ignored the fact that the formulas for heat index and wind chill are only valid under certain conditions.

- The dew point is only valid if the humidity is at least 50%.
- The wind chill is only valid if the temperature is at least 50 degrees. In addition, a calm wind (wind speed of 3 miles per hour or less) does not affect the wind chill. That is, the wind chill index is identical to the temperature when the wind speed is 3 miles per hour or less. Otherwise, the wind chill is defined using the formula from Chapter 9.

EXERCISE 11.17

Modify the `DewPoint` and `WindChill` functions in `weather.js` to implement these more robust definitions. In particular, both functions should return NaN if called with invalid inputs, and the `WindChill` function should be updated to handle calm winds. Test your modified functions in your `indexes.html` page (from Exercise 9.7) to verify that they behave as desired.

To a casual user planning his winter day, the meaning of the wind chill index might not be obvious. In particular, the average user might not recognize when extreme weather cold poses a health danger. The National Weather Service (`http://www.nws.noaa.gov`) issues health warnings when the wind chill index suggests potential danger (Figure 11.12).

Wind Chill Warnings	
≤ −60°	Extreme Danger — frostbite could occur within 5 minutes.
≤ −45°	Danger — frostbite could occur within 10 minutes.
≤ −25°	Caution — frostbite could occur within 30 minutes.

Figure 11.12 Warnings associated with extreme wind chill indexes.

EXERCISE 11.18

Augment your `indexes.html` page so that in addition to displaying the wind chill index when the user clicks the button, it also displays a health warning message when appropriate. For example, Figure 11.13 shows the appearance of the page when the wind chill reaches the Danger category (≤ –45º).

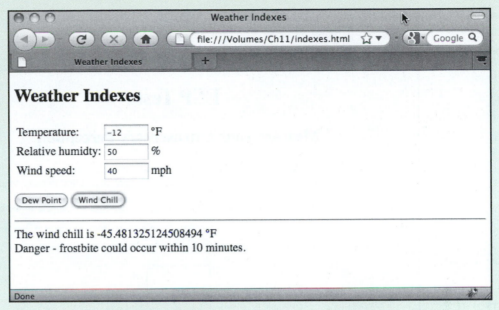

Figure 11.13 Sample appearance of the enhanced weather indexes page.

Example: Designing an ESP Test

Although no scientific evidence supports the existence of extrasensory perception (ESP), some people still believe in its legitimacy. A standard test for determining whether someone has ESP involves a deck of cards with various shapes on them. The test subject is shown the backs of cards and asked to guess the shapes on the reverse sides. If the subject is able to guess the correct shape more frequently than would be expected, then a claim of ESP might be made.

For example, suppose that each card in the deck displayed one of four different shapes. Guessing at random, a person could be expected to pick the correct shape 25% of the time. If the subject were able to consistently guess correctly more than 25% of the time, then some people might view this as evidence of ESP.

Chapter 9 presented two interactive Web pages that implemented rudimentary ESP tests. The first page (Figure 9.2) asked the user to think of a number and then displayed a randomly selected value at the click of a button. The second page (Figure 9.4) allowed the user to select his guess by clicking on one of four buttons, and that guess was displayed along with the random selection. In both of these pages, it was the responsibility of the user to check whether his guess was correct. Now that you know how to write an if statement, you can write a more advanced page that checks the user's guess automatically. Your new page can also include a counter to keep track of how many times the user is right during a sequence of guesses.

EXERCISE 11.19

Design and implement a Web page named `esp.html` that allows the user to conduct an ESP test. Your page should look something like the one in Figure 11.14. The rectangle containing a question mark represents the back of a card that is associated with a particular shape. After contemplating which shape appears on the front of the card, the user clicks the button corresponding to the shape he or she believes is on the card (here, four possibilities are assumed). After each guess, the question mark should be replaced by a randomly selected shape, and an alert box should notify the user as to whether the guess was correct. Statistics concerning the number and percentage of correct guesses should be maintained in text spans. After the statistics have been updated and the alert box has been closed, the page should restore the question-mark image, enabling the user to enter another guess.

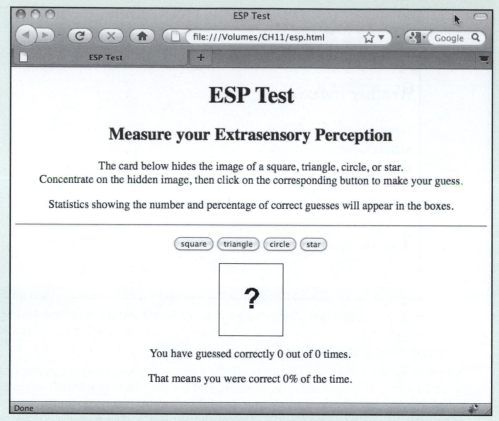

Figure 11.14 Sample appearance of the enhanced ESP test page.

Although you can create your own images for the cards, you can also use the images provided for you in the `http://balance3e.com/Images` directory. This directory contains images of four shapes—`square.gif`, `triangle.gif`, `circle.gif`, and `star.gif`—as well as `mystery.gif`, which displays the question mark.

EXERCISE 11.20

Using your `esp.html` page, test yourself for ESP. After 10 guesses, what is your percentage of correct guesses? After 20 guesses? After 50 guesses? How compelling do you find these percentages to be in deciding whether you have ESP? Justify your answer.

Example: Designing a Dot Race

A common event at sporting events is the running of dot races on the scoreboard. In a dot race, dots of different colors speed around a track, and members of the crowd are encouraged to cheer for different dots. Every few seconds, each dot moves forward a different random amount; the dot that reaches the finish line first is the winner.

EXERCISE 11.21

Design and implement a Web page named `dotrace.html` that allows the user to simulate a race between two dots. Your page should look something like the one in Figure 11.15. The length of the race (i.e., the goal distance) is entered by the user in a text box, and the positions of the two dots (initially 0) are displayed in text spans. Each time the user clicks the button labeled Take a Step,

Figure 11.15 Sample appearance of the dot race page.

each dot should move forward a random amount (either one, two, or three units). When one of the dots crosses the finish line—meaning that its current position is greater than or equal to the goal distance—an alert box should appear to identify the winner. Note that it is possible for the dots to tie if both cross the finish line on the same step. Thus, your code must be able to recognize a tied race and display an appropriate message in the alert box.

EXERCISE 11.22

Augment your `dotrace.html` page so that users can initiate repeated races without having to reload the page. You can accomplish this by adding a button labeled New Race; when a user clicks this button, the positions of the dots should be reset to 0. If the user clicks the Take a Step button after the current race is complete, an alert box should appear directing the user to click the New Race button and begin a new race.

12 Chapter

Data Representation

This chapter uses narrative, illustrations, hands-on experimentation, and review questions to introduce computer science and technology concepts.

Drama is life with the dull bits cut out.

Alfred Hitchcock

Digital is to analog as steps are to ramps.

Anonymous

There are only 10 different kinds of people in the world: those who know binary and those who don't.

Anonymous

In Chapter 1, we defined a computer as a device that receives, stores, and processes information. This chapter returns to the concepts of data and storage, detailing how data is represented inside a computer. Most computers store data as digital signals (i.e., sequences of 0s and 1s), but the technology used to retain these signals varies greatly, depending on the storage device and type of data. For example, we explained in Chapter 1 that RAM memory stores data as electrical currents in circuitry, whereas CD-ROMs store data as sequences of pits burned into the disk. However, despite differences among storage technologies, most employ the same sets of rules for converting data into 1s and 0s. For example, nearly all programs use the same coding standard for specifying text characters as 8-bit patterns. Similar conventions exist for representing other data types, including numbers and images.

This chapter describes common formats and standards that computers use to maintain data. After covering the basics of digital representation, we explain how specific data types such as integers, real numbers, and text are stored on computers. Because most data representations involve binary numbers, a review of binary-number systems is also provided. The chapter concludes by describing common techniques for storing complex data, including sound, images, and movies.

Analog vs. Digital

Data can be stored electronically in two ways, either as **analog** or **digital** signals. Analog signals represent data in a way that is *analog*ous to real life, in that such signals

Figure 12.1 Two radios with different frequency displays. On the old-fashioned radio to the left, the dial allows the user to select the frequency on a continuous scale. On the modern Bose® Wave® radio to the right, a digital display allows the user to select the frequency in predetermined increments.

can vary across an infinite range of values. By contrast, digital signals utilize only a discrete (finite) set of values.

For example, radio signals are inherently analog, as their frequencies are measured on a continuous scale. AM radio stations broadcast at frequencies ranging from 535 to 1,700 kilohertz, whereas FM radio stations broadcast at frequencies ranging from 88 to 108 megahertz. Older radio devices, such as the one pictured on the left in Figure 12.1, imitated radio's analog nature by representing frequency as a position on a dial. The user tuned the radio receiver by turning the dial, whose position could specify any value on a continuum. By contrast, most modern radios represent selected frequencies as discrete values, which appear as numbers on a display panel (as in the radio to the right in Figure 12.1). For example, users of most digital radios can select FM frequencies in increments of 0.1 megahertz, such as 106.7 and 106.8, and AM frequencies in increments of 10 kilohertz, such as 1480 and 1490. Frequencies between these increments are not representable on the radio and thus cannot be selected.

Like radio frequencies, many other types of data can be represented alternatively as analog or digital signals, depending on the particular device or technology involved. An analog thermometer, for instance, contains a column of liquid, such as alcohol or mercury, and specifies different temperatures as the height of the column changes. A digital thermometer is different in that it represents the temperature as a discrete number, usually measured in increments of 0.1 degrees. Similarly, an analog clock consists of hands that circle a numbered dial, where the hands' positions indicate the current time. By contrast, a digital clock displays the time as a series of discrete numbers specifying the hour, minutes, and possibly seconds. More complex data can also be represented in either analog or digital form. Later in this chapter, you will learn that audio cassettes store sound as analog signals on a magnetic tape, whereas compact disks (CDs) store sound as digital signals on the surface of a disk.

The primary trade-off between analog and digital data representation is variability versus reproducibility. Because an analog system encompasses a continuous range of values, a much greater number of unique signals can be represented. For example, the dial on an analog radio receiver allows you to find the exact frequency corresponding to the best possible reception for a particular station. However, this dial setting may be difficult to reproduce. If you switched to another station for a while and then wanted to return to the previous one, relocating the perfect frequency setting would involve fine-tuning the dial all over again. With a digital radio receiver, you might need to round the optimal frequency (such as 106.899) to the nearest represented alternative (106.9). However, a digital setting such as 106.9 megahertz can be remembered and reselected easily.

In general, analog representations are sufficient for storing data that is highly variable but does not have to be reproduced exactly. Analog radios are functional because station frequencies do not need to be precise—you can listen to a station repeatedly without specifying the perfect optimal frequency every time. Likewise, analog thermometers and clocks are adequate for most purposes, as a person rarely needs to reproduce the exact temperature or time—rough estimates based on looking at the devices usually suffice. However, the disadvantages of analog representation can cause problems under certain circumstances. For example, a radio astronomer might require a precise record of a frequency, or a scientist conducting an experiment might need to reproduce an exact temperature.

When it comes to storing data on a computer, reproducibility is paramount. If even a single bit is changed in a file, the meaning of the data can be drastically altered. Thus, modern computers are digital devices that save and manipulate data as discrete values. The specific means of storage depends on the technology used. For example, an electrical wire might carry voltage or no voltage, a switch might be open or closed, a capacitor might be charged or not charged, a location on a magnetic disk might be magnetized or not magnetized, and a location on a CD-ROM might be reflective or nonreflective. What all these technologies have in common is that they distinguish between only two possibilities. The simplest and most effective digital storage systems include two distinct (binary) states, typically referred to as 0 and 1. Thus, a voltage-carrying wire or a magnetized spot on a floppy disk can be thought of as a 1, whereas a wire with no voltage or a nonmagnetized spot can be thought of as a 0. Because these 1s and 0s—called binary digits, or bits—are central to computer data representation, the next section provides an overview of binary number systems.

Binary Numbers

As humans, we are used to thinking of numbers in their decimal (base 10) form, in which individual digits correspond to escalating powers of ten. When dealing with decimal integers, the rightmost digit is the 1s place ($10^0 = 1$), the next digit is the 10s place ($10^1 = 10$), the next is the 100s place ($10^2 = 100$), and so on. Our use of the decimal number system can be seen as a natural result of evolution, since humans first learned to count on ten fingers. Evolutionary bias aside, however, numbers can be represented using any base, including binary (base 2). In the binary number system, all values are represented using only the two binary digits, 0 and 1; these digits are called **bits**. As with decimal numbers, different digits in a binary number correspond to different powers—however, the digits specify ascending powers of 2, instead of 10. This means that the rightmost bit is the 1s place ($2^0 = 1$), the next bit is the 2s place ($2^1 = 2$), the next the 4s place ($2^2 = 4$), and so on. To distinguish binary numbers from their decimal counterparts, people typically add a subscript identifying the base. For example, 1101_2 would represent the binary number that is equivalent to 13 in decimal (Figure 12.2).

Converting a binary number to its decimal equivalent is easy: simply multiply each bit (either 1 or 0) by its corresponding power of 2 and then sum the results. The examples in Figure 12.3 illustrate the process of converting a number from binary (base 2) to decimal (base 10).

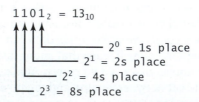

$$1101_2 = 13_{10}$$

2^0 = 1s place
2^1 = 2s place
2^2 = 4s place
2^3 = 8s place

Figure 12.2 Bit positions in a binary number.

Binary Number	Decimal Equivalent
$11_2 \rightarrow$	$1*2 + 1*1 = 3$
$1101_2 \rightarrow$	$1*8 + 1*4 + 0*2 + 1*1 = 13$
$10011_2 \rightarrow$	$1*16 + 0*8 + 0*4 + 1*2 + 1*1 = 19$
$100110_2 \rightarrow$	$1*32 + 0*16 + 0*8 + 1*4 + 1*2 + 0*1 = 38$

Figure 12.3 Converting from binary (base 2) to decimal (base 10).

```
Converting 19 to binary:

19 is odd   → B =       1,   D = Math.floor(19/2) = 9
 9 is odd   → B =      11,   D = Math.floor(9/2)  = 4
 4 is even  → B =     011,   D = Math.floor(4/2)  = 2
 2 is even  → B =    0011,   D = Math.floor(2/2)  = 1
 1 is odd   → B =   10011,   D = Math.floor(1/2)  = 0


Converting 116 to binary:

116 is even → B =       0,   D = Math.floor(116/2) = 58
 58 is even → B =      00,   D = Math.floor(58/2)  = 29
 29 is odd  → B =     100,   D = Math.floor(29/2)  = 14
 14 is even → B =    0100,   D = Math.floor(14/2)  = 7
  7 is odd  → B =   10100,   D = Math.floor(7/2)   = 3
  3 is odd  → B =  110100,   D = Math.floor(3/2)   = 1
  1 is odd  → B = 1110100,   D = Math.floor(1/2)   = 0
```

Figure 12.4   Converting from decimal (base 10) to binary (base 2).

The opposite conversion—from decimal to binary—is a little trickier, but still relatively straight-forward. The following algorithm describes the conversion of positive decimal numbers to binary. Because the algorithm is worded using computer terminology, it could be translated easily into a programming language.

Algorithm for converting positive decimal number D to binary number B:

1. Initialize B to be empty.
2. As long as D is nonzero, repeatedly:
   a. If D is even, add 0 to the left of B.
   b. If D is odd, add 1 to the left of B.
   c. Divide D by 2 and round down (i.e., D = Math.floor(D/2))

As an example, Figure 12.4 shows the steps required to convert the decimal values 19 and 116 into binary (10011_2 and 1110100_2, respectively).

Representing Integers

As computers retain all information as bits (0 or 1), binary numbers provide a natural means of storing integer values. When an integer value must be saved in a computer, its binary equivalent can be encoded as a bit pattern and stored using the appropriate digital technology. Thus, the integer 19 can be stored as the bit pattern 10011, whereas 116 can be stored as 1110100. However, because binary numbers contain varying numbers of bits, it can be difficult for a computer to determine where one value in memory ends and another begins. Most computers and programs avoid this problem by employing fixed-width integers. That is, each integer is represented using the same number of bits (usually 32 bits). Leading 0s are placed in front of each binary number to fill the 32 bits. Thus, a computer would represent 19 as:

00000000000000000000000000010011

Given that each integer is 32 bits long, $2^{32} = 4,294,967,296$ different bit patterns can be represented. By convention, the patterns are divided as evenly as possible between positive and negative integers. Thus, programs that use 32-bit integers can store $2^{32}/2 = 2^{31} = 2,147,483,648$ non-negative numbers (including 0) and $2^{32}/2 = 2^{31} = 2,147,483,648$ negative numbers. The mapping between integers and bit patterns is summarized in Figure 12.5.

While examining the integer representations in Figure 12.5, you may have noticed that the bit patterns starting with a 1 correspond to negative values, while those starting with a 0 bit correspond to

Bit Pattern	Decimal Value
10000000000000000000000000000000	$(-2^{31} = -2,147,483,648)$
10000000000000000000000000000001	$(-2^{31}+1 = -2,147,483,647)$
10000000000000000000000000000010	$(-2^{31}+2 = -2,147,483,646)$
.	
.	
.	
11111111111111111111111111111101	(-3)
11111111111111111111111111111110	(-2)
11111111111111111111111111111111	(-1)
00000000000000000000000000000000	$(\ 0)$
00000000000000000000000000000001	$(\ 1)$
00000000000000000000000000000010	$(\ 2)$
00000000000000000000000000000011	$(\ 3)$
.	
.	
.	
01111111111111111111111111111101	$(2^{31}-3 = 2,147,483,645)$
01111111111111111111111111111110	$(2^{31}-2 = 2,147,483,646)$
01111111111111111111111111111111	$(2^{31}-1 = 2,147,483,647)$

Figure 12.5   Representing integers as bit patterns.

non-negative values. Thus, the initial bit in each pattern acts as the ***sign bit*** for the integer. When the sign bit is 0, then the remaining bits are consistent with the binary representation of that integer. For example, the bit pattern corresponding to 3 begins with 0 (the sign bit) and ends with the 31-bit binary representation of 3: 00000000000000000000000000000011. Similarly, the bit pattern corresponding to 100 consists of a 0 followed by the 31-bit representation of 100: 00000000000000000000000001100100. If we wanted to encode negative integers using this method, we could write each as a 1 followed by the binary representation of the negative integer's absolute value. However, there are several drawbacks to such a representation. First, this system would identify the pattern 10000000000000000000000000000000 as representing negative zero. As actual number systems contain only one zero, which is neither positive nor negative, the inclusion of two zeros would be unnecessary and confusing. Second, the process of adding binary values would become unnecessarily complicated (see Chapter 14 for details).

To avert these difficulties, computers assign bit patterns to negative numbers in the exact opposite order. This means that the negative integer with the largest absolute value (2^{-31}) corresponds to the smallest bit pattern (10000000000000000000000000000000), whereas the negative integer with the smallest absolute value (-1) corresponds to the largest bit pattern (11111111111111111111111111111111). In addition to avoiding a negative zero, this notation, known as ***two's-complement*** notation, greatly simplifies binary addition. As you will learn in Chapter 14, adding binary numbers is a relatively simple generalization of adding decimal numbers, and this generalization holds with negative binary numbers as well, as long as they are represented in two's-complement notation.

Representing Real Numbers

Because digital computers store all data as binary values, the correlation between integers and their binary counterparts is relatively intuitive. Real (i.e., noninteger) values can also be stored in binary, but the mapping is not quite so direct. Recall that, in JavaScript, a real number can be specified in either decimal or scientific notation. For instance, the real number 1234.56 can be equivalently represented as 1.23456e3 (1.23456×10^3). When real numbers are written in scientific notation, their representation is normalized so that only one digit appears to the left of the decimal place. The following examples review the conversion of real numbers from decimal to scientific notation.

1234.56	→	1.23456×10^3
-50.0	→	-5.0×10^1
0.00099	→	9.9×10^{-4}

Any real value can be uniquely identified by the two components of this normalized form: the fractional part (the digits surrounding the decimal place) and the exponent (the power of 10). Furthermore, because the decimal point is always between the first and second digits of the fractional part, it is possible to ignore the decimal point when representing the number. Thus, each component of a real number in scientific notation can be treated as an integer value. For example, the real value 1234.56, which normalizes to 1.23456×10^3, could be represented by the integer pair (123456, 3). Similarly, −50.0, which normalizes to -5.0×10^1, could be represented by the pair (−5, 1); and 0.00099, which normalizes to 9.9×10^{-4}, could be represented by the pair (99, −4). Real numbers stored in this format are known as *floating-point numbers*, since the normalization process shifts (or floats) the decimal point until only one digit appears to the left.

In 1985, the Institute of Electrical and Electronics Engineers (IEEE) established a standard format for storing floating-point values that has since been adopted by virtually all computer and software manufacturers. According to the IEEE standard, a floating-point value can be represented using either 32 bits (4 bytes) or 64 bits (8 bytes). The 32-bit representation, known as *single precision*, allots 24 bits to store the fractional part (including the sign bit) and 8 bits to store the exponent, producing a range of potential positive values that spans from approximately 1.2×10^{-38} to 3.4×10^{38} (with an equivalent range for negative numbers). By contrast, the 64-bit representation, known as *double precision*, allots 53 bits for the fractional part (including the sign bit) and 11 bits for the exponent, yielding a much larger range of potential positive values (from approximately 2.2×10^{-308} to 1.8×10^{308}). (See Figure 12.6.)

Many details of the IEEE single-precision and double-precision formats are beyond the scope of this text. For our purposes, what is important is to recognize that a real value can be converted into a pair of integer values (a fraction and an exponent) that are combined to form a representative binary pattern. It is interesting to note, however, that certain bit patterns are reserved for special values, such as the NaN (Not a Number) value we have encountered in JavaScript.

As there are an infinite number of real values and only a finite number of 32- or 64-bit patterns, it is not surprising that computers are incapable of representing all real values, even among those that fall within the allotted range. When the result of a calculation yields a real value that cannot be represented exactly, the computer will round off the value to the pattern with the closest corresponding value. In a single-precision floating-point number, roughly 7 decimal digits of precision are obtainable. That is, the computer will round off any real value containing more than 7 significant digits.

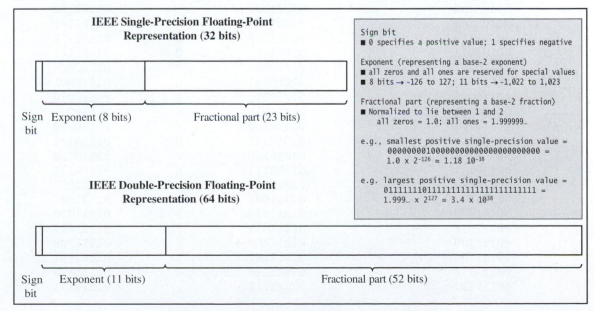

Figure 12.6 IEEE Floating-point representations.

Using double precision, approximately 16 decimal digits of precision are obtainable. The fact that JavaScript uses double precision to represent numbers explains why 0.9999999999999999 (with 16 9s to the right of the decimal) is represented exactly, whereas 0.99999999999999999 (with 17 9s) is rounded up to the value 1.

Most programming languages differentiate between integer and real values, using 32-bit patterns for storing integers and a floating-point format for storing real numbers. However, JavaScript simplifies number representation by providing only a single number type, which encompasses both integers and reals. Thus, all numbers in JavaScript are stored using the IEEE's double-precision floating-point format.

Representing Characters and Strings

Unlike integers and real values, characters have no natural correspondence to binary numbers. Thus, computer scientists must devise arbitrary systems for representing characters as bit patterns. The standard code for representing characters, known as ASCII (American Standard Code for Information Interchange), maps each character to a specific 8-bit pattern. The ASCII codes for the most common characters are listed in Figure 12.7.

ASCII Character Codes					
code	char	code	char	code	char
00100000	space	01000000	@	01100000	`
00100001	!	01000001	A	01100001	a
00100010	"	01000010	B	01100010	b
00100011	#	01000011	C	01100011	c
00100100	$	01000100	D	01100100	d
00100101	%	01000101	E	01100101	e
00100110	&	01000110	F	01100110	f
00100111	'	01000111	G	01100111	g
00101000	(	01001000	H	01101000	h
00101001	)	01001001	I	01101001	i
00101010	*	01001010	J	01101010	j
00101011	+	01001011	K	01101011	k
00101100	'	01001100	L	01101100	l
00101101	–	01001101	M	01101101	m
00101110	.	01001110	N	01101110	n
00101111	/	01001111	O	01101111	o
00110000	0	01010000	P	01110000	p
00110001	1	01010001	Q	01110001	q
00110010	2	01010010	R	01110010	r
00110011	3	01010011	S	01110011	s
00110100	4	01010100	T	01110100	t
00110101	5	01010101	U	01110101	u
00110110	6	01010110	V	01110110	v
00110111	7	01010111	W	01110111	w
00111000	8	01011000	X	01111000	x
00111001	9	01011001	Y	01111001	y
00111010	:	01011010	Z	01111010	z
00111011	;	01011011	[	01111011	{
00111100	<	01011100	\	01111100	|
00111101	=	01011101	]	01111101	}
00111110	>	01011110	^	01111110	~
00111111	?	01011111	_	01111111	delete

Figure 12.7 The ASCII character set.

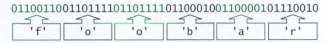

Figure 12.8   Representing a string as a sequence of ASCII codes.

Note that the three character subsets—digits, uppercase letters, and lowercase letters—are each represented using consecutive binary numbers. The digits are assigned the binary numbers with decimal values 48 through 57, the uppercase letters are assigned values 65 through 90, and the lowercase letters are assigned values 97 through 122. These orderings are important, because they enable programs to perform comparisons of character values. For example, the JavaScript expression:

    'a' < 'b'

evaluates to true, because the ASCII code for the character "a" is smaller than the ASCII code for "b". It is also clear from this system that uppercase letters have lower values than lowercase letters do. Thus, the JavaScript expression:

    'A' < 'a'

evaluates to true.

As strings are just sequences of characters, a string can be represented as a sequence of bytes, in which each byte corresponds to the ASCII code for a specific character. For example, the string 'foobar' is specified using the bit pattern listed in Figure 12.8. The first byte (8 bits) in this pattern is the ASCII code for 'f', the second byte is the code for 'o', and so on. This representation explains why, when Chapter 11 introduced JavaScript string comparison, it stated that the two strings are compared character by character, with the string that comes first in alphabetical order evaluating to "less than" the other string.

It should be noted that, although 8-bit ASCII codes are sufficient for representing English text, they are far too small to accommodate certain non-Roman alphabets. The Chinese language, for example, encompasses thousands of characters, and it would be impossible to differentiate between all of them using one byte of memory. As computing becomes more and more international, ASCII is being replaced by Unicode, a 16-bit encoding system capable of supporting most foreign-language character sets. To simplify the transition to Unicode, the designers of the new system made it backward compatible with ASCII; this means that the Unicode for an English-language character is equivalent to its ASCII code, preceded by eight leading 0s. Thus, 'f' is 01100110 in ASCII and 0000000001100110 in Unicode.

Representing Other Types of Data

So far, we have explained how basic data values—including integers, real numbers, characters, and strings—are stored as binary-number patterns inside a computer. When programs store and manipulate values of these types, they employ the representations we have described, along with some special-purpose variations. For example, word processing programs will store text using ASCII codes, but will insert special character symbols to denote formatting information. This technique is analogous to the process of inserting HTML tags within text to specify content and formatting information for the browser.

As you know, computers are capable of representing much more than numbers and characters. However, to store and manipulate complex data efficiently, computers require additional techniques and algorithms. Some of these algorithms allow the computer to convert data into binary, whereas others are used to compress the data, shortening its binary representation. The following sections describe commonly used methods of storing sound and images in computers.

Sounds

Sounds are inherently analog signals. Each particular sound produces a pressure wave with a unique amplitude (height, usually measured in pascals) and frequency (duration over time). For example,

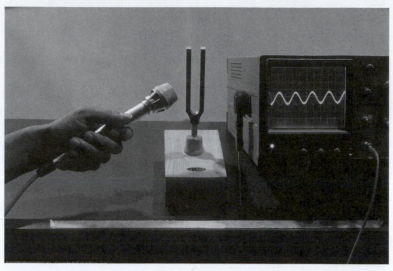

Figure 12.9 The sound produced by a tuning fork is displayed as an analog waveform on an oscilloscope.

Figure 12.9 portrays an *oscilloscope*, a device that records sounds and displays their corresponding waveforms on a screen. In this picture, the sound produced by a tuning fork is illustrated as a waveform on the oscilloscope screen. To demonstrate that different sounds produce different waveforms, Figure 12.10 compares the analog waveforms generated by a tuning fork, a violin, a flute, and a gong. When sound waves such as these reach your ear, they cause your eardrum to vibrate; your brain then interprets that vibration as sound.

The practice of using analog signals to store and manipulate sounds began with the invention of the telephone by Alexander Graham Bell (1875), which was followed almost immediately by Thomas Edison's phonograph (1877). Telephones translate a waveform into electrical signals of varying strengths, which are then sent over a wire and converted back to sound. By contrast, phonographs reproduce sounds by interpreting waveforms stored as grooves of varying depth and width on the surface of a disk. Audio-cassette technology employs a similar method of storing sounds as analog signals: each waveform is translated into signals of varying strengths and then saved as magnetized spots on a tape.

In most cases, the fact that the analog signal stored on a tape cannot always be reproduced exactly is not a major concern. This is because the human ear is unlikely to notice small inconsistencies in a sound recording. However, if a recording is duplicated repeatedly, then small errors can propagate. You may have noticed this if you have ever made a recording of a recording of a recording of a tape. Sound quality deteriorates as errors pile up during repeated recording. By contrast, digital recordings can be reproduced exactly, so a CD can be copied over and over without any deterioration in sound quality.

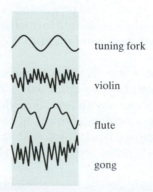

Figure 12.10 Waveforms corresponding to a tuning fork, a violin, a flute, and a gong.

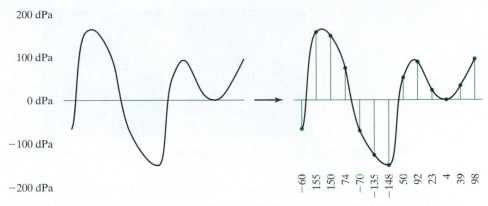

Figure 12.11 Digitizing an analog sound wave. At regular intervals, the amplitude of the waveform (here, measured in decipascals above or below normal air pressure) is recorded as an integer value.

Before a sound can be stored digitally, its analog waveform must be converted to a sequence of discrete values. This is accomplished via ***digital sampling***, in which the amplitude of the wave is measured at regular intervals and then stored as a sequence of discrete measurements (Figure 12.11). To reproduce sounds accurately, frequent measurements must be taken—as many as 44,100 readings per second are needed to achieve CD-quality sound. As a result, even short recordings can require massive amounts of storage. Various techniques have been developed to reduce the size of digital sound files, such as filtering out sounds beyond the range of human hearing, or recognizing when one sound will drown out another and filtering out the weaker sound. The MP3 format, for example, uses techniques such as these to reduce sound-file sizes by a factor of 10 or more without any noticeable reduction in sound quality. Because it enables sound files to be stored in a compact form, MP3 is extremely popular for portable music players and online music distribution (where smaller files allow for faster downloading). In addition to MP3, a variety of proprietary audio formats have been developed by companies for distributing online music. For example, Apple uses a variant of the MP3 format for music it distributes via iTunes.

Images

Like sounds, images are stored using a variety of formats and compression techniques. The simplest format for representing images on a computer is known as a ***bitmap***. A bitmap partitions an image into a grid of dots, called ***pixels*** (short for picture elements), and then converts each pixel into a bit pattern. In the case of black-and-white pictures, each pixel can be represented as a single bit: 0 for a black pixel and 1 for a white pixel. For example, Figure 12.12 shows how a simple black-and-white image can be partitioned into 64 pixels and then stored using 64 bits. It should be noted that the partitions in this example are fairly large, resulting in some pixels that are part white and part black. When this occurs, the pixel is usually assigned a bit value corresponding to the majority color, so a partition that is mostly black will be represented as a 0.

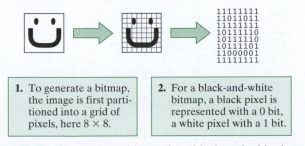

1. To generate a bitmap, the image is first partitioned into a grid of pixels, here 8 × 8.	2. For a black-and-white bitmap, a black pixel is represented with a 0 bit, a white pixel with a 1 bit.

Figure 12.12 Generating a bitmap for a black-and-white image.

Figure 12.13 An image stored using 72 pixels per square inch vs. 36 pixels per square inch.

Resolution is a term that refers to the sharpness or clarity of an image. Because each pixel is assigned a distinct color value, bitmaps that are divided into smaller pixels will yield higher-resolution images. However, every additional pixel increases the necessary storage by one bit. Figure 12.13 illustrates this by comparing the same picture at two different levels of resolution. When stored using 72 pixels per square inch, as shown on the left, the image looks sharp. If the number of pixels is reduced to 36 per square inch, as shown on the right, the image appears blocky, but the storage requirements are cut in half.

When creating a bitmap of a color image, more than one bit is required to represent each pixel. The most common system translates each pixel into a 24-bit code, known as that pixel's **RGB value**. The term RGB refers to the fact that the pixel's color is decomposed into the different intensities of red, green, and blue. Eight bits are allotted to each of the component colors, allowing for intensities ranging from 0 to 255 (with 0 representing a complete lack of that color and 255 representing maximum intensity). Figure 12.14 lists the RGB values for some common HTML colors. Note that different shades of red, such as darkred and maroon, are achieved by adjusting the intensity of the red component. Other colors, such as crimson and pink, require a mixture of the three component colors. Because each color component is associated with 256 possible intensities, $256^3 = 16,777,216$ different color combinations can be represented. Of course, color bitmaps require 24 times more storage than black-and-white bitmaps do, as each pixel requires 24 bits, instead of just one.

If you are familiar with the workings of the Microsoft Windows operating system, you have probably encountered bitmaps before. In Windows, bitmaps are commonly used to represent icons and background images, identified by the extension BMP. Although bitmaps are simple to describe and comprehend, they require a lot of memory to store complex images. For example, a photograph taken with a digital camera might contain as many as 10 megapixels, or 10 million pixels. If each pixel requires 24 bits, then a single photograph would require 30 MB of space. Fortunately, techniques have been developed for compressing images so that they can be stored using less space. The three most common image compression formats on the Web are GIF (Graphics Interchange Format), PNG (Portable Network Graphics), and JPEG (Joint Photographic Experts Group). All three

Common HTML Colors								
color	(R, G, B)		color	(R, G, B)		color	(R, G, B)	
red	(255,	0, 0)	green	(0, 128,	0)	blue	(0, 0, 255)	
darkred	(139,	0, 0)	darkgreen	(0, 100,	0)	darkblue	(0, 0, 139)	
maroon	(128,	0, 0)	forestgreen	(34, 139,	34)	royalblue	(65, 105, 225)	
crimson	(220, 20,	60)	olive	(128, 128,	0)	lightblue	(173, 216, 230)	
pink	(255, 192,	203)	lightgreen	(144, 238,	144)	purple	(128, 0, 128)	
violet	(238, 130,	238)	brown	(165, 42,	42)	gray	(128, 128, 128)	
orange	(255, 165,	0)	white	(255, 255,	255)	black	(0, 0, 0)	

Figure 12.14 Common HTML colors and their (R, G, B) representations.

formats apply algorithms that shorten an image's bit-pattern representation, thus conserving memory and reducing the time it takes to transmit the image over the Internet.

The GIF format uses techniques that identify repetitive patterns in an image and store those patterns efficiently. For example, the sample image in Figure 12.12 includes three entire lines of pixels that are all white. Using the GIF format, this pattern might be stored only once, with a special marker entered in place of each occurrence. By storing frequently occurring patterns only once, the size of the final representation can be reduced. Depending on the type of image, it is not uncommon for the GIF format to reduce the size of the image by a factor of 2 or 4, when compared with a bitmap representation.

While the GIF format has been used extensively on the Web, it has its limitations. Since the format represents each pixel using only 8 bits, a GIF image can display at most 256 different colors. In addition, legal questions surround the use of the format because of patents on parts of it compression algorithm. The PNG format was designed to improve upon the features of GIF and also avoid any patented techniques. It greatly expands the color range of images, allowing up to 64 bits per pixel. In addition, it uses more sophisticated compression techniques than GIF, which can further reduce the size of images (commonly 10% to 50% smaller than GIF).

GIF and PNG are known as *lossless* formats, as no information is lost during the compression. This means that the original image can be extracted exactly. Conversely, JPEG is a *lossy* format, as it employs compression techniques that are not fully reversible. For example, JPEG often compresses several neighboring pixels by storing their average color value. In a color photograph, where color changes tend to be gradual, this approach can greatly reduce the necessary storage for an image (by as much as a factor of 10 or 20) without noticeably degrading the image's quality. In practice, the GIF and PNG formats are typically used for line drawings and other images with discrete boundaries (where precision is imperative); the JPEG format, on the other hand, is most commonly used for photographs (where precision can be sacrificed for the sake of compression).

It is interesting to note that image formats such as GIF, PNG, and JPEG store additional information, or *metadata*, in the image file. For example, a digital image stored in one of these formats might contain metadata identifying its dimensions, the date it was created, and even the model and serial number of the camera or digital scanner that created it. This information can be useful for managing collections of digital images, such as organizing images by date or searching for identifying characteristics. Metadata has also been used as evidence in criminal cases involving copyright violations, assisting authorities in identifying the origin of a photograph.

Movies

In principle, a movie is nothing more than a sequence of still images, or *frames*, that are stored in a sequence. By displaying the frames sequentially at a rate faster than the human eye can distinguish, the illusion of continuity is achieved. For example, Figure 12.13 shows several frames from an old movie. Each frame is an image of a scene taken a fraction of a second later than the previous frame (typically, there are 24 frames per second). A projector displays the frames at the appropriate rate to produce the motion picture on a screen.

When storing a movie digitally, a variety of formats can be used to reduce its size. The most common digital video format on the Web, known as MPEG or MP4, uses many of the same techniques as JPEG to compress the individual frames. In addition, it utilizes complex algorithms to take advantage of similarities between successive frames. For example, note that the frames in Figure 12.15 are very similar, with only minute variations where motion is occurring. After storing the initial frame in its entirety, the MPEG format need only store the changes in each successive frame, greatly reducing the amount of redundant data. While the compression rate depends on the contents of the movie, storing a two-hour movie in roughly 500 MB (or roughly 3 KB per frame) is common using the MPEG format.

Elements of the MPEG format are included in the ATSC (Advanced Television Systems Committee) standard that is used for digital television broadcasts. Other related video compression formats are DVD, used for storing standard movies, and Blu-ray, used for storing high-definition movies.

Figure 12.15   Individual frames of a movie film.

How Computers Distinguish among Data Types

The obvious question you may be asking yourself at this point is: How does the computer know what type of value is stored in a particular piece of memory? If the bit pattern 01100110 is encountered, how can the computer determine whether it represents the integer 97, the character 'a', the exponent for a real number, or even a fragment of an image? The answer is that, without some context, it can't! If a program stores a piece of data in memory, it is up to that program to remember what type of data the particular bit pattern represents. For example, suppose you wrote JavaScript code that assigned the character 'a' to a variable. In addition to storing the corresponding bit pattern (01100110) in memory, the JavaScript interpreter embedded in the browser must accompany this pattern with information about its type, perhaps using additional bits to distinguish among the possible types. When the variable is accessed later in the program's execution, the bit pattern in memory is retrieved along with the additional bits, enabling the interpreter to recognize the data as a character.

The Web page data.html (accessible at http://balance3e.com/Ch12/data.html) illustrates how a computer can interpret the same bit pattern as representing different values, depending on context. The user can enter up to 32 bits in the text box, then click to see how that bit pattern would

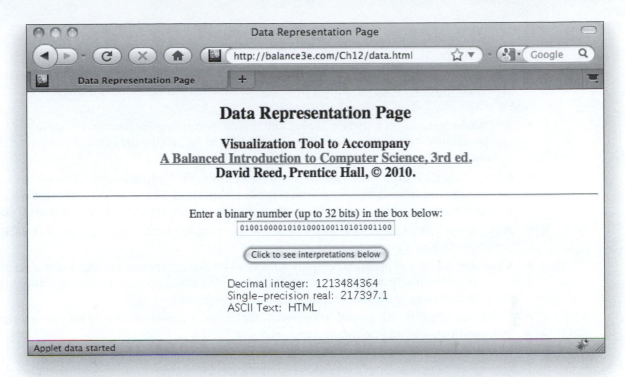

Figure 12.16   A 32-bit number can represent an integer, a real number, or four ASCII characters.

be interpreted as a decimal integer, a single-precision floating-point value, and a sequence of four ASCII characters. Figure 12.16 shows the page converting a sample 32-bit pattern into its corresponding integer, real, and text values.

Looking Ahead...

In this chapter, you studied various methods of representing data inside a computer. As the data operated on by computers must be accessed and reproduced exactly, computers store data as digital signals, which are represented as binary values—patterns of 1s and 0s. Because any numeric value can be represented in binary notation using 1s and 0s, there is a natural correspondence between numbers (both integers and reals) and the standard bit patterns used to identify them. The mapping of text to binary patterns is more arbitrary, but conventions such as the ASCII standard and Unicode ensure that character representations are consistent across machines. More complex data such as sound, images, and movies can also be stored as binary patterns, but advanced algorithms must be applied to such data in order to reduce the representation size.

Understanding how data is represented inside the computer can prove useful as you continue to program and develop Web pages. For example, knowing how characters are represented helps to explain the behavior of string comparisons in JavaScript. Likewise, knowing that not all numbers can be represented exactly inside the computer may help to explain potential errors that may occur in code attributable to rounding. And recognizing the trade-offs between lossy and lossless image formats can assist you in choosing the best format for images in a Web page.

Data representation will be revisited in Chapter 14, when we consider the internal workings of computers and the ways in which data and instructions are stored. But first, we will return to JavaScript programming and problem solving. Chapter 13 introduces an additional JavaScript control statement, the while loop, which will enable you to write programs involving repetition. A while loop is similar to an if statement in that it uses the result of a Boolean test to determine whether other statements are executed. Unlike an if statement, however, a while loop specifies that the statements in the loop are to be executed repeatedly, as long as the test succeeds. Thus, tasks that involve repeating an action over and over can be completed using while loops.

Chapter Summary

- Data can be stored electronically in two ways, either as analog signals (which can vary across an infinite range of values) or as digital signals (which use only a discrete set of values).

- The primary trade-off between analog and digital data representation is variability vs. reproducibility—analog representations are sufficient for storing data that is highly variable but does not have to be reproduced exactly.

- Because each bit of information on a computer is significant, modern computers are digital devices that store data as discrete, reproducible values. The simplest and most effective digital storage systems include two distinct (binary) states, typically referred to as 0 and 1.

- Any integer value can be stored as a binary number—a sequence of bits (0s and 1s), each corresponding to a power of 2.

- Most computers and programs employ a fixed-width integer representation, using a set number of bits (usually 32 bits) for each integer value. Using the two's-complement notation, bit patterns that begin with a 1 are interpreted as negative values.

- Using the IEEE floating-point standard, a real value is represented as a bit pattern that includes fractional and exponent components.

- ASCII (American Standard Code for Information Interchange) is a standard code for representing characters as 8-bit patterns. As computing becomes more and more international, ASCII is being replaced by Unicode, a 16-bit encoding system capable of supporting most foreign-language character sets.

- Before a sound can be stored digitally, its analog waveform must be converted to a sequence of discrete values via digital sampling.

- The MP3 format reduces the size of sound files by using a variety of techniques, such as filtering out sounds that are beyond the range of human hearing or are drowned out by other, louder sounds.

- The simplest digital format for representing images is a bitmap, in which a picture is broken down into a grid of picture elements, or pixels, and the color or intensity of each pixel is represented as a bit pattern.

- The three most common image formats on the Web, GIF (Graphics Interchange Format), PNG (Portable Network Graphics), and JPEG (Joint Photography Experts Group), start with a bitmap representation and then employ different methods of compressing the image.

- GIF and PNG are known as lossless formats, as no information is lost during the compression. Conversely, JPEG is a lossy format, as it employs compression techniques that are not fully reversible.

- The MPEG, or MP4, digital video format uses a variety of compression techniques, including some borrowed from JPEG, to compress movies.

- Because all types of data are stored digitally as bit patterns, any program that stores a piece of data in memory must remember its type in order to subsequently access and correctly interpret its meaning.

Review Questions

1. TRUE or FALSE? In contrast to digital signals, analog signals use only a discrete (finite) set of values for storing data.

2. TRUE or FALSE? The binary value 1101_2 represents the decimal number 27.

3. TRUE or FALSE? The decimal number 100 is represented as the binary value 110100_2.

4. TRUE or FALSE? Using the two's complement notation for representing integers, any bit pattern starting with a 1 must represent a negative number.

5. TRUE or FALSE? As the IEEE double-precision format use more bits than the single-precision format does, it allows for a wider range of real values to be represented.

6. TRUE or FALSE? ASCII code is a program written to convert binary numbers to their decimal equivalents.

7. TRUE or FALSE? Digital sampling is the process of converting an analog sound wave into digital values.

8. TRUE or FALSE? GIF and JPEG are examples of formats for representing and storing sounds.

9. TRUE or FALSE? In a bitmap, the number of pixels used to represent an image affects both how sharp the image appears and the amount of memory it requires.

10. TRUE or FALSE? If the bit pattern 001001100 appears at multiple places in a computer's memory, the pattern is guaranteed to refer to the same value each time.

11. Describe two advantages of storing data digitally, rather than in analog format.

12. In addition to the examples given in this chapter, describe a real-world device that can use either an analog or digital representation of data.

13. What decimal value is represented by the binary number 01101001_2? Show the steps involved in the conversion, then use the Data Representation Page to verify your answer.

14. What is the binary representation of the decimal value 92? Show the steps involved in the conversion, then use the Data Representation Page to verify your answer.

15. Using 32 bits to represent integers, the largest positive value that can be represented is $2^{31} - 1$, whereas the smallest negative value is 2^{31}. Why aren't these ranges symmetric? That is, why is there one more negative integer than there are positive integers?

16. It was mentioned in the chapter that having two representations of zero, both a positive zero and a negative zero, would be both wasteful and potentially confusing. How might the inclusion of both zeros cause confusion or errors within programs?

17. The IEEE floating-point format reserves several bit patterns for representing special values. For example, a 32-bit pattern that begins with 011111111 has a special meaning. Using the Data Representation Page, determine what 011111111 followed by all zeros represents. What if a pattern other than all zeros follows 011111111?

18. Assuming that a string is stored as a sequence of ASCII codes corresponding to individual characters, how would the string "CU#1" be represented?

19. Assuming that a string is stored as a sequence of ASCII codes corresponding to its individual characters, what string would be represented by the bit pattern 01001110110101110110110000001110011?

20. Suppose that a library has a taped recording of a historically significant speech. What advantages would there be to converting the speech to digital format?

21. A grayscale image is one in which each pixel can be white, or black, or various shades of gray in between. Assuming that there are 256 discernible shades of gray, how many bits would a bitmap require to represent a pixel in a grayscale image? How does this number compare to those for black-and-white and color bitmaps?

22. What is the difference between a lossless format and a lossy format for storing digital images? For what type of images might one or the other be preferable?

23. Is the MPEG compression format for storing video lossy or lossless? How did you determine your answer?

24. Estimate the average number of bytes per frame for an MPEG file you own. That is, divide the size of the file by the approximate number of frames (you may assume 24 frames per second). Is this average consistent across different movie files?

References

Abelson, Hal, Ken Ledeen and Harry Ellis. *Blown to Bits: Your Life, Liberty, and Happiness After the Digital Explosion.* Addison-Wesley, 2008.

Brain, Marshall. "How MP3 Files Work." January 2010. Online at `http://computer.howstuffworks.com/mp3.htm`.

Capron, H.L., and J.A. Johnson. *Computers: Tools for an Information Age*, 8th ed. Upper Saddle River, NJ: Prentice Hall, 2003.

Comer, Douglas E. *The Internet Book: Everything you need to know about computer networking and how the Internet works*, 4th ed. Upper Saddle River, NJ: Prentice Hall, 2006.

Dale, Nell, and John Lewis. *Computer Science Illuminated,* 4th ed. Sudbury, MA: Jones and Bartlett, 2009.

Harris, Tom. "How File Compression Works." January 2010. Online at `http://computer.howstuffworks.com/file-compression.htm`.

Harte, Lawrence. Introduction to MPEG, MPEG-1, MPEG-2 and MPEG-4. Althos Publishing, 2006.

Petzold, Charles. *Code: The Hidden Language of Computer Hardware and Software.* Redmond, WA: Microsoft Press, 2000.

Conditional Repetition

This chapter uses narrative, examples, and hands-on exercises to introduce programming concepts and Web development skills.

> *It is not true that life is one damn thing after another. It's one damn thing over and over.*
>
> Edna St. Vincent Millay
>
> *We cannot always control our thoughts, but we can control our words, and repetition impresses the subconscious, and we are then master of the situation.*
>
> Florence Scovel Shinn

In Chapter 11, you were introduced to conditional execution in the form of the JavaScript if statement. Known as a ***control statement***, an if statement is used to control the execution of other JavaScript statements. A simple if statement evaluates a condition and, on the basis of the result, determines whether a program will execute a particular statement or sequence of statements. When an else case is included, the if statement instead selects from among alternative sequences of statements. If statements are useful in solving problems that involve choices—for example, deciding what letter grade a student has earned or whether dice doubles have been rolled.

Closely related to the concept of conditional execution is that of conditional repetition. Many problems involve repeating some task over and over until a specific condition is met. For example, you might wish to roll dice repeatedly until you get doubles or repeatedly prompt a user until he or she enters a valid number. The JavaScript control statement that enables conditional repetition is called the ***while loop***. A while loop is similar to an if statement in that it uses a condition (i.e., a Boolean expression) to control the execution of a statement or sequence of statements. Unlike an if statement, however, a while loop repeatedly executes the statement or statements it controls as long as the condition holds true.

In this chapter, you will learn how while loops work and how they can be incorporated into Web pages. The first while loops that you will encounter repeat their tasks a varying number of times, depending on the data being processed and its effect on the Boolean condition controlling the loop. After mastering the design of these simple loops, you will move on to loops that iterate a predetermined number of times (such loops are commonly referred to as counter driven). In the final section, you will be asked to combine while loops and counters in a page that experiments with the hailstone sequence, an interesting numerical phenomenon that has puzzled mathematicians for years.

While Loops

In Chapter 11, you created a Web page that allowed the user to simulate random dice rolls by clicking a button. This page is sufficient for obtaining a few dice combinations, but using it becomes very tedious if a large number of rolls are required. For example, one exercise in Chapter 11 involved

```
1.  <!doctype html>
2.  <!-- roll.html                                          Dave Reed -->
3.  <!-- This page simulates dice rolls until doubles are obtained. -->
4.  <!-- ======================================================= -->
5.
6.  <html>
7.   <head>
8.     <title> Dice Roller </title>
9.     <script type="text/javascript" src="http://balance3e.com/random.js">
10.    </script>
11.    <script type="text/javascript">
12.       function RollUntilDoubles()
13.       // Assumes: outputDiv is available for output
14.       // Results: rolls and displays dice until doubles are obtained
15.       {
16.         var roll1, roll2;
17.
18.         roll1 = RandomInt(1, 6);                // ROLL AND DISPLAY DICE
19.         roll2 = RandomInt(1, 6);
20.         document.getElementById('outputDiv').innerHTML=roll1+'-'+roll2+'<br>';
21.
22.         while (roll1 ! = roll2) {               // WHILE NOT DOUBLES,
23.            roll1 = RandomInt(1, 6);             // ROLL AGAIN AND DISPLAY AT
24.            roll2 = RandomInt(1, 6);             // THE END OF THE PAGE DIVISION
25.            document.getElementById('outputDiv').innerHTML =
26.                 document.getElementById('outputDiv').innerHTML+
27.                 roll1+'-'+roll2+'<br>';
28.         }
29.
30.         document.getElementById('outputDiv').innerHTML =
31.              document.getElementById('outputDiv').innerHTML+'DOUBLES!';
32.       }
33.    </script>
34.   </head>
35.
36.   <body>
37.     <h2>Dice Roller</h2>
38.     <input type="button" value="Roll until doubles"
39.            onclick="RollUntilDoubles();">
40.     <hr>
41.     <div id="outputDiv"></div>
42.   </body>
43.  </html>
```

Figure 13.1 Web page for rolling dice until doubles are obtained.

rolling dice and counting the number of doubles obtained. Although a counter freed you from tallying the total number of rolls, you were forced to click the button over and over again to generate a reasonable number of dice rolls.

Fortunately, JavaScript provides an additional control statement for specifying that a task should be performed repeatedly. A *while loop* resembles an if statement in that its behavior is dependent on a Boolean condition, but the statements inside a while loop's curly braces are executed repeatedly as long as the condition remains true. The general form for a while loop is as follows:

```
while (BOOLEAN_TEST) {
    STATEMENTS_EXECUTED_AS_LONG_AS_TRUE
}
```

The statements inside the curly braces are known as the *loop body*, because these statements are controlled by the loop. When the browser encounters a while loop, it first evaluates the Boolean test. If that test succeeds (i.e., evaluates to `true`), then the statements inside the loop are executed in order, just as if they were enclosed in an if statement. Unlike an if statement, however, a while loop does not stop there. Once all the statements in the loop body have been executed, program control returns to the beginning of the loop. That is, the loop test is evaluated again and, if it succeeds, the statements inside the loop body are executed a second time. This process repeats until the Boolean test fails (i.e., evaluates to `false`).

For example, the Web page in Figure 13.1 contains a while loop that simulates the repeated rolling of two dice until doubles are obtained. The `RollUntilDoubles` function begins by simulating the initial dice rolls, storing their values in variables `roll1` and `roll2` (lines 18–19) and displaying the results in a page division (line 20). Upon reaching the while loop, the browser first evaluates the loop test to determine whether the two rolls are different (line 22). If so, then the loop test succeeds (evaluates to `true`), and the statements inside the loop body are executed. After completing an iteration of the loop body, the browser evaluates the loop test again to determine whether the new dice values are different. As long as the rolls do not equal each other, the browser will repeatedly execute the loop body, rolling the dice and displaying their values (lines 23–27). Eventually, the dice combination will be doubles, causing the loop test to fail (evaluate to `false`) and the loop to terminate. When this finally occurs, the browser will reach the last statement, which displays the message "DOUBLES!" (lines 30–31). Figure 13.2 shows the `roll.html` page rendered in a Web browser.

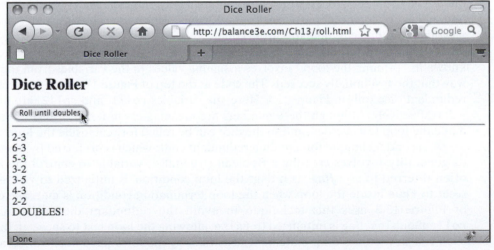

Figure 13.2 `roll.html` rendered in a Web browser.

EXERCISE 13.1

Enter the `roll.html` text from Figure 13.1 into a new Web page. After loading this page, click the button to verify that the code repeatedly simulates and displays dice rolls until doubles are obtained.

Perform repeated simulations using your page. What was your shortest sequence of rolls that ended in doubles? What was your longest sequence?

Common errors to avoid...

Beginning students often confuse if statements and while loops. This mistake is somewhat understandable, as the two control statements look so much alike. Don't be thrown by this apparent similarity—if statements and while loops are very different. Depending on the result of an if statement's Boolean test, the corresponding statements are executed either once or not at all. By contrast, a while loop implies repetition. The statements in the loop body are executed repeatedly as long as the loop test succeeds.

Technically, the curly braces in a while loop are optional if the loop body contains only one statement to be executed. As was the case with if statements, however, we strongly recommend that you include curly braces in every while loop you write. This practice maintains consistency and prevents you from introducing errors if you modify the code later on. We also suggest that you indent the statements inside each loop to emphasize the structure of the code.

Avoiding Redundancy

One troublesome feature of the code in `roll.html` is redundancy. Before the while test can be evaluated the first time, the page must roll the dice and display the result. Then the same code for simulating and displaying dice rolls must be placed inside the loop. In programming, redundancy is not just annoying, it's dangerous. Imagine that, after writing the code in Figure 13.1, you wanted to modify its behavior—for example, by switching from six-sided to eight-sided dice. To successfully implement the new version, you would need to change the code at multiple locations (first altering the initial `roll1` and `roll2` assignments, then making the same adjustments to the assignments inside the loop body). In this particular example, accommodating the redundant code might seem trivial, but as you begin to work on larger applications, it becomes increasingly difficult to ensure that you've updated every copy of a particular code sequence. To avoid such consistency problems, it is always desirable to remove redundancy from code.

Two different techniques are commonly used to avoid code redundancy such as this. The first, known as "priming the loop," involves assigning values to the variables from the loop test in such a way that the test initially succeeds. The code at the top of Figure 13.3 uses this technique to avoid the redundant dice rolls in Figure 13.1. Here, the variables `roll1` and `roll2` are initialized to −1 and −2, respectively. Although these numbers are meaningless in terms of dice rolls, they do suffice to make the loop test succeed, and so the dice can be rolled for real inside the loop.

A second technique for avoiding redundant code, which is preferred by many programmers for its generality, involves creating a Boolean (true/false) variable to control the loop. This variable, often referred to as a *flag*, as it flags the loop condition, is initialized to `false` and subsequently reset to `true` inside the loop when the loop termination condition is met. The code at the bottom of Figure 13.3 uses this technique to avoid the redundant dice rolls in Figure 13.1. The `rolledDoubles` flag is initialized to `false`, allowing the loop test to succeed. Inside the loop, after each roll of the dice, an if statement tests to see if doubles have been rolled and sets the flag to `true` in that case.

```
roll1 = -1;                              // PRIME THE LOOP BY ASSIGNING
roll2 = -2;                              // INITIAL VALUES TO THE VARIABLES
document.getElementById('outputDiv').innerHTML = '';

while (roll1 != roll2) {                 // AS LONG AS YOU DON'T HAVE DOUBLES,
    roll1 = RandomInt(1, 6);             // ROLL AGAIN AND DISPLAY THE ROLLS
    roll2 = RandomInt(1, 6);
    document.getElementById('outputDiv').innerHTML =
        document.getElementById('outputDiv').innerHTML+roll1+'-'+roll2+'<br>';
}

_____

rolledDoubles = false;                   // INITIALIZE A BOOLEAN FLAG
document.getElementById('outputDiv').innerHTML = '';

while (rolledDoubles == false) {         // AS LONG AS IT IS FALSE,
    roll1 = RandomInt(1, 6);             // ROLL AGAIN AND DISPLAY THE ROLLS
    roll2 = RandomInt(1, 6);
    document.getElementById('outputDiv').innerHTML =
        document.getElementById('outputDiv').innerHTML+roll1+'-'+roll2+'<br>';

    if (roll1 == roll2) {                // IF DOUBLES WERE ROLLED, SET THE FLAG
        rolledDoubles = true;            // SO THAT THE LOOP WILL TERMINATE
    }
}
```

Figure 13.3 Two alternative loops that roll dice until doubles are obtained, without redundant code.

EXERCISE 13.2

Modify your roll.html page so that it incorporates one of the two techniques, either priming the loop or a flag, from Figure 13.3. Then load the page and verify that the code behaves as before.

As mentioned in Chapter 11, there is a 1 in 6 (or 16.7%) chance of obtaining doubles when you roll two dice simultaneously. If you don't get doubles on the first roll, there is a 5/6 * 1/6 = 5/36 = 13.9% chance of obtaining doubles on the second roll. Thus, your chances of getting doubles within two rolls are 16.7% + 13.9% = 30.6%. Continuing this analysis:

chance of getting doubles in 1 roll:	16.7%
chance of getting doubles within 2 rolls:	30.6%
chance of getting doubles within 3 rolls:	42.1%
chance of getting doubles within 4 rolls:	51.8%
chance of getting doubles within 5 rolls:	59.8%
chance of getting doubles within 6 rolls:	66.5%
chance of getting doubles within 7 rolls:	72.1%
...	
chance of getting doubles within 20 rolls:	97.4%

This analysis shows that while you might get lucky and obtain doubles in one or two rolls, those instances will be balanced out by the times where it takes many more rolls. More than half of the time (51.8%), you should obtain doubles within four rolls. However, it is possible that more rolls will be required. In fact, there is a 2.6% chance that it will take more than 20 rolls to obtain doubles!

EXERCISE 13.3

Add a counter to your roll.html page to record the number of rolls that occur before doubles are obtained. Recall that a counter consists of a variable that is initialized to zero and incremented every time some event occurs. In this case, you should declare and initialize the counter variable in the `RollUntil` function, then add code to increment the counter each time the dice are rolled. When doubles are finally obtained, your page should display the counter's current value in a page division.

Use your page to conduct 20 different experiments, counting how many times it takes to obtain doubles each time. Are your results consistent with the universal odds of rolling doubles?

Designer Secrets

In your `stats.html` page from Chapter 11, you integrated counters directly into the page. That is, for each type of roll you wanted to count (e.g., doubles, sevens), you added a text span that initially contained 0 and incremented those contents each time the roll was obtained. By contrast, your `roll.html` page (Exercise 13.1) used a local variable to keep count of the number of rolls, displaying the final of that counter once doubles were obtained.

In most applications involving loops, this latter technique is preferable. Since you only care about the final value of the counter once the loop has terminated, there is no reason to display the intermediate values of the counter. In fact, most Web browsers will not display intermediate changes to the page but will instead wait until the loop terminates before updating the page contents. Thus, there is no reason to slow the loop down by trying to update the page directly from inside the loop. Instead, it is clearer and probably faster just to update a variable inside the loop and then display the final value of that variable when the loop terminates.

The while loop in your `roll.html` page causes the dice to be rolled repeatedly until doubles are obtained, but by modifying the loop test, you could use the same code to roll for any dice combination. For example, changing the loop test to (`roll1 + roll2 != 7`) would cause the code to loop as long as the sum of the dice is not 7. This means that the page would continue rolling until a combination totaling 7 appeared.

EXERCISE 13.4

Modify your `roll.html` page so that it rolls the dice until their combined sum equals 7. Then use this new page to conduct 20 different experiments, counting how many rolls it takes to obtain a 7 each time. Report your results. On average, a 7 should appear within four rolls. Do your results support this claim? Explain.

Make a similar modification to your page, causing it to roll the dice until their combined sum equals 2. Use your page to conduct 20 different experiments, counting how many rolls it takes to obtain a 2 each time. Report your results. On average, a 2 should appear within 25 rolls. Do your results support this claim? Explain.

Example: Lottery Combinations

Lotteries have been described as "a tax on the gullible." In general, the odds of winning a lottery are so infinitesimal that the cost of the lottery ticket far exceeds the expected payoff. For example, consider the Pick-4 lottery that you simulated in Chapter 7. Four digits are selected at random and the player must predict all four in order to win. Because any number between 0000 and 9999 might appear, the likelihood that any particular four-digit sequence will be drawn is 1 in 10,000. If the payoff the winner receives is less than $10,000 on a $1 ticket, then the odds are not in the player's favor.

A common misconception about lotteries is that a distinctive sequence, such as 0-0-0-0, is less likely to occur than a random-looking sequence, such as 3-7-5-2. In reality, each number sequence has the same probability of appearing. It just so happens that there are many more "random-looking" sequences than there are distinctive sequences.

EXERCISE 13.5

Create a Web page named `lottery.html` that repeatedly simulates Pick-4 lottery drawings until a specific sequence is obtained. The user should be able to enter the desired sequence in a series of four text boxes and then click a button to see how many drawings the page had to perform before their sequence came up. The appearance of your page should resemble that of Figure 13.4.

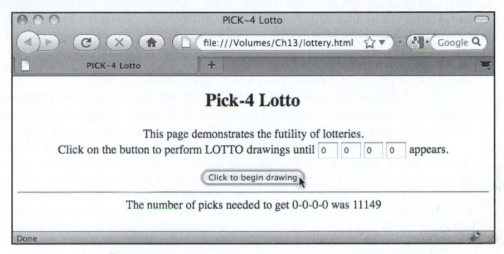

Figure 13.4   Sample appearance of `lottery.html` page.

Use your page to conduct 20 different experiments, each time counting how many drawings it takes to obtain 0-0-0-0. Report your results.

Next, pick your favorite four-digit combination and conduct an additional 20 experiments. Report your results. On average, did it require a smaller number of picks to acquire this sequence than were needed to obtain 0-0-0-0? Should it?

Common errors to avoid...

In English, descriptions of repetitive tasks usually focus on the stopping condition for the loop—an activity recurs *until something happens*. Conversely, the loop test in a while loop specifies the condition under which the loop continues—an activity recurs *as long as something does not happen*. Thus, when you define a test for conditional repetition, the condition you specify should be the exact opposite of the condition as you would state it in English. For example, the task of rolling dice until doubles are obtained requires a while loop whose test is (`roll1 != roll2`), which tells the page to keep rolling as long as you *don't* have doubles. Likewise, the task of rolling until a 7 is obtained requires the loop test (`roll1 + roll2 != 7`)—that is, the page keeps rolling as long as the dice values *don't* total 7.

Deriving the appropriate loop test can be especially tricky if the stopping condition involves logical connectives. For example, consider the task of rolling dice until either a 7 or 11 is obtained. The loop test must specify the condition under which neither total has occurred:

```
(roll1+roll2 != 7 && roll1+roll2 != 11)
```

Note that we employ the `&&` operator here, representing AND. As long as both conditions hold (the total is not 7 and also not 11), the loop should continue to execute.

Counter-Driven Loops

While loops facilitate conditional repetition within a program, allowing you to specify a sequence of statements that you want repeatedly executed as long as some condition holds. Because a while loop is controlled by a condition, it is usually impossible to predict the number of repetitions that will occur. As an example, consider your roll.html page that simulated rolling dice until doubles were obtained. In some instances, the first dice roll might produce doubles, causing the loop to terminate after one iteration. On the other hand, it might take tens or even hundreds of rolls to obtain doubles.

Although this kind of unpredictable repetition is ideal for some problems, others involve a pre-determined number of loop iterations. In these cases, some action must be carried out a certain number of times to complete a task. For example, instead of rolling dice until you obtain doubles, you might want to roll the dice a specific number of times and record the number of doubles that appear. If you rolled the dice 1,000 times, you would expect to obtain roughly 167 doubles (one out of every six rolls). Alternatively, you could roll the dice 1,000 times and compare the number of rolls that equaled 7 to the number of rolls that equaled 2. As six times as many combinations yield 7 as yield 2, you would expect your twos count to be roughly one-sixth of your sevens count.

If you want to perform a task involving a specific number of repetitions, you can implement a *counter-driven loop*—that is, a while loop whose test is based on a counter. The counter associated with a counter-driven loop is designed to record the number of times the loop has executed, so we can think of it as a repetition counter. The loop test should be tied to the counter, stopping the loop once the counter's value equals the desired number of repetitions. In general, the following loop structure can be used to execute a sequence of statements some predefined number of times:

```
repCount = 0;
while (repCount < DESIRED_NUMBER_OF_REPETITIONS) {
    STATEMENTS_FOR_CARRYING_OUT_DESIRED_TASK
    repCount = repCount + 1;
}
```

Note that the repetition counter is initialized to 0 before the loop begins and then incremented at the end of the loop body. Thus, the counter will keep track of how many times the statements in the loop body have been executed. When the number of repetitions reaches the number indicated in the condition, the loop test will fail, and the loop will terminate.

```
repCount = 0;                                    // INITIALIZE THE REP COUNTER
while (repCount < 10) {                           // AS LONG AS < 10 REPETITIONS
    document.getElementById('outputDiv').innerHTML =
        document.getElementById('outputDiv').innerHTML+'HOWDY<br>';

    repCount = repCount + 1;                      // INCREASE THE REP COUNTER
}
_____

repCount = 0;                                    // INITIALIZE THE REP COUNTER
while (repCount < 100) {                           // AS LONG AS < 100 REPETITIONS
    roll1 = RandomInt(1, 6);                       // SIMULATE AND DISPLAY THE ROLLS
    roll2 = RandomInt(1, 6);
    document.getElementById('outputDiv').innerHTML =
        document.getElementById('outputDiv').innerHTML+roll1+'-'+roll2+'<br>';

    repCount = repCount + 1;                      // INCREASE THE REP COUNTER
}
```

Figure 13.5   Examples of counter-driven loops.

Figure 13.5 provides two examples of counter-driven while loops. In the first example, the statements in the loop body are executed 10 times, displaying the word "HOWDY!" on a separate line each time. In the second example, the statements in the loop body are executed 100 times, simulating a dice roll and displaying the result each time.

Example: Dice Rolls

The Web page in Figure 13.6 incorporates a counter-driven loop similar to the second example in Figure 13.5. To initiate the loop code, the user enters a desired number of dice rolls in a text box and then clicks

```html
1.  <!doctype html>
2.  <!-- repstats.html                                    Dave Reed -->
3.  <!-- This page simulates repeated dice rolls and maintains stats. -->
4.  <!-- ============================================================= -->
5.
6.  <html>
7.   <head>
8.     <title> Dice Stats </title>
9.     <script type="text/javascript" src="http://balance3e.com/random.js">
10.    </script>
11.    <script type="text/javascript">
12.      function RollRepeatedly()
13.      // Assumes: repsBox contains a non-negative integer
14.      // Results: simulates that many dice rolls, displays # of doubles
15.      {
16.         var totalRolls, doubleCount, repCount, roll1, roll2;
17.
18.         totalRolls = parseFloat(document.getElementById('repsBox').value);
19.
20.         doubleCount = 0;                        // INITIALIZE THE COUNTERS
21.         repCount = 0;
22.         while (repCount < totalRolls) {         // REPEATEDLY,
23.             roll1 = RandomInt(1, 6);            // SIMULATE THE DICE ROLLS
24.             roll2 = RandomInt(1, 6);
25.             if (roll1 == roll2) {               // IF DOUBLES,
26.                 doubleCount = doubleCount + 1;   // INCREMENT THE COUNTER
27.             }
28.
29.             repCount = repCount + 1;            // INCREMENT THE REP COUNTER
30.         }
31.                                                 // DISPLAY THE RESULTS
32.         document.getElementById('outputDiv').innerHTML =
33.             'The number of doubles obtained was ' + doubleCount;
34.      }
35.    </script>
36.   </head>
37.
38.   <body>
39.     <h2>Dice Stats</h2>
40.     <p>
41.      Desired number of rolls:
42.      <input type="text" id="repsBox" size=6 value=1000>
43.     </p>
44.     <input type="button" value="Click to Roll" onclick="RollRepeatedly();">
45.     <hr>
46.     <div id="outputDiv"></div>
47.   </body>
48.  </html>
```

Figure 13.6 Counter-driven loop for rolling dice a specific number of times.

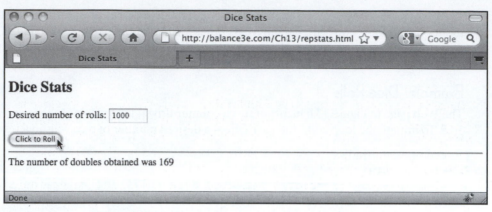

Figure 13.7 `repstats.html` rendered in a Web browser.

a button. This event invokes function `RollRepeatedly`, which simulates the specified number of rolls. The if statement inside the loop body tests the result of each roll and, if doubles are obtained, increments a separate counter. After performing the desired number of rolls, the loop terminates, and the value of the doubles counter is displayed in a page division. The resulting Web page is shown in Figure 13.7.

EXERCISE 13.6

Enter the `repstats.html` text from Figure 13.6 into a new Web page. After loading this page, click the button to verify that the code behaves as described.

Use your page to count the number of doubles that occur during 60 dice rolls. Conduct this experiment 10 times and report the results. Are the counts from the 10 different experiments fairly consistent? Is each result close to the expected number of doubles (60∗1/6 = 10)?

Increase the number of rolls from 60 to 600, and then perform 10 more experiments. Are the counts more consistent than those you obtained from 60 rolls? Are they closer to the expected number of doubles (600∗1/6 = 100)? Should they be? Explain.

Increase the number of rolls from 600 to 6,000 and then perform 10 more experiments. Are the counts more consistent than those you obtained from 600 rolls? Are they closer to the expected number of doubles (6,000∗1/6 = 1,000)? Should they be? Explain.

EXERCISE 13.7

Modify your `repstats.html` page so that, in addition to recording the number of doubles, it also counts the number of sevens and the number of twos obtained. This will require adding two counters to the `RollRepeatedly` function and modifying the code to display these additional counters when the loop terminates.

If you roll the dice a large number of times, roughly 1/6th of the rolls should equal 7 and 1/36th of the rolls should equal 2. Conduct several experiments with your page to verify this outcome. Are the counts more consistent as you increase the number of rolls?

Common errors to avoid...

As explained above, the browser will repeatedly execute statements in the body of a while loop as long as the loop test succeeds (evaluates to `true`). Therefore, it is possible to define a while loop that never terminates. For example, suppose you wrote a counter-driven while loop but forgot to increment the repetition counter inside the loop.

```
repCount = 0;
while (repCount < 10) {
    document.getElementById('outputDiv').inerHTML =
        document.getElementById('outputDiv').inerHTML + 'HOWDY<br>';
}
```

Because the repetition counter is initialized to 0 and never incremented, the loop test (`repCount < 10`) will always be true. Such a loop is known as an ***infinite loop***, or, more colorfully, a ***black hole loop***. If you are not familiar with astronomy, a black hole is a collapsed star whose gravitational field is so strong that it pulls matter and even light into it. Once inside the "event horizon" of a black hole, there is no way to escape its gravitational pull. Similarly, after the above while loop's test succeeds, execution becomes trapped in the loop and can never move on. When defining while loops, you must be very careful to avoid infinite loops. In particular, the loop body must contain code that affects the loop test in some way (e.g., a counter-driven loop must include statements that modify the repetition counter). Otherwise, an infinite loop is sure to occur.

If you accidentally write a page that contains an infinite loop, clicking the browser's `Stop` button will sometimes break the loop, allowing you to fix the logic error and reload the page. If the `Stop` button doesn't work, you will need to close the browser completely and then restart.

Variables and Repetition

As demonstrated in the previous section, you can design a while loop that iterates a specific number of times by using a counter variable to control the loop test. However, this represents only one option for creating while loops with predictable executions. In fact, any variable can be employed to control the number of loop repetitions, and the variable can be updated in various ways. For example, consider the while loop in Figure 13.8, which displays a simple countdown in a Web page. The while loop is controlled by the test (`count > 0`). As long as this test evaluates to `true`, the code in the loop body will be executed repeatedly. Assume that the user entered 10 in the text box. Because `count`'s initial value is 10, the loop test succeeds and the loop body is executed: the statements inside the loop display `10` in the page (lines 20–21) and then decrement the value of `count` (line 22). After the loop body completes, the loop test is evaluated again using the current value of `count` (i.e., 9). As the test still succeeds, the code inside the loop is executed: 9 is displayed and the value of `count` is decremented. This process repeats until the tenth iteration through the loop, when the value 1 is displayed and `count` is decremented to become 0. At this point, the loop test fails and the while loop terminates. The browser then advances to the statement immediately following the while loop (lines 25–26), which displays the message "BLASTOFF!" Figure 13.9 shows the page rendered in a Web browser.

EXERCISE 13.8

Enter the `countdown.html` text from Figure 13.8 into a new Web page. After loading this page, experiment with it by changing the contents of the text box and verifying that the code behaves as described.

Once you have done this, modify the page so that, instead of decrementing `count` by 1, the code halves `count`'s value during each loop iteration (any fractional values should be rounded down). For example, the starting value 10 would be halved to 5, then 2, then 1, and finally 0.

EXERCISE 13.9

Recall that Chapter 8 described the binary search algorithm for finding a particular entry in an ordered list. The idea behind binary search is to begin looking in the exact center of the list. If the desired entry comes before the middle entry in the list's organizational scheme, then you can

```
1.  <!doctype html>
2.  <!-- countdown.html                                    Dave Reed -->
3.  <!-- This page displays a countdown from a specified number. -->
4.  <!-- ==================================================== -->
5.
6.  <html>
7.   <head>
8.     <title> Countdown </title>
9.     <script type="text/javascript">
10.       function Countdown()
11.       // Assumes: countBox contains a non-negative integer
12.       // Results: displays a countdown from that number in outputDiv
13.       {
14.         var count;
15.
16.         count = parseFloat(document.getElementById('countBox').value);
17.         document.getElementById('outputDiv').innerHTML = '';
18.
19.         while (count > 0) {
20.           document.getElementById('outputDiv').innerHTML =
21.           document.getElementById('outputDiv').innerHTML + count + '<br>';
22.           count = count - 1;
23.         }
24.
25.         document.getElementById('outputDiv').innerHTML =
26.             document.getElementById('outputDiv').innerHTML + 'BLASTOFF!';
27.       }
28.     </script>
29.   </head>
30.
31.   <body>
32.     <p>
33.       Start of the countdown:
34.       <input type="text" id="countBox" size=4 value=10>
35.     </p>
36.     <input type="button" value="Begin Countdown" onclick="Countdown();">
37.     <hr>
38.     <div id="outputDiv"></div>
39.   </body>
40.  </html>
```

Figure 13.8   Web page with a counter-driven loop for displaying a countdown.

eliminate all entries beyond the middle and repeat the process on the remaining half of the list. Similarly, if the desired entry comes after the middle entry, you can eliminate all entries before the middle and repeat the process on the remaining half. Every time you perform a comparison, you reduce the size of the list by one-half. Eventually, you either locate the desired entry or determine that it isn't in the list.

Now that you understand how the binary search algorithm works, you can use your modified countdown.html page to determine how many checks are needed to locate an item in a particular ordered list. If you enter a list size in the text box, the sequence of numbers displayed in the text area will represent the remaining size of the list to be searched after each successive inspection. Thus, the number of values in the text area will be one more than the number of checks required to find an entry in the worse case. To more easily identify this necessary number of checks, add a counter to your countdown.html page that records how many times the value is halved before reaching 0.

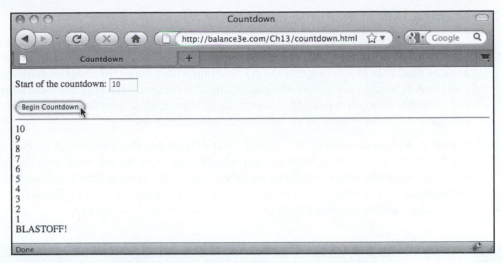

Figure 13.9 countdown.html rendered in a Web browser.

When the countdown completes, the browser should display the counter's value below the sequence in the text area. For example, if the initial value of count were 10, your page would produce the following output:

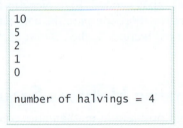

```
10
5
2
1
0

number of halvings = 4
```

Use your modified countdown.html page to determine how many times the following numbers must be halved (and, if necessary, rounded down) before reaching 0:

32

64

128

6000

308000000

6800000000

The last three numbers in this exercise approximate the size of a small university's student body, the U.S. population, and the world population, respectively. Thus, the results you obtained represent the maximum number of binary search comparisons required to find an entry in listings of these populations.

Exercise 13.9 demonstrated that repeatedly halving a number (and rounding down) reduces it to 0 very quickly. For example, a large number such as 1,000 needs to be halved only 10 times before reaching 0. Note that every time you double the size of the starting number, the number of halvings needed to reach 0 increases by 1. This means that even extremely large values can be reduced to 0 in a relatively small number of halvings (e.g., 2,000 is reduced to 0 in 11 halvings, 4,000 is reduced to 0 in 12 halvings, . . . 10 billion is reduced to 0 in 34 halvings). As the following exercise demonstrates, the opposite principle is also true—if you start with a small number and repeatedly double it, it doesn't take long for that number to get extremely large.

EXERCISE 13.10

Consider a sheet of paper. If you fold the paper in half, the resulting doubled sheet is twice as thick. Likewise, if you fold the sheet in half again, the thickness is doubled again (and becomes four times greater than that of the original sheet). Starting with a standard sheet of paper, how many folds do you think it would take before the paper's thickness equaled the distance between the earth and the sun (roughly 93 million miles)? Of course, this hypothetical question assumes that the original sheet is large enough and that you are strong enough to keep folding!

Create a Web page named `fold.html` that determines the number of folds required for a folded paper's thickness to reach from the earth to the sun. You should start with the initial thickness of a piece of paper (assume 0.002 inch) and then repeatedly double that value until it reaches 93 million miles (recall that a mile equals 5,280 feet and a foot equals 12 inches). Declare a counter variable to record the number of folds, and report the final count as your answer.

Designer Secrets

Like if statements, while loops control the execution of other statements. Whenever a program needs to perform some task (potentially) more than once, you should include a while loop. The loop test must specify the logical condition under which the program should keep looping.

If the task involves a specific number of repetitions that can be determined ahead of time, then a counter-driven while loop is needed. To implement a counter-driven loop, you must initialize the counter variable before the loop, compare the counter's value against the desired number of repetitions in the loop test, and increment the counter at the end of the loop.

Example: Generating Hailstone Sequences

An interesting unsolved problem in mathematics concerns what is called the "hailstone sequence." The following algorithm defines this sequence:

1. Start with any positive integer.
2. If that number is odd, then multiply it by 3 and add 1; otherwise, divide it by 2.
3. Repeat as many times as desired.

For example, the hailstone sequence starting with 5 is:

   5, 16, 8, 4, 2, 1, 4, 2, 1, . . .

Note that this hailstone sequence eventually reaches the pattern 4-2-1, which then loops indefinitely. Similarly, the hailstone sequence starting with 15 is:

   15, 46, 23, 70, 35, 106, 53, 160, 80, 40, 20, 10, 5, 16, 8, 4, 2, 1, 4, 2, 1, . . .

It is conjectured that, no matter what positive integer you start with, you will always end up in the 4-2-1 loop. In experimenting with hailstone sequences, mathematicians have proven that this hypothesis holds for all starting values up to 5,764,607,523,034,234,880 (and probably higher by the time you read this). However, the conjecture has yet to be proven true for all numbers.

EXERCISE 13.11

Create a Web page named `hail.html` that computes and displays hailstone sequences. The user should be able to enter a positive integer in a text box and then click a button. When the button is clicked, the hailstone sequence starting with the input number should appear in a separate text area, one number per line. If the sequence gets to 1 (meaning it is stuck in the 4-2-1 loop), then your code should print the word "STUCK!" in the text area and terminate. Include a variable that records and displays the length of the hailstone sequence (up to the point where 1 is reached). For example, the hailstone sequence starting with 5 would be displayed as:

```
5
16
8
4
2
1
STUCK!
Hailstone sequence length: 6
```

Hint: There are many different ways to test whether a number is even or odd. For example, if `num/2` is equal to `Math.floor(num/2)`, then `num` is an even number. Likewise, because the % operator computes the remainder left over after division, the expression `(num % 2 == 0)`, evaluates to `true` only if `num` is even.

EXERCISE 13.12

Using your `hail.html` page, answer the following questions:

- What is the length of the hailstone sequence starting at 100? Starting at 200? Starting at 400?
- What is the smallest starting number that generates a hailstone sequence with a length of at least 15?
- Identify a starting number for which the hailstone sequence is at least 30 numbers long. What is the length of the sequence? If you add or subtract 1 from this starting number, how long are the hailstone sequences associated with the new starting numbers?
- In general, if the hailstone sequence starting at some number N has length L, how long would the hailstone sequence starting at 2N be? Explain your reasoning.

Looking Ahead...

In this chapter, you were introduced to the while loop, which specifies conditional repetition in JavaScript code. Like an if statement, a while loop is a control statement that relies on a Boolean test. However, a while loop is functionally different in that it specifies repetition—the statements in the body of a while loop will be executed repeatedly as long as the loop test evaluates to `true`. While loops are useful for any situation in which some task must be executed more than once. Often, the number of repetitions that the loop will perform is not known ahead of time but is instead based on some condition—for example, a loop that rolls dice repeatedly as long as doubles haven't been obtained. Other while loops are designed to repeat a predetermined number of times—for example, a loop that rolls dice 1,000 times and counts doubles. In either case, a while loop can control the repeated execution of the necessary statements.

The next chapter, Chapter 14, returns to the hardware side of computing, focusing on how the physical components of a computer work together to produce the complex behaviors we observe. As we first observed in Chapter 8, repetition plays a central role in this process. The CPU repeatedly fetches and executes machine-language instructions from memory. Although each instruction represents a simple operation (such as adding two numbers or moving data from one memory location to another), the overall effect of executing billions of such instructions in a second can be exceedingly complex. In Chapter 14, you will study the internal workings of the computer, focusing on the components defined by the von Neumann architecture (CPU, memory, and input/output devices) and their interactions. Using software simulators that accompany the chapter, you will be able to visualize and experiment with the behavior of the components.

Chapter Summary

- A while loop is a control statement that specifies conditional repetition. A while loop is similar to an if statement in that its behavior is dependent on a Boolean condition. Unlike an if statement, however, a while loop repeatedly executes the statement(s) it controls as long as the condition remains true.

- The general form for a while loop is as follows:

```
while (BOOLEAN_TEST) {
    STATEMENTS_EXECUTED_AS_LONG_AS_TRUE
}
```

  The statements inside the curly braces are known as the loop body. If the loop test succeeds (evaluates to true), then the statements in the loop body are executed. After iterating through the loop, the browser returns to the beginning of the while loop and reevaluates the loop test. This process repeats until the loop test fails (evaluates to false).

- Even though they look similar, while loops and if statements are very different control statements—an if statement executes the statement(s) it controls either once or not at all, whereas a while loop can execute its statement(s) repeatedly.

- A counter-driven while loop can be used to repeat some programmatic task a specified number of times. The general form for a counter-driven loop is as follows:

```
repCount = 0;
while (repCount < DESIRED_NUMBER_OF_REPETITIONS) {
    STATEMENTS_FOR_CARRYING_OUT_DESIRED_TASK

    repCount = repCount + 1;
}
```

- Infinite loops (or black hole loops) are while loops that never terminate—that is, their conditions never evaluate to false. To avoid creating an infinite loop, you must ensure that the loop body contains code that affects the loop test in some way (e.g., by incrementing the repetition counter).

Supplemental Material and Exercises

More Practice with Loops

EXERCISE 13.13

Predict the output sequences that would be produced by each of the following while loops:

```
count = 10;
while (count > 0) {
    document.getElementById('outputDiv').innerHTML =
        document.getElementById('outputDiv').innerHTML + count + '<br>';
    count = count - 2;
}
document.getElementById('outputDiv').innerHTML =
    document.getElementById('outputDiv').innerHTML + 'DONE WITH 1ST!<br>';
```

```
num = 1;
while (num <= 5) {
    document.getElementById('outputDiv').innerHTML =
        document.getElementById('outputDiv').innerHTML + num + '<br>';
    num = num + 1;
}
document.getElementById('outputDiv').innerHTML =
    document.getElementById('outputDiv').innerHTML + 'DONE WITH 2ND!<br>';

x = 1;
y = 10;
while (x < y) {
    document.getElementById('outputDiv').innerHTML =
        document.getElementById('outputDiv').innerHTML + x + ' ' + y + '<br>';
    x = x + 1;
    y = y - 2;
}
document.getElementById('outputDiv').innerHTML =
    document.getElementById('outputDiv').innerHTML + 'DONE WITH 3RD!<br>';
```

EXERCISE 13.14

In the spirit of the "Old MacDonald" page you wrote in Chapter 9, create a Web page named `bottles.html` that displays verses of the song "100 Bottles of Root Beer on the Wall" (you may insert your favorite beverage). The page should contain a text box in which the user can enter the initial number of bottles. You should also provide a button that, when clicked, calls a function to display (in a page division) the sequence of verses starting with the specified number of bottles. For example, if the user entered the number 100, your page might display:

```
100 bottles of root beer on the wall.
100 bottles of root beer.
Take one down, pass it around.
99 bottles of root beer on the wall.

99 bottles of root beer on the wall.
99 bottles of root beer.
Take one down, pass it around.
98 bottles of root beer on the wall.

...

1 bottle of root beer on the wall.
1 bottle of root beer.
Take one down, pass it around.
0 bottles of root beer on the wall.
```

Hint: The variable that drives your loop test should be initialized to the number of bottles entered by the user and then decremented during each iteration of the loop. Within the loop body, include statements that display the verse associated with the variable's current value.

More Dice Examples

Numerous exercises in this chapter demonstrated that some dice totals are more likely to occur than others. For example, if you rolled a pair of dice repeatedly, you would expect to obtain roughly six

Dice Total	Number of Combinations	Possible Combinations
2	1	1-1
3	2	1-2, 2-1
4	3	1-3, 2-2, 3-1
5	4	1-4, 2-3, 3-2, 4-1
6	5	1-5, 2-4, 3-3, 4-2, 5-1
7	6	1-6, 2-5, 3-4, 4-3, 5-2, 6-1
8	5	2-6, 3-5, 4-4, 5-3, 6-2
9	4	3-6, 4-5, 5-4, 6-3
10	3	4-6, 5-5, 6-4
11	2	5-6, 6-5
12	1	6-6

Figure 13.10   Probability of obtaining various dice combinations.

times more 7s than 2s. This is because six different dice combinations total to 7, whereas only one combination totals to 2. Figure 13.10 lists every total that can be obtained by rolling two dice, as well as the combinations that yield each total.

The symmetry associated with the dice combinations suggests that 7, in addition to being the most likely roll, is also the most likely average of multiple rolls. Because there is an equal probability of your combination totaling 2 and 12, 3 and 11, and so on, these numbers balance out. If you rolled the dice many times and averaged the results, you would expect to get 7 (or a value very close to 7).

EXERCISE 13.15

Create a Web page named `repavg.html` that simulates a large number of dice rolls and computes the average of the dice totals. The user should be able to enter a number of rolls in a text box and then click a button, which should call a function to simulate the rolls and compute the average. Once calculated, the average should be displayed in a separate text box.

Hint: To compute the average, you must maintain a running sum of the dice rolls. Start by declaring a variable and initializing it to 0 (as you would with a counter). Each time the page simulates a dice roll, add the combined total of the two dice to the variable. Once the loop terminates, divide the sum of all your dice combinations by the number of dice rolls to determine the average roll.

After implementing your page, use it to answer the following questions: What is the average of 100 dice rolls? 1,000 dice rolls? 10,000 dice rolls? Is there a pattern to the numbers you obtain? Should there be?

If you have ever been to a casino or watched a gangster movie, you are probably familiar with the game of craps. Craps is a game in which players win or lose depending on the dice combinations they roll. The player's initial roll is known as his point. The point can be an immediate winner (7 or 11) or an immediate loser (2 or 3). If the player's point does not equal one of these game-ending totals, then the player must continue rolling until he either rolls his point again (a winner) or obtains a 7 (a loser).

For example, the following sequence of rolls would cause the player to win:

```
Initial roll:  6 (player's point)
Next roll:    10
Next roll:     4
Next roll:     6
WINNER!
```

Generalized code for representing a craps game is provided in Figure 13.11.

```
myPoint = SUM OF TWO DIE ROLLS
if (myPoint IS 7 OR 11) {
    WINNER!
}
else if (myPoint IS 2 OR 3) {
    LOSER!
}
else {
    while (HAVEN'T ROLLED myPoint OR 7) {
        ROLL THE DICE
    }
    if (ROLLED myPoint) {
        WINNER!
    }
    else {
        LOSER!
    }
}
```

Figure 13.11 Generalized code for determining the outcome of a craps game. Actual JavaScript code must replace capitalized text in the appropriate places before this code could be executed.

EXERCISE 13.16

Create a Web page named `craps.html` that simulates a game of craps. When the user clicks a button, this event should call a function that rolls the dice until the player wins or loses. When implementing this function, use the generalized code from Figure 13.11 as a guide. The value of each roll should be displayed in a page division, along with a message indicating whether the player won or lost.

For Loops

In this chapter, you examined several examples of counter-driven while loops in which the following basic form was used to repeat a sequence of code a specific number of times:

```
repCount = 0;
while (repCount < DESIRED_NUM_OF_REPETITIONS){
    STATEMENTS_FOR_CARRYING_OUT_THE_TASK
    repCount = repCount + 1;
}
```

By specifying different code in the loop body and a desired number of repetitions, you were able to implement various counter-driven applications. As this kind of counter-driven loop is common, JavaScript provides a variant of while loops that captures the pattern more succinctly. The following represents the general form of this variant, which is called a *for loop*:

```
for (repCount=0; repCount<DESIRED_NUM_OF_REPETITIONS; repCount=repCount+1) {
    STATEMENTS_FOR_CARRYING_OUT_THE_TASK
}
```

A for loop incorporates all the components of a counter-driven loop but also makes the loop more compact and easier to read. In particular, the steps involving the loop counter—initialization, testing, and incrementing—are isolated on one line, separated by semicolons. Because these statements control the behavior of the loop, listing them together emphasizes the loop's characteristics. In addition, separating the loop control statements from the actual code to be executed in the body (i.e., inside the curly braces) makes it easier for someone reviewing the code to focus on the actions performed by the loop.

```
for (repCount = 0; repCount < 10; repCount=repCount + 1) {
    document.getElementById('outputDiv').innerHTML =
        document.getElementById('outputDiv').innerHTML+'HOWDY<br>';
}
_____
for (repCount = 0; repCount < 100; repCount=repCount + 1) {
    roll1 = RandomInt(1, 6);          // SIMULATE AND DISPLAY THE ROLLS
    roll2 = RandomInt(1, 6);
    document.getElementById('outputDiv').innerHTML =
        document.getElementById('outputDiv').innerHTML+
        roll1+'-'+roll2+'<br>';
}
```

Figure 13.12 Examples of counter-driven for loops.

Despite these formatting differences, the behavior of a for loop is identical to that of its while loop counterpart. Upon encountering a for loop, the browser executes the first component of the loop header, which initializes the value of the loop counter. Then the loop test (the loop header's second component) is evaluated; if the test succeeds, then the statements inside the loop body are executed. After iterating through the loop body, the browser increments the loop counter (this action is represented by the loop header's third component). Finally, the loop test is reevaluated, possibly causing the loop body to execute again.

To illustrate the interchangeability of for loops and counter-driven while loops, the for loops in Figure 13.12 perform tasks identical to those of the counter-driven while loops in Figure 13.5.

EXERCISE 13.17

Reimplement your `repstats.html` page, replacing the while loop with an equivalent for loop. Test the page repeatedly to verify that it behaves identically to the while loop version.

EXERCISE 13.18

Reimplement your `repavg.html` page, replacing the while loop with an equivalent for loop. Test the page repeatedly to verify that it behaves identically to the while loop version.

Inside the Computer—The von Neumann Architecture

This chapter uses narrative, illustrations, hands-on experimentation, and review questions to introduce computer science and technology concepts.

> *Any sufficiently advanced technology is indistinguishable from magic.*
>
> Arthur C. Clarke
>
> *John von Neumann draws attention to what seemed to him a contrast. He remarked that for simple mechanisms, it is often easier to describe how they work than what they do, while for more complicated mechanisms, it is usually the other way around.*
>
> Edsger Dijkstra

As was discussed in Chapter 1, virtually all modern computers have the same basic layout, known as the von Neumann architecture. This layout divides the hardware of a computer into three main components: memory, a CPU and input/output devices. The first component, memory, provides storage for data and program instructions. The CPU is in charge of fetching instructions and data from memory, executing the instructions, and then storing the resulting values back in memory. Input devices (such as the keyboard, mouse, and microphone) allow a person to interact with the computer by entering information and commands, whereas output devices (such as the screen, speakers, and printer) are used to communicate data, instructions, and the results of computations.

This chapter explores the details of the von Neumann architecture by describing the inner workings of a computer. We develop our explanation incrementally, starting with a simple representation of the CPU datapath and then adding main memory and a control unit. When combined with input and output devices, these components represent an accurate (albeit simplified) model of a modern, programmable computer. Software simulators (originally developed by Grant Braught at Dickinson College) are provided for each model to facilitate experimentation and hands-on learning.

CPU Subunits and Datapath

As we saw in Chapter 1, the CPU acts as the brain of the computer. It is responsible for obtaining data and instructions from memory, carrying out the instructions, and storing the results back in memory. Each computer's CPU can understand and execute a particular set of instructions, known as that computer's **machine language**. In Chapter 8, we explained that programmers can control a computer by defining instructions for its CPU—this is accomplished either by writing programs directly in machine language, or by writing programs in a high-level language and then translating them into machine language. Even programs that exhibit complex behavior are specified to the CPU as sequences of simple machine-language commands, each performing a task no more complicated than adding two numbers or copying data to a new location. However, the CPU can execute these instructions at such a high speed that complex programmatic behavior is achieved.

CPU Subunits

The CPU itself is comprised of several subunits, each playing a specific role in the processor's overall operation. These subunits are the arithmetic logic unit, the registers, and the control unit (Figure 14.1).

- The **arithmetic logic unit (ALU)** is the collection of circuitry that performs actual operations on data. Basic operations might include addition, subtraction, and bit manipulations (such as shifting or combining bits).

- **Registers** are memory locations that are built into the CPU. As registers are integrated directly into the CPU circuitry, data in registers can be accessed more quickly (as much as 5 to 10 times faster) than data in main memory. However, because of the limited number of registers in the CPU (commonly 16 or 32), these memory locations are reserved for data that the CPU is currently using. To function efficiently, the computer must constantly copy data back and forth between registers and main memory. These transfers occur across a collection of wires called a **bus**, which connects the registers to main memory. A separate set of buses connects the registers to the ALU, allowing the ALU to receive data for processing and then store the results of computations back in the registers.

- The **control unit (CU)** can be thought of as "the brain within the brain," in that it oversees the various functions of the CPU. The control unit is the circuitry in charge of fetching data and instructions from main memory, as well as controlling the flow of data from the registers to the ALU and back to the registers.

Together, these three subunits form the **core** of the CPU. As we saw in Chapter 1, many of today's commercial CPUs are multi-core processors, meaning they have two or more cores embedded on the same chip. While the cores may share some internal resources (e.g., cache), they operate semi-independently and so allow for multiple instructions to be executed concurrently.

Since a multi-core CPU can be thought of as multiple single-core CPUs combined, the rest of this chapter will focus on the simpler model of a single-core CPU. To generalize the model to multiple cores, you need only envision multiple copies of the core datapath operating concurrently within the CPU.

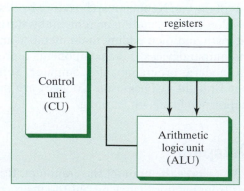

Figure 14.1 CPU subunits. Because ALU operations such as addition and subtraction operate on two values, there are two buses connecting the registers to the ALU. The result of the ALU operation is passed back to the registers via a single bus.

CPU Datapath Cycles

The path that data follows within the CPU, traveling along buses from registers to the ALU and then back to registers, is known as the **CPU datapath**. Every task performed by a computer, from formatting a document to displaying a page in a Web browser, is broken down into sequences of simple operations; the computer executes each individual operation by moving data from the registers to the ALU, performing computations on that data within the ALU, and then storing the result in the registers. A single rotation around the CPU datapath is referred to as a **CPU datapath cycle**, or **CPU cycle**.

Recall that, in Chapter 1, we defined CPU speed as measuring the number of basic instructions that a CPU can carry out in one second. As each instruction requires a single CPU cycle to execute, we can infer that a CPU's speed will equal the number of CPU cycles that occur per second. For example, an 1.6 GHz CPU can perform 1.6 billion CPU cycles per second, whereas a 3.2 GHz CPU can perform 3.2 billion CPU cycles per second. However, CPUs cannot be compared solely on the basis of their processor speeds. This is because two machine languages might divide the same task into different sets of instructions, and one set might be more efficient than the other. That is, one CPU might be able to complete a task in a single cycle, whereas another might require several cycles to complete the same task. To accurately evaluate a CPU's performance, we must consider the instruction set for that CPU, as well as the number of registers and the size of the buses that carry data between components.

Obviously, the number of cores within a CPU affects performance as well. In theory, a dual core CPU, such as Intel's Core 2 Duo or AMD's Athlon X2, could double the amount of work performed by executing two instructions concurrently on the two cores. In practice, however, an optimal speedup factor of 2 is rarely achieved, due to technical overhead and potential imbalances between the workloads of the cores.

Datapath Simulator

To help you visualize the behavior of the CPU datapath, a simple simulator has been designed to accompany the text. The CPU Datapath Simulator (accessible at `http://balance3e.com/Ch14/datapath.html`) models a simple CPU containing four registers. Using this simulator, you can follow the progress of data as it traverses the CPU datapath, from the registers to the ALU and back to the registers. To keep things simple, we have avoided including an explicit control unit in this simulator. Instead, the user must serve as the control unit, selecting the desired input registers, ALU function, and output register by clicking the knob images. Note that not all features of the simulator will be demonstrated in this chapter. In particular, the ALU has two bit-manipulation operations, & and |, which involve combining individual bits in the two input values. Likewise, there are status boxes within the ALU that identify when an operation results in a negative number, zero, or an overflow (a value too large to be represented). You are free to experiment with these features, but all of the examples in this chapter will involve simple addition and subtraction.

Figures 14.2 through 14.5 demonstrate using the simulator to add two numbers together—a task that can be completed during a single CPU cycle.

- This simulator uses text boxes to represent registers, enabling the user to enter data by typing in the boxes. The knobs, which allow the user to specify how data moves along the CPU datapath and what operations the ALU performs on the data, are images that change when the user clicks them. In Figure 14.2, the user has entered the numbers 43 and −296 in registers R0 and R1, respectively. After inputting these values, the user clicks the A Bus knob so that it selects R0 and the B Bus knob so that it selects R1. This will cause the numbers stored in these two registers to be transferred along the indicated buses to the ALU, which will perform an operation on them. Because the user has set the ALU Operation knob to addition and the C Bus knob to R2, the ALU will add the two numbers together, and the result will travel along the C Bus to be stored back in register R2.

- After entering the desired settings, the user initiates a CPU cycle within the simulator by clicking the button labeled Execute. Figure 14.3 depicts the state of the CPU as the values in R0 and R1

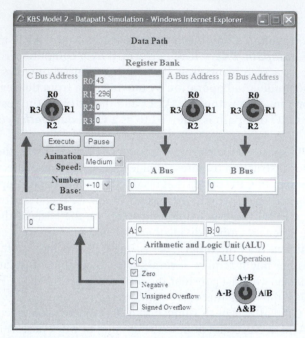

Figure 14.2 Initial settings of the simulator.

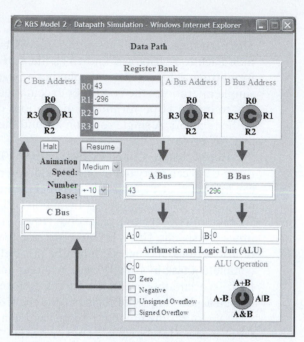

Figure 14.3 Data traveling from registers to the ALU.

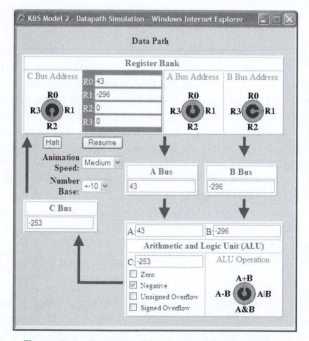

Figure 14.4 Data traveling from ALU to registers.

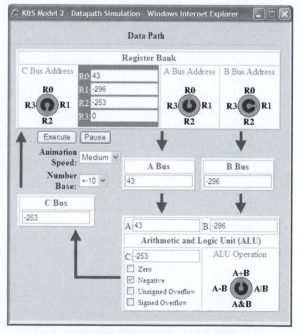

Figure 14.5 Final result of the CPU cycle.

travel along the A and B buses to the ALU. The arrows that represent the buses blink red, and the numbers being transferred are displayed in text boxes next to the buses.

- Figure 14.4 illustrates the state of the CPU after the ALU has received the numbers and performed the specified operation. Because the user set the ALU Operation knob to addition, the ALU adds the two numbers, 43 and −296. The result, −253, is then sent out along the C Bus.

- Finally, Figure 14.5 shows the end result of the CPU cycle. Because the user set the C Bus knob to R2, the value −253 (which travels along the C Bus) is ultimately stored in register R2.

HANDS-ON EXERCISES:

Experiment with this simulator until you are familiar with the CPU datapath and the events that occur within a CPU cycle. Then, use the simulator to answer the following questions:

14.1. What would happen if you placed the number 100 in R0, then set the knobs so that A Bus = R0, B Bus = R0, ALU = A − B, and C Bus = R0?

14.2. Describe the settings that would cause the value stored in R2 to be doubled.

14.3. How many cycles are required to add the contents of R0, R1, and R2 and then place the sum in R3? Describe the settings for each cycle.

CPU and Main Memory

Although the CPU datapath describes the way in which a computer manipulates data stored in registers, we have not yet explained how data gets into the registers in the first place, or how the results of ALU operations are accessed outside the CPU. Both these tasks involve connections between the CPU and main memory. Recall from Chapter 1 that all active programs and data are stored in the main memory of a computer. We can think of main memory as a large collection of memory locations, in which each location is accessible via an address. Similar to the way in which a street address (e.g., 27 Maple Drive) allows a mail carrier to find and access a mailbox, a memory address (e.g., memory location 27) allows the CPU to find and access a particular piece of main memory. A bus connects main memory to the CPU, enabling the computer to copy data and instructions to registers and then copy the results of computations back to main memory. Figure 14.6 illustrates the interaction between a computer's main memory and CPU.

Transferring Data to and from Main Memory

As a program is executed, the control unit processes the program instructions and identifies which data values are needed to carry out the specified tasks. The required values are then fetched from main memory along the main memory bus, loaded into registers, and used in ALU operations.

As a concrete example, imagine that you had a file containing 1,000 numbers and needed to compute the sum of those numbers. To begin, the computer would need to load the data from the file into main memory—for example, at memory locations 500 through 1499. Then, the control unit would carry out the following steps to add the numbers and store the resulting sum back in main memory:

1. Initialize one of the registers, say R0, to 0. This register will store the running total of the numbers.
2. For each number stored at memory addresses 500 through 1499:
   a. Copy the number from main memory to another register, say R1.
   b. During one cycle around the CPU datapath, add the contents of R0 and R1 and store the result back in R0.
3. When all the numbers in the file have been processed, the value in R0 will represent their sum. This value can then be copied back to a main memory location.

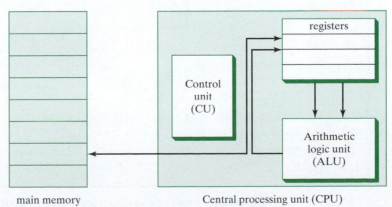

registers

Control unit (CU)

Arithmetic logic unit (ALU)

main memory

Central processing unit (CPU)

Figure 14.6 A bus connects main memory to the CPU.

Note that each number must be transferred into a register before it can be added to the sum. In practice, transferring data between main memory and the CPU takes much longer than executing a single CPU cycle. This is mainly because the electrical signals must travel a greater distance—for example, from a separate RAM chip to the CPU chip. In the time it takes for data to traverse the main memory bus and reach the registers, several CPU cycles may actually occur. Modern processors compensate for this delay with special hardware that allows multiple instructions to be fetched at once. By fetching several instructions ahead, the processor can often identify instructions that are not dependent on the current one, and execute them while the current data transfer is in progress. Thus, the CPU can perform useful computations rather than sitting idle while an instruction waits for data to be copied from main memory to the registers.

Datapath with Memory Simulator

Our next version of the CPU Datapath Simulator has been augmented so that it illustrates the relationship between the CPU and main memory. The main memory incorporated in this extended simulator (accessible at `http://balance3e.com/Ch14/dpandmem.html`) can store up to 32 16-bit numbers, with addresses 0 through 31. A new bus, labeled `Main Memory Bus`, connects the main memory to the CPU, allowing data and computation results to be transferred between the main memory and the registers. As in our previous example, this version of the simulator does not contain an explicit control unit. The user must serve as the control unit, selecting the desired settings on the Main Memory Bus and C Bus to control the data flow. Note that these buses can move data either between main memory and the registers or from the ALU to main memory, depending on how the user sets the switches. The user can open and close these bus switches by clicking them, effectively disconnecting and connecting the buses.

Figures 14.7 through 14.9 demonstrate using the simulator to add two numbers stored in main memory.

• When the CPU must add two numbers stored in main memory, the first step is to copy one of the numbers into a register. In Figure 14.7, the user has selected the first number to be added, currently in main memory location 0, by clicking the R/W button next to that location (R/W refers to the fact

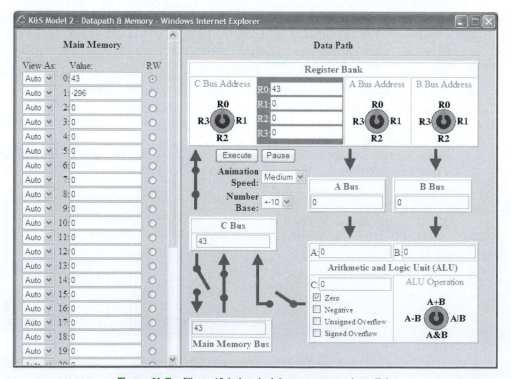

Figure 14.7 First, 43 is loaded from memory into R0.

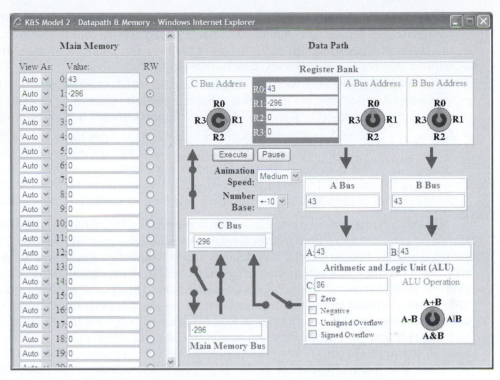

Figure 14.8 Second, −296 is loaded from main memory into R1.

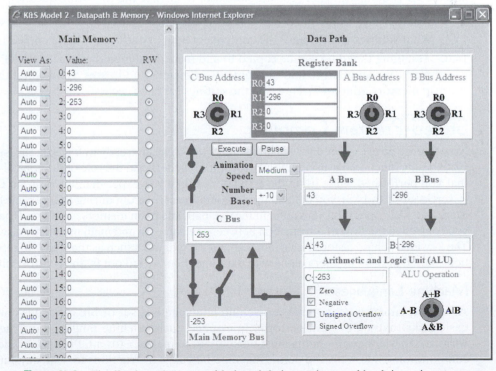

Figure 14.9 Finally, the values are added, and their sum is stored back in main memory.

that the button selects which memory location will be *read from* or *written to*). The user has also configured the arrows surrounding the Main Memory Bus so that they connect main memory to the registers. Once inside the CPU, the Main Memory Bus connects to the C Bus, which loads the number into register R0 (as the C Bus knob is set to R0).

- Figure 14.8 illustrates the next step in our example, which involves copying the second number into a register. Because the user has highlighted the R/W button next to main memory location 1 and set the C Bus knob to R1, the contents of location 1 are fetched and stored in register R1.

- Figure 14.9 depicts the CPU cycle during which the ALU adds the contents of R0 and R1. Note that the A Bus, B Bus, and ALU Operation knob settings are the same as those in Figures 14.3 through 14.6; this is because the two examples portray the same task (i.e., adding the numbers stored in R0 and R1). In Figure 14.9, however, the switches on the Main Memory bus are set so that the result of the addition is sent to main memory, rather than to the registers.

Two interesting observations can be made concerning the behavior of the simulator. First, the simulator requires more time to transfer data between main memory and the CPU than it does to perform a CPU datapath cycle. This delay is meant to simulate the slower access times associated with main memory. In a real computer, as many as 10 CPU cycles might occur in the time it takes to transfer data between the CPU and main memory. The second observation is that, even while data is being fetched from main memory, operations are still performed on the CPU datapath. For example, in Figure 14.8, the number in R0 (43) is sent along both the A and B Buses to the ALU, yielding the sum 86. This might seem wasteful, since the result of the ALU operation is ignored (due to the disconnected C Bus). Surprisingly, this is an accurate reflection of a CPU's internal workings. It is more efficient for the ALU to perform needless computations while data is being transferred to or from main memory than it would be to add extra circuitry to recognize whether the C Bus is connected.

HANDS-ON EXERCISES:

Experiment with this simulator until you are familiar with the interactions between main memory and the CPU datapath. Then, use the simulator to answer the following questions:

14.4. What settings would result in the sum of registers R0 and R3 being stored in memory location 4?

14.5. What settings would cause the contents of memory address 4 to be copied into register R0?

14.6. Assuming that data can be copied to and from main memory in a single CPU cycle, how many cycles are required to add the contents of memory addresses 5 and 6 and then store the result in memory address 7? Describe the settings for each cycle.

Stored-Program Computer

Now that we have explored how main memory works, we are ready to focus on the last component of the CPU: a fully functioning, automatic control unit. To understand the role of the control unit, recall the tasks that you performed while using the simulators. When you experimented with the Datapath Simulator (Exercises 14.1 to 14.3), you defined the computation carried out during a CPU cycle by selecting the registers and ALU operation via knobs. In the datapath and main memory simulator (Exercises 14.4 to 14.6), you controlled the flow of information between the datapath and main memory via switches on the buses. The key idea behind a stored-program computer is that tasks such as these can be represented as instructions, stored in main memory along with data, and then carried out by the control unit.

Machine Languages

As we explained in Chapter 8, a machine language is a set of binary codes corresponding to the basic tasks that a CPU can perform. In essence, each machine-language instruction specifies how various hardware components must be configured in order for a CPU cycle to perform a particular computation. Thus, we could define machine-language instructions for our simulator by enumerating all the physical settings of the knobs and switches. For example, the settings:

```
A Bus = R0          ALU Switch = closed
B Bus = R1          MMIn Switch = open
ALU = A+B           MMOut Switch = open
C Bus = R2          C Switch = closed
```

would define a configuration in which the contents of R0 and R1 are added and stored back in R2. This notation might suffice to control the behavior of a very simple machine, such as the one represented in our simulator; however, real-world CPUs contain an extremely large number of physical components, and specifying the status of all these parts during every CPU cycle would be impossible. Furthermore, because machine-language instructions are stored in memory along with data, the instructions must ultimately be represented as bit patterns.

Figure 14.10 describes a simple machine language that has been designed for our simulator. As the main memory locations in our simulator can hold a maximum of 16 bits, our language represents each instruction as a 16-bit pattern. The initial bits indicate the type of task that the CPU must perform, whereas the subsequent bits indicate the registers and/or memory locations involved in the task. Because there are only four registers, two bits suffice to represent a register number; because there are 32 main memory locations, five bits suffice to represent a memory address. For instance, all instructions that involve adding the contents of two registers begin with the bit pattern 1010000100. The final six bits of an addition instruction represent the destination register (i.e., the register where the result will be stored) and the source registers (i.e., the registers whose contents will be added by the ALU), respectively. As an example, suppose that you wanted to add the contents of R0 and R1 and then store the result in R2—i.e., R2 = R0 + R1. The bit patterns for R2 ($2 = 10_2$), R0 ($0 = 00_2$), and R1 ($1 = 01_2$) would be appended to the initial bit pattern for addition (1010000100), yielding the machine-language instruction 1010000100100001. Similarly, if the intent were R3 = R0 + R1, then the bit pattern for R3 ($3 = 11_2$) would replace that of R2: 1010000100110001.

The first two machine-language instructions in Figure 14.10 correspond to tasks that users can perform with the CPU Datapath Simulator—i.e., selecting an ALU operation to be executed and the

Operation	Machine-Language Instruction	Example
Add contents of two registers, store result in another register e.g., R0 = R1 + R2	1010000100 RR RR RR	1010000100 00 01 10 will add contents of R1 (01) and R2 (10), then store the result in R0 (00)
Subtract contents of two registers, store result in another register e.g., R0 = R1 - R2	1010001000 RR RR RR	1010001000 00 01 10 will take contents of R1 (01), subtract R2 (10), then store the result in R0 (00)
Load contents of memory location into register e.g., R3 = M[5]	100000010 RR MMMMM	100000010 11 00101 will load contents of memory location 5 (00101) into R3 (11)
Store contents of register in memory location e.g., M[5] = R3	100000100 RR MMMMM	100000100 11 00101 will store contents of memory location 5 (00101) in R3 (11)
Move contents of one register into another register e.g., R1 = R0	100100010000 RR RR	100100010000 01 00 will move contents of R0 (00) to R1 (01)
Halt the machine	1111111111111111	N/A

Figure 14.10 Machine language for Computer Simulator.

registers to be operated on during a CPU cycle. The next three instructions correspond to tasks that users can perform with the datapath and memory version of the simulator—i.e., controlling the flow of information between the main memory and the datapath. The last instruction, HALT, tells the control unit when a sequence of instructions terminates. Of course, a real CPU would require many more instructions than these. For example, if a CPU executes programs that include conditional statements (such as JavaScript if statements and while loops), its machine language must support branching instructions that allow the CPU to jump from one instruction to another. However, Figure 14.10's limited instruction set is sufficient to demonstrate the workings of a basic CPU and its control unit.

Control Unit

Once a uniform machine language for a particular CPU is established, instructions can be stored in main memory along with data. It is the job of the control unit to obtain each machine-language instruction from memory, interpret its meaning, carry out the specified CPU cycle, and then move on to the next instruction. Because instructions and data are both stored in the same memory, the control unit must be able to recognize where a sequence of instructions begins and ends. In real computers, this task is usually performed by the operating system, which maintains a list of each program in memory and its location. For simplicity, our simulator assumes that the first instruction is stored in memory location 0. The end of the instruction sequence is explicitly identified using the HALT bit pattern.

To track the execution of an instruction sequence, the control unit maintains a ***program counter (PC)***, which stores the address of the next instruction to be executed. As we are assuming that all programs start at address 0, the PC's value is initialized to 0 before program execution begins. When the control unit needs to fetch and execute an instruction, it accesses the PC and then obtains the instruction stored in the corresponding memory location. After the control unit fetches the instruction, the PC is incremented so that it identifies the next instruction in the sequence.

The steps carried out by the control unit can be defined as a general algorithm, in which instructions are repeatedly fetched and executed:

Fetch-Execute Algorithm carried out by the control unit:

1. Initialize PC = 0.
2. Fetch the instruction stored at memory location PC, and set PC = PC + 1.
3. As long as the current instruction is not the HALT instruction, repeatedly:
   a. Decode the instruction—that is, determine the CPU hardware settings required to carry it out.
   b. Configure the CPU hardware to match the settings indicated in the instruction.
   c. Execute a CPU datapath cycle using those settings.
   d. When the cycle is complete, fetch the next instruction from memory location PC, and set PC = PC + 1.

For example, suppose that main memory contained the program and data shown in Figure 14.11. The first five memory locations (addresses 0 through 4) contain machine-language instructions for adding two numbers and storing their sum back in memory. The numbers to be added are stored in memory locations 5 and 6. To execute this program, the control unit would carry out the following steps:

1. First, the program counter is initialized: PC = 0.
2. The instruction at memory location 0 (corresponding to the current value of PC) is fetched, and the PC is incremented: PC = 0 + 1 = 1.
3. Because this instruction (1000000100000101) is not a HALT instruction, it is decoded: the CPU hardware is configured so that it will load the contents of memory location 5 into register R0, and a CPU cycle is executed.
4. The next instruction (at memory location 1, corresponding to the current value of PC) is fetched, and the PC is incremented: PC = 1 + 1 = 2.
5. Because this instruction (1000000100100110) is not a HALT instruction, it is decoded: the CPU hardware is configured so that it will load the contents of memory location 6 into register R1, and a CPU cycle is executed.

```
0: 1000000100000101        // load memory location 5 into R0
1: 1000000100100110        // load memory location 6 into R1
2: 1010000100100001        // add R0 and R1, store result in R2
3: 1000001001000111        // copy R2 to memory location 7
4: 1111111111111111        // halt
5: 0000000000001001        // data to be added: 9
6: 0000000000000001        // data to be added: 1
7: 0000000000000000        // location where sum is to be stored
```

Figure 14.11   Machine-language program for adding two numbers in memory.

6. The next instruction (at memory location 2, corresponding to the current value of PC) is fetched, and the PC is incremented: PC = 2 + 1 = 3.

7. Because this instruction (1010000100100001) is not a HALT instruction, it is decoded: the CPU hardware is configured so that it will add the contents of registers R0 and R1 and store the result in register R2, and a CPU cycle is executed.

8. The next instruction (at memory location 3, corresponding to the current value of PC) is fetched, and the PC is incremented: PC = 3 + 1 = 4.

9. Because this instruction (1000001001000111) is not a HALT instruction, it is decoded: the CPU hardware is configured so that it will copy the contents of register R2 to memory location 7, and a CPU cycle is executed.

10. The next instruction (at memory location 4, corresponding to the current value of PC) is fetched, and the PC is incremented: PC = 4 + 1 = 5.

11. Because this instruction (1111111111111111) is a HALT instruction, the control unit recognizes the end of the program and stops executing.

Stored-Program Computer Simulator

The Stored-Program Computer Simulator (accessible at http://balance3e.com/Ch14/machine.html) models the behavior of a complete, stored-program computer. Instructions and data can be entered into memory, with the first instruction assumed to be at memory location 0. The control unit is responsible for fetching and interpreting the machine-language instructions, as well as carrying out the tasks specified by those instructions.

The simulator contains several display boxes to illustrate the control unit's inner workings. As we described in the previous section, the program counter (PC) lists the address of the next instruction to be executed. In addition to the PC, CPUs also maintain an ***instruction register (IR)***, which lists the instruction that the control unit is currently executing. The IR is displayed in the simulator as an additional text box. Above these boxes, the simulator exhibits the actual knob and switch settings defined by the current instruction—this makes the correspondence between the machine-language instruction and the CPU hardware settings more obvious. Knob settings are specified as two-bit binary numbers: 00 represents a knob pointing straight up, 01 represents a knob pointing to the right, 10 represents a knob pointing down, and 11 represents a knob pointing to the left. The four switch settings are represented by a four-bit pattern, with a 1 bit indicating a closed switch and a 0 bit an open switch (the topmost switch in the simulator, the C Bus, corresponds to the first bit, followed by the three remaining switches from left to right).

Figures 14.12 through 14.17 demonstrate using the simulator to execute the example machine-language program from Figure 14.11.

• Figure 14.12 depicts the initial state of the simulator. The machine-language instructions are stored in main memory, starting at address 0. The data required to execute the instructions is

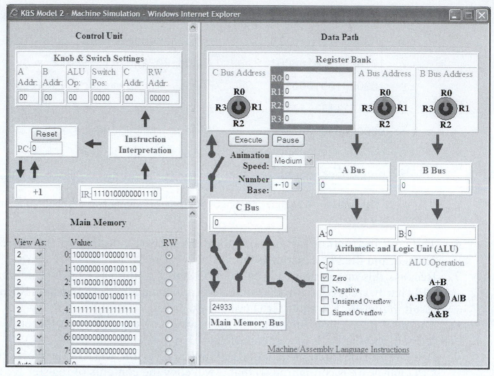

Figure 14.12 Initial state of the simulator, with program stored in main memory.

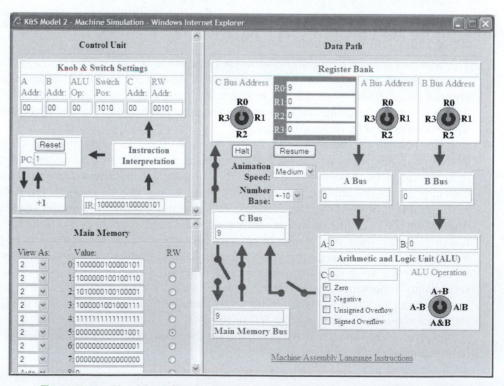

Figure 14.13 Simulator after the first instruction has been executed (R0 = MM5).

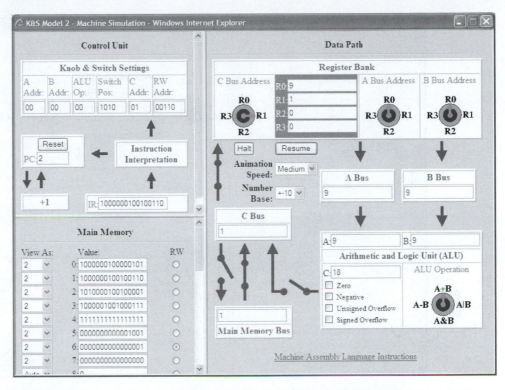

Figure 14.14 Simulator after the second instruction has been executed (R1 = MM6).

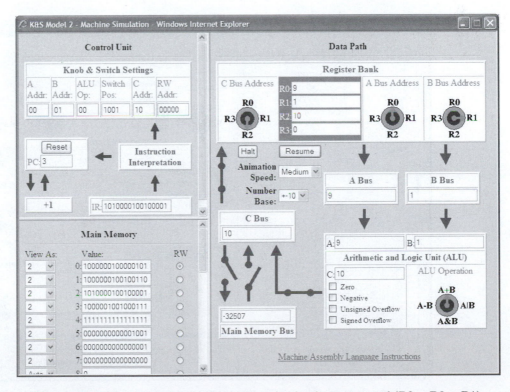

Figure 14.15 Simulator after the third instruction has been executed (R2 = R0 + R1).

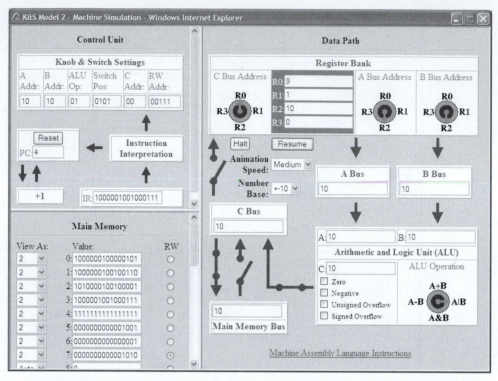

Figure 14.16 Simulator after the fourth statement has been executed (MM7 = R2).

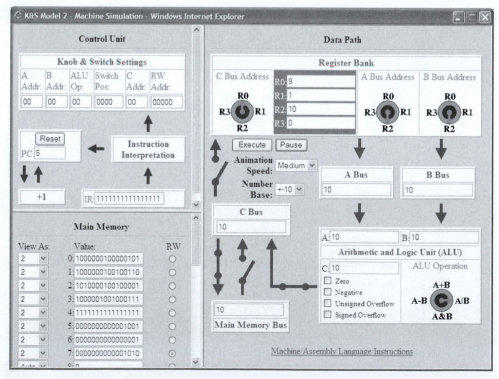

Figure 14.17 Simulator after the fifth statement has been executed (HALT).

also stored in memory, at addresses 5 and 6, immediately following the last instruction. Within the control unit, the program counter (PC) is initialized to 0, so the instruction at address 0 will be the first to be loaded and executed. To assist the user, the page includes a link to a reference page that summarizes all of the machine- and assembly-language instructions, labeled "Machine/Assembly Language Instructions."

- Figure 14.13 portrays the simulator after the first instruction has been executed. Within the control unit, the instruction from address 0 has been loaded into the instruction register and translated into the knob and switch settings required to carry out the specified CPU datapath cycle. Once the control unit determines the correct knob and switch settings, it carries out the corresponding CPU datapath cycle. In this case, the value from memory location 5, the number 9, is loaded into register R0. Note that the PC is automatically incremented when the instruction is executed so the next instruction to be fetched and executed will be the instruction at address 1.

- Figure 14.14 shows the simulator after the next instruction, from memory location 1, has been executed. Here, the value from memory location 6, the number 1, is loaded into register R1.

- Figure 14.15 depicts the result of executing the next instruction, from memory location 2, which adds the contents of registers R0 and R1 and stores the result in register R2.

- Figure 14.16 portrays the result of executing the next instruction, from memory location 3, which copies the result of the addition, stored in R2, into memory location 7.

- Finally, Figure 14.17 shows the computer after the program terminates. Recall that the HALT instruction 1111111111111111 tells the control unit to stop processing. As no datapath cycle is executed once the HALT instruction is recognized by the control unit, the knob and switch settings within the datapath are not changed from the previous cycle.

The simulator is designed so that the user can enter values in main memory as either decimal or binary numbers. By default, values entered by the user are assumed to be decimal numbers. However, the user can always select 2 from the View As box to the left of a memory location in order to view the contents in binary. Before entering a machine-language instruction in a memory cell, the user must first set the value of the View As box to 2, because machine-language instructions are represented in binary.

HANDS-ON EXERCISES:

Experiment with this simulator until you are familiar with its behavior. Then, use the simulator to answer the following questions:

14.7. What task would the following machine-language program perform?

```
0: 1010001000000000
1: 1000001000000011
2: 1111111111111111
```

14.8. What sequence of machine-language instructions would cause the contents of the four registers to be copied into memory locations 7, 8, 9, and 10, respectively?

14.9. What sequence of machine-language instructions would cause the simulator to add the contents of memory locations 10, 11, and 12 and then store the result in memory location 13?

14.10. What do you think would happen if you forgot to place a HALT instruction at the end of a machine-language program? How would the control unit react? Use the simulator to test your prediction, then report the results.

The Role of Input/Output Devices

To complete our description of the stored-program computer, we must at least briefly discuss the role of input and output devices. Input devices such as keyboards, mice, and scanners allow the user to communicate with the computer by entering data and instructions, which are then stored in memory and accessed by the CPU. Likewise, output devices such as display screens, speakers, and printers allow the user to view the current status of the computer and access computation results that are stored in memory.

Computers that are designed to run one program at a time, such as the first programmable computers (introduced in the 1950s) and the first personal computers (introduced in the 1970s), provide relatively straightforward methods of user interaction. The user enters program instructions and data directly into main memory locations via input devices such as keyboards or tape readers. Then, by flipping a switch or entering a specific command, the user instructs the CPU to fetch the program instructions from memory and execute them in sequential order. Once a particular computation has been completed, the user can view its result by sending the contents of memory to a printer or display screen. This process is closely modeled by our simulator, in which the user enters instructions and data by typing them in main memory boxes, then initiates execution by clicking a button. In the case of the simulator, however, the final step of sending results to an output device is not necessary—the contents of the registers and main memory are already visible.

As we discussed in Chapters 6 and 10, most modern computers allow for multitasking, meaning that multiple programs can be loaded in main memory and be active simultaneously. When multiple programs are to be executed, user interactions and the computations that result from those interactions become more complex. In particular, the instructions and data associated with each program must be loaded into separate portions of main memory. When the user switches from one program to another (say, by clicking on a different window in the graphical user interface), the CPU must save the state of the current program and be able to locate the portion of memory associated with the new program. These tasks, and many others involving the coordination of programs and CPU processing, are managed by the operating system.

Machine vs. Assembly Languages

It is important to note that the machine language and hardware configurations associated with our simulator are much simpler than those of any actual computer. A real machine language might encompass tens or hundreds of instructions, and a real CPU might contain hundreds or thousands of configurable components. However, our model is sufficient to demonstrate computer behavior at its lowest level.

The simulator is also useful in representing the difficulty and tedium of programming in a machine language. As you learned in Chapter 8, writing, debugging, and understanding bit-sequence instructions can be mind-numbing work. Over the past fifty years, computer programming has advanced significantly, and most modern programmers are able to avoid direct machine-language programming. Some of the earliest programmer tools were assembly languages, which substitute words for bit patterns, allowing the programmer to write:

```
ADD R0 R1 R2
```

instead of the machine-language instruction:

```
1010000100000110
```

It is much easier for programmers to remember and understand assembly-language instructions than patterns of 0s and 1s. Furthermore, most assembly languages support the use of variable names, enabling programmers to specify memory locations by descriptive names, rather than by numerical addresses. This greatly simplifies the programmer's task, as she no longer needs to worry about the physical location of data and how locations might shift as new instructions are inserted into memory. Figure 14.18 lists one possible set of assembly-language instructions that correspond to the machine-language instructions from Figure 14.11.

Within the Stored Program Computer Simulator, the user may enter assembly-language instructions directly in memory. The default mode for displaying the contents of memory locations, labeled "Auto" in the View As box, will automatically recognize assembly-language instructions and will display them as text (changing the label to "Inst" to acknowledge that they are instructions).

Operation	Machine-Language Instruction	Assembly-Language Instruction
Add contents of two registers, then store result in another register e.g., R0 = R1 + R2	1010000100 RR RR RR e.g., 1010000100 00 01 10	ADD [REG] [REG] [REG] e.g., ADD R0 R1 R2
Subtract contents of two registers, then store result in another register e.g., R0 = R1 − R2	1010001000 RR RR RR e.g., 1010001000 00 01 10	SUB [REG] [REG] [REG] e.g., SUB R0 R1 R2
Load contents of memory location into register e.g., R3 = MM5	100000010 RR MMM e.g., 100000010 11 00101	LOAD [REG] [MEM] e.g., LOAD R3 5
Store contents of register into memory location e.g., MM5 = R3	100000100 RR MMMMM e.g., 100000100 11 00101	STORE [MEM] [REG] e.g., STORE 5 R3
Move contents of one register into another register e.g., R1 = R0	100100010000 RR RR e.g., 100100010000 01 00	MOVE [REG] [REG] e.g., MOVE R1 R0
Halt the machine	1111111111111111	HALT

Figure 14.18   Assembly-language instructions.

After inputting the instructions, the user can switch between viewing the instruction in assembly- or machine-language form by selecting Inst (for assembly-language instructions) or 2 (for machine-language instructions in binary form) in the View As box to the left of the instruction. For example, Figure 14.19 depicts the same program that is pictured in Figure 14.12, but here the instructions are formatted as Inst.

HANDS-ON EXERCISES:

Experiment with the simulator until you are comfortable with the correspondence between machine-language and assembly-language instructions. Then, use the simulator to answer the following questions:

14.11. What sequence of assembly-language instructions corresponds to the machine-language instruction set from Exercise 14.7?

14.12. What sequence of assembly-language instructions corresponds to the machine-language instruction set you wrote in Exercise 14.9?

14.13. Write a sequence of assembly-language instructions that multiplies the contents of memory location 10 by four. For example, if the number 10 were stored in memory location 10, executing your instructions would cause the simulator to store 40 there. *Note:* Although the ALU Operation knob does not provide a multiplication setting, a number can be multiplied via repeated additions (e.g., 10*4 = 10 + 10 + 10 + 10).

Looking Ahead...

In this chapter, you studied the internal workings of computers, focusing on the CPU, main memory, and their interactions. By experimenting with the various simulators, you saw how the CPU breaks up even the most complex computing tasks into sequences of very simple instructions, each of which can be executed during a single CPU datapath cycle. Although buses that connect the CPU to main memory enable the manipulation of large amounts of data, the computer must transfer each data

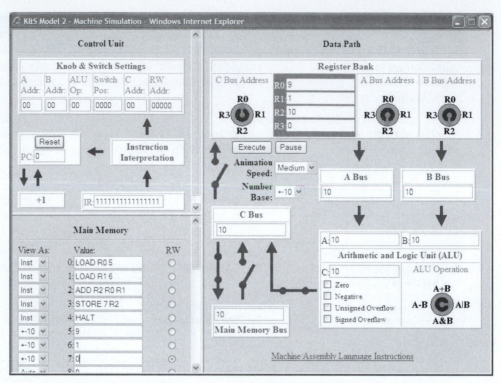

Figure 14.19 Assembly-language program displayed in computer simulator.

value into a CPU register, perform operations on the value within the ALU, and then store the result of the computation back in main memory. The combination of a control unit and main memory allows computers to process stored programs. This behavior was modeled by our most sophisticated simulator, in which programs consisting of machine-language instruction sequences were stored in memory, fetched and decoded by the control unit, then executed in a series of CPU datapath cycles.

Building upon your general understanding of computer components and their organization, Chapter 16 will delve deeper into the details of their design and construction. In particular, you will study the construction and behavior of transistors and integrated circuits. However, before you consider how these technologies are used to build the hardware components of computer, Chapter 15 will describe a general methodology for designing and implementing software components. The object-oriented approach to software development attempts to simplify the task of designing and testing software systems by focusing on programming structures that model real-world objects. For example, a JavaScript string is an object that models a word or phrase, with useful operations on a string (such as capitalizing it or extracting a substring) provided as part of the language. Chapter 15 will describe the JavaScript string type, and explore applications that involve storing and manipulating text.

Chapter Summary

- Virtually all modern computers use the von Neumann architecture, which divides the hardware into three main components: memory, a central processing unit (CPU), and input/output devices.

- The CPU is responsible for obtaining data and instructions from memory, carrying out the instructions, and storing the results back in memory.

- The CPU is comprised of the arithmetic logic unit (ALU), registers, and the control unit. The ALU is the collection of circuitry that performs actual operations on data. Registers are memory locations that are built into the CPU and used to store data for fast access. The control unit is the circuitry in charge of fetching data and instructions from main memory, as well as controlling the flow of data from the registers to the ALU and back to the registers.

- The path that data follows within the CPU, traveling along buses from registers to the ALU and then back to registers, is known as the CPU datapath. A single rotation around the CPU datapath is referred to as a CPU datapath cycle, or CPU cycle.

- A bus connects main memory to the CPU, enabling the computer to copy data and instructions to registers and then copy the results of computations back to main memory.

- As a program is executed, the control unit processes the program instructions, identifies which data values are needed to carry out the specified tasks, and loads those values from main memory into registers.

- In practice, transferring data between main memory and the CPU takes much longer than executing a single CPU cycle.

- A machine language is a set of binary codes corresponding to the basic tasks that a CPU can perform.

- To execute a program stored in memory, the control unit must repeatedly fetch the next machine-language instruction from memory, interpret its meaning, carry out the specified CPU cycle, and then move on to the next instruction.

- To track the execution of an instruction sequence, the control unit maintains a program counter (PC), which stores the address of the next instruction to be executed.

- Computers that are designed to run one program at a time provide relatively straightforward methods of user interaction, such as having the user enter instructions and data directly into main memory locations via a keyboard and viewing the results of computations on a screen.

- Computers that support multitasking—the ability to load and execute multiple programs simultaneously—require support from the operating system to coordinate programs and manage shared resources.

- Since assembly languages substitute words for the bit patterns used in machine languages, they make it much easier for the programmer to write, understand, and debug code.

Review Questions

1. TRUE or FALSE? Any piece of memory that is used to store the sum of numeric values is known as a register.

2. TRUE or FALSE? The path that data follows within the CPU, traveling along buses from registers to the ALU and then back to registers, is known as the CPU datapath.

3. TRUE or FALSE? All modern CPUs provide the same set of basic operations that can be executed in a single CPU cycle.

4. TRUE or FALSE? The size of main memory is generally measured in MHz or GHz.

5. TRUE or FALSE? Suppose you wish to add two numbers that are stored in memory. Before the arithmetic logic unit (ALU) can add the numbers, they must first be transferred to registers within the CPU.

6. TRUE or FALSE? In real computers, it takes roughly the same amount of time to transfer data from main memory to registers as it does to add two numbers in registers.

7. TRUE or FALSE? Within the CPU, the control unit is responsible for fetching machine-language instructions from memory, interpreting their meaning, and carrying out the specified CPU cycles.

8. TRUE or FALSE? Suppose a CPU contains eight registers. Within a machine-language instruction, at least 3 bits would be required to uniquely identify one of the registers.

9. TRUE or FALSE? In a multitasking computer, the program counter keeps track of how many programs are currently loaded into main memory.

10. TRUE or FALSE? In a stored-program computer, both machine-language instructions and the data operated on by those instructions can reside in main memory at the same time.

11. Name the three subunits of the CPU, and describe the role of each subunit in carrying out computations.

12. Describe how data values move around the CPU datapath and what actions occur during a single CPU cycle. How does the datapath relate to CPU speed?

13. Consider two computer systems that are identical except for their CPUs. System 1 contains a 1.8GHz Pentium 4, whereas System 2 contains a 1.8GHz PowerPC processor. Will these two systems always require the same amount of time to execute a given program? Justify your answer.

14. Consider the following tasks: (1) adding 100 numbers stored in main memory, and (2) adding a number to itself 100 times. Although both tasks require 100 additions, the second would be executed much more quickly than the first would. Why?

15. Machine languages are machine specific, meaning that each type of computer has its own machine language. Explain why this is the case.

16. Within the control unit, what is the role of the program counter (PC)? That is, how is the PC used in fetching and executing instructions?

17. In a stored-program computer, both instructions and data are stored in main memory. How does the control unit know where the program instructions begin? How does it know where the instructions end?

18. Describe two advantages of assembly languages over machine languages.

References

Brain, Marshall. "How Microprocessors Work." *HowStuffWorks*, December, 2009. Online at `http://www.howstuffworks.com/microprocessor.htm`.

Braught, G. "Computer Organization in the Breadth First Course." *Journal of Computing in Small Colleges*, 16(4), 2001.

Braught, Grant, and David Reed. "The Knob & Switch Computer: A Computer Architecture Simulator for Introductory Computer Science." *ACM Journal of Educational Resources in Computing*, 1(4), 2001.

Malone, Michael. *The Microprocessor: A Biography*. New York: Springer-Verlag, 1995.

"The PC Technology Guide—Components/Processors." *PCTechGuide*, December, 2009. Online at `http://www.pctechguide.com/02Processors.htm`.

Stallings, William. *Computer Organization and Architecture: Designing for Performance*, 8th ed. Upper Saddle River, NJ: Prentice Hall, 2009.

Tanenbaum, Andrew S. *Structured Computer Organization*, 5th ed. Upper Saddle River, NJ: Prentice Hall, 2006.

JavaScript Strings

This chapter uses narrative, examples, and hands-on exercises to introduce programming concepts and Web development skills.

The basic tool for the manipulation of reality is the manipulation of words. If you can control the meaning of words, you can control the people who must use the words.

Philip K. Dick
I Hope I Shall Arrive Soon

Words form the thread on which we string our experiences.

Aldous Huxley
Brave New World

Throughout this book, you have written numerous interactive Web pages that manipulate numbers. These pages have read in numbers entered by the user (via text boxes), performed calculations using mathematical operators and functions, and displayed the results of computations (via alert windows or page divisions). You have also written pages that process words and phrases, but your tools for handling string values have been more limited. Although you have learned to read in string values and display them in a page, the only operation that you have performed on strings is concatenation using the + operator.

This chapter explores features of the JavaScript string type, including ways to manipulate text within interactive Web pages. You will learn that strings are different from numbers and Booleans in that they are *objects*, software units that encapsulate both data and operations that can be performed on that data. The techniques introduced in this chapter will allow you to access various components of a string, construct new strings by modifying existing ones, and traverse strings in search of desired sequences or patterns. By the end of this chapter, you will be able to solve numerous complex problems that involve storing and modifying text.

Strings as Objects

As commercial software projects have become larger and more complex, the designers of programming languages have searched for methods of organizing software that will ease the software development process and, at the same time, be intuitive for programmers.

In the 1970s and early 1980s, the ***procedural programming*** approach, which was supported by languages such as Pascal and C, encouraged programmers to design programs around actions—the programmer would identify the main actions to be carried out by the program and would then implement functions for each action. Although this approach was effective when programs were relatively small (hundreds or perhaps thousands of lines long), it did not always scale well to larger projects involving teams of developers. Today, the predominant approach to software development is ***object-oriented programming***, which is supported by modern languages such as C++ and Java. Object-oriented languages encourage programmers to design programs around software objects—the programmer identifies the real-world objects involved, such as a bank account or customer, and models those objects with programming structures. The object-oriented approach has proven effective at managing large systems, because individual objects can be assigned to different programming teams and developed independently. The development of self-contained software objects can also cut development costs by supporting code reuse, as the same or similar objects can be combined in different ways to solve different kinds of problems.

To better understand what a software object consists of, consider the analogy of a common real-world object: a doorbell. A thorough description of a doorbell encompasses not only the bells physical components (a button, a bell, and wires) but also its functionality. When a doorbell is pressed, the noise generated by the bell alerts you that someone is at the door. A software object represents a similar combination of data and behaviors. For example, we have seen that an HTML button, when combined with JavaScript code, serves as a software model of a doorbell. Each button has properties, including a name and a label, and predefined functionality, as defined by the JavaScript code that is executed when a user clicks the button.

Although JavaScript does not provide the full functionality of advanced languages such as C++ and Java, it does support the development and use of simple software objects. In addition to providing the functionality for HTML objects such as buttons, JavaScript provides its own software objects that aid the programmer in developing code. For example, the `Math` object (first introduced in Chapter 7) contains many useful properties (e.g., constants representing `PI` and `E`) as well as functions (e.g., `sqrt` for computing the square root of a number and `random` for generating a random value). As you will learn in this chapter, a JavaScript string is an object that models words and phrases, encompassing both properties (characteristics of the string, such as its length and the characters that compose it) and functionality (operations that can be performed on the string value, such as concatenation and character access).

Properties and Methods

In previous chapters, we defined a string as a sequence of characters enclosed in quotes. However, strings also possess a set of ***properties*** that describe a string and ***operations*** that can be applied to a string to trigger various actions. For example, each string has a `length` property that records the number of characters in the string. To access the length of a string, you specify the name of the variable that stores the string value, followed by a period and `length`, which is the name of the property. Thus, if `word = 'foo'`, then the expression `word.length` would evaluate to 3, as there are three characters in `foo`. Figure 15.1 depicts another example, in which `str = 'Foo 2 You'`, causing `str.length` to evaluate to 9.

In addition, there are numerous operations (i.e., functions) that are predefined for use with JavaScript strings. For example, when the `toUpperCase` function is applied to a string, it returns a copy of that string in which all lowercase letters are converted to uppercase. Likewise, the `toLowerCase` function returns an entirely lowercase version of a given string. Unlike other JavaScript functions, which may be called with any type of input, functions such as `toUpperCase` and `toLowerCase` are explicitly associated with strings. In fact, it is natural to think of each string value as having its own copy of these functions, in the same way that each string has its own `length` property.

To differentiate them from stand-alone functions, functions that belong to an object are known as ***methods*** of that object. As was the case with properties, programmers apply the methods associated with an object to that object by specifying the objects name, a period, and then the method (function) call. Figure 15.1 demonstrates the effects of applying the `toUpperCase` and `toLowerCase`

str = 'Foo 2 You'; | 'Foo 2 You' |
                        str

len = str.lenght; | 'Foo 2 You' | | 9 |
                        str   len

upStr = str.toUpperCase (); | 'Foo 2 You' | | 9 | | 'FOO 2 YOU' |
                                 str   len   upStr

downStr = str.toLowerCase (); | 'Foo 2 You' | | 9 | | 'FOO 2 YOU' | | 'foo 2 you' |
                                   str   len   upStr   downStr

Figure 15.1 Tracing the effects of string manipulations.

methods to the string variable `str`. Note that instead of modifying the original string value stored in `str`, these method calls simply return new copies of the string in which all letters are uppercase or lowercase.

The Web page in Figure 15.2 demonstrates accessing a string's `length` property and `toUpperCase` method within a program. The page contains a text box in which the user can enter a string. When the button is clicked, the length of that string and an uppercase version are displayed in the page division. Figure 15.3 shows the resulting Web page.

```
1.  <html>
2.  <!-- strdemo.html                                          Dave Reed -->
3.  <!-- This page demonstrates several string properties and operations -->
4.  <!-- ============================================================ -->
5.
6.  <head>
7.    <title> String Fun </title>
8.    <script type="text/javascript">
9.      function Process()
10.     // Assumes: strBox contains a string
11.     // Results: displays the outcome of string operations in outputDiv
12.     {
13.       var str;
14.
15.       str = document.getElementById('strBox').value;
16.
17.       document.getElementById('outputDiv').innerHTML =
18.         'length: ' + str.length + '<br>' +
19.         'uppercase: ' + str.toUpperCase() + '<br>';
20.     }
21.   </script>
22. </head>
23.
24. <body>
25.   <h2>String Demo</h2>
26.   <p>
27.     Enter a string: <input type="text" id="strBox" size=20 value="">
28.   </p>
29.   <input type="button" value="Click to Process" onclick="Process();">
30.   <hr>
31.   <div id="outputDiv"></div>
32. </body>
33. </html>
```

Figure 15.2 Web page that demonstrates the `length` property and `toUpperCase` method.

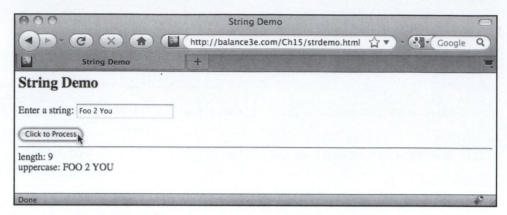

Figure 15.3 `strdemo.html` rendered in a Web browser.

EXERCISE 15.1

Enter the `strdemo.html` text from Figure 15.2 into a new Web page, then load this page to verify that it behaves as described.

After experimenting with `strdemo.html`, augment the page so that a lowercase version of the string is also displayed in the page division.

Common errors to avoid...

Note that the string methods `toUpperCase` and `toLowerCase` do not in any way change the string value on which they operate. Instead, these methods return a copy of the original string in which all characters are either uppercase or lowercase. As such, a call to one of these methods in a statement by itself serves no real purpose. For example, consider the statement:

```
str.toUpperCase();
```

This call would return a copy of the string value stored in the variable `str`, but with all letters converted to uppercase. However, as this returned value is not saved in a variable or otherwise incorporated into a larger expression, the value is lost. To actually modify the value of `str`, making it uppercase, you must place the method call on the right-hand side of an assignment to that variable. For example, the following statement would replace `str`'s value with an uppercase version of `str`:

```
str = str.toUpperCase();
```

In general, the only way to change the value of a variable is via an assignment statement in which that variable appears on the left-hand side.

Common String-Manipulation Methods

The `toUpperCase` and `toLowerCase` methods described above are only two of many methods defined for strings. For example, other useful methods allow programmers to access and manipulate individual components of a string. Such components are identifiable via indices, or numbers that correspond to the order in which individual characters occur in a string. Indices are assigned in ascending order from left to right, so that the first character in the string is considered to be at index 0, the second character at index 1, and so on. The `charAt` method takes an index as input and returns the character stored at that particular index of the string. For example, the call `str.charAt(0)` will return the character at `str`'s index 0 (i.e., the first character in `str`), and `str.charAt(1)` will return the character at str's index 1 (i.e., the second character in str). Because string indices start at 0, the last character in a string str can be accessed via the call str.charAt(str.length - 1).

Whereas the charAt string method enables you to access a single character within a string, the substring method returns a sequence of characters within a string—that is, a substring. The substring method takes two numbers as inputs, representing the starting (inclusive) and ending (exclusive) indices that delimit the substring. For example, the call str.substring(0, 2) will return the substring consisting of the first two characters in the string str (from indices 0 and 1), and str.substring(1, 4) will return the substring consisting of the second, third, and fourth characters (from indices 1, 2, and 3).

EXERCISE 15.2

Assuming word = 'smarmy', predict the values that each of the following method calls would return:

```
word.charAt(0)
word.charAt(5)
word.charAt(word.length-1)
word.substring(0, 5)
word.substring(4, 5)
word.substring(1, word.length)
word.substring(0, word.length-1)
```

Common errors to avoid...

The string methods charAt and substring are very forgiving with respect to invalid indices, and this leeway can lead to undetected logic errors. If you call charAt with an index that is either too small (less than 0) or too big (greater than or equal to the string length), no error occurs. Instead, an empty string is returned. Likewise, if you call substring with indices that extend beyond the valid range for that string, the excess range will be ignored. For example, if word = 'smarmy', then word.substring(-1, 2) will return 'sm', just as the call word.substring(0,2) would. Similarly, the call word.substring(2, word.length+10) will return 'army', just as the call word.substring(2, word.length) would.

Thus, if you are writing code that employs these string methods, you cannot assume that the browser will catch errors related to invalid indices. Check your program's output carefully to ensure that each method call is accessing the intended value(s).

String Concatenation

As we have explained, the charAt and substring methods can be used to break a string into component parts. Conversely, the concatenation (+) operator, introduced in Chapter 5, can rejoin these parts and reassemble the original string. For example, assuming that the variable word stores a string, the following assignment would leave word's value unchanged:

```
word = word.charAt(0) + word.substring(1, word.length);
```

Here, the method calls to charAt and substring divide the string into two parts, one consisting of the string's first character and the other consisting of the rest of the string. However, the assignment statement concatenates the two parts back together and assigns the result back to word. For example, if word = 'smarmy', then the effect of this assignment would be word = 's' + 'marmy' = 'smarmy'.

Although the assignment statement above effectively demonstrates string concatenation, it does not serve any particular purpose, as word's value is not modified. The function defined in Figure 15.4 performs a similar but more useful task. Function Capitalize takes a string as input and returns a

```
function Capitalize(str)
// Assumes: str is a word
// Returns: str with first letter capitalized, all others lowercase
{
    var firstLetter, restString, cap;
    firstLetter = str.charAt(0);                  // GET FIRST CHAR
    restString = str.substring(1, str.length);    // GET REST OF WORD
    cap = firstLetter.toUpperCase() + restString.toLowerCase();
                                                  // PUT BACK TOGETHER

    return cap;
}
```

Figure 15.4   Function that capitalizes a string.

capitalized version of that string. Using the charAt and substring methods, the function divides the string into separate substrings containing the first character and the rest of the string, as before. However, the first character is made uppercase (using the toUpperCase method) and the rest of the string is made lowercase (using the toLowerCase method) before the function concatenates the two components back together.

EXERCISE 15.3

Create a text file named string.js and enter the Capitalize function into that file. Then modify your strdemo.html page so that it loads this library file. When the button in the page is clicked, in addition to displaying the previous values, it should also call the Capitalize function and display the capitalized word in the page.

Once you have done this, test the page using various string inputs to verify that the function produces the desired results. How does the function behave when given a string containing characters other than letters (e.g., digits, spaces, punctuation marks)? Explain your observations.

EXERCISE 15.4

Define a function named Rotate that takes a string as input and returns a copy of that string in which all characters are rotated one position to the left. This means that the second character should be shifted from index 1 to index 0, the third character should be shifted from index 2 to index 1, and so on. The first character should be shifted so that it appears at the end of the string. For example, the function call Rotate('abcde') should return the string 'bcdea'. Insert this function definition into your string.js library file. Then modify your strdemo.html page so that it also displays the rotated string when the button is clicked.

Searching Strings

The final string method that we will examine is the search method, which traverses a string in order to locate a given character or substring. The search method takes a character or string as input and then returns the index at which that character or string first occurs in the larger string. For example, if str = 'banana', then the call str.search('n') will return 2, because the character 'n' first occurs in str at index 2. Likewise, the call str.search('ana') will return 1, because the first occurrence of the substring 'ana' begins at index 1. If the desired character or substring does not occur in the string, the search method returns –1.

A simple application of the search method is to determine whether a string is a single word or a phrase. If the string contains no spaces, the call str.search(' ') will return –1, indicating that the string value consists of a single word. However, if str.search (' ') returns a non-negative value, then the presence of spaces signifies a phrase containing multiple words.

EXERCISE 15.5

Define a function named Classify that takes a string as input and then determines whether the string is a single word (containing no spaces) or a phrase (containing one or more spaces). The function should return a string value, either 'word' or 'phrase', depending on whether the input string contains any spaces. Once you have developed this function, insert its definition into your string.js library file. Then, modify your strdemo.html page so that it also displays whether the entered text is a word or phrase.

General Searches

As the previous examples demonstrate, the search method can be used to locate the first occurrence of a single character (such as a space) within a string. There are times, however, when you might wish to search for a type of character, such as vowels or punctuation marks, rather than a specific value. For example, consider the task of converting a word into Pig Latin. As you may recall from your childhood, Pig Latin is a silly variation on the English language in which words are translated as follows:

- If a word contains no vowels or begins with a vowel, the characters "way" are appended to the end of the word. Thus, the word *nth* is translated as "nthway" in Pig Latin, and *apple* is translated as "appleway."

- If a word begins with a consonant, its initial sequence of consonants is shifted to the end of the word and followed by "ay." Thus, the word *banana* is translated as "ananabay" in Pig Latin, and *cherry* is translated as "errychay."

For a program to translate a word into Pig Latin, it must find the first vowel in the word. If the word doesn't contain a vowel or the first vowel is at index 0, then the program should translate the word by concatenating "way" onto the end of the original string. If the first vowel in the word occurs at an index other than 0, then the substring of characters preceding that index should be concatenated onto the substring starting with that index, followed by "ay."

One option for locating the first vowel in a string is to conduct five different searches. That is, you could perform a search to find the first occurrence of an *a* (if any), another search to find the first occurrence of an *e* (if any), and additional searches for *i, o,* and *u*. Then you would have to compare the indices returned by these searches to determine the smallest, which would represent the first occurrence of a vowel. Fortunately, JavaScript provides a simpler means of searching for a class of characters. If you specify a sequence of characters between /[and]/, the search method will traverse the string and find the first occurrence of any character in that sequence. For example, the call phrase.search(/[aeiou]/) would return the index of the first occurrence of a lowercase vowel in phrase. If phrase contains no vowels, the search method will return –1, as before. Figure 15.5 lists several other search method calls that employ the /[ ]/ notation. Note that a hyphen can be used to more succinctly represent a range of characters, such as all lowercase letters (*a-z*) or all digits (0-9).

Common errors to avoid...

Although they look similar, the method calls phrase.search('aeiou') and phrase.search(/[aeiou]/) have very different meanings. When given a string (a sequence of characters surrounded by quotes) as input, the search method looks for the first occurrence of that string. When given a class of characters (a sequence of characters surrounded by /[and]/) as input, the search method looks for the first occurrence of any single character from that class.

As you experiment with the search method, make sure that you do not confuse these two types of searches.

`phrase.search(/[aeiou]/)`	returns the index of the first occurrence of a lowercase vowel in `phrase`; returns −1 if not found
`phrase.search(/[aeiouAEIOU]/)`	returns the index of the first occurrence of a lowercase or uppercase vowel in `phrase`; returns −1 if not found
`phrase.search(/[a-z]/)`	returns the index of the first occurrence of lowercase letter in `phrase`; returns −1 if not found
`phrase.search(/[a-zA-Z]/)`	returns the index of the first occurrence of lowercase or uppercase letter in `phrase`; returns −1 if not found
`phrase.search(/[0-9]/)`	returns the index of the first occurrence of a digit in `phrase`; returns −1 if not found
`phrase.search(/[ .,;:'!\?]/)`	returns the index of the first occurrence of a space or punctuation mark in `phrase`; returns −1 if not found

Figure 15.5 search method calls to locate classes of characters.

EXERCISE 15.6

Define a function named `PigLatin` that takes a string as input and returns the Pig Latin translation. For example, the call `PigLatin('oops')` should return `'oopsway'`, whereas `PigLatin('foo')` should return `'oofay'`. Insert this function definition into your `string.js` library file. Then create a Web page named `piglatin.html` in which the user can enter a word in a text box and click a button to see the Pig Latin translation.

Using your page, determine the Pig Latin translation of each of the following words:

```
scheme
3rd
shortstop
abracadabra
```

EXERCISE 15.7

Technically speaking, the Pig Latin rules that we have established apply only to words, not phrases. However, your current `piglatin.html` page does nothing to prevent users from entering a string containing spaces. Thus, a user could enter "foo bar" in the text box and be told that the Pig Latin translation is "oo barfay."

Modify your `PigLatin` function so that, before the string is translated, the function checks whether the input is a single word (i.e., whether it contains any spaces). If there are spaces in the input, the function should return the string "ILLEGAL INPUT".

Hint: the `Classify` function you wrote in Exercise 15.5 should prove useful here.

String Manipulations and Repetition

Although this chapter has introduced multiple string-manipulation techniques, none has involved conditional repetition. Capitalizing a word required dividing a string into pieces (using `charAt` and `substring`), modifying the pieces (using `toUpperCase` and `toLowerCase`), and then rejoining them (using the + operator). Likewise, converting a word into Pig Latin required finding a vowel (using `search`), splitting up the word (using `substring`), and putting it back together again (using +). However, certain manipulations, such as reversing a string's character sequence or replacing all the vowels in a string, involve repeatedly performing the same operations. To accomplish such tasks, we can combine while loops (introduced in Chapter 13) with string methods such as `charAt` and `search`.

```
str = 'abcd';
copy = '';                          // INITIALIZE copy TO EMPTY STRING

i = 0;                              // START AT BEGINNING OF str
while (i < str.length) {            // AS LONG AS CHARS LEFT IN str
    copy = copy + str.charAt(i);    //   ADD CHAR TO END OF copy
    i=i+1;                          //   GO TO NEXT CHAR
}
```

	copy	i	str.charAt(i)
before loop	''	0	'a'
after 1st loop pass	'a'	1	'b'
after 2nd loop pass	'ab'	2	'c'
after 3rd loop pass	'abc'	3	'd'
after 4th loop pass	'abcd'	4	''

Figure 15.6   Tracing code that copies a string character by character.

The JavaScript code segment in Figure 15.6 illustrates how a while loop can be used to access and process each individual character in a string. In this example, the characters that compose the string str are concatenated one-by-one onto another string, resulting in an exact copy. Initially, str is 'abcd' and copy is the empty string. During each while-loop iteration, another character from str is accessed and concatenated onto the end of copy, yielding the strings 'a', then 'ab', then 'abc', and finally 'abcd'. The variable i, which represents the index of the character currently being processed, is initialized to 0 and then incremented at the end of the loop body. The table below the code traces the values of i and copy during each pass through the loop.

EXERCISE 15.8

Consider a variation on the code in Figure 15.6, in which the string concatenation inside the while loop is reversed:

```
str = 'abcd';
copy = '';                   // INITIALIZE copy TO EMPTY STRING
i = 0;                       // START AT BEGINNING OF str
while (i < str.length) {     // AS LONG AS CHARS LEFT IN str
    copy = str.charAt(i) + copy; // ADD CHAR TO FRONT OF copy
    i=i+1;                   // GO TO NEXT CHAR
}
```

Trace the behavior of this modified code in the table below:

	copy	i	str.charAt(i)
before loop	''	0	'a'
after 1st loop pass			
after 2nd loop pass			
after 3rd loop pass			
after 4th loop pass			

EXERCISE 15.9

Define a function named `Reverse` that takes a string as input and returns a copy of that string in reverse order. For example, the function call `Reverse('abcd')` should return the string `'dcba'`. Once you have developed this function, insert its definition into your `string.js` library file. Then, modify your `strdemo.html` page so that it also displays the reversed string when the button is clicked.

EXERCISE 15.10

Consider the following code segment, which removes all spaces and punctuation marks from a given phrase. The first statement performs a search to determine whether the phrase contains a space or punctuation mark. If such a character is found, then its index will be stored in the variable `index` and the loop test will succeed. The while loop removes the character from the phrase by concatenating the pieces of `phrase` that occur before and after that character and then assigning the result back to `phrase`. The last statement inside the loop body searches for an additional space or punctuation mark in the modified `phrase`. If one is found, the loop test will succeed again and the character will be deleted. This process repeats until all spaces and punctuation marks have been removed.

```
index = phrase.search(/[ .,;:'!\?]/);    // LOOK FOR SPACE/PUNCT.
while (index ! = -1) {                    // IF FOUND, REMOVE IT
    phrase = phrase.substring(0,index) +
             phrase.substring(index+1, phrase.length);
    index = phrase.search(/[ .,;:'!\?]/); // LOOK FOR ANOTHER
}
```

Using this code, define a function named `Strip` that takes a string as input and returns a copy of that string from which all spaces and punctuation marks have been removed. For example, the function call `Strip('Foo 2 You!')` should return `'Foo2You'`.

Insert the `Strip` function definition into your `string.js` library file. Then modify your `strdemo.html` page so that it also displays the stripped string when the button is clicked.

Example: Recognizing Palindromes

A *palindrome* is a word or phrase that reads the same backward and forward. For example, the words *madam* and *toot* are both palindromes. Generally, spaces and punctuation marks in a word or phrase are ignored when testing for a palindrome, and case is irrelevant. Thus, the phrase "Madam, I'm Adam" is considered a palindrome. Using the `toUpperCase` method, as well as the `Reverse` and `Strip` functions you wrote earlier, you can design a page that recognizes palindromes.

EXERCISE 15.11

Design and implement a Web page named `pal.html` that tests whether a word or phrase is a palindrome. Your page should allow the user to enter a word or phrase and then display a string indicating whether that word or phrase is a palindrome. The code that evaluates the users input should be case insensitive and should ignore any spaces or punctuation marks within the string. Thus, the following words and phrases would all be considered palindromes:

```
Bob
Able was I ere I saw Elba.
A man; a plan; a canal: Panama!
```

Example: Substitution Ciphers

The use of codes (or *ciphers*) as a means of hiding the meaning of messages traces its roots to ancient history. The first documented use of codes was by Hebrew scribes in approximately 500 B.C. The *Atbash cipher* specified that each letter in a message would be encoded using the corresponding letter in the alphabet reversed. For example, *A* would be encoded as *Z*, *B* would be encoded as *Y*, *C* would be encoded as *X*, and so on. The first known military use of codes was by Julius Caesar in 50–60 B.C. The ***Caesar cipher*** specified that each letter in the alphabet would be encoded using the letter three later in the alphabet. For example, *A* would be encoded as *D*, *B* would be encoded as *E*, *C* would be encoded as *F*, and so on. The code wraps around at the end of the alphabet, so *X*, *Y*, and *Z* would be encoded as *A, B*, and *C*, respectively.

Both the Atbash and Caesar ciphers are examples of **substitution ciphers**, codes in which one letter of the alphabet is substituted for another. A substitution cipher can be described succinctly by specifying its key—that is, the sequence of letters to which the alphabet is mapped. For example, the keys for the Atbash and Caesar ciphers are listed below. To encode a specific letter using one of these ciphers, you simply find the corresponding letter in the key below it.

```
Atbash cipher:                          Caesar cipher:

ABCDEFGHIJKLMNOPQRSTUVWXYZ              ABCDEFGHIJKLMNOPQRSTUVWXYZ

⇓⇓⇓⇓⇓⇓⇓⇓⇓⇓⇓⇓⇓                           ⇓⇓⇓⇓⇓⇓⇓⇓⇓⇓⇓⇓⇓

ZYXWVUTSRQPONMLKJIHGFEDCBA              DEFGHIJKLMNOPQRSTUVWXYZABC
```

For example, the Atbash cipher would encode the word *CODE* as XLWV, whereas the Caesar cipher would encode it as FRGH. Although both of these ciphers were effective at their time (when very few people could read at all), their simple patterns of encoding letters seem pretty obvious today. In principle, though, a substitution cipher can specify any mapping from letters to letters. For example:

```
Mystery cipher:

ABCDEFGHIJKLMNOPQRSTUVWXYZ

⇓⇓⇓⇓⇓⇓⇓⇓⇓⇓⇓⇓⇓

QWERTYUIOPASDFGHJKLZXCVBNM
```

Substitution ciphers have several attractive features. For one, they are relatively simple to understand and use. They are also reasonably effective. There are more than 4×10^{26} different arrangements of the 26 letters in the alphabet. Since each of these arrangements may be used as a key for a substitution cipher, there are more than 4×10^{26} different codes that can be used. By selecting one of these keys, the corresponding cipher can be used to encode messages. As long as the recipient of the message has that same key, the message can be easily decoded. Without the key, however, decoding a message can be extremely difficult.

EXERCISE 15.12

For each of the three ciphers listed above, give the corresponding encodings:

message	Atbash	Caesar	Mystery
ABCDE			
FOO			
SECRET			

Encoding Messages

As the previous section showed, encoding messages using a substitution cipher is relatively straightforward. The following steps must take place:

for as many letters as there are in the message
    get the next character in the message
    find its position in the *alphabet*
    find the corresponding letter in the *key*
    use that letter to encode the original letter in the message

These steps are implemented in the Encode function in Figure 15.7. The while loop that spans lines 23–34 processes each character in the message and appends the corresponding encoded character onto the variable coded. Note that each individual character in the message is accessed using the charAt method (line 25), with the loop variable starting at 0 (the index of the first character) and ranging to message.length–1 (the index of the last character). The indexOf method is called (line 26) to determine where the character appears in the alphabet (i.e., by finding its index in the alphabet string). If that character does not appear in the alphabet string, meaning it is not an uppercase letter, then that character is appended to coded without change (line 28). If it is an uppercase letter, however, the corresponding letter in the key string is appended (line 31) to coded. When the loop finally terminates, each character will have been processed, producing the encoded message that is displayed in the page division (line 36).

The BODY of the ciper.html page contains an HTML element that we have not previously encountered. A *text area* is similar to a text box, except that it can span multiple lines. The general form of a text area element is:

```
<textarea id="AREA_ID" rows=HEIGHT cols=WIDTH>
     INITIAL CONTENTS OF THE TEXT AREA
</textarea>
```

where AREA_ID is a name that identifies the text area, HEIGHT is the number of rows, and COLS is the number of columns in the text area. For example, the text area in ciper.html is 8 rows high and 40 columns wide (as shown in Figure 15.8). Since there is no text in between the opening and closing TEXTAREA tags, the text area is initially empty.

Functionally, text areas behave the same as text boxes—you access and modify their contents using an expression of the form:

```
document.getElementById('AREA_ID').value
```

In fact, the statement in Figure 15.6 that accesses the text area (line 18) would be unchanged if messageArea were defined to be a text box instead of a text area.

EXERCISE 15.13

Enter the ciper.html text from Figure 15.6 into a new Web page, then load this page to verify that it behaves as described.

Use this page to verify your predictions from Exercise 15.12. That is, encode each of the messages using the different cipher keys and verify that you obtain the predicted encoding.

Designer Secrets

Text boxes and text areas perform the same function in a Web page—they provide a space within the page where the user can enter text. The choice of which to use is dependent upon the amount of input to be entered. A text box can only span one line, so it is appropriate when the text to be entered is short. If the input is potentially long—that is, too long to fit on one line—then a text area is required.

As it is currently written, the ciper.html page will encode all capital letters in the message and leave all other characters unchanged. If we wanted to be able to handle both uppercase and lowercase letters, there are a variety of approaches that could be taken. For example, we might modify the if statement inside the loop (lines 27–32 in Figure 15.6) so that it searches for the uppercase version of a character if the character is not already uppercase. A simpler approach, however, would be to

```
1.  <html>
2.  <!-- cipher.html                                      Dave Reed -->
3.  <!-- This page encodes messages using a simple substitution -->
4.  <!-- cipher (with message and key entered by the user)      -->
5.  <!-- ======================================================= -->
6.
7.  <head>
8.    <title> Substitution Cipher </title>
9.
10.   <script type="text/javascript">
11.     function Encode()
12.     // Assumes: the message to be encoded is in messageArea (all caps),
13.     //          the key for encoding is in keyBox (all caps)
14.     // Results: the coded version of message is displayed in outputDiv
15.     {
16.       var message, key, alphabet, coded, i, ch, index;
17.
18.       message = document.getElementById('messageArea').value;
19.       key = document.getElementById('keyBox').value;
20.       alphabet = 'ABCDEFGHIJKLMNOPQRSTUVWXYZ';
21.       coded = '';
22.
23.       i = 0;
24.       while (i < message.length) {      // FOR AS MANY LETTERS AS THERE ARE
25.         ch = message.charAt(i);         // ACCESS EACH LETTER IN MESSAGE
26.         index = alphabet.indexOf(ch);   // FIND ITS POSITION IN ALPHABET
27.         if (index == -1) {              // IF NOT A CAPITAL LETTER,
28.           coded = coded + ch;           // THEN ADD IT UNCHANGED
29.         }                               // OTHERWISE,
30.         else {                          // ADD THE CORRESPONDING LETTER
31.           coded = coded + key.charAt(index); // IN THE KEY STRING
32.         }
33.         i = i + 1;
34.       }
35.
36.       document.getElementById('outputDiv').innerHTML = coded;
37.     }
38.   </script>
39. </head>
40.
41. <body>
42.   <h2>Substitution Cipher</h2>
43.   <p>
44.     Key: <input type="text" id="keyBox" size=26
45.                 value="ZYXWVUTSRQPONMLKJIHGFEDCBA">
46.   </p>
47.   <p>
48.     Enter your message below: <br>
49.     <textarea id ="messageArea" rows=8 cols=30></textarea> <br>
50.       <input type="button" value="Encode the Message" onclick="Encode();">
51.   </p>
52.   <hr>
53.   <div id="outputDiv"></div>
54. </body>
55. </html>
```

Figure 15.7 Web page for encoding a message using a substitution cipher.

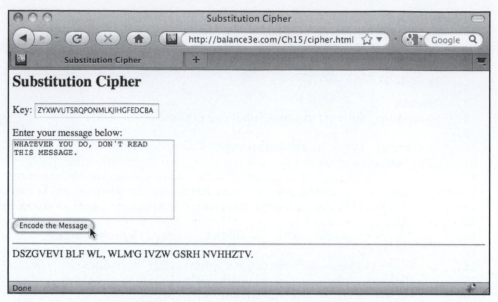

Figure 15.8 `cipher.html` rendered in a Web browser.

expand the alphabet and key to include both uppercase and lowercase letters. This can be done by adding lowercase letters to the end of the alphabet string literal (line 20) and also requiring the user to enter uppercase and lowercase letters in the key string. Fortunately, a more elegant solution is possible using string methods. Consider the two assignments below:

```
alphabet = alphabet + alphabet.toLowerCase();
key = key + key.toLowerCase();
```

The first assignment updates the alphabet variable by taking its current value (the uppercase letters *A . . . Z*) and appending the lowercase version of the alphabet (*a . . . z*) to the end. Similarly, the second assignment updates the key variable, appending a lowercase version of the key string to the end of the uppercase letters. If these two assignments are inserted into the `cipher.html` page (after the variables have been given their initial values), then the existing loop will suffice for encoding both uppercase and lowercase letters. Uppercase letters in the message will be encoded precisely as before, using the first halves of the updated alphabet and key variables. Lowercase letters in the message will now be encoded using the second halves of the alphabet and key variables, which are lowercase copies of the first halves.

EXERCISE 15.14

Add the above two assignment statements to your `cipher.html` page so that it properly encodes messages containing both uppercase and lowercase letters. As before, any non-letters (including spaces and punctuation marks) should be left unchanged by the encoding.

Decoding Messages

Given an encoded message and the key by which it was encoded, decoding a message is a straightforward process. The steps in the encoding must simply be performed in reverse. That is, each coded letter must be mapped back into the corresponding letter of the alphabet. Consider the Atbash cipher, for example:

```
Atbash cipher:

ABCDEFGHIJKLMNOPQRSTUVWXYZ

⇓ ⇓ ⇓ ⇓ ⇓ ⇓ ⇓ ⇓ ⇓ ⇓ ⇓ ⇓ ⇓ (mapping to encode)

ZYXWVUTSRQPONMLKJIHGFEDCBA
--------------------------

ZYXWVUTSRQPONMLKJIHGFEDCBA

⇓ ⇓ ⇓ ⇓ ⇓ ⇓ ⇓ ⇓ ⇓ ⇓ ⇓ ⇓ ⇓ (mapping to decode)

ABCDEFGHIJKLMNOPQRSTUVWXYZ
```

Since the letter *A* is encoded as *Z*, the letter *Z* is decoded by performing the reverse mapping back to *A*. For each letter in a coded message, this reverse mapping can be made to recover the original letter. The steps involved in decoding an encoded message can be described as follows:

> for as many letters as there are in the message
> > get the next character in the message
> > find its position in the *key*
> > find the corresponding letter in the *alphabet*
> > use that letter to decode the original letter in the message

Note that this decoding algorithm is identical to the earlier encoding algorithm, except that the roles of the key and alphabet are reversed. That is, when decoding a message, you find its position in the key (instead of the alphabet) and then access the corresponding character in the alphabet (instead of the key).

EXERCISE 15.15

Augment your `cipher.html` page so that it can both encode and decode messages. You will need to define a new function named `Decode`, which decodes the message in the text area using the entered cipher key. You should also add a second button labeled `Decode the message` that calls this new function when it is clicked.

Once you have done this, test the page by decoding the messages you encoded in Exercise 15.13. As an additional test, decode the following message using the Mystery cipher defined in a previous section:

```
Egfukqzxsqzogfl - ngx rtegrtr zit dtllqut!
```

Looking Ahead...

In this chapter, you learned that JavaScript represents strings as objects and that certain properties and operations (methods) are associated with every string value. The properties and methods of strings include the `length` property, which can be accessed to determine the number of characters in a string, and the `charAt` and `substring` methods, which can be used to retrieve individual components of a string. By combining these methods with the concatenation (+) operator, you were able to write pages that manipulate text in complex ways. Toward the end of the chapter, we introduced another string method: `search`. The `search` method's ability to locate a character, substring, or range of characters within a string added to your expressive power when manipulating text.

In Chapter 17, you will study another type of JavaScript object: arrays. Similar to a string object, which encompasses properties and methods for describing and modifying a sequence of characters, an array encapsulates a list of arbitrary items and provides properties and methods for manipulating those items. Before we continue our examination of objects, however, Chapter 16 returns to the study of the computer's internal workings. If you recall, Chapter 14 described the internal workings of the computer at a relatively high level of abstraction. In particular, the components of the CPU, its connections to main memory, and the flow of information between the components were studied. In Chapter 16, you will learn about computer hardware at a more detailed level, starting with transistors and building up to the complex circuitry composing these key components of modern computer systems.

Chapter Summary

- A software object is a programming structure that models an object in the real world. An object encompasses data (properties) along with the operations (functions) that can be performed on that data.

- To distinguish them from stand-alone functions, functions that belong to an object are known as methods of that object.

- In JavaScript, strings are objects with numerous predefined properties and methods:
    - The `length` property specifies the number of characters in the string.
    - The `toUpperCase` method returns a copy of the string in which all lowercase letters have been replaced with their uppercase equivalents.
    - The `toLowerCase` method returns a copy of the string in which all uppercase letters have been replaced with their lowercase equivalents.
    - The `charAt` method returns the character stored at a particular index of a string.
    - The `substring` method returns a sequence of characters from a string, specified by starting and ending indices.
    - The `search` method returns the index of the first occurrence of a character, substring, or class of characters within a given string.

- Programmers access the properties and methods of an object by placing a period after the object's name and following the period with the desired property name or method call. For example, `str.length` will return the number of characters in `str`, whereas `str.charAt(0)` will return the first character in `str`.

- Using a while loop and the `charAt` method, a string can be traversed and modified/replaced character by character. Similarly, programmers can use a while loop and the `search` method to repeatedly search for characters and modify/replace them.

- Whereas a text box is limited to a single line of text, a text area can contain any number of lines. The following represents a generalized text area element:

```
<textarea id="AREA_ID" rows=HEIGHT cols=WIDTH>
    INITIAL CONTENTS OF THE TEXT AREA
</textarea>
```

Supplemental Material and Exercises

More Practice with Strings

This chapter contains several exercises in which you traced code that traversed and manipulated strings. Because string manipulation can be confusing at first, additional exercises may prove beneficial.

EXERCISE 15.16

Consider a variation on the code in Figure 15.5:

```
str = 'foobar';
copy = '';

i = 0;
while (i < str.length) {
    copy = copy + str.charAt(i) + '-';
    i = i + 1;
}
```

Trace the behavior of this modified code in the table below:

	copy	i	str.charAt(i)
before loop	`' '`	0	`'f'`
after 1st loop pass			
after 2nd loop pass			
after 3rd loop pass			
after 4th loop pass			
after 5th loop pass			
after 6th loop pass			

EXERCISE 15.17

Consider a variation on the code in Figure 15.5:

```
str = foobar;

i = str.search(/[aeiou]/);
while (i != -1) {
    str = str.substring(0, i) + '*' + str.substring(i+1, str.length);
    i = str.search(/[aeiou]/);
}
```

Trace the behavior of this modified code in the table below:

	str	i
before loop	`'foobar'`	1
after 1st loop pass		
after 2nd loop pass		
after 3rd loop pass		

Example: Translating Phone Numbers

Advertisers have found that people remember words much more easily than they remember numbers. Thus, we are continually bombarded with phone numbers that are expressed using letters. To help people dial alphabetic phone numbers, most phone buttons list the letters along with their corresponding digits. In case your phone doesnt provide this information, the following list maps letters to their numeric equivalents:

2	ABC	6	MNO
3	DEF	7	PRS
4	GHI	8	TUV
5	JKL	9	WXY

Note that the digits 1 and 0 do not have corresponding letters. Also, the letters Q and Z are not represented.

EXERCISE 15.18

Design and create a Web page named `phoney.html` that converts alphabetic phone numbers into entirely numeric ones. Your page should allow the user to enter the number (possibly containing letters) in a text box. When the user clicks a button, the page should call a function to translate the input, generating a version of the phone number in which all letters have been replaced by their corresponding digits. For example, 1-800-IAM-DAVE should be translated to 1-800-426-3283.

Example: Roman Numerals

The ancient Romans developed a system for representing number values alphabetically. This "Roman numeral" system employed the following letters to symbolize the indicated numeric values:

$$M = 1{,}000, \ D = 500, \ C = 100, \ L = 50, \ X = 10, \ V = 5, I = 1$$

To convert an ancient Roman numeral to its numeric equivalent, you must sum up the values represented by each of the letters in the numeral. For example, MCVII represents $1{,}000 + 100 + 5 + 1 + 1 = 1{,}107$, whereas CCIIII represents $100 + 100 + 1 + 1 + 1 + 1 = 204$. By convention, letters are always listed in decreasing order of value.

EXERCISE 15.19

Design and create a Web page named `roman.html` containing a text box in which the user can enter an ancient Roman numeral. When the user clicks a button, the number represented by that Roman numeral should appear in the page.

Once you have completed your page, use it to convert the following Roman numerals to numeric values:

    MCLXVI   XXXX   MM   MXXIIII   LXXXXVIIII

EXERCISE 15.20

Add elements to your `roman.html` page so that the user can perform the opposite conversion, translating a number into an ancient Roman numeral.

Hint: One approach to building the Roman numeral would be to write a series of while loops. As long as the number entered by the user is greater than or equal to 1,000, add the letter *M* to a string representing the Roman numeral and subtract 1,000 from the value. If the resulting number is greater than or equal to 500, add *D* to the string and subtract 500. Then, repeatedly add *C*s and subtract 100 until the number becomes less than 100, and so on.

EXERCISE 15.21

A more challenging programming exercise would be to modify your `roman.html` page so that it uses the modern style of Roman numerals. In this system, I can appear before V and X to represent 4 and 9, respectively; X can appear before L and C to represent 40 and 90, respectively; and C can appear before D and M to represent 400 and 900, respectively.

Example: Rotating Ciphers

In practice, substitution ciphers can often be broken (decoded without the key) using insight and computational power. As a good example of this, you may be familiar with cryptographic puzzles that appear in many newspapers. These puzzles use a substitution cipher to encode a quotation, and the challenge is to decode the quotation. This can be done by analyzing the patterns of words and the frequency of letters in the quotation. For example, if the same three-letter sequence appears numerous times in the coded quotation, you might work under the assumption that it represents the common word *the*.

The weakness of substitution ciphers is that they always map the same letter of the alphabet to the same key letter. Thus, it is possible to look at the coded message and look for patterns. An interesting variation on substitution ciphers was adopted by Nazi Germany during World War II. The Germans used a machine called an Enigma for encoding all military messages. The Enigma machine utilized a series of interconnected rotors to encode letters. In essence, the rotors defined a substitution cipher, mapping one letter to another. What made the Enigma machine so effective, however, was that the rotors were rotated after each letter was encoded, essentially changing the substitution cipher after every letter! This added wrinkle made the Enigma codes virtually impossible to break (until electronic computers were built).

This same effect can be obtained in a simple substitution cipher by rotating the key after each letter is encoded (ignoring non-letters). For example, suppose you are using the Atbash cipher to encode AAA. After mapping A to Z, the key ZYXWVUTSRQPONMLKJIHGFEDCBA would be rotated to obtain YXWVUTSRQPONMLKJIHGFEDCBAZ. Thus, the second A would be mapped to Y. Similarly, another rotation of the key would cause the third A to be mapped to X. Using a rotating key, each occurrence of a letter in the message is mapped to a different letter, and so pattern analysis is more difficult.

EXERCISE 15.22

Modify your cipher.html page from Exercise 15.15 so that it implements a rotating substitution cipher.

Hint: This should require only minimal changes to the code. After each character in the message has been encoded/decoded, your Rotate function (from Exercise 15.4) should be called to rotate the key.

The Math and Document Objects

In this chapter, we have already explained that strings, as well as buttons and other form elements, represent objects. However, you may not remember that you encountered a JavaScript object in Chapter 7, when we introduced mathematical functions such as Math.sqrt and Math.random. We are now able to recognize Math as an object that encapsulates various useful mathematical functions and constants. A set of common mathematical functions, including Math.sqrt and Math.random, are implemented as methods of the Math object. In addition to these methods, the Math object encompasses properties that represent standard mathematical constants, such as Math.PI for $\pi = 3.14159. . . .$

EXERCISE 15.23

Whenever you order a pizza, you are faced with the decision of which size to order. Is a large pizza a good deal, or would you be better off ordering two mediums?

Create a Web page named pizza.html that determines the cost per square inch of any pizza. The page should contain text boxes in which the user can enter the diameter of the pizza (i.e., the number of inches across) and its price. Given this input, the cost per square inch can be computed as:

$$\text{cost per square inch} = \text{cost}/(\pi * (\text{diameter}/2)^2)$$

Using the Math.PI property and the Math.pow method, your page should compute and display the cost per square inch for any specified pizza.

Once you have completed the page, use it to determine which would be the better deal: a 16-inch pizza for $18.99 or two 12-inch pizzas for $10.99 each.

The other object that you have employed in your JavaScript programs is the document object. The document object encapsulates information and operations associated with the Web page itself. For example, the document.getElementById method, which we have used in numerous pages, accesses an element of the page by its identifier. One property of the document object is URL, which specifies the URL (Web address) of the page. While surfing the Web, you may have noticed Web pages that display their URLs at the bottom. This is useful information, in that it reminds users of the pages location and documents that location when the user prints the page contents. Although you could include this information as plain text within a page, ensuring the accuracy of the information would require updating the text every time the page was moved. If you display the values by accessing the URL property, however, the information is automatically updated within the page.

As we have seen previously, one way to dynamically embed text within a Web page is to use a JavaScript statement to assign the INNERHTML attribute of a page division or text span. When the text only needs to be assigned once, however, another `document` method makes this task even simpler. The `document.write` method can be called directly within a page (embedded within SCRIPT tags) to display a value when the page loads. For example, placing the following text at the bottom of a Web page will result in its URL being automatically displayed:

```
<script type="text/javascript">
    document.write('<p>Page location: ' + document.URL + '</p>');
</script>
```

EXERCISE 15.24

Using the `document.URL` property, modify your home page (and any other pages you wish) so that the page URL is displayed at the bottom.

Inside the Computer— Transistors and Integrated Circuits

16

Chapter

This chapter uses narrative, illustrations, hands-on experimentation, and review questions to introduce computer science and technology concepts.

Think of it! With VLSI we can pack 100 ENIACS in 1 sq. cm.

Alan Perlis

What we didn't realize then was that the integrated circuit would reduce the cost of electronic functions by a factor of a million to one; nothing had ever done that for anything before.

Jack Kilby

I went to my first computer conference at the New York Hilton about 20 years ago. When somebody there predicted the market for microprocessors would eventually be in the millions, someone else said, "Where are they all going to go? It's not like you need a computer in every doorknob!"

Years later, I went back to the same hotel. I noticed the room keys had been replaced by electronic cards you slide into slots in the doors.
There was a computer in every doorknob.

Danny Hillis

In Chapter 14, you were introduced to the hardware inside a computer at a relatively high level of abstraction. The chapter described components of the von Neumann architecture, such as the CPU and main memory; the buses that connect these components; and the way in which various pieces are assembled to produce a general-purpose, programmable computer. In this chapter, you will delve further into the workings of computer hardware, focusing on the basic technology used to construct hardware components.

Recall from Chapter 6 that early computing devices, such as Pascal's calculator (1642) and Babbage's Analytical Engine (1833), were purely mechanical. Such devices stored information as different settings on dials and cogs and then processed this information in response to physical actions (e.g., turning a crank to spin interlocking wheels). Modern computers, by contrast, are powered by electricity, using electrical signals to store and manipulate information. This chapter begins by reviewing the fundamental properties of electricity, as well as the importance of electrical switches to computing technology. After covering these basics, the chapter describes transistors, the building blocks of modern computers, and the ways in which transistors can be combined into circuits that store values and perform operations. We end the chapter with a discussion of integrated circuits, microprocessors, and the manufacturing techniques used to create computer chips.

Electricity and Switches

Computers, along with most modern machines, are electrical devices. The components of a computer require electrical power to carry out their assigned tasks. For example, electricity generates the light that shines through a computer screen, illuminating the individual pixels that make up images and letters. Electricity also runs the motor that spins the hard-drive disk, allowing information to be accessed. In addition, the main memory and CPU employ electrical signals to store and manipulate data. For example, numbers are stored in main memory or transferred to the CPU as bit patterns, in which the individual 1s and 0s are represented by the presence or absence of electrical current along a wire. Although we are all familiar with electricity in that we use it every day, understanding the details of electrical currents and their properties requires significant knowledge of physics.

Electricity Basics

Simply stated, electricity is a flow of *electrons*—the negatively charged particles in atoms—through a medium. Elements such as copper, silver, and gold are especially good at conducting electricity, meaning that their molecular structure can accommodate the flow of electrons with little resistance. To ensure the efficient delivery of electricity, most power and phone lines are constructed from copper wire (Figure 16.1), whereas computers often use gold for connecting electrical components over small distances. Other elements, especially nonmetals such as carbon and oxygen, are poor conductors of electricity.

Electricity can be quantified in various ways. An *ampere*, or amp, is a unit that gauges electron flow: 1 amp of current is equal to 6.24 quintillion (6.24×10^{18}) electrons flowing past a given point each second. Another common measure of electricity is *voltage*, which corresponds to the physical force produced by the flow of electrons. In the United States, standard household outlets carry 110 or 120 volts; in Europe, 220-volt outlets are more typical.

Switches

The most basic tool for controlling the flow of electricity is a switch. A *switch* is a device designed to connect or disconnect two wires, thus regulating the flow of electricity between them. For example, a light switch on a wall serves as an intermediary between the power line entering your home and the outlet that operates a lighting fixture. If the switch is in the "on" position, then the wires that link the outlet to the power line are connected and the lighting fixture receives electricity. However, if the switch is turned off, then the connection is interrupted and no power reaches the outlet. Figure 16.2 depicts the relationship between a light switch and the electrical connection it regulates. In this and subsequent figures, a blue line symbolizes a wire carrying electrical current, whereas a black line symbolizes a wire carrying no current.

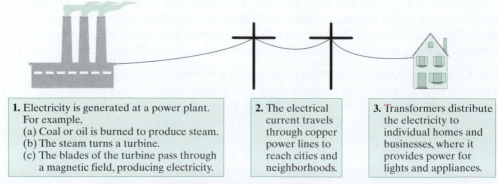

1. Electricity is generated at a power plant. For example,
   (a) Coal or oil is burned to produce steam.
   (b) The steam turns a turbine.
   (c) The blades of the turbine pass through a magnetic field, producing electricity.

2. The electrical current travels through copper power lines to reach cities and neighborhoods.

3. Transformers distribute the electricity to individual homes and businesses, where it provides power for lights and appliances.

Figure 16.1   Electricity flowing from a power plant to homes.

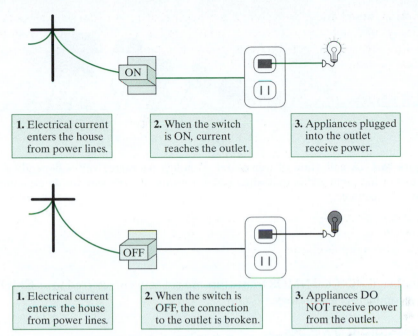

1. Electrical current enters the house from power lines.

2. When the switch is ON, current reaches the outlet.

3. Appliances plugged into the outlet receive power.

1. Electrical current enters the house from power lines.

2. When the switch is OFF, the connection to the outlet is broken.

3. Appliances DO NOT receive power from the outlet.

Figure 16.2 A light switch controls the flow of electricity from outside power lines to household appliances.

Transistors

As we have established in previous chapters, computers store and manipulate information as electrical signals. Because switches are integral to controlling electrical flow, it should not be surprising that computer components such as main memory and the CPU incorporate switches. In fact, advances in switching mechanisms have defined the first five generations of computer technology (see Chapter 6 for a detailed analysis of computer history). The first electronic computers (Generation 0) were built in the 1930s using switches called electromagnetic relays. These relays were physical switches whose on/off positions were controlled by voltage to a magnet. In the 1940s, the replacement of relays with vacuum tubes launched computer history's Generation 1. Although vacuum tubes could be turned on and off as if they were a mechanical switches, the tubes' lack of moving parts enabled them to shift between states much more quickly than relays could. However, vacuum tubes had a downside—they generated large amounts of heat and tended to burn out frequently. In 1948, John Bardeen, Walter Brattain, and William Shockley at AT&T Bell Labs invented the transistor, ushering in yet another generation of computer technology (Generation 2). A *transistor*, considered by many to be the most important invention of the 20th century, is a solid piece of metal attached to a wire that serves as a switch by alternatively conducting or resisting electricity (Figure 16.3). Transistors are similar to vacuum tubes in that they contain no moving parts; however, transistors are smaller, more reliable, and more energy efficient than vacuum tubes. Because of these advantages, transistors enabled hardware experts to design smaller, faster machines at a drastically lower cost.

Although the first transistor was made of gold and germanium, modern transistors are constructed from silicon instead of germanium. Both germanium and silicon belong to a category of elements called *semiconductors*, or metals that can be manipulated to be either good or bad conductors of electricity. Through a process known as *doping*, impurities can be added to a slab of germanium or silicon, causing the metal to act as an electrical switch. Today, most transistors are built using metaloxide semiconductor (MOS) technology. A positively doped metal-oxide semiconductor (PMOS) transistor contains silicon doped with impurities that make it conduct electricity, but it can be made nonconductive by applying current to a separate control wire. Conversely, a negatively doped metaloxide semiconductor (NMOS) transistor contains silicon doped with impurities that make it nonconductive, but it can be made conductive by applying current to a control wire. When implemented

Figure 16.3 A collection of transistors. Although packaging varies depending on the manufacturer, each transistor has input and output wires, and at least one control wire for determining whether the transistor will conduct electricity.

together, PMOS and NMOS transistors are collectively referred to as CMOS (combined metal-oxide semiconductor) technology.

Transistors as Switches

Figures 16.4 and 16.5 are abstractions that illustrate the behavior of PMOS and NMOS transistors. In practice, each transistor acts as a switch that can be opened or closed to control the flow of electricity through a wire. A control wire determines whether the switch is closed, allowing current to move through the connection, or open, halting the flow of electricity. In the case of a PMOS transistor, the switch is closed when there is no current (0 volts) on the control wire, but opens when current (5 volts) is applied. Conversely, the switch on an NMOS transistor is open when there is no current (0 volts) on the control wire, but closes when there is a current (5 volts).

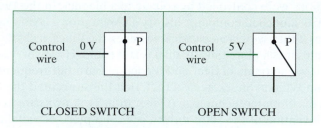

Figure 16.4 PMOS transistor.

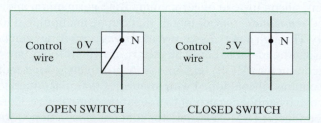

Figure 16.5 NMOS transistor.

The Web page `logic.html` (accessible at `http://balance3e.com/Ch16/logic.html`) provides an interactive tool for studying the behavior of PMOS and NMOS transistors. By accessing the pull-down menu to the left of each simulated transistor and selecting the desired voltage for its control wire (0 volts or 5 volts), the user can open and close the switches and observe their behavior.

Although transistors were initially more expensive than their vacuum tube counterparts, the benefits that transistors offered in terms of size, power consumption, heat dispersal, and longevity far outweighed the cost disadvantage. The year 1953 marked the launch of the first transistor-powered commercial product, a hearing aid, which was followed by the transistor radio in 1954. A year later, researchers at Bell Labs constructed the first computer built entirely with transistors. As mass production techniques improved throughout the 1950s, the cost of manufacturing transistors dropped steadily, and transistors soon replaced vacuum tubes in virtually all electronic appliances. In addition to commercial success, the invention of the transistor brought scientific recognition to Shockley, Brattain, and Bardeen, earning them the 1956 Nobel Prize in Physics (Figure 16.6).

From Transistors to Gates

At first glance, it is not obvious how a transistor—or any electric switch, for that matter—can serve as the building block of modern computers. After all, computers are powerful machines that perform billions of complex mathematical and logical operations per second—how can a simple switch contribute to this impressive behavior? However, as this book has demonstrated, even the most intricate computer functionality is produced by combining sequences of simpler components. For example, Chapter 1 taught you that, although a single bit can differentiate between only two different values, a collection of 8 bits (a byte) can represent any character on a keyboard. Likewise, in Chapter 7, you saw that simple JavaScript statements can be joined to create functions that carry out complex computations. In much the same way, transistors can be combined to form *circuits*, which perform the underlying operations of computers.

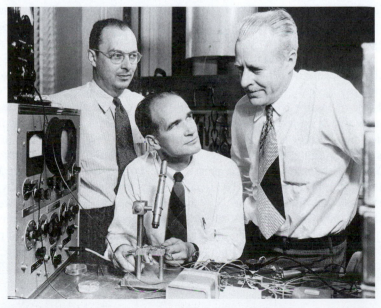

Figure 16.6   John Bardeen, William Shockley, and Walter Brattain looking at an early transistor through a microscope.

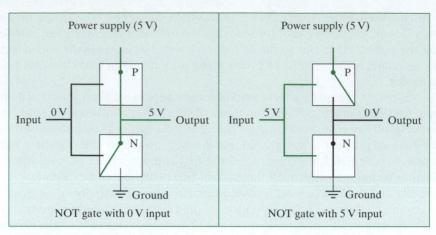

Figure 16.7 CMOS circuitry for a NOT gate.

A circuit is a collection of transistors (and possibly other electronic devices) wired together to produce a particular behavior. For example, a hardware designer might combine an NMOS transistor and a PMOS transistor to form the circuit shown in Figure 16.7. We can think of the wire on the left as carrying an input signal and the wire on the right as producing a corresponding output signal. A consistent electrical current is supplied to this circuit at the top (labeled 5 V), and the circuit is grounded at the bottom so that any electrical current is carried harmlessly away. Note that the input wire to the left of the circuit serves as the control wire for the two transistors. If no current is applied to the input wire, then the PMOS transistor will close to allow current to travel on the output wire, and the NMOS transistor will open to disconnect the ground (as shown on the left-hand side of Figure 16.7). Likewise, if current is applied to the input wire, then the PMOS transistor will open to disconnect the output wire and the NMOS transistor will close to ground the input (as shown on the right-hand side of Figure 16.7). This example represents the simplest circuit that performs a useful function: producing an output signal that is the opposite of the input signal. A circuit of this type is known as a NOT gate.

Gates and Binary Logic

The term "gate" suggests a simple circuit that controls the flow of electricity in much the same way that an iron gate might control traffic flow through a fence. In the case of a NOT gate, the flow of electricity is manipulated so that the output signal is always the opposite of the input signal (input voltage → no output voltage, no input voltage → output voltage). Although it is accurate to describe a gates' inputs and outputs as voltage levels, we can think of these inputs and outputs more abstractly in terms of binary values: 0 represents no current and 1 represents current. From this perspective, we can think of a gate as computing a function on binary values. The table on the right-hand side of Figure 16.8 lists each possible input value for a NOT gate, along with its corresponding output value. The left-hand side of the figure depicts a symbol—a large triangle connected to a smaller circle—that is often used to represent a NOT gate; this notation abstracts away all the circuit's underlying details, allowing a designer to draw the circuit simply and easily.

You may have noticed a similarity between the NOT gate and the JavaScript logical connective ! from Chapter 11. In fact, the NOT gate inverts voltages in the same way that the NOT (!) operator inverts Boolean values (!true → false, !false → true). If we replaced 0 with false and 1 with true, the table from Figure 16.8 would perfectly describe the behavior of the NOT operator. For this reason, tables that describe the mapping from circuitry inputs to outputs are known as **truth tables**.

NOT gate

Input ─▷o─ Output

input	NOT output
0	1
1	0

Figure 16.8 Behavior of a NOT gate.

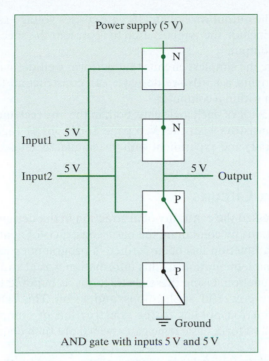

Figure 16.9 CMOS circuitry and behavior of an AND gate.

In addition to the NOT gate, many other simple circuits can be defined to perform useful tasks. Figure 16.9 shows how two NMOS transistors and two PMOS transistors can be wired together to form an AND gate, which corresponds to the JavaScript connective && (AND). The resulting circuit contains two input wires and produces voltage on its output wire only if both input wires carry voltage. Figure 16.10 depicts the circuitry and behavior of an OR gate, which corresponds to the

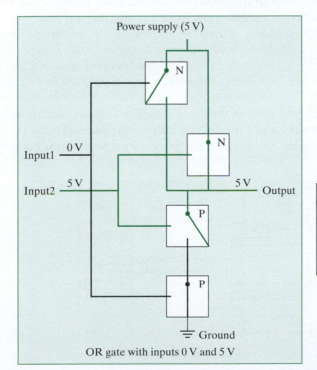

Figure 16.10 CMOS circuitry and behavior of an OR gate.

JavaScript connective | | (OR). The output wire of an OR gate carries voltage as long as either input wire carries voltage. Both figures include the symbols used to represent the specified gates, as well as truth tables describing the gates' output.

AND, OR, and NOT gates are the simplest circuits that perform well-defined logical operations. By combining these primitive circuits, a hardware designer can construct all the logic required to store and manipulate information within a computer.

To better understand the behavior of each logic gate, both in the abstract and as complex circuits involving NMOS and PMOS transistors, visit the Web page `logic.html` (accessible at `http://balance3e.com/Ch16/logic.html`) and experiment with the simulated gates.

From Gates to Complex Circuits

Throughout this text, we have stressed the centrality of abstraction in the design of software. For example, programmers define functions by combining the basic constructs of a language, such as variables and operators. Once such a function has been defined, a programmer can invoke it without understanding the details of its implementation, as this information was abstracted away when the behavior was encapsulated as a function. Using these abstractions as building blocks, the programmer is able to define even more powerful applications, and so on. This same pattern of ever-increasing complexity and abstraction applies to the construction of computer hardware. For instance, transistors are connected to form basic logic gates, which are then combined to build more advanced circuitry.

To demonstrate the process of designing logical circuitry, let us consider the task of adding two numbers. As we saw in Chapter 14, the CPU's ALU contains circuitry for adding numbers. Input buses carry numbers as binary signals to the ALU, where the sum of those numbers is calculated and represented as a series of signals on an output bus. Suppose we wished to design circuitry that would perform addition within the ALU. For simplicity, we will initially limit ourselves to the task of adding 4-bit numbers. Figure 16.11 depicts the input and output signals involved in adding 0101 and 1100, which yield the sum 10001 (since $0101_2 + 1001_2 = 10001_2$).

Before we continue, it might help to quickly review the rules of binary addition. In principle, adding binary (base 2) numbers is no different from adding decimal (base 10) numbers. Recall that, in decimal, corresponding columns of digits are added together, starting from the right. If the sum of any two digits yields a 2-digit number (a number ≥ 10), then the 1 is carried over to the next column. Similarly, in binary, corresponding bits are added together, starting from the right. If the sum of any two bits yields a 2-bit number (a number $\geq 10_2$), then the 1 is carried over to the next column.

For example, Figure 16.12 portrays two different examples of binary addition. In the example on the left, adding the rightmost bits 1 and 1 produces a sum of 10_2 (decimal value two). Thus, a 0 is written in the rightmost column of the result and a 1 is carried over to the next column. The sum of the

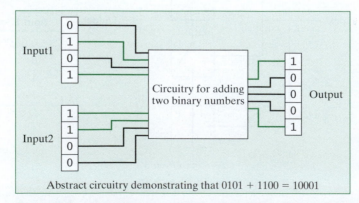

Abstract circuitry demonstrating that 0101 + 1100 = 10001

Figure 16.11   Abstract view of circuitry for adding binary numbers.

$$
\begin{array}{r}
1\ 1 \\
1\ 0\ 1\ 1_2 \\
+\ \ \ \ \ \ \ \ \ 1_2 \\
\hline
1\ 1\ 0\ 0_2
\end{array}
\qquad\qquad
\begin{array}{r}
1\ 1 \\
1\ 1\ 0\ 0_2 \\
+\ \ \ \ 1\ 0\ 1_2 \\
\hline
1\ 0\ 0\ 0\ 1_2
\end{array}
$$

Figure 16.12 Examples of binary addition.

second set of bits then becomes 10_2 because of the previous carry, causing a second 0 to be written in the result and a 1 to be carried over to the third addition. In the example on the right, a 1 is carried over after adding the leftmost bits. In such an instance, the sum of the numbers will contain one more bit than the largest input value (in the same way that $9 + 9 = 18$, and 18 has one more digit than 9 does).

Although binary addition is a relatively straightforward operation, designing a circuit for adding binary numbers is far from trivial. If we attempted to design such a circuit from scratch using transistors, the complexity involved could become overwhelming. However, if we think of circuit design in terms of multitiered complexity, then the underlying layers can establish abstractions that simplify the upper layers. For example, instead of starting at the transistor level, we can use logical gates AND, OR, and NOT as building blocks to create a simple circuit for adding 2 bits. Such a circuit would contain two input lines, representing the bits to be added, and two outputs, representing the sum of the inputs and a possible carry. This functionality can be implemented using only four gates, as illustrated in Figure 16.13. In the pictured configuration, the first input has a value of 1 and the second input has a value of 0, yielding a sum of 1 and a carry of 0. This type of circuit is known as a *half-adder*.

The term "half-adder" refers to the fact that, when you add binary numbers containing more than one bit, summing the corresponding bit pairs by column is only half the job. As you add up each column, you must also consider that a bit might be carried over from the previous addition. Thus, adding corresponding bits in a number actually requires the ability to add 3 bits: the two input values and a possible carry. Using half-adders and logical gates as building blocks, we can design a circuit that performs this task. Figure 16.14 depicts such a circuit, which is known as a *full-adder* and consists of two half-adders and an OR gate. In the pictured configuration, two of the inputs have values of 1, yielding a sum of 0 and a carry of 1.

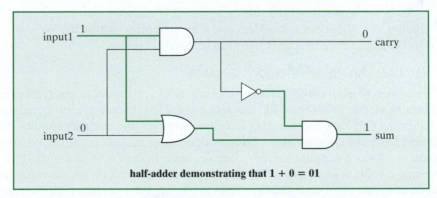

half-adder demonstrating that 1 + 0 = 01

Figure 16.13 Half-adder circuit.

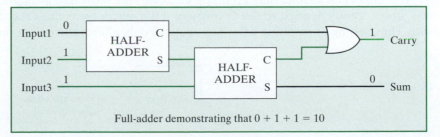

Full-adder demonstrating that 0 + 1 + 1 = 10

Figure 16.14 Full-adder circuit.

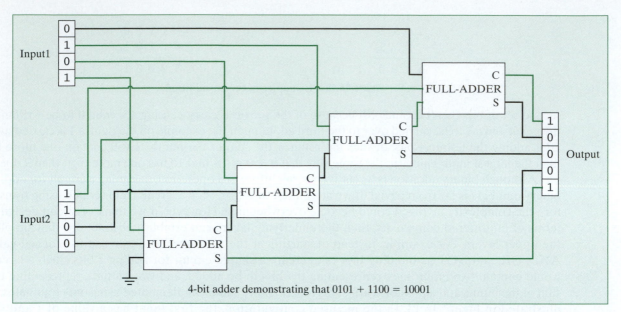

4-bit adder demonstrating that 0101 + 1100 = 10001

Figure 16.15 4-bit adder circuit.

Finally, using full-adders as building blocks, we can design a more complex circuit that sums two 4-bit numbers. Because a full adder is required to add each corresponding bit pair together (along with a possible carry from the previous addition), the appropriate circuit will encompass four full-adders wired together (Figure 16.15). In the pictured configuration, the two input numbers are 0101 and 1100, yielding a sum of 10001.

From this basic design, you can see how hardware designers produce circuits that add arbitrarily large binary numbers. For example, to add 8-bit numbers, you could wire eight full-adders together in a similar pattern. You could also achieve this functionality by combining two copies of the 4-bit adder circuit.

To better understand the intricacies of ALU circuitry, you can observe and experiment with the behavior of half-adders, full-adders, and 4-bit adders by visiting the Web page `logic.html` (accessible at `http://balance3e.com/Ch16/logic.html`).

Example: Designing Memory Circuitry

In addition to performing calculations such as adding numbers, electronic circuitry is also used to implement memory that the CPU can access quickly. For example, both main memory and the registers within the CPU are composed of circuitry. However, the circuitry used to store bits in memory is different from the circuitry that performs operations such as addition. Whereas adders manipulate inputs to produce outputs, memory circuits must maintain values over time. The simplest circuit for storing a value is known as a *flip-flop*. A flip-flop stores a bit whose value can be set to 1 by applying current to one input wire and then reset to 0 by applying current to another input wire. In Figure 16.16, these input wires are labeled Set and Reset, respectively.

It is important to note that a flip-flop maintains the last value assigned to it, either a 1 if current was most recently applied to the Set wire or a 0 if current was most recently applied to the Reset wire. Thus, setting or resetting a flip-flop requires only a brief current on the appropriate input wire,

Figure 16.16 Flip-flop for storing a bit.

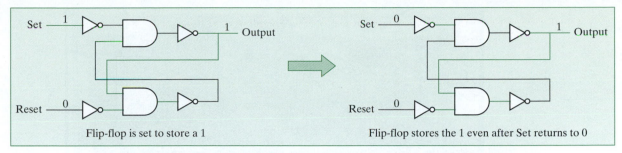

Figure 16.17 Flip-flop being set (storing a 1 bit), then maintaining that value.

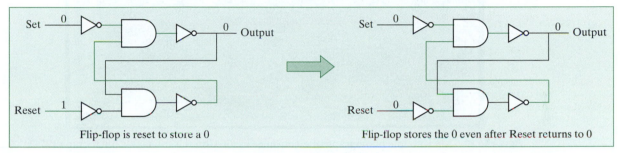

Figure 16.18 Flip-flop being reset (storing a 0 bit), then maintaining that value.

and once set or reset, the output of the circuit is constant. This behavior is achieved within the circuitry via a feedback loop, which causes the output of the circuit to circle back and refresh the inputs. For example, Figures 16.17 and 16.18 portray a flip-flop that is constructed from two AND gates and four NOT gates. Note that, in each diagram, the outputs of the rightmost NOT gates loop back and serve as inputs for the AND gates. On the left-hand side of Figure 16.17, a current is applied to the Set wire so that the flip-flop stores a 1. On the right-hand side of the figure, the current on the Set wire has stopped flowing, but the flip-flop circuitry retains the output 1. Similarly, Figure 16.18 shows a flip-flop being reset to store a 0 (in the left-hand diagram) and then maintaining that bit value even after the input current has stopped (in the right-hand diagram).

In much the same way that full-adders can be wired together to produce the ALU's complex circuitry, flip-flops can be wired together to construct the registers and main-memory cells of a computer. You can observe and experiment with the behavior of flip-flops at the Web page `logic.html` (accessible at `http://balance3e.com/Ch16/logic.html`).

From Circuits to Microchips

Initially, circuits were built by wiring together individual transistors. If a hardware designer wished to create a new computer component, he or she would assemble a large number of transistors and physically connect them using wire and a soldering iron. In addition to being extremely tedious and error prone, this approach did not lend itself to mass production. Every time a particular circuit was needed, it had to be constructed from scratch out of transistors and wire. Furthermore, there were limitations to the minimum size of circuits built from individual transistors. As the spacing of transistors within circuits had to accommodate the human hands that inserted and soldered the wires, even simple circuits consisting of tens or hundreds of transistors were quite large.

The Integrated Circuit

In 1958, two researchers independently developed techniques for manufacturing mass-produced, smaller circuitry. Jack Kilby at Texas Instruments and Robert Noyce at Fairchild Semiconductor Corporation both realized that, to enable the mass production of circuits, all the components (including transistors and their connections) would have to be constructed as a single unit. Each

Figure 16.19 Microscopic photograph of electronic circuitry on the Intel 4004 microchip (1971).

researcher proposed a manufacturing process in which circuitry is layered onto a single wafer of silicon, known as a *microchip*. Because every component of the circuit was integrated onto the same microchip, these circuits became known as *integrated circuits* (Figure 16.19).

In 1959, both Texas Instruments and Fairchild Semiconductor applied for and were awarded patents on their microchip-manufacturing techniques. After several years of legal battles, the two companies agreed to cross-license their technologies, which marked the beginning of the computer microchip industry. After leaving Fairchild Semiconductor, Noyce went on to cofound Intel, today's dominant microchip producer. Kilby was awarded the 2000 Nobel Prize in Physics in recognition of his contribution to the development of the integrated circuit.

Manufacturing Integrated Circuits

The production of integrated circuits is perhaps the most complex engineering process in the world. The transistors that are manufactured on a microchip can be as small as 65 nanometers (65×10^{-6} meters), or roughly 1/1,500th the width of a human hair. To achieve precision on such a small scale, integrated-circuit manufacturing relies heavily on techniques normally associated with photography. As you may already know, photographic images are created by exploiting chemicals whose physical properties change upon exposure to light. When someone takes a picture, chemicals on the film react to incoming light. These chemical changes are then translated to color intensities when the photograph is developed.

To produce the incredibly small and precise circuitry on microchips, hardware manufacturers use similar light-sensitive chemicals. Initially, the silicon chip is covered with a semiconductor material, then coated with a layer of *photoresist*—a chemical sensitive to ultraviolet light. The pattern of transistors to be layered onto the chip is printed on a mask, a transparent surface on which an opaque coating has been applied to form patterns. Ultraviolet light is filtered through the mask, passing through the transparent portions and striking the surface of the chip in the specified pattern. The photoresist exposed to ultraviolet light reacts, hardening the layer of semiconductor below it. Once exposure is completed, the photoresist not exposed and the soft layer of semiconductor below are etched away, leaving only the desired pattern of semiconductor material on the surface of the chip (Figure 16.20). This process may be repeated 20 or 30 times, depositing layer upon layer of semiconductor material to form the circuit's transistors and their connections. Even the "wires" that connect the transistors are formed by depositing conductive material on the surface of the chip.

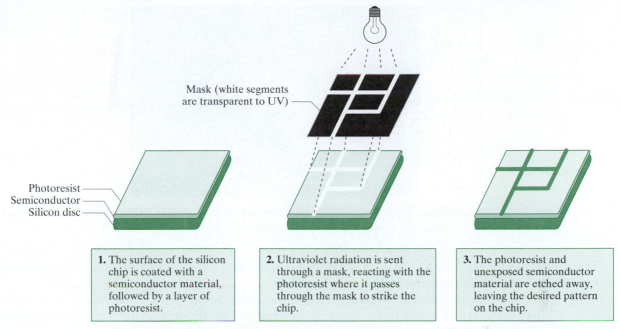

Mask (white segments are transparent to UV)

Photoresist
Semiconductor
Silicon disc

1. The surface of the silicon chip is coated with a semiconductor material, followed by a layer of photoresist.

2. Ultraviolet radiation is sent through a mask, reacting with the photoresist where it passes through the mask to strike the chip.

3. The photoresist and unexposed semiconductor material are etched away, leaving the desired pattern on the chip.

Figure 16.20 Adding a single layer of circuitry to a silicon chip.

Not surprisingly, manufacturing microchips requires extreme care and cleanliness. A single human hair or fleck of skin could damage thousands of transistors if it came in contact with the circuit. To prevent such problems, microchip production takes place in "clean rooms," where sealed ventilation systems remove airborne contaminants and workers wear protective suits that contain loose hair and skin cells (Figure 16.21).

Packaging Microchips

Because a silicon chip containing an integrated circuit is fragile, it is encased in plastic for protection (Figure 16.22). Metal pins are then inserted on both sides of the packaging, facilitating easy connections to other microchips.

It is safe to say that the microchip has revolutionized the way in which computers are designed and built. Useful circuits are implemented and mass produced as microchips. As microchips can be manufactured in bulk, their invention has drastically lowered the cost of constructing circuitry. Furthermore, the tiny circuits on microchips are much closer to one another, which increases the speed of operations by shortening the distances over which electrical signals must travel. Today, the designers of computer systems do not even need to consider the low-level details of transistors and

Figure 16.21 Workers use specialized equipment to produce and inspect the circuitry on microchips. Note that protective clothing is worn not for the benefit of the worker, but to protect the microchip circuitry from contaminants such as skin cells and loose hairs.

Figure 16.22 An early microchip, with circuitry visible in the cutaway portion of the plastic case. Two rows of metal pins are used connect the circuitry to other components of the computer.

other electrical devices. Instead, they can simply select prebuilt microchips that contain the needed circuitry and wire those microchips together.

Improvements in manufacturing techniques and technologies are constantly reducing the scale of integrated circuits. In the early 1960s, a microchip one inch across might have contained the circuitry for five to ten logic gates. By the early 1970s, the space required to hold circuitry had shrunk to the point where a complete CPU could be manufactured on a single microchip, known as a ***microprocessor***. The first CPU contained entirely on a microchip was the Intel 4004. Released in 1971, the 4004 consisted of roughly 2,300 transistors and their connections. By the early 1980s, the era of VLSI was begun, where hundreds of thousands of transistors could fit on a single chip. For example, the Intel 80286, which was released in 1982 and used in many early personal computers, encompassed more than 134,000 transistors. By the 1990s, microprocessors with millions of transistors were manufactured, with the Pentium 4 microprocessor (released in 2000) encompassing more than 42 million transistors. In 2006, the Core 2 Duo contained 291 million transistors, while Intel's high-end server processor contained an astounding 1.7 billion transistors. Moore's Law—named after its originator, Intel's Gordon Moore—describes this remarkable evolution of technology and manufacturing. Moore noted as early as 1965 that the number of transistors that can fit on a microchip doubles every 18 to 24 months. As Figure 16.23 demonstrates, this pattern

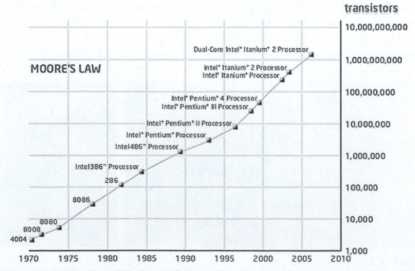

Figure 16.23 This graph (with a logarithmic scale) shows how Intel's family of processors has followed Moore's Law, doubling the number of transistors every 18 to 24 months. (Reprinted with permission of Intel Corporation.)

has been maintained over the past 30 years, and industry analysts predict that it will continue to hold for the near future.

Looking Ahead...

In this chapter, you studied the low-level functionality of computer hardware, including various implementations of electrical switches. After describing the behavior of electrical currents, the chapter explained that a transistor is a solid piece of silicon doped with impurities to make it act as a semiconductor. Transistors are designed to either conduct electricity or not, depending on whether an electrical current is applied to an input wire; this functionality allows each transistor to act as an electrical switch. When wired together, transistors can form circuits that perform computational tasks. The simplest such circuits, known as logic gates, process electrical inputs and produce output signals according to logical functions such as AND, OR, and NOT. In turn, logic gates can be wired together to form more complex circuits, eventually building to the circuitry that makes up the ALU, main memory, and other computer components. Modern technology makes it possible to integrate complex circuitry, consisting of millions of transistors and their connections, on a single microchip that can be mass produced.

With this deeper understanding of computer hardware in mind, Chapter 17 completes our coverage of fundamental programming skills by discussing applications that involve storing and manipulating large amounts of data. Arrays, which are explored in Chapter 17, are lists of items that can be stored and accessed efficiently, allowing programmers to process sequences of words or numbers. As you will discover, arrays have many common features with strings, which were studied in Chapter 15. Both are examples of JavaScript objects, with properties and operations (methods) associated with them. Both also represent sequences of items that can be accessed via indices. However, arrays are much more flexible than strings, in that they are not limited to sequences of characters only—the values stored in an array can be of any type (including numbers, strings, and even other arrays). As such, they prove to be useful in a variety of applications that require storing and processing collections of related information.

Chapter Summary

- Computers are electrical devices, requiring electricity to perform tasks such as illuminating the screen, powering the hard drive, and transferring data as electrical impulses.

- Electricity is a flow of electrons—the negatively charged particles in atoms—through a medium. Gold and copper are especially good at conducting electricity, and so they are often used to connect computer components.

- An electrical switch is a device designed to connect or disconnect two wires, thus regulating the flow of electricity between them. Switches can be implemented using a variety of technologies, including electromagnetic relays, vacuum tubes, and transistors.

- A transistor, considered by many to be the most important invention of the 20th century, is a solid piece of metal attached to a wire that serves as a switch by alternatively conducting or resisting electricity.

- Transistors were invented by John Bardeen, Walter Brattain, and William Shockley at AT&T Bell Labs in 1948.

- Transistors are constructed from semiconductors—metals that can be doped with impurities to make them either good or bad conductors of electricity. The most common semiconductor used in modern transistors is silicon.

- A Negatively-doped Metal-Oxide Semiconductor (NMOS) transistor serves as a switch that is closed when electrical current is applied to its control wire; otherwise, it is open.

Conversely, a Positively-doped Metal-Oxide Semiconductor (PMOS) transistor is open when current is applied to its control wire; otherwise, it is closed.

- Because transistors were smaller, lasted longer, and required less power than vacuum tubes, they began replacing vacuum tubes in consumer devices in the 1950s (e.g., transistorized hearing aid in 1953, transistor radio in 1954, Bell Labs transistor computer in 1955).

- A circuit is a collection of transistors (and possibly other electronic devices) wired together to produce a particular behavior. The simplest circuits that perform well-defined logical operations are the NOT gate, AND gate, and OR gate.

- Tables that describe the mapping from circuitry inputs to outputs are known as truth tables.

- Simple circuits can be wired together to form more complex circuits. For example, starting with simple NOT, AND, and OR gates, the complex circuitry of the ALU can be designed and implemented.

- The simplest circuit for storing a value is known as a flip-flop. A flip-flop stores a bit whose value can be set to 1 by applying current to one input wire and then reset to 0 by applying current to another input wire.

- In 1958, Jack Kilby and Robert Noyce independently proposed manufacturing processes in which circuitry is layered onto a single wafer of silicon, known as a microchip. Because every component of the circuit was integrated onto the same microchip, these circuits became known as integrated circuits.

- To produce the incredibly small and precise circuitry on microchips (transistors can be 1/1,500th the width of a human hair), hardware manufacturers use light-sensitive chemicals to etch circuitry into layers of semiconductor materials.

- To protect the fragile silicon chip containing an integrated circuit, it is encased in plastic and packaged with metal pins to facilitate connections to other microchips.

- Moore's Law predicts that the number of transistors that can fit on a chip will double every 18 to 24 months.

Review Questions

1. TRUE or FALSE? Nonmetals such as carbon and oxygen tend to be good conductors of electricity.

2. TRUE or FALSE? A semiconductor is a metal that can be manipulated to be either a good or a bad conductor of electricity.

3. TRUE or FALSE? A circuit is a collection of transistors (and possibly other electronic devices) wired together to produce a particular behavior.

4. TRUE or FALSE? NMOS and PMOS were two competing companies that manufactured microchips in the early 1960s.

5. TRUE or FALSE? If there is no electrical current on the input wire to a NOT gate, then there will be current on its output wire.

6. TRUE or FALSE? The sum of the binary numbers 101_2 and 1_2 is 110_2.

7. TRUE or FALSE? A flip-flop is a circuit that serves to store a single bit.

8. TRUE or FALSE? Jack Kilby and Robert Noyce are credited with independently inventing the integrated circuit.

9. TRUE or FALSE? The main reason that workers wear protective clothing when manufacturing integrated circuits is to protect them from exposure to dangerous chemicals.

10. TRUE or FALSE? Moore's Law dictates that integrated circuitry must be manufactured out of silicon, as opposed to other semiconductors such as germanium.

11. Name three different technologies that, over the years, have served as electrical switches in computers. How were these technologies similar, and how were they different? What advantages or disadvantages did each provide?

12. Electricians commonly wear rubber shoes and gloves to protect themselves when working with live wiring. Would this suggest that rubber is an efficient or inefficient conductor of electricity? Explain your answer.

13. Describe the difference between an NMOS transistor and a PMOS transistor.

14. It is possible to develop truth tables for logic circuits, just as we did for individual gates. For example, the logic circuit shown here combines an AND gate and an OR gate. Complete the corresponding truth table by calculating the output value for each set of inputs. [*Hint:* Figure out the output of the AND gate in each case and then use the result to determine the overall output.]

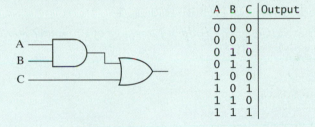

A	B	C	Output
0	0	0	
0	0	1	
0	1	0	
0	1	1	
1	0	0	
1	0	1	
1	1	0	
1	1	1	

15. The logic circuit shown here is similar to the one in Question 14, except that the AND and OR gates are in reversed positions. Complete the corresponding truth table by calculating the output value for each set of inputs.

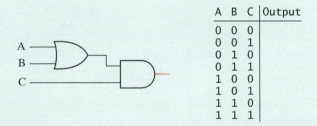

A	B	C	Output
0	0	0	
0	0	1	
0	1	0	
0	1	1	
1	0	0	
1	0	1	
1	1	0	
1	1	1	

16. What is the sum of the binary numbers 100101_2 and 1011_2? Show the steps you used to calculate your answer.

17. Explain why the circuitry for adding two 4-bit numbers must be constructed by combining full-adders, rather than half-adders.

18. What is the total number of gates required to build a 4-bit adder? Assuming two transistors per NOT gate (as in Figure 16.8) and four transistors per AND and OR gate (as in Figures 16.9 and 16.10, respectively), what is the total number of transistors in the circuitry of the 4-bit adder?

19. Describe how a flip-flop is able to retain the last bit value assigned to it.

20. Does it make any sense for both of a flip-flop's input wires to carry current at the same time? What would happen within the circuit if this were to happen?

21. In what way is integrated-circuit manufacturing similar to photography?

22. Can Moore's Law continue to hold forever? That is, can technology continue to advance at its current rate indefinitely, causing the number of transistors that fit on a microchip to double every 12 to 18 months? Explain.

References

Augenbraun, Eliene, and P. W. Hammer, Executive Producers. *Transistorized!: The History of the Invention of the Transistor.* ScienCentral, Inc., and the American Institute of Physics, 1999. Online at `http://www.pbs.org/transistor/`.

Brain, Marshall. "How Semiconductors Work." *How Stuff Works*, April 2001. Online at `http://electronics.howstuffworks.com/diode.htm`.

Malone, Michael S. *The Microprocessor: A Biography.* New York: Springer-Verlag, 1995.

Mano, M. Morris, and Charles R. Kime. *Logic and Computer Design Fundamentals*, 4th ed. Upper Saddle River, NJ: Prentice Hall, 2007.

Petzold, Charles. *Code: The Hidden Language of Computer Hardware and Software.* Redmond, WA: Microsoft Press, 1999.

JavaScript Arrays

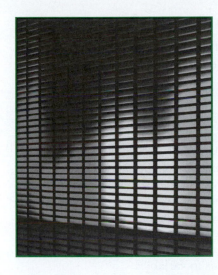

This chapter uses narrative, examples, and hands-on exercises to introduce programming concepts and Web development skills.

17

Chapter

Why can't somebody give us a list of things that everybody thinks and nobody says, and another list of things that everybody says and nobody thinks.

Oliver Wendell Holmes, Sr.
The Professor at the Breakfast-Table

Enough organization, enough lists and we think we can control the uncontrollable.

John Mankiewicz
House, The Socratic Method

In Chapter 15, you were introduced to the concept of software objects—programming structures that encompass both data (properties) and operations (methods) that can be performed on that data. A string object, for example, has properties that provide information about the string (e.g., the sequence of characters, length) and methods that can be called to manipulate the string's value (e.g., toUpperCase, charAt). In this chapter, you will learn about another type of JavaScript object, the *array*. JavaScript uses an array structure to represent a list; each array stores and indexes a sequence of items, allowing users to access individual list items by specifying their corresponding indices. Arrays are useful for handling arbitrarily long user input, as well as for organizing large amounts of data. For example, imagine a program that asks a user to enter a phrase and then displays an acronym consisting of the first letter of every word in that phrase. If the user's input were stored as an array consisting of individual words, the program could process the words individually, copying the first letter of each to form the acronym.

Early exercises in this chapter emphasize a conceptual understanding of arrays, including what they are and how they are stored. While tracing code that assigns values to arrays, you will be asked to draw the memory cells associated with various array values. Eventually, you will apply this knowledge to developing Web pages that process both words and numbers in arrays, including an application for storing dice statistics and another for storing and displaying animation frames.

Arrays as Objects

In Chapter 9, you created several Web pages that incorporated the `RandomOneOf` function from the `random.js` library. This function takes a list of items as input and returns a random item from that list. For example, the call:

```
RandomOneOf(['yes', 'no', 'maybe'])
```

would return either `'yes'`, `'no'`, or `'maybe'`, each with equal likelihood.

In JavaScript, lists of items that are enclosed in square brackets and separated by commas are known as **arrays**. Like strings, arrays are objects that encapsulate multiple values and their associated properties and methods. However, unlike strings (which store only text characters), the items in an array can be of any data type. Although the example just mentioned `['yes', 'no', 'maybe']` contains three string values, an array can also store numbers, Booleans, nested arrays, or any combination thereof. As JavaScript places no limitations on arrays' contents or organization, programming with arrays can provide incredible flexibility.

For example, the following statements assign valid array values to variables:

```
responses = ['yes', 'no', 'maybe'];
nums = [1, 2, 3, 2+1, 7*7, 2*5-1];
misc = [1.234, 'foo', 7-5, true, 3, 'foo'];
empty = [ ];
```

These examples demonstrate that:

- The items in an array do not have to be of the same type.
- An item can appear in an array more than once.
- An array item can be specified as an expression—in such cases, the array actually stores the expression's equivalent value.
- An array can be empty.

Accessing Items in an Array

Because an array stores a series of values, its associated memory cell is divided into components, each containing an individual value. For example, consider the array assigned to the `misc` variable in the examples above. Figure 17.1 depicts the organization of `misc`'s memory cell, in which array items are stored in separate components of the cell. Like the characters in a string, array items are assigned sequential indices, allowing programmers to retrieve any item by specifying its corresponding index. Instead of providing a method such as `charAt`, however, arrays use a bracket notation for allowing access to individual items. Thus, the first item in `misc` is accessed as `misc[0]`, the second as `misc[1]`, and so on. Similar to strings, arrays have a `length` property, which identifies the number of items in the array. This means that the last item in the array `misc` is accessible as `misc[misc.length-1]`. Note that any expression that evaluates to an integer (such as `misc.length-1`) can be used to index an array.

In addition to being flexible, arrays are especially forgiving data structures. If you specify an index that is beyond the scope of a given array, the array simply returns `undefined`. For example, `misc[6]` and `misc[100]` will both evaluate to `undefined`.

	misc[0]	misc[1]	misc[2]	misc[3]	misc[4]	misc[5]
misc	1.234	'foo'	2	true	3	'foo'

Figure 17.1 Memory cell for the `misc` array.

EXERCISE 17.1

Assume that the following statements have assigned arrays to variables:

```
responses = ['yes', 'no', 'maybe'];
nums = [1, 2, 3, 2+1, 7*7, 2*5-1];
misc = [1.234, 'foo', 7-5, true, 3, 'foo'];
empty = [ ];
```

Predict the value that would be accessed by each of the following expressions:

```
responses[0]
responses[responses.length-1]
nums.length
nums[0]
nums[0] + nums[1] + nums[2]
empty.length
empty[0]
misc[nums[0]]
```

Now that you know how to create an array and access its values, you can understand the workings of the RandomOneOf function from Chapter 9. The RandomOneOf function (Figure 17.2) uses the length property and bracket notation associated with arrays to retrieve a random item from an array. First, RandomOneOf calls the RandomInt function to select a number between 0 and the last index in the array (i.e., the list length minus 1). After the random number is returned, the function uses bracket notation to obtain the array item stored at that index.

EXERCISE 17.2

Suppose that the assignment to randomIndex in the RandomOneOf function (Figure 17.2) were replaced by the following:

```
randomIndex = RandomInt(0, list.length);
```

Would this modification cause the function to return an error? Would the function still behave appropriately every time it is called? Explain.

Assigning Items in an Array

In addition to accessing an existing item in an array, bracket notation can also be used to assign a value to an array component. For example, suppose that misc has been assigned the same array value as in the previous examples:

```
misc = [1.234, 'foo', 7-5, true, 3, 'foo'];
```

```
function RandomOneOf(list)
// Given : list is a nonempty list (array)
// Returns: a random item from the list
{
    var randomIndex;

    randomIndex = RandomInt(0, list.length-1);

    return list[randomIndex];
}
```

Figure 17.2 Function for selecting a random item from an array (from random.js).

	misc[0]	misc[1]	misc[2]	misc[3]	misc[4]	misc[5]
misc	1000	'foo'	2	true	3	'foo'

Figure 17.3 Memory cell for the `misc` array, after assigning `misc[0] = 1000`.

	misc[0]	misc[1]	misc[2]	misc[3]	misc[4]	misc[5]	misc[6]	misc[7]	misc[8]
misc	1000	'foo'	2	true	3	'foo'	undefined	undefined	'oops'

Figure 17.4 Memory cell for the `misc` array, after assigning `misc[8] = 'oops'`.

The assignment

```
misc[0] = 1000;
```

would store the value 1000 as the first item in the array `misc`, overwriting the value that was previously stored there. Figure 17.3 portrays the effect of this assignment on `misc`'s corresponding memory cell.

If the index in an assignment statement is beyond the array's current length, the array will be automatically expanded to accommodate the new item. Any components in between the new item and the original array will be considered `undefined`. For example, the assignment

```
misc[8] = 'oops';
```

would expand the `misc` array so that its memory cell resembles Figure 17.4.

EXERCISE 17.3

For each of the following statements, draw the memory cell associated with the variable after the assignment has been made:

```
vals = [1, 5.3, 'house'];
vals[0] = vals[1];
vals[2] = vals[2] + 'hold';
blank = [];
blank[0] = 'foo';
blank[3] = 'bar';
blank[blank.length] = 'biz';
blank[blank.length] = 'baz';
```

Common errors to avoid...

As was mentioned earlier, arrays are like strings in that attempts to access invalid array indices do not by themselves cause errors. Instead, the array returns the value `undefined` if you specify an index that is negative or higher than that of the last item in the array. In most cases, however, an error will occur as soon as the code attempts to perform an action using the `undefined` value, such as displaying it or incorporating it into an expression.

For example, suppose that you wanted to add together every value in an array of numbers named `nums`. The following code attempts to accomplish this task but in fact loops one time too many:

```
sum = 0;
i = 0;
while (i <= nums.length) {
    sum = sum + nums[i];
    i = i + 1;
}
```

Because the while loop test uses <= instead of <, the last value for which the test succeeds will be nums[nums.length], which is beyond the actual bounds of the array. Although this mistake doesn't generate an immediate error, the code does not behave as desired during the final loop-body iteration. As soon as the code adds the undefined value to the sum of the array, the sum becomes NaN, signifying that the result is "Not a Number."

From Strings to Arrays

Throughout this text, you have written interactive Web pages that accept and process user input. For example, in your story.html page (Exercise 5.5.) the user entered words and phrases in text boxes, which were incorporated into a story in the page. Similarly, in your tip.html page (Exercise 7.3), the user entered a check amount in a text box, which was used to calculate and display the appropriate tip amount. In your cipher.html page (Exercise 15.13), the user entered a message in a text area, which was accessed and encoded using a substitution cipher. In all of these pages, each value entered by the user was accessed as a single string, which could be converted to a number using parseFloat if appropriate.

The inability to treat user inputs as anything other than single strings or numbers is limiting, as numerous programming tasks involve separately processing an arbitrary number of words or numbers entered by a user. For example, imagine that you need to define a page that generates an acronym for a given phrase by combining the first letter of each word in the phrase. Similarly, you might want to generalize your Pig Latin page (Exercise 15.6) so that it translates entire phrases, instead of just words, into Pig Latin. Accomplishing these tasks would be difficult, if not impossible, using your current set of programming tools.

The split Method for Strings

Although arrays are useful for organizing and manipulating large amounts of data, no mechanism in JavaScript enables a user to input a series of values directly as an array. As we have seen, JavaScript treats anything entered via a text box or text area as a string. Even if the user enters a sequence of words or numbers, those words or numbers are automatically joined together in a single string. Technically, the individual items could be extracted using string methods such as search and substring, but such processing would be tedious. Fortunately, JavaScript strings provide a method, split, for easily accessing the components of a string.

The only input required by the split method is a character or sequence of characters that serves as a delimiter for breaking apart the string. The split method separates the string into component substrings at each occurrence of the delimiter and then returns an array consisting of those substrings (the delimiter character or substring is lost during this process). For example, if user1 = 'Grace Murray Hopper', then the method call user1.split(' ') would break the string every time a space occurs, returning the array ['Grace', 'Murray', 'Hopper']. Likewise, if user2 = 'Hopper, Grace Murray', then user2.split(', ') would split the string every time that a comma is followed by a space, returning the array ['Hopper', 'Grace Murray'].

As was the case with the search method, split will also accept a collection of characters as input, any of which will then act as the delimiter. When the split method is given a collection of characters between /[and]/, the method splits the string every time it encounters a single character from that collection. If a + symbol is added before the final backslash, the split method will recognize arbitrarily long sequences of characters from the collection. For example, if user2 = 'Hopper, Grace Murray', then user2.split(/[,]+/) would split the string at each sequence of commas and/or spaces, returning the array ['Hopper', 'Grace', 'Murray']. Figure 17.5 lists several other split method calls and describes the arrays returned by these calls.

`phrase.split(' ')`	breaks the string `phrase` into an array of items, delimited by a single space
`phrase.split(': ')`	breaks the string `phrase` into an array of items, delimited by a colon followed by a space
`phrase.split(/[ \t\n,]/)`	breaks the string `phrase` into an array of items, delimited by a single space, tab (`\t`), newline (`\n`), or comma
`phrase.split(/[ \t\n,]+/)`	breaks the string `phrase` into an array of items, delimited by any sequence of spaces, tabs (`\t`), newlines (`\n`), and/or commas

Figure 17.5 Examples of `split` array method calls, which divide strings into arrays.

EXERCISE 17.4

The first statement that follows assigns a string to variable `people`, whereas the subsequent four assignments split `people` into various arrays. For each of these statements, draw the memory cell associated with the variable after the assignment has been made:

```
people = 'von Neumann, John 1903\n' + 'Turing, Alan 1913';
split1 = people.split(' ');
split2 = people.split(', ');
split3 = people.split(/[ ,\n]/);
split4 = people.split(/[ ,\n]+/);
```

Example: Generating Acronyms

One useful application of the `split` method is to derive acronyms. Although acronyms appear throughout our daily lives, they are especially popular in the computing field. For example, RAM is an acronym for "random access memory," GUI is an acronym for "graphical user interface," and WWW is an acronym for "World Wide Web." In addition, many computer companies are known by acronyms, such as IBM (International Business Machines) and HP (Hewlett Packard). The function in Figure 17.6, which is contained in the `arrays.js` library file, takes a phrase as input and returns the acronym associated with that phrase.

```
function Acronym(phrase)
// Assumes: phrase is a string of words
// Returns: the acronym made up of first letters from the phrase
{
    var words, acronym, index, nextWord;

    words = phrase.split(/[ \t,]+/);            // CONVERT phrase TO AN ARRAY
    acronym = '';                               // INITIALIZE THE acronym

    index = 0;                                  // START AT FIRST WORD
    while (index < words.length) {              // AS LONG AS WORDS LEFT
      nextWord = words[index];                  //    GET NEXT WORD
      acronym = acronym + nextWord.charAt(0);   //    ADD FIRST CHAR OF WORD
      index = index + 1;                        //    GO ON TO NEXT WORD
      }

    return acronym.toUpperCase();               // RETURN UPPER CASE acronym
}
```

Figure 17.6 Function that returns an acronym for a given phrase.

	acronym	index	nextWord (words[index])	nextWord.charAt(0)
before loop	''	0	'What'	'W'
after 1st pass	'W'	1	'you'	'y'
after 2nd pass	'Wy'	2	'see'	's'
after 3rd pass	'Wys'	3	'is'	'i'
after 4th pass	'Wysi'	4	'what'	'w'
after 5th pass	'Wysiw'	5	'you'	'y'
after 6th pass	'Wysiwy'	6	'get'	'g'
after 7th pass	'Wysiwyg'	7	undefined	
return value:	'WYSIWYG'			

Figure 17.7 Tracing the behavior of acronym('What you see is what you get').

First, the function calls the split method to convert the phrase into an array of words, using spaces, tabs, and commas as delimiters. Then a while loop traverses the array, extracting the first letter of each word (via charAt) and adding it to a new string named acronym. When the loop terminates, the toUpperCase method is applied to acronym, yielding an entirely uppercase version of acronym as the function's return value. For example, the phrase "What you see is what you get" is often represented by the acronym WYSIWYG. If this phrase were provided as input to the Acronym function, then the variable words would be assigned:

    ['What', 'you', 'see', 'is', 'what', 'you', 'get']

Traversing the array, the function would extract each word's first letter and combine them into a new string, as shown in Figure 17.7.

EXERCISE 17.5

Create a Web page named acronym.html that derives an acronym from a given phrase. The page should load the arrays.js library file (accessible at http://balance3e.com/arrays.js) and contain a text box in which the user can enter the phrase. When the user clicks the button in the page, the Acronym function is called to construct the appropriate acronym and display it in a page division (see Figure 17.8).

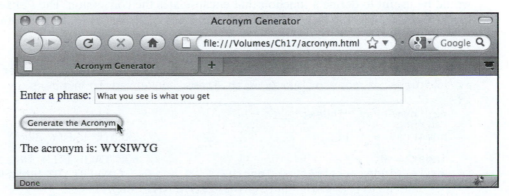

Figure 17.8 Sample appearance of acronym.html page.

EXERCISE 17.6

Modify your PigLatin function (Exercise 15.7) so that it can translate entire phrases of words into Pig Latin. Similar to the Acronym function from Exercise 17.5, your function should break the input string into words using the `split` method. It should then translate each word as before and combine the translated words into a new phrase (with a space between each word). Modify your `piglatin.html` page so that it instructs the user to enter a phrase for translation (see Figure 17.9).

Figure 17.9 Sample appearance of the revised `piglatin.html` page.

Arrays of Numbers

As demonstrated by your `acronym.html` and modified `piglatin.html` pages, certain programming tasks involve treating user input as a sequence of separate words, rather than as one long string. The `split` method is useful in such cases, because this method breaks a string into an array of component substrings. As you might imagine, there are also applications in which user input must be handled as a sequence of separate numbers. For example, Chapter 7 asked you to create a Web page named `grades.html` that computed a student's grade in a course (Exercise 7.10). Using this page, individuals could enter various averages (for lessons, labs, discussions, etc.) in text boxes and then view their overall average for the course in a page division. However, this page was limited, in that it expected the user to provide a precomputed average for each category. A more comprehensive page would accept a list of the user's individual grades for each category (e.g., lesson grades) and then automatically compute the associated category averages.

It is important to note that the `split` method takes a string as input and returns an array of strings as output. Even if the input string contains numerical digits, `split` returns each array item as a string. For example, if `str = '1 2 3'`, then `str.split(' ')` would return the array `['1', '2', '3']`. Of course, it is possible to convert the values in this array to numbers by accessing each one and `parseFloating` it. However, as processing a sequence of numbers is a fairly common task, it would be useful to define a function that encapsulates the conversion. The `ParseArray` function in the `arrays.js` library (Figure 17.10) takes an array of strings as input and returns a copy of that

```
function ParseArray(strArray)
// Assumes: strArray is an array of strings representing numbers
// Returns: a copy of array with items converted to numbers
{
  var numArray, index;

  numArray = [ ];                           // CREATE EMPTY ARRAY TO STORE NUMS

  index = 0;                                // FOR EACH ITEM IN strArray
  while (index < strArray.length) {         //   CONVERT TO NUMBER AND STORE
      numArray[index] = parseFloat(strArray[index]);
      index = index + 1;
  }

  return numArray;                          // FINALLY, RETURN THE NUMS
}
```

Figure 17.10 The `ParseArray` function, from the `arrays.js` library file.

```
function Average(numArray)
// Assumes: numArray is an array of numbers
// Returns: average of the numbers in numArray
{
  var sum, index;

  sum = 0;                                // INITIALIZE sum

  index = 0;                              // FOR EACH NUM IN numArray
  while (index < numArray.length) {       //    ADD NUMBER to sum
      sum = sum + numArray[index];
      index = index + 1;
  }

  return sum/numArray.length;             // RETURN AVERAGE
}
```

Figure 17.11 Library file `arrays.js`, containing functions for manipulating arrays of values.

array in which each item has been converted to a number. The function assumes that each string in the array encompasses a sequence of digits (possibly including a decimal point) that represents a number.

The `ParseArray` function works by traversing an array of strings, applying `parseFloat` to each array item, and returning a corresponding array of numbers. For example, the call `ParseArray(['123', '3.14159', '-99', '0'])` will return the array of numbers `[123, 3.14159, -99, 0]`.

The `Average` function, also defined in `arrays.js` (Figure 17.11) similarly uses a loop to traverse through an array of values. In this case, the function takes an array of numbers as input and calculates their average. It does this by first traversing the array values and adding each successive value to a variable named `sum`. Once the final sum is obtained, it is divided by the size of the array to calculate the average.

The Web page in Figure 17.12 demonstrates a particular use of the `ParseArray` and `Average` functions. The page contains a text box in which the user can enter a sequence of numbers, each separated by commas and/or spaces. At the click of a button, the `ShowAvg` function is called (line 33) to access the numbers in the text box and calculate the average of those numbers. Within the `ShowAvg` function, the `split` method is called to split the input string into an array (line 19). The resulting array of strings is converted into an array of numbers by calling the `ParseArray` function (line 20). Finally, the `Average` function is called on that array of numbers to calculate their average, which is displayed in the page (lines 22–23). Figure 17.13 shows the resulting Web page.

EXERCISE 17.7

Enter the `average.html` text from Figure 17.12 into a new Web page, then load this page to verify that it behaves as described. What happens if you click on the button without entering any numbers in the text box?

Calling the `split` method on an empty string produces an empty array—i.e., an array with length 0. Thus, clicking the button in this page without entering any numbers will result in a call to the `Average` function with an empty array as input. When the function attempts to calculate the average of an empty array, a division by 0 occurs, causing the function to return NaN. Modify the `Average` function so that it returns 0, rather than NaN, if its input is empty. Then verify that your `average.html` page displays 0 for the average if the user leaves the text box empty.

```
 1. <!doctype html>
 2. <!-- average.html                                    Dave Reed -->
 3. <!-- This page utilizes the arrays.js library file to store -->
 4. <!-- an array of numbers and compute their average.       -->
 5. <!-- ======================================================== -->
 6.
 7. <html>
 8.  <head>
 9.    <title> Average Numbers </title>
10.    <script type="text/javascript" src="arrays.js"></script>
11.    <script type="text/javascript">
12.      function ShowAvg()
13.      // Assumes: numsBox contains a sequence of numbers
14.      // Results: displays the average of the numbers in outputDiv
15.      {
16.        var str, strArray, numArray;
17.
18.        str = document.getElementById('numsBox').value;
19.        strArray = str.split(/[ ,]+/);   // SPLIT STRING INTO AN ARRAY
20.        numArray = ParseArray(strArray); // CONVERT ARRAY ELEMENTS TO NUMS
21.
22.        document.getElementById('outputDiv').innerHTML =
23.            'The average of [' + numArray + '] is ' + Average(numArray);
24.      }
25.    </script>
26.  </head>
27.
28.  <body>
29.    <p>
30.      Enter numbers: <input type="text" id="numsBox" size=40 value="">
31.    </p>
32.    <p>
33.      <input type="button" value="Compute the Average" onclick="ShowAvg();">
34.    </p>
35.    <div id="outputDiv"></div>
36.  </body>
37. </html>
```

Figure 17.12 Web page that uses the `ParseArray` and `Average` functions to average numbers.

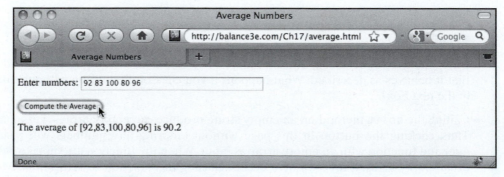

Figure 17.13 average.html rendered in a Web browser.

Designer Secrets

When using the `split` method to convert user input into an array of values, it is important to recognize that the resulting array might be empty. If the input is the empty string or a string containing only those characters recognized as delimiters, then the `split` method will return an empty array (i.e., an array whose `length` is 0). This means that, when a program uses the `split` method, you must make sure that the surrounding code accounts for the possibility of an empty array. For example, code that computed the average of an array of numbers would need to check for an empty array to avoid division by 0 (yielding `NaN`). In such a case, 0 might be returned as the average or the user might be prompted to reenter the numbers.

EXERCISE 17.8

Reimplement your `grades.html` page from Chapter 7 (Exercise 7.10). Instead of requiring users to provide precomputed averages, your modified page should provide text boxes in which users can enter a series of grades for each category (e.g., all homework grades obtained by the user could be listed in a text box).

Common errors to avoid...

Chapters 5 and 7 demonstrated that, in certain instances, a program will treat a user input as a number, even if you fail to `parseFloat` the value. In particular, the browser will automatically convert a string of digits into a number if a purely numerical operator (such as * or /) is applied to the value. However, because the + operator is compatible with both strings and numbers, string concatenation will be performed whenever + is applied to string values. To avoid confusion, we strongly recommended that you always call `parseFloat` to explicitly convert numbers before processing them.

For these same reasons, it is strongly suggested that you call `ParseArray` to explicitly convert any array of numbers before attempting to process the numbers. Otherwise, if the + operator is applied to items from the array, the operator would be interpreted as representing concatenation, rather than addition.

Example: Maintaining Dice Statistics (Approach 1)

In Chapter 13, you created a Web page that simulated repeated dice rolls and recorded the number of times that a specific total was obtained (Exercise 13.7). For example, this page allowed you to roll a pair of dice 1,000 times and count the number of 7s obtained. By changing a few numbers in the code, you could modify the page to count occurrences of any potential dice total. Statistical analysis predicts that, given a large number of dice rolls, the distribution of totals will mirror the percentages listed in Figure 17.14.

If you were using the page you created in Exercise 13.7, verifying this expected distribution of dice totals would involve performing 11 different experiments—one for each possible total. For example, you could roll the dice 1,000 times, count the number of 2s obtained, and verify that the number was close to 28 (2.8%). Then, you could roll the dice another 1,000 times, count the number of 3s obtained, and verify that the number was close to 56 (5.6%). If you repeated this process for every number up to 12, you would generate a complete set of dice statistics. However, as each experiment involves an independent sequence of 1,000 dice rolls, the total distribution might be

Dice total	Likelihood of Obtaining That Total
2	2.8%
3	5.6%
4	8.3%
5	11.1%
6	13.9%
7	16.7%
8	13.9%
9	11.1%
10	8.3%
11	5.6%
12	2.8%

Figure 17.14 Likelihood of possible dice totals.

skewed. That is, if you added up the counts from each of the 11 experiments, the total might not equal 1,000.

To obtain a valid distribution of dice totals, you would need to simulate a large number of rolls and simultaneously count the occurrences of every different total. This could be accomplished by defining 11 counters, each corresponding to a particular total (see Figure 17.15).

This approach would work (assuming that you inserted appropriate code in place of the '. . .'s), but it is incredibly tedious. After separate assignments initialize each of the 11 counters to 0, a cascading if-else statement containing 11 cases must identify every dice total and increment the corresponding

```
count2 = 0;                              // INITIALIZE EACH
count3 = 0;                              // COUNTER
count4 = 0;                              // (CORRESPONDING TO
.                                        // THE NUMBER OF 2'S,
.                                        // 3'S, 4'S, ... 12'S)
.
count12 = 0;

rep = 0;                                 // INITIALIZE rep COUNTER
while (rep < 1000) {                     // AS LONG AS ROLLS REMAIN
    roll = RandomInt(1, 6) + RandomInt(1, 6); // GET NEXT ROLL
    if (roll == 2) {                     // IF ROLLED 2,
        count2 = count2 + 1;             // ADD 1 TO 2'S COUNT
    }
    else if (roll == 3) {                // ELSE IF ROLLED 3,
        count3 = count3 + 1;             // ADD 1 TO 3'S COUNT
    }
    else if (roll == 4) {                // ELSE IF ROLLED 4,
        count4 = count4 + 1;             // ADD 1 TO 4'S COUNT
    }
    .                                    // SIMILAR CASES FOR
    .                                    // ROLLS 5 THROUGH 11
    .
    else if (roll == 12) {               // ELSE IF ROLLED 12,
        count12 = count12 + 1;           // ADD 1 TO 12'S COUNT
    }

    rep = rep + 1;                       // GO ON TO NEXT REP
}
```

Figure 17.15 Code that uses 11 counters to keep dice statistics.

```
count = [0,0,0,0,0,0,0,0,0,0,0];          // INITIALIZE ALL COUNTERS

 rep = 0;                                  // INITIALIZE REP COUNTER
 while (rep < 1000) {                       // AS LONG AS ROLLS REMAIN
     roll = RandomInt(1, 6) + RandomInt(1, 6);  //  GET RANDOM ROLL OF DICE
     count[roll-2] = count[roll-2] + 1;    //  ADD 1 TO COUNTER
     rep=rep+1;                            //  GO ONTO NEXT REP
}
```

Figure 17.16   Code that uses an array of counters to keep dice statistics.

counter. Furthermore, once the counts have been obtained, 11 separate statements would be required to display each counter value.

As if this code were not complex enough, now consider the task of generalizing the page so that it could handle dice with additional sides. Rolling and keeping statistics on eight-sided dice would involve 15 different counters and a cascading if-else with 15 cases. For 12-sided dice, 23 counters and if-else cases would be required. Surely, there must be a better way.

Example: Maintaining Dice Statistics (Approach 2)

After contemplating the use of separate counters to track dice statistics, you can see how arrays would provide an attractive alternative in such cases. Instead of representing each counter as a separate variable, you can define the counters as items in an array. That is, all 11 counters could be stored in a single array and initialized via a single assignment. This approach would also enable each individual counter to be accessed and updated via its corresponding index. Because the smallest possible dice total is two, its counter will be at index 0. The counter for 3s will be at index 1, and each subsequent index will store a counter for a sequentially higher total (up to the 12s counter at index 10). Figure 17.16 depicts an array that keeps dice statistics. Although the code performs the same task as the code in Figure 17.15, this version is much simpler because of the array of counters.

Note that the assignment statement at the top of the code segment defines an array of 11 counters and initializes all of them to 0. As the loop body is executed, the code accesses the appropriate counter for each `roll` via the statement `count[roll-2]`, as each counter index is two less than the dice total it tracks. Clearly, this approach is much more efficient than using separate counters, and it would be easier to adapt this code for dice with a different number of sides. Furthermore, displaying the counts generated by this code would be less tedious, because a single loop could step through the array and display the count stored at each index (from 0 to 10).

EXERCISE 17.9

Design and create a Web page named `stats.html` that simulates a number of dice rolls and displays statistics on those rolls. The user should be able to specify the number of dice rolls via a text box and then click a button to view the resulting counts. Figure 17.17 portrays one possible layout for the page.

EXERCISE 17.10

Augment your `stats.html` page so that, in addition to displaying the counts for each dice total, the page also represents the counts as percentages of the total number of rolls. To compute each percentage, you must divide the count by the total number of rolls and then multiply by 100. For example, if 162 out of 1,000 rolls were 2s, then that's 16.2% of the rolls. For our purposes, it is sufficient to round percentages to the nearest integer value, so 162 out of 1,000 would be displayed as 16%.

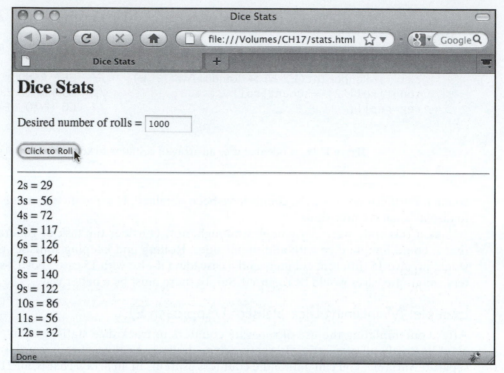

Figure 17.17 Sample appearance of `stats.html` page.

EXERCISE 17.11

Using your `stats.html` page, perform 100 dice rolls and report the results. Are your percentages close to the expected ones listed in Figure 17.14? Should they be?

Now, perform 1,000 dice rolls using your page and report the results. Are the percentages from this experiment closer to the expected percentages? Should they be?

Now, perform 10,000 dice rolls using your page and report the results. Are the percentages from this experiment closer to the expected percentages? Should they be?

Example: ASCII Animations

In an age of 3-D graphics and video games, what could be more retro than returning to the olden days of character-based art? Pictures made up of typed or printed characters have existed for more than a century, but they became widespread in the 1970's and 1980's due to character-based monitors and the growth of the Internet. For example, drawings such as the following might appear at the end of an email message:

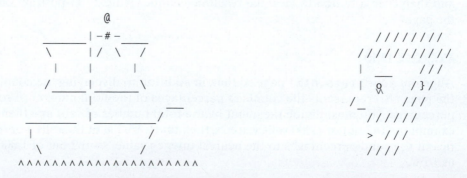

These character-based drawings became known as ASCII art, in reference to the ASCII code for representing characters (see Chapter 12).

The concept of ASCII art can easily be extended to moving animations. As we saw in Chapter 12, movies are nothing more than sequences of picture frames, displayed one after another to give the appearance of motion. An ASCII animation is a movie in which each individual frame is a piece of ASCII art. For example, consider the following repeating sequence of ASCII drawings. If these two stickperson figures are alternately displayed, it gives the appearance of the person performing jumping jacks.

The Web page in Figure 17.18 provides a framework for creating and displaying ASCII animations. The page contains two text areas (as shown in Figure 17.19). In the text area on the left, the user can enter the ASCII art that makes up the frames of an animation. Individual frames are separated by a line containing '====='. For example, the default content of the text area is the two-frame animation of the stickperson performing jumping jacks, but the user can change the animation by entering new ASCII art frames in the text area. When the user clicks the button labeled "Play the Animation," the PlayAnimation function is called to access the frames and display the animation in the text area to the right.

The PlayAnimation function begins by accessing the content of the text area (line 16) and splitting the string into individual frames using the split method (lines 17–22). Because different operating systems and browsers represent text lines differently (some end lines with '\n' while others use '\r\n'), the function must identify which type of line formatting is being used. If a search for '=====\r\n' matches a frame divider, then the string is split using that pattern; otherwise, it is split using '=====\n'. Once the sequence of frames is stored in the frameSeq array, the setInterval function is called to display the successive frames at quarter-second intervals (line 25).

EXERCISE 17.12

Enter the ascii.html text from Figure 17.18 into a new Web page, then load this page to verify that it behaves as described. Note that the only way to stop an animation once it has begun is to reload the page (e.g., by clicking the Reload button in the browser).

Design and create your own ASCII animation. You may enter the frames directly in the text area in the page, or instead use a separate text editor and then copy-and-paste the completed frame sequence into the page when done. Use your imagination!

Looking Ahead...

In this chapter, you learned how to store and manipulate data in JavaScript arrays. An array is a collection of items in which each item is accessible via an index. For example, the first value in the array nums is stored at index 0 and is represented as nums[0]. Arrays are especially flexible structures—for example, if you specify an array index that has no corresponding value in the array, the array will return the value undefined, rather than an error. Furthermore, if you assign a value to an index outside the current scope of the array, the array will be automatically extended to accommodate the assignment. Arrays are useful for storing and manipulating large amounts of data, particularly if that data represents user input. For example, if a user enters a sequence of words or numbers in a text box or text area, then the input can be converted from a string into an array using the string method split. Once in array form, the data can be easily traversed and processed, as this chapter's various examples have demonstrated.

```
 1.  <!doctype html>
 2.  <!-- ascii.html                              Dave Reed -->
 3.  <!-- Page for entering and viewing ASCII animations. -->
 4.  <!-- ================================================= -->
 5.
 6.  <html>
 7.   <head>
 8.     <title>ASCII Animation</title>
 9.     <script type="text/javascript">
10.       function PlayAnimation()
11.       // Assumes: frameArea contains the text of an ASCII animation
12.       // Results: displays each frame of the animation in succession (0.25 sec apart)
13.       {
14.         var frameStr;
15.
16.         frameStr = document.getElementById('frameArea').value;
17.         if (frameStr.indexOf('\r\n') != -1) {        // SOME BROWSERS/PLATFORMS
18.             frameSeq = frameStr.split('=====\r\n');   // USE \r\n FOR LINE ENDINGS,
19.         }                                             // OTHERS USE \n
20.         else {                                        // MUST HANDLE BOTH CASES
21.             frameSeq = frameStr.split('=====\n');
22.         }
23.
24.         currentFrame = 0;
25.         setInterval('ShowNextFrame();', 250);
26.       }
27.
28.       function ShowNextFrame()
29.         // Assumes: frameSeq is an array of animation frames, and
30.         //          currentFrame is the index of the current frame
31.         // Results: displays the current frame in displayArea & increments the index
32.       {
33.         document.getElementById('displayArea').value = frameSeq[currentFrame];
34.         currentFrame = (currentFrame + 1) % frameSeq.length;
35.       }
36.     </script>
37.   </head>
38.
39.   <body style="text-align:center">
40.     <h2>ASCII Animation Editor/Viewer</h2>
41.     <table style="margin-left:auto;margin-right:auto">
42.       <tr><td style="text-align:center">
43.         Enter the frames below, separated by "=====".</td>
44.         <td style="text-align:center">
45.         <input type="button" value="Play the Animation" onclick="PlayAnimation();">
46.       </tr>
47.       <tr><td><textarea id="frameArea" rows=25 cols=55 style="font-size:8pt">
48.          o
49.         /#\
50.         _|_
51.        =====
52.         \o/
53.          #
54.        _/ \_ </textarea></td>
55.         <td><textarea id="displayArea" rows=25 cols=55 style="fontsize:8pt">
56.         </textarea></td>
57.       </tr>
58.     </table>
59.   </body>
60.  </html>
```

Figure 17.18 Web page that displays ASCII animations in a text area.

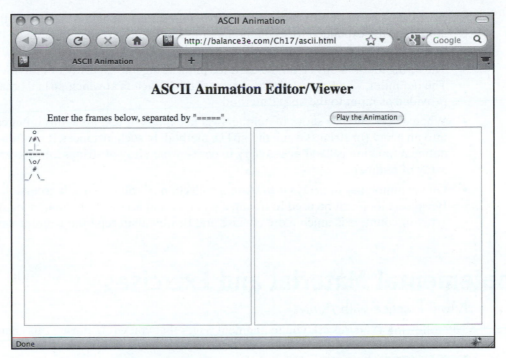

Figure 17.19 ascii.html rendered in a Web browser.

This chapter completes the text's coverage of programming concepts. Through the design and implementation of interactive Web pages, you have developed an impressive set of programming and problem-solving skills. Among other tools, you have used variables to store values; buttons, text boxes, text areas, and page divisions to handle input and output; functions to manage and encapsulate complexity; if statements and while loops to control the execution of other statements; and finally strings and arrays to manipulate complex data. In Chapter 18, you will look back on the broader material from this text to examine the role of computers in our society.

Chapter Summary

- An array is a list in which individual items are accessible via indices. Arrays are specified in JavaScript by enclosing items in square brackets, separated by commas. For example, misc = [1, 'foo', 3].

- Like strings, arrays are composite structures, in that multiple values are contained in a single object. Unlike strings, however, the items in an array can be of any type.

- The individual items in an array are accessed by specifying the array name, followed by a bracketed index. For example, the first item in the array misc is accessed as misc[0], the second item as misc[1], and so on.

- Similar to strings, all arrays have a length property, which identifies the number of items in the array. For example, the last item in the array misc would be misc[misc.length-1].

- If you attempt to access an array index that is beyond the length of an array, undefined is returned.

- Bracket notation can be used to assign a value to an array component. For example, the assignment misc[0] = 1000; will store 1,000 in the first component of the array misc, overwriting the value that was previously stored there.

- If you assign a value to a component beyond the current length of the array, the array will be automatically expanded to accommodate the new value. Any components in between the new item and the original array will be considered `undefined`.

- The string method `split` can be used to split a string into an array of individual components. The delimiter, which specifies the character or characters at which `split` breaks the string, is provided as input to the `split` method.

- When a user enters a series of numbers via a text box or text area, this input can be divided into an array (of strings) using the `split` method. In such instances, it is often useful to define a function called `ParseArray` to convert the array of strings into a corresponding array of numbers.

- One common use of arrays is to store a collection of counters, each accessible via an index. Because a loop can be used to traverse an array and access each counter by its index, an array of counters is much more concise and flexible than separate counter variables.

Supplemental Material and Exercises

More Practice with Arrays

The following exercises ask you to augment pages that you wrote during this chapter.

EXERCISE 17.13

Define a function named `Minimum` that is similar to the `Average` function from Figure 17.11, but that takes an array of numbers as input and returns the smallest value from that array. For example, the call `Minimum([33, 12, 5, 17, 8])` should return 5. After inserting this function into your `arrays.js` page, modify your `average.html` page so that it displays the minimum input value along with the average.

Hint: To find the minimum value in an array, your function should traverse the array and record the smallest value it encounters. Start by initializing a variable to the first value in the array. Then, compare each subsequent value in the array to the variable, updating the variable whenever a smaller value is found.

EXERCISE 17.14

When a course has numerous assignments, a kindly instructor may drop a student's lowest grade to allow for one bad day. Modify your `grades.html` page from Exercise 17.8 so that the lowest lesson grade is ignored.

Hint: To compute the average of a collection of grades while dropping the lowest grade, you can use the following formula:

    ((avg_of_grades * number_of_grades) - minimum_grade)/(number_of_grades - 1)

EXERCISE 17.15

Modify your `stats.html` page so that it simulates repeatedly rolling a pair of eight-sided dice and then collects statistics on the dice totals obtained. Because the array of counters provides extreme flexibility, only minimal changes should be required to adapt the page.

Searching an Array

In life, we are constantly searching for things. Looking up a number in the phone book, rifling through a stack of papers to find a particular one, scanning the index of a book for a topic—these are all examples of searching. In computer science, searching is an especially common task. Many problems involve storing, accessing, and updating large collections of data. For example, consider a database program for maintaining a library's inventory of books. In addition to storing an entry for each book, such a program must be able to sort and retrieve these entries by author, title, Library of Congress number, or subject.

As we saw in Chapter 8, the simplest way to search for some item in a list is to scan the list in order, starting at the beginning. If the desired item is not first in the list, then you look at the second item, then the third, and so on until the item is found. This strategy is known as *sequential search*, since it involves searching through list items in sequence. As an example, consider the following array of words:

```
words = ['if', 'else', 'function', 'while', 'for', 'var', 'return'];
```

If we were looking for the word 'function' in this array, a sequential search would inspect the first component ('if'), then the second ('else'), and finally the third before finding the desired word.

The SeqSearch function in Figure 17.20 performs a sequential search on a list of items. The two inputs required by this function are the list to be searched (an array) and the desired item. When called on a particular array, the function compares the desired item with each item in the array, starting at the beginning (i.e., at index 0). If the function encounters an item that matches the desired item, it immediately returns the index at which the match was found. If the desired item isn't found by the time the while loop reaches the last index, then the item is not in the list, and –1 will be returned.

EXERCISE 17.16

Add the SeqSearch function to the arrays.js library file and then create a Web page named seq.html that utilizes the SeqSearch function to perform sequential searches on user input. The page should contain a text area in which the user can enter a sequence of words separated by white space, as well as a text box in which the user can enter the word to be searched for. When the user clicks a button, SeqSearch should be called to search for the desired word in the sequence and display the result (either the index at which the word was found or else –1) in a separate text box.

```
function SeqSearch(list, desired)
// Assumes: list is an array of items
// Returns: index of list where desired first appears, or -1 if not found
{
    var index;

    index = 0;                          // START AT FIRST ITEM
    while (index < list.length) {       // AS LONG AS ITEMS LEFT
        if (list[index] == desired) {   //    IF NEXT ITEM IS THE DESIRED ONE,
            return index;               //    THEN RETURN INDEX WHERE FOUND
        }
        index = index + 1;              //    GO ON TO NEXT ITEM
    }
    return -1;                          // IF FAILED TO FIND DESIRED, RETURN -1
}
```

Figure 17.20 Function for sequentially searching an array of items.

EXERCISE 17.17

After experimenting with `seq.html`'s sequential search capabilities, answer the following questions:

- What is the minimum number of inspections required to find an item in an array using sequential search? Where must the desired item occur in the array for the page to perform this minimum number of inspections?

- What is the maximum number of inspections required to find an item in an array using sequential search? Where must the desired item occur in the array for the page to perform this maximum number of inspections?

Although sequential search is sufficient for searching small lists, the fact that your program might have to examine every list item before completing a search makes this approach infeasible for large lists. As we saw in Chapter 8, however, a list can be searched much more efficiently if the items in the list are ordered. The **binary search** algorithm searches for a particular item in a sorted list by first checking the list's middle entry. The middle entry is compared to the desired item and, if the two are equal, then the search terminates successfully. If the middle entry comes after the desired item in the list's ordering scheme, then all items in the list beyond the middle entry are eliminated from consideration. Likewise, if the middle entry comes before the desired item in the list's ordering scheme, then the items before the middle entry are eliminated. The search then continues by repeatedly checking the middle entry of the remaining half of the list, eventually honing in on the desired entry.

For example, suppose that we were looking for the name "Jack" in the following array of names, which is sorted alphabetically:

```
['Charlie','Dave','Jack','Jerald','Jerroll','Laura','Lois','Winnie']
```

According to the binary search algorithm, we begin by looking at the middle entry of the array. Since the array indices range from 0 to 7, we will select index 3 as the middle (the average of 0 and 7, rounded down). If the name we are looking for were stored at index 3, then we would be done. Since it is not, we compare the names and find that "Jerald" comes after "Jack". Thus, we know that "Jack" must come before "Jerald" in the list (i.e., our desired item occurs before index 3 in the array). We then repeat the process, this time focusing on the sublist starting at index 0 and ending at index 2. The midpoint in this sublist is at index 1 (the average of 0 and 2), which contains the name "Dave". Since "Dave" comes before "Jack" alphabetically, we know that "Jack" must come after index 1. Finally, the desired name is found at index 2.

To help us better understand binary search, we can define a set of generalized variables to use in our description of the algorithm. In this context, let `left` always refer to the leftmost or lowest possible index at which the desired array item could be located. Likewise, `right` will refer to the rightmost or highest possible index. Before a binary search begins, `left` is 0 and `right` is the last index in the array. During each step of the binary search, the midpoint mid between `left` and `right` is inspected. If the item stored at `mid` is the desired item, then the search terminates successfully. If the item at `mid` occurs after the desired item in the ordering scheme, then `right` becomes `mid-1`. Likewise, if the item at `mid` occurs before the desired item, then `left` becomes `mid+1`. Since each step either increases `left` or decreases `right`, the binary search will eventually locate the desired item if it is in the array. If the array doesn't contain a match for the desired item, then the `left` and `right` indices will ultimately cross, indicating that there is no more array to search.

For example, Figure 17.21 traces the steps in the binary search for "Jack" in the array of names listed above. Likewise, Figure 17.22 traces the steps in the binary search for "Sue" in the same array.

```
name = ['Charlie','Dave','Jack','Jerald','Jerroll','Laura','Lois','Winnie'];
                left      right     mid      names(mid)
```

	left	right	mid	names(mid)
1st inspection	0	7	3	'Jerald'
2nd inspection	0	2	1	'Dave'
3rd inspection	2	2	2	'Jack'

On the third inspection, the desired name is found, and the search terminates.

Figure 17.21 Trace of a binary search for the name "Jack."

```
name = ['Charlie','Dave','Jack','Jerald','Jerroll','Laura','Lois','Winnie'];
                left      right     mid      names(mid)
```

	left	right	mid	names(mid)
1st inspection	0	7	3	'Jerald'
2nd inspection	4	7	5	'Laura'
3rd inspection	6	7	6	'Lois'
4th inspection	6	5	–	–

On the fourth inspection, the right index becomes smaller than the left index, signifying that all indices in the array have been eliminated from consideration. At that point, the binary search can terminate, since the desired name is not present.

Figure 17.22 Trace of a binary search for the name "Sue."

EXERCISE 17.18

Using the array of names from the previous examples (repeated below), perform the following traces:

```
name = ['Charlie','Dave','Jack','Jerald','Jerroll','Laura','Lois','Winnie'];
```

a. Trace the binary search for "Dave" in the table below:

	left	right	mid	names(mid)
1st inspection				
2nd inspection				
.				
.				
.				

b. Trace the binary search for "Jerroll" in the table below:

	left	right	mid	names(mid)
1st inspection				
2nd inspection				
.				
.				
.				

c. Trace the binary search for "Zoe" in the table below:

	left	right	mid	names(mid)
1st inspection				
2nd inspection				
.				
.				
.				

EXERCISE 17.19

The sort method, when applied to an array of strings, returns a copy of that array in which the strings appear in alphabetical order. For example, if the variable words stored the array ['foo', 'bar', 'biz'], then the call words.sort() would return ['bar', 'biz', 'foo'].

Define a function named BinSearch that implements binary search and store it in arrays.js. Then, create a Web page named bin.html that performs binary searches. Like seq.html, this page should contain a text area in which the user can enter a sequence of words and a text box for specifying the word to search for. When the user clicks a button, the page should sort the words in alphabetical order (using the array method sort) and then call BinSearch to perform the search. As in seq.html, the result of the search (either the index at which the word was found or else –1) should be displayed in a separate text box.

EXERCISE 17.20

After experimenting with bin.html's binary search capabilities, answer the following questions:

• What is the minimum number of inspections required to find an item in an array using binary search? Where must the desired item occur in the array for the page to perform this minimum number of inspections?

• What is the maximum number of inspections required to find an item in an array using binary search? Where must the desired item occur in the array for the page to perform this maximum number of inspections?

Parallel and Nested Arrays

Suppose that you wanted to create a Web page that quizzed the user on state capitals. The page would need to select states at random, ask the user to guess each state's capital, and then compare the user's guesses against the correct answers. To accomplish this, the page must store the names of all 50 states and their capitals. In addition, the page must be able to select a random state and locate the corresponding capital.

Clearly, the easiest way to store state and capital names would be in arrays, as shown in Figure 17.23.

```
STATES =    ['Alabama', 'Alaska', 'Arizona', 'Arkansas', 'California',
             'Colorado', 'Connecticut', 'Delaware', 'Florida', 'Georgia',
             'Hawaii', 'Idaho', 'Illinois', 'Indiana', 'Iowa',
             'Kansas', 'Kentucky', 'Louisiana', 'Maine', 'Maryland',
             'Massachusetts', 'Michigan', 'Minnesota', 'Mississippi', 'Missouri',
             'Montana', 'Nebraska', 'Nevada', 'New Hampshire', 'New Jersey',
             'New Mexico', 'New York', 'North Carolina', 'North Dakota', 'Ohio',
             'Oklahoma', 'Oregon', 'Pennsylvania', 'Rhode Island', 'South Carolina',
             'South Dakota', 'Tennessee', 'Texas', 'Utah', 'Vermont',
             'Virginia', 'Washington', 'West Virginia', 'Wisconsin', 'Wyoming'];
CAPITALS =  ['Montgomery', 'Juneau', 'Phoenix', 'Little Rock', 'Sacramento',
             'Denver', 'Hartford', 'Dover', 'Tallahassee', 'Atlanta',
             'Honolulu', 'Boise', 'Springfield', 'Indianapolis', 'Des Moines',
             'Topeka', 'Frankfort', 'Baton Rouge', 'Augusta', 'Annapolis',
             'Boston', 'Lansing', 'St. Paul', 'Jackson', 'Jefferson City',
             'Helena', 'Lincoln', 'Carson City', 'Concord', 'Trenton',
             'Santa Fe', 'Albany', 'Raleigh', 'Bismarck', 'Columbus',
             'Oklahoma City', 'Salem', 'Harrisburg', 'Providence', 'Columbia',
             'Pierre', 'Nashville', 'Austin', 'Salt Lake City', 'Montpelier',
             'Richmond', 'Olympia', 'Charleston', 'Madison', 'Cheyenne'];
```

Figure 17.23 Arrays for storing states and capitals.

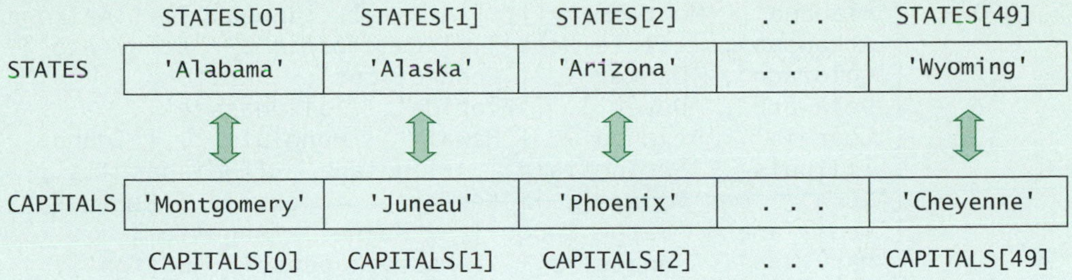

Figure 17.24 Memory cells corresponding to the parallel arrays from Figure 17.23.

As you may have noticed, the order in which the states and capitals appear is not random. The states are listed in alphabetical order, and the capitals are listed so that their order mirrors that of their associated states. This means that the city at CAPITALS[0] (Montgomery) is the capital of STATES[0] (Alabama), the city at CAPITALS[1] (Juneau) is the capital of STATES[1] (Alaska), and so on. In general, the city at a particular index of the CAPITALS array corresponds to the state at the same index of the STATES array.

When two separate arrays store related items of data at corresponding indices, they are called **parallel arrays**. You can visualize this concept by drawing the memory cells for the parallel arrays, one above the other (Figure 17.24). When parallel arrays are drawn this way, it is clear that each data entry in one array is related to the corresponding data entry in the other array.

EXERCISE 17.21

Design and create a Web page named states.html that quizzes the user on state capitals. The layout of the page is entirely up to you. However, the page should contain a text box in which the user can specify the number of questions on the quiz. After processing this input, the page should repeatedly ask the user to identify the capitals of randomly selected states until the desired number of questions has been posed. Once the quiz is complete, the user's score (number of correct answers and percentage correct) should be displayed in the page.

Hint: your page should store the states and state capitals in parallel arrays, as shown in Figure 17.23. To select a state for each quiz question, your page will need to generate a random index from 0 to 49 and assign it to a variable (e.g., stateIndex). Then the state name can be accessed as STATES [stateIndex]. Once the user enters a guess, this input should be checked against the state capital stored at CAPITALS[stateIndex].

Since arrays can store values of any type, it is possible to nest arrays inside other arrays. This capability can be useful in structuring related data, such as states and state capitals. As an alternative to parallel arrays, we could store each state and its capital together in an array of length 2. All 50 state/capital pairs could then be stored in a single array, as shown in Figure 17.25. The memory cell for this nested structure is depicted in Figure 17.26.

The advantage of using such nested arrays is that you can explicitly group related information together. That is, all the information about a particular state (which could be expanded to include population, state flower, etc.) is stored in one item of the STATE_INFO array. Of course, two levels of access are now required to look at a state name or capital. For example, the assignment

```
state = STATE_INFO[0];
```

assigns the array ['Alabama', 'Montgomery'] to the variable state. To access the state name from this pair, the first index must be accessed: state[0]. Likewise, the corresponding capital can be accessed at the second index: state[1].

```
STATE_INFO = [['Alabama', 'Montgomery'], ['Alaska', 'Juneau'], ['Arizona', 'Phoenix'],
              ['Arkansas', 'Little Rock'], ['California', 'Sacramento'],
              ['Colorado', 'Denver'], ['Connecticut', 'Hartford'],
              ['Delaware', 'Dover'], ['Florida', 'Tallahassee'],
              ['Georgia', 'Atlanta'], ['Hawaii', 'Honolulu'], ['Idaho', 'Boise'],
              ['Illinois', 'Springfield'], ['Indiana', 'Indianapolis'],
              ['Iowa', 'Des Moines'], ['Kansas', 'Topeka'], ['Kentucky', 'Frankfort'],
              ['Louisiana', 'Baton Rouge'], ['Maine', 'Augusta'],
              ['Maryland', 'Annapolis'], ['Massachusetts', 'Boston'],
              ['Michigan', 'Lansing'], ['Minnesota', 'St. Paul'],
              ['Mississippi', 'Jackson'], ['Missouri', 'Jefferson City'],
              ['Montana', 'Helena'], ['Nebraska', 'Lincoln'],
              ['Nevada', 'Carson City'], ['New Hampshire', 'Concord'],
              ['New Jersey', 'Trenton'], ['New Mexico', 'Santa Fe'],
              ['New York', 'Albany'], ['North Carolina', 'Raleigh'],
              ['North Dakota', 'Bismarck'], ['Ohio', 'Columbus'],
              ['Oklahoma', 'Oklahoma City'], ['Oregon', 'Salem'],
              ['Pennsylvania', 'Harrisburg'], ['Rhode Island', 'Providence'],
              ['South Carolina', 'Columbia'], ['South Dakota', 'Pierre'],
              ['Tennessee', 'Nashville'], ['Texas', 'Austin'],
              ['Utah', 'Salt Lake City'], ['Vermont', 'Montpelier'],
              ['Virginia', 'Richmond'], ['Washington', 'Olympia'],
              ['West Virginia', 'Charleston'], ['Wisconsin', 'Madison'],
              ['Wyoming', 'Cheyenne']];
```

Figure 17.25 Nested array structure for storing states and capitals.

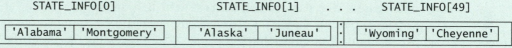

Figure 17.26 Memory cell corresponding to the nested arrays from Figure 17.25.

EXERCISE 17.22

Modify your `states.html` page so that it uses the nested array structure `STATE_INFO` to store the names of the states and their capitals. Then experiment with the new version to verify that the page behaves as before.

Computers and Society

This chapter uses narrative, illustrations, and review questions to introduce computer science and technology concepts.

Technology is neither good nor bad, nor even neutral. Technology is one part of the complex of relationships that people form with each other and the world around them; it simply cannot be understood outside of that concept.

Samuel Collins

We've all heard that a million monkeys at a million keyboards could produce the complete works of Shakespeare; now, thanks to the Internet, we know that is not true..

Robert Wilensky.

Computing is not about computers any more. It is about living.

Nicholas Negroponte

This chapter explores the effects of technology on the society in which we live. Computers and the Internet have changed the ways in which people carry out daily tasks, access information, communicate with each other, and conduct business. Having completed this book, you are better prepared to place computing in an appropriate historical context and to assess computers' potential for improving quality of life. Of course, the widespread adoption of computer technology also introduces the potential for abuses and unwanted consequences. For example, overreliance on high-tech tools can lead to disaster when complex systems fail. Likewise, as more personal communications and business transactions move online, privacy and security become major concerns. By examining both the positive and potentially negative societal role of computers, this chapter intends to call your attention to computers' wide-ranging influence while helping you become a more knowledgeable technology consumer.

Positive Impact of Technology

In the article "The Greatest Inventions in the Past 1000 Years," historian Larry Gormley ranked technological developments according to their impact on modern life.[1] Although any such list leaves room for debate, there is no doubt that the inventions listed by Gormley (Figure 18.1) have influenced the way in which society is structured. For example, the automobile changed the face of America by increasing personal mobility. When people

	Invention	Year	The Greatest Inventions in the Past 1000 Years[1] Inventor	Notes
1	Printing Press	1450	Johannes Gutenberg	allowed literacy to greatly expand
2	Electric Light	1879	Thomas Edison	powered countless social changes
3	Automobile	1885	Karl Benz	increased personal mobility and freedom
4	Telephone	1876	Alexander Graham Bell	spread communication across wide areas
5	Radio and Television	1895 & 1926	Guglielmo Marconi and John Baird	made the world smaller
6	Vaccination	1796	Edward Jenner	protected people from disease
7	Computer	1939	John Atanasoff et al.	transformed business world; predecessor to the Internet
8	Airplane	1903	Orville and Wilbur Wright	allowed people and products to quickly move across wide areas
9	Gas-powered Tractor	1892	John Froelich	started agricultural mechanization
10	Anesthesia	1844	Horace Wells	provided a great leap forward for medicine

Figure 18.1 Greatest inventions, as listed by Larry Gormley.

obtained their own affordable mode of transportation, they were able to move away from urban areas and still drive to their jobs, which led to American suburbanization and the rise of today's "commuter culture." The availability of telephone service also contributed to the decentralization of American society, in that phones enabled people to communicate and conduct business over large distances.

More than any other invention in Figure 18.1, computer technology is still evolving, which means that it continues to impact society in new ways. As we saw in Chapter 6, the first electronic computers made immediate contributions to world affairs during the 1940s. The COLOSSUS, developed by the British government, was instrumental in breaking the Nazi Enigma code and providing the Allies with an intelligence advantage in World War II. In the United States, the ENIAC and subsequent computers performed the calculations and simulations that enabled American scientists to develop nuclear technology, which shaped the politics of the subsequent Cold War. More recently, computers have become common in homes and businesses, changing the way in which we communicate and driving today's information-based economy. As computer scientists continue to augment existing technology and develop new applications, the potential for computers to influence daily life appears unlimited.

The sections that follow describe some of the ways in which computers, most notably through the Internet, have improved the quality of modern life.

Computers and Programs for Everyday Tasks

Over the past few years, computer technology has become so pervasive that it is now difficult to imagine life without it. One obvious example is the way in which computers have changed the nature of monetary transactions. When most products and services were bought for cash, people were forced to carry large amounts of money on their person. In addition to being inconvenient, a cash-based society invited crime, because muggings were likely to net thieves large quantities of untraceable funds. Today, many consumers are replacing cash with credit and debit cards, thanks to a computerized banking network that enables the electronic transfer of funds from one banking institution to another. Because of the proliferation of automated teller machines (ATMs) and debit-card scanners, people can access their money around the clock from almost any location, even while traveling (Figure 18.2). As a result, people are no longer dependent on cash reserves to purchase goods. From pay-at-the-pump gas stations to vending machines with credit-card readers, computing technology makes it easier for consumers to make purchases without carrying cash. In addition, the new system discourages traditional theft, as credit-card purchases are traceable. Unfortunately, the electronic era has inspired new forms of illegal activity, including credit-card fraud and identity theft, where a criminal uses false identification to pose as another person in order to make purchases or obtain credit.

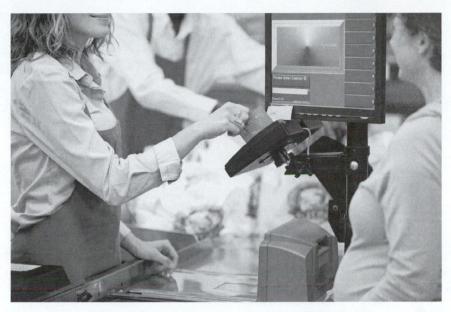

Figure 18.2 Debit-card readers provide retail shoppers with direct access to checking-account funds or credit-card accounts.

Although ATMs and debit-card readers serve as visible reminders of our reliance on technology, modern life also depends on thousands of less obvious, hidden computer applications. ***Embedded processors***, computer chips built into appliances and machinery to control their workings, account for more than 90% of all computer processors. Modern houses contain hundreds of embedded processors, concealed in devices such as microwave ovens, television remote controls, cordless phones, and automatic thermostats. Similarly, automobiles employ embedded processors to control fuel injectors, antilock brakes, and other components (see Figure 18.3). In fact, some 2010 automobiles have more computing power than fighter jets, with more than 100 embedded processors driven by 100 million lines of code.[2]

Society has also been affected by the availability of personal computers and easy-to-use software, which enable individuals to accomplish tasks previously reserved for highly trained professionals. For example, word processing and desktop publishing software have made it simple for anyone to produce professional-looking documents, such as business cards and flyers. Similarly, most personal computers now come with video-editing software, which allows users to create, edit, and augment digital video images on their computers. In addition, many software companies market specialized applications that capture human expertise and make it available to users. For example, tax preparation programs such as TaxCut by H&R Block integrate graphics, sound, and video to guide users

Microprocessors in Automobiles[3]		
speech technology	high-intensity discharge lamps	lighting system
electronic-memory seat	electric windows	mirror control
premium audio system	door module	climate control
digital radio	transmission control	navigation/GPS
immobilization	alarm systems	trip computer
head-up display	one-way data pager	right-of-cluster display
cruise control	Internet access	integrated cell phone
central body controllers	rain sensor	engine controller
vehicle-to-roadside communications	central locking and remote keyless entry	analog and digital instrumentation

Figure 18.3 Common uses of microprocessors in automobiles, as listed by Warren Webb.

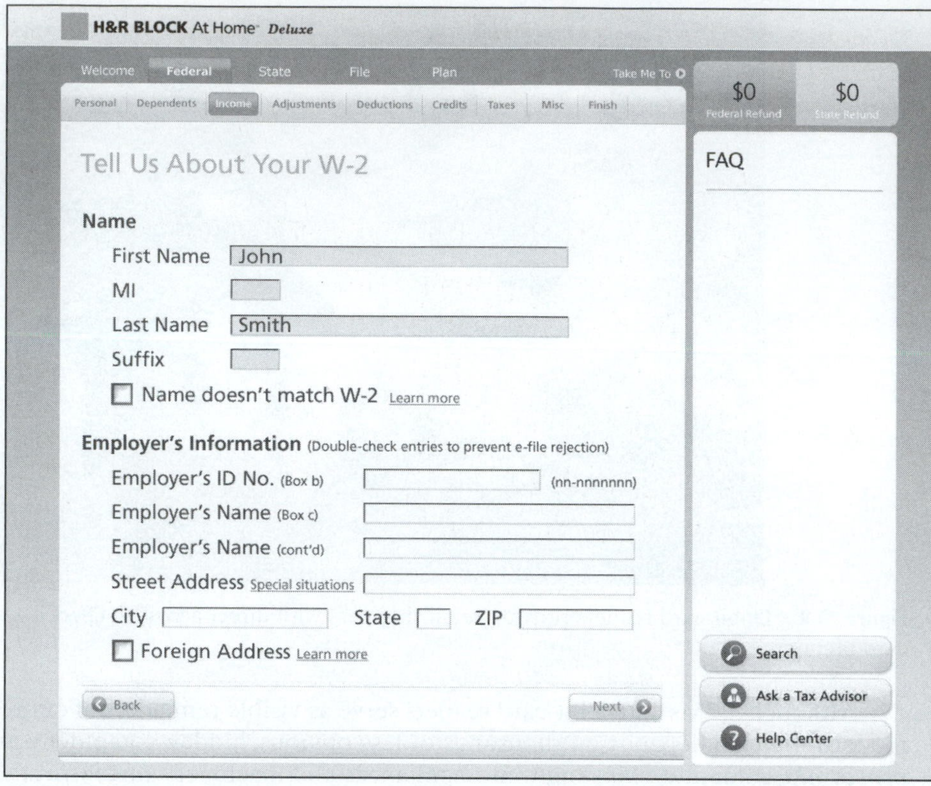

Figure 18.4 TaxCut by H&R Block guides the user in the preparation of his or her income taxes. The program uses specialized tax knowledge and even integrates sound and video to provide tax tips. (Copyright © 2010 HRB Digital LLC. All Rights Reserved.)

through the process of completing various tax forms (Figure 18.4). Over the past few years, many of these applications that capture human expertise have become available as Internet-based services. By offering access to such services over the Web on a pay-per-use basis, software companies can drastically reduce the cost to users while ensuring that all included information is regularly updated.

In recent years, new technologies have led to new types of software. Smart phones and hand-held computers such as the Apple iPad have driven the development of mobile applications, or apps, that run on theses devices. In June 2010, Apple's online App Store offered more than 225,000 apps for the iPhone and iPad.[4] Digital readers such as Amazon's Kindle and Sony's Reader allow users to download books and read them on small, portable displays.

The Internet and Web as Information Sources

As more people gain access to the Internet, online resources are quickly replacing traditional sources of information. Unlike print media such as newspapers and magazines, Web sites can be updated 24 hours a day, allowing online publishers to report stories as soon as they break. News sites can also integrate text and pictures with other types of media, such as video footage and interactive polls. The immediacy of the online delivery system has been especially appealing during crises, such as the September 11 terrorist attacks and the war in Iraq. According to Nielsen/NetRatings, over 10 million users accessed the CNN.com news site (Figure 18.5) from work during the first week of the Iraq war, constituting a 58% increase in visitors over the previous week.[5] Other online news sources, such as MSNBC.com and Yahoo!® News, experienced similar upsurges in traffic.

In an effort to compete with increasingly popular Internet media, many newspapers and magazines have expanded their offerings to include online versions. For example, *The Washington Post* (www.washingtonpost.com) and *The New York Times* (www.nytimes.com) both publish online editions. In addition, independent media organizations have used the Web to present stories and opinions that might not otherwise reach a mainstream audience (Figure 18.6). And because the Internet

Figure 18.5 Many traditional media outlets, such as television networks, newspapers, and magazines, now have a presence on the Web. Shown here is the CNN.com homepage from January 24, 2007. (© 2007 Cable News Network. Turner Broadcasting System, Inc. All Rights Reserved.)

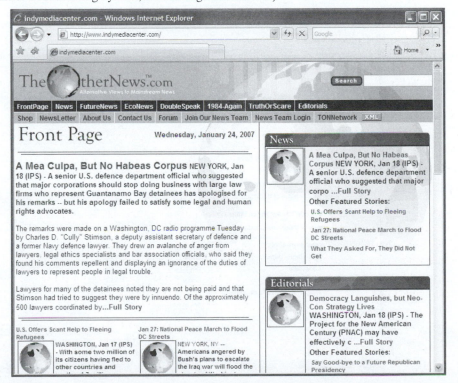

Figure 18.6 In addition to traditional media sources, alternative voices can be expressed on the Web because of its open-access nature. Shown here is the *TheOtherNews.com* homepage from January 24, 2007. (© 2007 TheOtherNews.com. All Rights Reserved. Reprinted with permission.)

crosses international borders, it has been instrumental in enabling the citizens of repressive governments to read objective news and communicate with the world.

Traditional media have approached the Internet in a variety of ways—some providing limited services online for free, others providing full services online but at a fee. Responding to the widespread availability of online reference material, the *Encyclopedia Britannica* (`www.eb.com`) now sells access to its encyclopedia as a subscription service over the Web. In the public sector, the U.S. government has led the campaign to move key data online by posting draft legislation, public service announcements, and various other documents on its network of Web sites. With the increasing popularity of smart phones and small, handheld computers many companies and organizations are customizing their Web sites for the mobile viewer. Such sites are able to recognize when a viewer is accessing the site via a mobile device and display pages in a format designed for smaller screens.

Although many traditional publications repurpose their content for the Web, the majority of Web pages are unique resources created by individuals and private organizations. As you learned in Chapter 1, anyone with minimal HTML skills and access to a Web server can design pages and make them available to the world. Given the diversity of opinion, perspective, and interests represented by today's online community, it is possible to find Web content on virtually any topic. For example, Web users can locate information about their favorite sports teams (`www.cubs.com`), directions to a local disc golf course (`www.pdga.com`), an explanation of how antilock brakes operate (`www.iihs.org/research/qanda/antilock.html`), the complete works of William Shakespeare (`shakespeare.mit.edu`), updates on the Kilauea volcanic eruption in Hawaii (`hvo.wr.usgs.gov`), and the schedule for the ferry connecting Hatteras and Ocracoke, North Carolina (`www.hatteras-nc.com/ferry/`). To help navigate this vast sea of information, search engines such as Google (`google.com`), Microsoft Bing (`bing.com`), and Yahoo!® Search (`search.yahoo.com`) automatically catalog Web pages and allow users to search for data by topic or keywords. Figure 18.7 depicts the advanced search options available to Google users.

Figure 18.7 Google's advanced search options allow users to look for any word, exact phrase, or combination of words, and can even limit the scope of the search based on file formats, dates, or location. (© 2010 Google, Inc.)

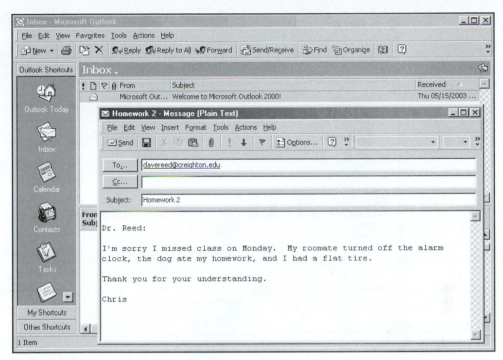

Figure 18.8 Email applications, such as Microsoft Outlook, enable users to send and receive messages, as well as organize contacts and plan their schedules. (Microsoft Outlook® is a registered trademark of Microsoft. All Rights Reserved.)

The Internet and Web as Communications Media

As we explained in Chapter 3, the exponential growth of the Internet during the 1970s was fueled in part by a proliferation of communications-based applications. Countless scientists, government workers and college faculty were drawn to the Internet by the availability of electronic mail and newsgroups. When Internet access became more widespread in the 1990s, a broad group of nontechnical users began going online to exchange business and personal information. According to a 2009 survey conducted by the Pew Internet & American Life Project, 74% of American adults use the Internet regularly, with almost 90% of those communicating via email.[6] On average, 247 billion emails were sent and received each day in 2009. Unfortunately, more than 80% of those emails were spam, unsolicited messages advertising some product or service.[7]

Today, it is common for Internet service providers (ISPs) to bundle email accounts with other services, making it easy for their customers to use the Internet for both Web access and email communications. One of the most popular email-management programs for Windows-based PCs is Microsoft Outlook, in which individuals send and receive email messages via an intuitive, Web-inspired interface (Figure 18.8). Users who want the ability to check their email from any Internet-enabled computer can take advantage of Web-based email services, such as Microsoft Hotmail (www.hotmail.com) and Yahoo!® Mail (mail.yahoo.com).

In addition to email, the growing popularity of mobile devices has led to the development of more direct communication tools. ***Instant messaging***, or ***chat***, applications enable users to conduct virtual conversations by typing messages and reading immediate responses on a computer or hand-held device. ***Text messaging***, or ***texting***, applications enable users to send short messages from one cell phone to another. By 2008 the number of text messages sent on cell phones (357 per month, on average) exceeded the number of phone calls made (204 per month, on average). For teens, the gap between texting and calling is even more pronounced, 1,742 texts vs. 231 phone calls per month, on average.[8]

Figure 18.9 Social networking sites such as Facebook allow users to post information and share with friends. (© 2010 Facebook, Inc. All Rights Reserved.)

Social networking applications that combine Internet or cell phone communications with community building have also evolved and grown in popularity, especially among younger users. Twitter, a social networking application that enables users to post short messages from cell phones or computers and subscribe to read others' posts, claimed to serve more than 100 million users in 2008. Facebook, a social networking Web site that enables users to post biographies, photographs, and messages online and connect with other posters, claimed to serve more than 400 million users in 2008.

The Internet and Web for Commerce

Another popular function of the Web is to facilitate electronic commerce, or *e-commerce*. As the number of Internet users has grown, businesses have recognized the Web's potential as an advertising medium and tool for reaching new customers. Today, almost every company maintains a Web presence, varying from information-based sites—at which the company provides data regarding its mission or products—to transaction-based sites—at which consumers can actually purchase goods.

Online shopping offers numerous benefits to consumers. Instead of searching through the mall and standing in long lines, shoppers can make purchases from the comfort of their homes at any time of day or night. Web-based commerce also makes it easier to comparison shop—i.e., compare the products, features, and prices offered by various companies. Furthermore, online stores provide more detailed product descriptions and reviews than would be available through conventional stores, which helps consumers make more informed purchasing decisions. Many of the largest e-commerce sites are online offshoots of traditional retailers, such as www.barnesandnoble.com (Barnes & Noble booksellers), www.circuitcity.com (Circuit City electronics stores), and www.sears.com (Sears department stores). In addition, many banks and retailers provide online services such as account tracking and online bill payments for the convenience of their customers.

Figure 18.10 Online retail outlets, such as Amazon.com, allow consumers to research products as well as purchase them. (© 1996-2010, Amazon.com, Inc. All Rights Reserved.)

Although companies such as these use the Internet to complement their traditional sales and services, some online companies are strictly Internet ventures. These companies have proven to be a much riskier venture, attributable in part to their lack of other revenue streams to support startup and development. In fact, many of the companies founded during the e-commerce boom of the late 1990s failed to turn a profit and have since folded. However, the largest e-commerce site in terms of yearly sales, Amazon.com, is a strictly online company that was founded in 1994 (Figure 18.10). According to the U.S. Census Bureau, online sales for the entire e-commerce sector exceeded $133 billion in 2008, an increase of 4.6% over 2007. Amazon.com by itself generated more than $19.1 billion in sales for 2008.[9]

The Web has also provided a new advertising channel for businesses and organizations. The most common method of Internet-based advertising involves the owners of popular Web sites charging fees in exchange for hosting advertising banners on their pages. These so-called *banner ads* are clickable images that promote a particular company's product or service. Users who click an ad are typically directed to the company's Web site, where they can make purchases or review additional product-related information. Some marketers have turned to more aggressive means of capturing the consumer's attention, such as animated, interactive ads or pop-up ads that pop open a new window that the user must manually close. To help combat intrusive advertising, modern browsers incorporate a variety of tools, including pop-up window blockers and fraudulent Website registries. From a publicity perspective, Internet-based advertising offers potential advantages over other, more traditional channels, as the Web's structure makes targeted marketing easier and allows direct connections between ads and related purchasing interfaces.

In addition to facilitating *business-to-consumer (B2C)* transactions, the Internet is extensively used for communication and information exchanges within and among businesses. *Business-to-business (B2B)* transactions allow companies to manage inventory more dynamically, improve efficiency by linking various data channels, and form partnerships based on sharing resources and information.

Potential Dangers of Technology

In conjunction with the benefits we have mentioned, the widespread adoption of technology also introduces the potential for abuses and undesirable consequences. The following sections outline some of the dangers that computers pose for individuals, businesses, and society at large.

Reliance on Complex Systems

As society becomes dependent on complex, computer-based products and services, the effects of computer errors or system failures become far-reaching. Whereas errors in the programs you wrote for this book might cause you frustration or earn you a bad grade, errors in software for air traffic control, electrical power relays, and banking systems can endanger lives and cost companies millions of dollars. The following list describes situations in which computer-system bugs produced dire and unexpected consequences.

- Between 1985 and 1987, six cancer patients received massive radiation overdoses when a Therac-25 radiation therapy machine malfunctioned. These malfunctions were eventually traced to a single coding error in the control mechanism for the machine. Four of the accidents resulted in patient deaths, whereas the other two resulted in patient disfigurement and disability.

- In 1990, AT&T's long-distance telephone network was crippled for nine hours, because of a misplaced statement in the electronic switching software. An estimated 60,000 customers were without long-distance service during this period, costing AT&T more than $60 million in lost revenue and damage to its reputation.

- In 1991, 28 soldiers were killed when a Scud missile struck a U.S. Army barracks near Dharan, Saudi Arabia. It was later determined that a Patriot missile battery failed to track and intercept the incoming Scud missile because of a software error. The control software for the Patriot missiles performed a repeated computation involving the value 1/10, which is a nonterminating number when represented in binary. The resulting round-off error, when compounded over 100 hours of active use, amounted to a .34 second timing error that caused the Patriot missile to miss its target.

- In 1999, NASA's *Mars Climate Orbiter* went off course and was destroyed in the Martian atmosphere. The navigational error that caused the crash was traced to inconsistencies in the software-development process at NASA. Apparently, some development teams on the project designed code using Imperial units (e.g., pounds), whereas other teams used metric units (e.g., kilograms). No one working on the project noticed this inconsistency, and the required measurement conversions were never made. The cost of the *Orbiter* was $125 million.

- In 2007, 17.000 planes were grounded at Los Angeles International Airport (LAX) due to a bug in U.S. Customs and Border Protection (USCBP) agency software. Passengers were unable to leave or enter the country through the airport for more than eight hours until the problem was resolved.

- In 2010, Toyota was forced to recall more than 400,000 hybrid vehicles to replace faulty software that controlled anti-lock brakes. Industry experts estimated that the cost of the recall, when combined with lost sales, could exceed $6 billion.

To avoid errors such as these, the software industry uses design and testing methodologies aimed at minimizing costs while improving the quality of large applications. However, as the size and complexity of software grows, design and testing become significantly more difficult. For example, it might be feasible for an experienced programmer to carefully study a 1,000-line program and ensure that it behaves as expected. However, performing the same type of analysis on a 10,000-line program would require significantly more than 10 times as much work, because each section of code must be tested not only in isolation, but also in relation to the other sections of code. As more software components are added to a system, the number of potential interactions between them grows exponentially. Software bugs are inevitable when the scale of a project renders it too complex for detailed study. For example, when Windows 2000 was released, the operating system was known to contain more than 63,000 bugs in its 35 million lines of code.[10] However, these bugs were not considered critical, as most were extremely unlikely to occur in everyday use and, at worst, required the user to reboot the computer. Clearly, critical systems—such as those that control aircraft or financial networks—necessitate more careful testing and debugging to protect human lives and property.

Information Overload

Although the impressive range of information available online can be viewed as a strength, it is also one of the medium's greatest weaknesses. The fact that individuals can add content to the Web ensures that all ideas and perspectives can be heard. However, the massive volume of data created by the online community isn't particularly organized, which makes finding any single piece of information difficult. As of 2009, various sources have estimated the size of the Web to exceed 50 billion pages. Search engines are useful in narrowing down an Internet search, but users must carefully select their search criteria to find specific resources. For example, suppose that a programmer wanted to learn more about the JavaScript `alert` function. A search for "JavaScript" produces 525 million matches using Google, whereas a more refined search for "JavaScript alert function" reduces the number of matching pages to 2,680,000. In the results of the second search, the first 10 pages include both general-purpose JavaScript tutorials and documentation on the `alert` function.

Even after a user locates Web pages related to a desired topic, judging the reliability of those pages is not always easy. Unlike traditional media sources, which have editors and reviewers to ensure at least some degree of accuracy and impartiality, the Web is neither monitored nor censored. Because anyone can be a Web author, there is always a chance that the author is uninformed, misinformed, or biased. Moreover, professional writers are familiar with the idea that complex questions require complex answers, whereas Web authors may settle for short answers that, although not entirely inaccurate, lack context and justification. For example, a Web search on the simple question "What is the capital of Missouri?" returns numerous pages that provide the answer (Jefferson City). However, entering a more complex question such as "Who invented the computer?" produces pages with a variety of answers, including Alan Turing, Konrad Zuse, Charles Babbage, John Atanasoff, and John von Neumann. As you learned in Chapter 6, each of these figures contributed to the development of computing technology in a different way. Responsible researchers would need to explain these answers in context to justify them. Figure 18.11 lists several criteria that can be applied to online content to evaluate its credibility.

It is important to note that even search engine results must be viewed critically. Companies that advertise through the browser company are often given preferential placemet on the search results page. In addition, there are techniques that Web developers can use to artificially inflate

Author Reputation	Is the author well known or well regarded in his field? If this information is not apparent, try to access biographical information or related works that reference the author to determine credibility.
Author Objectivity	Is there reason to believe that the author is objective? If the author has a political agenda or personal history with the topic, there is a greater danger of bias.
Content Review	Has the page been edited or reviewed by other parties? If so, there is more reason to trust its accuracy. Even the reputation of the organization hosting the page can be considered as supporting evidence, because a reputable organization will exert some control over content to protect the organization's integrity.
Content Verifiability	Does the author demonstrate scholarship and knowledge of the field by properly referencing other works? If evidence is strictly anecdotal or sources are untraceable, the content may reflect personal opinions that are not supported by the facts.
Content Timeliness	Is the information provided in the material timely? If the sources are old or are not accompanied by explicit dates, then the content may be out of date or contradictory to current practices.

Figure 18.11 Criteria for evaluating online content.

their ranking in the search results. Thus, when conducting research using a search engine, the user needs to look carefully at the source of the information and seek independent, corroborating sources when accuracy is essential.

Privacy and Security

When using credit cards or shopping online, consumers must often sacrifice their privacy for the sake of convenience. Most credit-card companies and online retailers maintain detailed records of customer purchases in an effort to identify patterns and predict future sales. Although such records can be used to improve customer service, there is significant potential for misuse. By analyzing a person's credit-card records, a company can infer many otherwise private details of the person's life, including hobbies, travel patterns, and personal contacts. Companies commonly sell customer profiles to marketing firms and other retailers, which use the information to contact potential buyers and deliver targeted advertising. However, Web users can limit the exploitation of their personal data by interacting only with reputable online businesses. Most such companies have established privacy policies outlining the way in which they handle customer information, and many explicitly promise not to sell data to third parties (Figure 18.12). To ensure that companies follow their own privacy policies, third-party organizations such as TRUSTe.com have been formed that evaluate companies' privacy procedures and offer accreditation seals.

Email also raises privacy concerns in our technology-driven society. When an email message is received, it is commonly stored in a file on the recipient's computer. If that message contains sensitive personal or business information, there is a danger that unauthorized users might get access to that file. Whereas legislation explicitly protects the privacy of letters and packages sent through the U.S. Postal Service, there are few laws that apply directly to electronic privacy. Furthermore, courts have overwhelmingly favored employers over employees in invasion-of-privacy suits involving email. Unless a company or organization explicitly states its policy on electronic privacy, it may be assumed that the company has the right to access any content on company-owned machines. This has been ruled to include emails written or received by employees, even if the emails are unrelated to company business.

Figure 18.12 Most companies provide an online policy describing the type of information recorded for a customer or site visitor, and the acceptable uses of such information. Shown here is the privacy policy for Amazon.com. (© 1996-2010, Amazon.com, Inc. All Rights Reserved.)

In recent years, a growing threat to user privacy is ***phishing***, the act of obtaining sensitive information (e.g., credit card numbers, usernames, or passwords) by masquerading as a trusted entity in an email. These emails may claim to be banks seeking account confirmation, Internet service providers attempting to verify account information, or lost acquaintances hoping to reconnect. By responding with sensitive information, user's are susceptible to financial loss or identity theft. It was estimated that as many as 5 million users were victims of successful phishing attacks in 2008.[11] In addition to direct financial losses, email accounts compromised via phishing are commonly used as platforms for spam attacks.

Privacy is closely linked to the issue of security—i.e., the assurance that Internet transmissions will travel from a verified sender to a verified recipient without being intercepted or corrupted in any way. As email messages travel across the Internet, they pass through numerous routers that direct the messages to their destinations. Each router represents a security risk, because someone could gain access to the router and eavesdrop on messages that are relayed. Although all Internet communications require security, e-commerce is particularly dependent on the ability to conduct secure transactions, as customers must submit credit-card numbers and other vulnerable data. Various security-related technologies have been developed to validate the identities of online customers and to encrypt data broadcast over the Internet (see Chapter 10 for details regarding encryption methods). Despite these efforts, however, online fraud is a continuing problem that affects customers and companies alike. CyberSource Corporation, a leading security management firm, has estimated that fraudulent online purchases cost companies more than $4 billion in 2008.[12]

The Digital Divide

An especially troubling aspects of recent technological developments is that the benefits associated with computers are not shared equally by all. According to a 2010 report by the Pew Internet & American Life Project, Americans with minority ancestry, lower incomes, and less education are still less likely to be online than are Americans without these factors (Figure 18.13). As we have outlined in this chapter, Internet access can provide numerous advantages in our society—in addition to helping

How Internet Access Has Changed in America[13] The percentage of each group with Internet access.					
By Gender	**2000**	**2009**	**By Race**	**2000**	**2009**
Men	51%	74%	Whites	50%	76%
Women	46%	74%	Blacks	34%	70%
			Hispanics	43%	64%
By Age	**2000**	**2006**	**By Household Income**	**2000**	**2006**
18–29	69%	93%	less than $30,000	31%	60%
30–49	60%	81%	$30,000–$50,000	52%	76%
50–64	45%	70%	$50,000–$75,000	67%	83%
64 +	14%	38%	$75,000 and above	78%	94%
By Education	**2000**	**2006**			
Did not graduate high school	17%	39%			
High school grad	34%	63%			
Some college	63%	87%			
College +	75%	94%			

Figure 18.13   Statistics on the Digital Divide, from Pew Internet & American Life Project (2010). The Project bears no responsibility for the interpretations presented or conclusions reached based on analysis of the data.

people become better informed, knowledge of the Web is a prerequisite for jobs in a variety of fields. Many experts worry that discrepancies in Internet access will widen the socioeconomic gap between the advantaged and disadvantaged in our society.

Numerous groups are addressing the digital divide in an effort to ensure that all people can enjoy the benefits of Internet access. During the Clinton administration, the U.S. government made Internet connectivity a priority in public schools. A major part of this campaign was the E-rate program, through which schools received government funding earmarked for computer technology and Internet service. By 2003, nearly all public schools in the United States were connected to the Internet, as compared to 35% in 1994. In addition, the number of connected classrooms in public schools has increased dramatically, from only 3% of classrooms in 1994, to 93% in 2003, to 97% in 2008.[14] Following this trend, most public libraries and community centers now provide Internet-enabled computers; in conjunction with nonprofit organizations such as TechSoup Global (`www.techsoupglobal.org`), these organizations have been instrumental in supplying Internet access and technical assistance to minority groups and lower-income individuals. Although the digital divide continues to affect Americans, there is no doubt that the situation has improved over the last decade. Hopefully, public- and private-sector organizations will continue to work together in the quest for universally available Internet access.

It should be noted that the digital divide also exists on a global scale. In 2004, it was estimated that the G8 countries (Canada, France, Germany, Italy, Japan, Russia, the United Kingdom, and the United States) accounted for almost half of all Internet users in the world, despite containing only 15% of the world's population.[15] Because high-tech jobs are a major force in the world economy, lack of Internet access places less developed nations at a significant disadvantage and compounds their other economic problems. International organizations such as the United Nations (`www.un.org`) and World Economic Forum (`www.weforum.org`) are working to address the global digital divide. One promising approach from the private sector is the One Laptop Per Child (OLPC) program, organized by Nicholas Negroponte and colleagues at the MIT Media Lab in 2005. The OLPC organization is committed to the development and dissemination of low-cost, low-power laptops to school children in third-world countries. By 2010, more than 1.5 million laptops have been manufactured and distributed to developing countries, including 594,000 to Peru, 480,000 to Uruguay, and 110,000 to Rwanda.[16]

Looking Beyond...

Clearly, computing technology has significantly impacted society over the last 70 years, both positively and negatively. In addition to teaching programming skills, this book has tried to make you a knowledgeable consumer of technology in your personal and professional life. Now that you have studied the structure and behavior of computers, you are better prepared to evaluate and effectively use new technology. Furthermore, your familiarity with computer history should help you recognize and appreciate the impact that new technology can have in your life. Having explored the methodologies employed by programmers and computer professionals, you are equipped with a better understanding of the computer science field and how it relates to other disciplines.

The programming component of this book has also contributed to your development as a student and user of computing technology. In learning to build interactive Web pages using HTML and JavaScript, you have acquired practical Web-development skills that will prove useful for many information-based careers. Through the process of writing JavaScript code, you have mastered fundamental concepts of programming, which can be applied to learning other, more complex programming languages. In a broader context, programming also fosters critical-thinking and problem-solving skills, which pertain to many facets of daily life.

It is the author's hope that this book has empowered you to be an active participant in a future in which computing technology improves our quality of life.

Chapter Summary

- Computers and the Internet have changed the ways in which people carry out daily tasks, access information, communicate with each other, and conduct business. For example, electronic banking has changed the way people access money, and applications software has enabled individuals to accomplish tasks previously reserved for highly trained professionals.

- Embedded processors, computer chips that are built into appliances and machinery to control their workings, account for more than 90% of all computer processors.

- The Internet and World Wide Web provide alternative sources of news and information that can be updated easily and accessed by people worldwide.

- It has been estimated that 74% of American adults use the Internet regularly, with almost 90% of those communicating via email.

- In 2008, online sales for the entire electronic commerce, or e-commerce, sector exceeded $133 billion. Online shopping can be more convenient for consumers, and it makes product research and comparison shopping easier.

- Banner ads are clickable images that promote a particular company's product or service.

- As society becomes dependent on complex, computer-based products and services, the effects of computer errors or system failures become far-reaching (e.g., failure of medical machinery controls can lead to patient deaths, bugs in switching software can lead to telephone network outages).

- As of 2009, various sources have estimated the size of the Web to exceed 50 billion pages.

- Because the Web is large and there are few controls on the quality of page content, finding desired information on the Web and verifying its authenticity can be difficult.

- Criteria that can be applied to online content to evaluate its credibility include author reputation, author objectivity, content review, content verifiability, and content timeliness.

- Privacy and security are concerns, as electronic banking and online shopping provide records of individual activities and preferences. Most reputable companies establish privacy policies outlining the way in which they handle customer information and use encryption techniques to protect private information as it is transmitted.

- The "digital divide" refers to the fact that the benefits associated with computers are not shared equally by all. Americans with minority ancestry, lower incomes, and less education are less likely to be online than are other Americans. On a global scale, America, western Europe and certain Asian countries have much greater Internet connectivity than other parts of the world.

Review Questions

1. TRUE or FALSE? Computer technology has greatly impacted the banking industry, to the extent that credit cards and debit cards have reduced consumers' reliance on cash.

2. TRUE or FALSE? Embedded processors are computer chips that are built into appliances and machinery to control their workings.

3. TRUE or FALSE? Instant messaging software allows users to send and receive messages almost instantaneously, allowing for interactive conversations between remote users.

4. TRUE or FALSE? Commercial software systems are thoroughly tested so that all programming errors are identified and fixed before the system is marketed.

5. TRUE or FALSE? Search engines such as `Google.com` verify the accuracy of information on Web pages before they report those pages.

6. TRUE or FALSE? `Amazon.com` is the largest e-commerce site in terms of yearly online sales.

7. TRUE or FALSE? Because of budget constraints, public schools are less likely to have Internet access today than they were 10 years ago.

8. TRUE or FALSE? The "digital divide" refers to the fact that the disadvantaged in society (e.g., minorities, the poor, and uneducated citizens) are less likely to have access to the Internet.

9. Do you think that Gormley's list (Figure 18.1) represents the 10 most important inventions of the last 1,000 years? If not, what inventions do you think are missing from this list? What possible developments in computer technology might increase the relative importance of computers?

10. In addition to the examples listed in this chapter, describe two other aspects of society that have been greatly impacted by computer technology. Within these areas, what specific activities or jobs were most affected? On the whole, has the impact been positive or negative? Justify your answers.

11. Describe two advantages of online newspapers over their print counterparts. Do you think that electronic newspapers will completely replace printed papers in the near future? Why or why not?

12. Perform a Web search on your name. That is, enter your name into a search engine, such as Google or Yahoo!® Search, and then search the Web for occurrences of that name. How many matching pages did the search engine find? If you have your own Web page, did the search engine find it? You may need to include additional search parameters if your name is relatively common.

13. Use a search engine to research and answer the following questions. Identify the site at which you obtained your answer, as well as the search parameters you used to locate the page.
    a. Who invented the programming language PHP?
    b. In what year did the Battle of Hastings take place?
    c. Who won the Academy Award for best actress in 1996?
    d. How many number-one hits did the Beatles have?

Endnotes

1. Gormley, Larry. "The Greatest Inventions in the Past 1000 Years." eHistory.com, 2003. Online at `http://www.ehistory.com/world/articles/ArticleView.cfm?AID=20`.

2. Motavalli, Jim. "The Dozens of Computers that Make Modern Cars Go (and Stop)." *New York Times*, p. B6, February 5, 2010.

3. Webb, Warren. "Embedded Technology Transforms the Automobile." *EDN Magazine*, August 19, 1999.

4. AppleInsider Staff. "*eBusiness Essentials: Technology and Network Requirements for the Electronic Marketplace.*" AppleInsider, June 7, 2010. Available online at http://www.appleinsider.com/articles/10/06/07/apple_says_app_store_ has_made_developers_over_1_billion.html.

5. *Round-The-Clock News Coverage of the War In Iraq Draws Surfers Online.* Nielsen/NetRatings, March 2003. Online at `http://www.nielsen-netratings.com/pr/pr_030327.pdf`.

6. Pew Internet & American Life Project: Latest Trends. Pew Research Center, December 2009. Online at `http://www.pewinternet.org/Trend-Data/Online-Activites-Total.aspx`.

7. Radicati, Sara. "Email Statistics Report, 2009–2013." Radicati Group, 2009.

8. Covey, Nic. Flying Fingers. Nielsen Telecom Consumer Insights, November 2008. Online at `http://en-us.nielsen.com/content/nielsen/en_us/insights/consumer_insight/issue_12/flying_fingers.html`.

9. *United States Department of Commerce News*. February 2006. Online at `http://www.census.gov/mrts/www/data/pdf/08Q4.pdf`.

10. Farr, John. "HOW Many Bugs, Did You Say??" Applelinks.com, February 2000. Online at `http://www.applelinks.com/articles/2000/02/20000212012612.shtml`.

11. Gartner Says Number of Phishing Attacks on U.S. Consumers Increased 40 Percent in 2008. Gartner Research Press Release, April 14, 2009. Online at http://www.gartner.com/it/page.jsp?id=936913.

12. CyberSource 10th Annual Online Fraud Report. CyberSource Corporation, 2009.

13. Pew Internet and American Life Project: Latest Trends. Pew Research Center, December 2009. Online at `http://www.pewinternet.org/Trend-Data/Online-Activites-Total.aspx`.

14. Linda Gray, Nina Thomas and Laurie Lewis. *Educational Technology in U.S. Public Schools: Fall 2008.* National Center for Education Statistics, 2008.

15. World Telecommunication/ICT Indicators Database, International Telecommunication Union, 2004.

16. Deployments. One Laptop Per Child Wiki, June 2010. Online at http://wiki.laptop.org/go/ Deployments.

References

Abelson, Hal, Ken Ledeen and Harry Ellis. *Blown to Bits: Your Life, Liberty, and Happiness After the Digital Explosion.* Addison-Wesley, 2008.

Baase, Sara. *A Gift of Fire: Social, Legal and Ethical Issues in Computing*, 3rd ed. Upper Saddle River, NJ: Prentice Hall, 2008.

Cavazos, Edward, and Gavino Morin. *Cyber-space and the Law: Your Rights and Duties in the On-line World.* Cambridge, MA: MIT Press, 1994.

Huckle, Thomas. "Collection of Software Bugs." May 2010. Online at `http://wwwzenger.informatik.tu-muenchen.de/persons/huckle/bugse.html`.

Margolis, Jane, Rachel Estrella, Joanna Goode, Jennifer Jellison Holme, and Kimberly Nao. *Stuck in the Shallow End: Education, Race, and Computing.* Cambridge, MA: MIT Press, 2008.

Negroponte, Nicholas. Being Digital. New York: Vintage Books, 1995.

Norris, Mark, Steve West, and Kevin Gaughan. *eBusiness Essentials: Technology and Network Requirements for the Electronic Marketplace.* New York: John Wiley & Sons, 2000.

Appendix A
Browser Basics

As Chapters 1 and 3 explained, a Web browser is a program for accessing and displaying Web pages. The two most popular Web browsers are Microsoft Internet Explorer and Mozilla Firefox, both of which are free. Other freely available browsers are Safari, Chrome, Opera, and Konquerer. While any of these suffices for viewing most pages, some subtle differences between them may affect the display of pages, especially with respect to newer features of the Web. The sections that follow describe how to perform common tasks using Internet Explorer and Firefox. The steps may vary slightly for the other browsers, and you are encouraged to read documentation pertaining to your browser of choice.

Microsoft Internet Explorer

Microsoft Internet Explorer (IE) is the most popular browser in the world today. It is automatically installed on all computers with Microsoft Windows operating systems, and it can also be downloaded for free from Microsoft's site: `http://www.microsoft.com`. Prior to 2006, Microsoft produced versions of Internet Explorer for both the Windows and Mac operating systems. Currently, however, Internet Explorer is only supported for Windows. As of March 2010, the latest version available was Internet Explorer 8. Figures A.1 and A.2 show the appearance of a Web page in Internet Explorer 8, running under Windows XP.

Starting Up the Browser

Since browsing the Web is a common task, your computer may have an Internet Explorer icon on the desktop or in the taskbar at the bottom of the screen.

If an IE icon appears in the desktop or the taskbar:
1. Double-click on the icon to start up the browser.

If an icon does not appear on the desktop or taskbar, then the browser program must be started through the system menus.

To start IE:
1. Click on the `Start` menu that appears in the bottom-left corner of the screen.
2. Click on the Internet Explorer icon to start up the browser.

When the browser window opens, the home page for that computer is automatically loaded. On a new computer, the home page is usually either Microsoft's site or else the Web site for the manufacturer of that computer. However, you can change the home page along with other settings (such as default fonts and colors).

To change the home page:
1. Click on the browser's `Tools` menu.
2. From that menu, select `Internet Options`.
3. In the Home Page box that appears, enter the desired Web address.
4. Click OK to close the window and save the new settings.

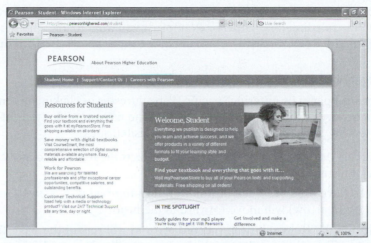

Figure A.1 A Web page rendered by Internet Explorer 8 running under the Windows XP operating system.

Figure A.2 A Web page rendered by Internet Explorer 8, with the Menu Bar displayed.

Opening a Web Page

To direct the browser to load the page at a particular Web address, the simplest way is to directly enter the Web address in the Address box at the top of the browser window. Alternatively, you may go through the File menu to open a page.

To open a page in the browser (quick method):

1. Type the Web address for that page in the Address box at the top of the browser window.
2. Hit the Enter key to load that page.

To open a page in the browser (general method):

1. Click on the browser's `File` menu.
2. From that menu, select Open.
3. In the box that appears, enter the desired Web address. If the page is stored locally on the same machine, you may click on the Browse button to select the folder and file name.

When opening a page that is stored on a remote Web server, you can omit the `http://` prefix to the Web address—the browser will automatically add it. Thus, the addresses `http://balance3e.com` and `balance3e.com` are equivalent.

When opening a page stored on the same computer that the browser is executing on, you must specify the full directory path. For example, if you want to load the file `personal.html` that is stored on a flash drive (the E: drive), you can enter `E:\personal.html` in the Address box.

Navigating the Web

As you visit pages by entering specific Web addresses or clicking on links in pages, the browser maintains a history of the sites you have visited. The navigation buttons at the top of the browser can be used to move quickly among these recently visited sites.

- Clicking the Back button (left arrow) instructs the browser to move back in the history—that is, to the most recently visited Web page.
- If you have used the Back button to return to previously viewed pages, clicking the Forward button (right arrow) will move forward in the history.
- Clicking the Reload button (curved arrows) will reload the page that is currently in the browser window. This is especially useful when you are developing a Web page, since you can load the page, make changes to it in a separate editor, and then view those changes by clicking the Reload button.
- Clicking the Cancel button (the X) will cause the browser to stop loading the current page.
- Clicking the Home button (the house) will load the home page for the browser.

Viewing the Source of a Web Page

One of the attractive features of the Web, from a developer's standpoint, is its openness. Often you can learn by viewing the source code of other people's Web pages.

To view the HTML source for a Web page:
1. Click on the browser's `View` menu.
2. Select `Source`. The HTML source code for the current page will appear in a separate editor window.

Once the HTML source code for a page appears in the editor window, you are free to study that code, cut and paste sections (if the content is freely available), and even save a copy on your computer.

Downloading/Saving a Web Page

You can also download pages or their elements and save them on your own computer. In doing so, you must be careful not to violate copyrights or otherwise infringe upon the rights of the owner. Unless explicitly stated otherwise, you should assume that any image or page on the Web is private property.

To download a public image:
1. Click on the desired image using the right mouse button.
2. From the resulting menu, select `Save Picture As....`
3. A window will then open in which you can browse and select the folder and file name where you want the image stored.

Similarly, you can download an entire HTML document and save it on your computer. The simplest way is to download the page and all supporting files (e.g., images that appear in the page) at the same time.

To download a Web page and all supporting files:
1. Click on the browser's `File` menu.
2. From the resulting menu, select `Save As....`
3. A window will then open in which you can browse and select the folder and file name where you want the page stored.

With this sequence of commands, all of the supporting files are stored in a separate folder, and links within the page are adjusted to point to it. If you wish to download only the page itself, with the original links intact, you should instead follow the above instructions to view the source of that page, then save that source code directly from the text editor.

Mozilla Firefox

The second most popular Web browser is Mozilla Firefox. This browser is produced by the Mozilla Foundation, a non-profit organization that formed out of the now defunct Netscape Corporation. In fact, the Firefox browser is built upon the code base of the Netscape Navigator browser, which was made public in 1998. It can be downloaded for free from Mozilla's site: `http://www.mozilla.com`. As of March 2010, the latest version available was Firefox 3.6 for the Windows, Mac, and Linux operating systems. Figure A.3 shows the appearance of Mozilla Firefox 3.6 running under Mac OS X.

Starting Up the Browser

Since browsing the Web is a common task, your computer may have a Mozilla Firefox icon on the desktop or in the taskbar at the bottom of the screen.

If a Firefox icon appears in the desktop or the taskbar:

1. Double-click on the icon to start up the browser.

If an icon does not appear on the desktop or taskbar, then the browser program must be started through the system menus.

To start Firefox under the Windows operating system:

1. Click on the `Start` menu that appears in the bottom-left corner of the screen.
2. From that menu, select `All Programs`.
3. Then, select Mozilla Firefox from the list of programs, and click on the Firefox icon to start up the browser.

To start Firefox under the Mac OS:

1. Click on the `Finder` icon in the tool bar at the bottom of the screen.
2. In the window that appears, select `Applications` from the `Places` menu on the left.
3. Click on the Firefox icon to start up the browser.

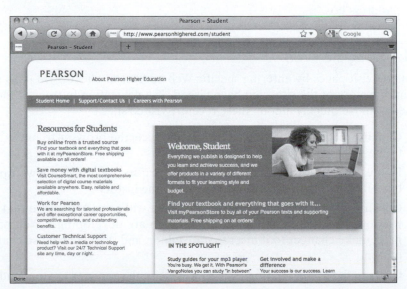

Figure A.3 A Web page rendered by Firefox 3.6 running under the Mac OS X operating system.

When the browser window opens, the home page for that computer is automatically loaded. On a new computer, the home page is usually either Mozilla's site or else the Web site for the manufacturer of that computer. However, you can change the home page along with other settings (such as default fonts and colors).

To change the home page for the browser:
1. Select `Preferences` from under the `Firefox` menu at the top left.
2. Select the Main tab to view the startup options.
3. In the Home Page box that appears, enter the desired Web address.
4. Close the Preferences window to save the new settings.

Opening a Web Page

To direct the browser to load the page at a particular Web address, the simplest way is to directly enter the Web address in the Address box at the top of the browser window. Alternatively, you may go through the `File` menu to open a page.

To open a page in the browser (quick method):
1. Type the Web address for that page in the Address box at the top of the browser window.
2. Hit the Enter key to load that page.

To open a page in the browser (general method):
1. Click on the browser's `File` menu.
2. If the desired page is stored on a remote Web server, select `Open Location...` and enter the Web address in the box that appears.
3. If the desired page is stored locally on the same machine, select `Open File...` and either enter the file name for that page, or else browse in order to select the folder and file location.

When opening a page that is stored on a remote Web server, you can omit the `http://` prefix to the Web address—the browser will automatically add it. Thus, the addresses `http://balance3e.com` and `balance3e.com` are equivalent.

When opening a page that is stored on the same computer that the browser is executing on, you must specify the full directory path for the file. For example, if you want to load the file `personal.html` that is stored on a flash drive (the E: drive), you can enter `E:\personal.html` in the Address box.

Navigating the Web

As you visit pages by entering specific Web address or clicking on links in pages, the browser maintains a history of the sites you have visited. The navigation buttons at the top of the browser can be used to move quickly among these recently visited sites.

- Clicking the Back button (left arrow) instructs the browser to move back in the history—that is, to the most recently visited Web page.
- If you have used the Back button to return to previously viewed pages, clicking the Forward button (right arrow) will move forward in the history.
- Clicking the Reload button (curved arrow) will reload the page that is currently in the browser window. This is especially useful when you are developing a Web page, since you can load the page, make changes to it in a separate editor, and then view those changes by clicking the Reload button.
- Clicking the Cancel button (the X) will cause the browser to stop loading the current page.
- Clicking the Home button (the house) will load the home page the for browser.

Viewing the Source of a Web Page

One of the attractive features of the Web, from a developer's standpoint, is its openness. Often you can learn by viewing the source code of other people's Web pages.

To view the HTML source for a Web page:

1. Click on the browser's View menu.
2. Select Page Source. The HTML source code for the current page will appear in a separate editor window.

Once the HTML source code for a page appears in the editor window, you are free to study that code, cut and paste sections (if the content is freely available), and even save a copy on your computer.

Downloading/Saving a Web Page

You can also download pages or their elements and save them or your own computer. In doing so, you must be careful not to violate copyrights or otherwise infringe upon the rights of the owner. Unless explicitly stated otherwise, you should assume that any image or page on the Web is private property.

To download a public image:

1. Click on the desired image using the right mouse button (Control + click on a Mac).
2. From the resulting menu, select Save Image As....
3. A window will then open in which you can browse and select the folder and file name where you want the image stored.

Similarly, you can download an entire HTML document and save it on your computer. The simplest way is to download the page and all supporting files (e.g., images that appear in the page) at the same time.

To download a Web page and all supporting files:

1. Click on the browser's File menu.
2. From the resulting menu, select Save Page As....
3. A window will then open in which you can browse and select the folder and file name where you want the page stored.

With this sequence of commands, all of the supporting files are stored in a separate folder, and links within the page are adjusted to point to it. If you wish to download only the page itself, with the original links intact, you should instead follow the above instructions to view the source of that page, then save that source code directly from the text editor.

Appendix B
Common Text Editors

Since a Web page is nothing more than a text file that contains special HTML tags, any text editor that can save documents as plain text files will suffice for developing your own Web pages. Both the Windows and Mac operating systems come with basic, general-purpose text editors: NotePad for Windows and TextEdit for the Mac. This appendix describes the basic operations of creating and editing Web pages using these two editors. However, you are strongly encouraged to obtain and use a special-purpose editor that is customized for Web pages. Web-customized text editors such as HTML-Kit (`http://www.chami.com/html-kit`) and Text Wrangler (`http://www.barebones.com/products/textwrangler`) use different colors and fonts to display HTML and JavaScript elements in a document, and thus make editing and debugging a Web page much simpler. Links to many freely available, Web-customized text editors can be found online at `http://webdevelopersjournal.com/software/html_editors.html`.

NotePad for Windows

NotePad is the basic text editor that comes preinstalled in the Windows operating system. While it lacks many of the advanced features of word processing programs and even Web-customized editors, it is simple to use and sufficient for creating and editing Web pages.

Starting Up NotePad

To start NotePad:
1. Click on the `Start` menu that appears in the bottom-left corner of the screen.
2. From that menu, select `All Programs`.
3. From the menu that appears, select `Accessories`.
4. Select NotePad from the list of accessories to start up the text editor.

Creating a New File

To create a new file:
1. Click on NotePad's `File` menu.
2. From that menu, select `New`.
3. An untitled document will appear in the editor window, and you can start typing in that document.

Opening an Existing File

To open an existing file:
1. Click on NotePad's `File` menu.
2. From that menu, select `Open`.
3. In the window that appears, click on the box labeled `Look in:` to select the directory where the file is stored.
4. Click on the icon for the desired file to select it. The name of that file will appear in the `File name:` box at the bottom of the window.
5. Click the Open button to open that file.

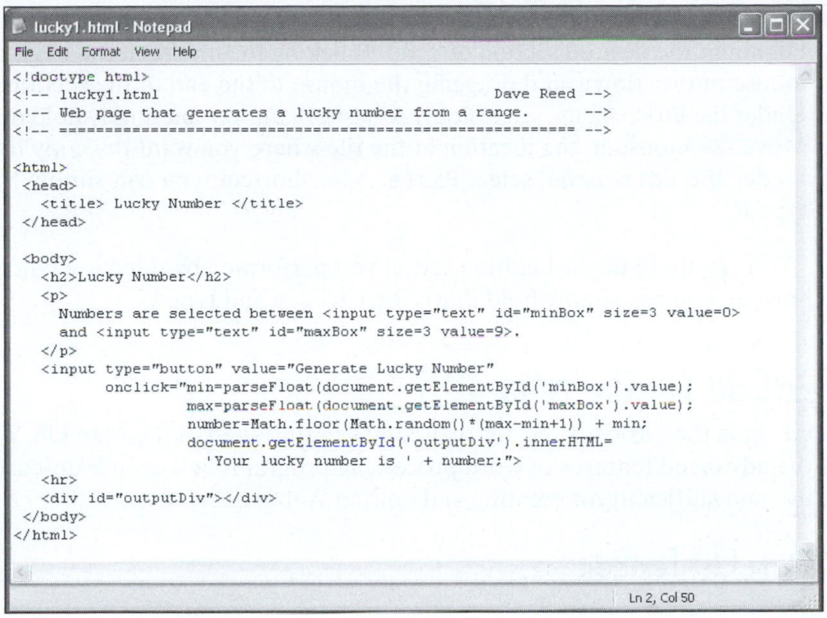

```
<!doctype html>
<!-- lucky1.html                                        Dave Reed -->
<!-- Web page that generates a lucky number from a range.         -->
<!-- ========================================================== -->

<html>
 <head>
   <title> Lucky Number </title>
 </head>

 <body>
   <h2>Lucky Number</h2>
   <p>
     Numbers are selected between <input type="text" id="minBox" size=3 value=0>
     and <input type="text" id="maxBox" size=3 value=9>.
   </p>
   <input type="button" value="Generate Lucky Number"
          onclick="min=parseFloat(document.getElementById('minBox').value);
                   max=parseFloat(document.getElementById('maxBox').value);
                   number=Math.floor(Math.random()*(max-min+1)) + min;
                   document.getElementById('outputDiv').innerHTML=
                     'Your lucky number is ' + number;">
   <hr>
   <div id="outputDiv"></div>
 </body>
</html>
```

Figure B.1 The NotePad text editor running under the Windows XP operating system.

Saving a File

To save the file currently in the editor:

1. Click on NotePad's `File` menu.
2. From that menu, select `Save`. If this is a new file, you will be prompted for a file name. Enter the name in the `File name:` box. If you want the file stored in a location other than the default directory, click on the `Save In:` box to select the desired location (e.g., the `a:\` drive). When saving a Web page, be sure to specify an extension of `.html` or `.htm`, as these extensions are automatically recognized by the browser when loading a page.
3. Click the Save button to save the file.

Copying a File

To save the file currently in the editor under a different name:

1. Click on NotePad's `File` menu.
2. From that menu, select `Save As...`.
3. In the window that appears, click on the box labeled `Save in:` to select the directory where the file is be saved.
4. Enter the desired file name in the box labeled `File name:`. Again, be sure to specify an extension of `.html` or `.htm`, as these extensions are automatically recognized by the browser when loading a page.
5. Click the Save button to save the file.

Copy and Paste

When typing text into the editor, you can use the Enter key to move to the next line, and the Backspace key to back up and erase mistyped text. In addition, the arrow keys can be used to move from line to line and subsequently edit text.

For repetitive tasks, it is often useful to be able to copy entire sequences of text and then edit them as desired.

To copy and paste a section of text:

1. Highlight the desired section of text by clicking the mouse at the beginning of the text, holding the mouse button down, and dragging the mouse to the end of the section.
2. Under the Edit menu, select Copy. As a shortcut, you can simply hold down the Ctrl key and type C.
3. Move the mouse to the location in the file where you want the copy to be inserted.
4. Under the Edit menu, select Paste. As a shortcut, you can simply hold down the Ctrl key and type P.

You can undo the last editing action you performed by selecting Undo under the Edit menu. As a shortcut, you can simply hold down the Ctrl key and type U.

TextEdit for the Mac OS

TextEdit is the basic text editor that comes preinstalled in the Mac OS. While this editor lacks many of the advanced features of word processing programs and even Web-customized editors, it is simple to use and sufficient for creating and editing Web pages.

Starting Up TextEdit

To start TextEdit:

1. If the TextEdit icon appears in the tool bar at the bottom of the screen, click on the icon to start up the editor.
2. If not, click on the Finder icon in the tool bar, and select Applications to locate the TextEdit icon.

Configuring TextEdit to Create and Edit Text Files

By default, TextEdit is configured to create files using the Rich Text Format (rtf). In order to create and edit plain text files, which are what you need for Web pages, you must alter the TextEdit Preferences.

To alter TextEdit Preferences for Web development:

1. Click on TextEdit menu.
2. From that menu, select Preferences.

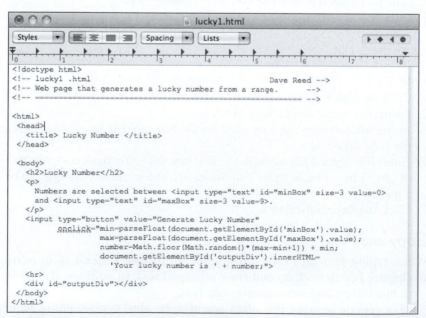

Figure B.2 The TextEdit text editor running under the Mac OS X operating system.

3. Under the category New Document, click on the button next to Plain text so that a dot appears there instead of by Rich text.
4. Under the category Open and Save, click on the box next to Ignore rich text commands in HTML files so that a check mark appears in the box.
5. Similarly, click on the box next to Add ".txt" extension to plain text files so that the check mark disappears.

Creating a New File

To create a new file:
1. Click on TextEdit's File menu.
2. From that menu, select New.
3. An untitled document will appear in the editor window, and you can start typing in that document.

Opening an Existing File

To open an existing file:
1. Click on TextEdit's File menu.
2. From that menu, select Open.
3. In the window that appears, browse to select the desired file.
4. Click the Open button to open that file.

Saving a File

To save the file currently in the editor:
1. Click on TextEdit's File menu.
2. From that menu, select Save. If this is a new file, you will be prompted for a file name. Enter the name in the Save as: box. If you want the file stored in a location other than the default directory, browse to select the desired location. When saving a Web page, be sure to specify an extension of .html or .htm, as these extensions are automatically recognized by the browser when loading a page.
3. Click the Save button to save the file.

Copying a File

To save the file currently in the editor under a different name:
1. Click on TextEdit's File menu.
2. From that menu, select Save As....
3. In the window that appears, browse to select the desired location.
4. Enter the desired file name in the box labeled Save as:. Again, be sure to specify an extension of html or .htm, as these extensions are automatically recognized by the browser when loading a page.
5. Click the Save button to save the file.

Copy and Paste

When typing text into the editor, you can use the Enter key to move to the next line, and the Backspace key to back up and erase mistyped text. In addition, the arrow keys can be used to move from line to line and subsequently edit text.

For repetitive tasks, it is often useful to be able to copy entire sequences of text and then edit them as desired.

To copy and paste a section of text:

1. Highlight the desired section of text by clicking the mouse at the beginning of the text, holding the mouse button down, and dragging the mouse to the end of the section.
2. Under the `Edit` menu, select `Copy`. As a shortcut, you can simply hold down the ⌘ key and type C.
3. Move the mouse to the location in the file where you want the copy to be inserted.
4. Under the `Edit` menu, select `Paste.` As a shortcut, you can simply hold down the ⌘ key and type P.

In addition, you can undo the last editing action you performed by selecting `Undo` under the `Edit` menu. As a shortcut, you can simply hold down the ⌘ key and type Z.

Appendix C
HTML Reference

Document Structure

`<html>  . . .  </html>`	**HTML:** top-level structure of a Web page.
`<head>  . . .  </head>`	**Head:** section at the top of the document, specifying elements that should be interpreted first when the page loads.

`<body>  . . .  </body>`
 	
optional attributes:
`onload="JAVASCRIPT_CODE"`
`onunload="JAVASCRIPT_CODE"`
	Body: section at the bottom of the document, specifying text and other HTML elements that will be rendered in the page. Code specifying actions to take place when the page loads or unloads can be specified using the `onload` or `onunload` attribute, respectively.

`<title> ... </title>`	**Page Title:** text that will appear in the Title Bar at the top of the browser window.
`<!-- . . . -->`	**Comment:** text that is ignored by the browser when rendering the page.

Text Spacing and Formatting

` `	**Break:** a line break that causes subsequent text to begin on the next line in the page.
` `	**Nonbreaking Space:** a space character that is explicitly rendered, overriding the automatic layout of text by the browser.
`<hr>`	**Horizontal Rule:** a line that is displayed across the browser window.
`<b>  . . .  </b>`	**Bold:** text that is to be rendered in bold.
`<i>  . . .  </i>`	**Italics:** text that is to be rendered in italic.
`<u>  . . .  </u>`	**Underline:** text that is to be underlined.

Text Grouping and Headings

`<h1>  . . .  </h1>`
`<h2>  . . .  </h2>`
`. . .`
`<h6>  . . .  </h6>`
	Headings: section headings that are rendered with blank lines before and after. The smaller the heading number, the larger the font used.

`<p> . . . </p>`	**Paragraph:** a grouping of text that is rendered with blank lines before and after.
`<div> . . . </div>`	**Page Division:** a grouping of text and/or page elements that can be formatted uniformly. A page division is rendered with blank lines before and after.
`<span> . . . </span>`	**Text Span:** a grouping of text and/or HTML elements that can be formatted uniformly. A text span is not separated from surrounding text.

All grouping and heading elements have optional style attributes:
 	
`style="text-align:center"`
`style="text-align:left"`
`style="text-align:right"`
`style="text-align:justify"`
`style="color:COLOR_NAME"`
	The style attribute can be used to align elements in the page (centered, left justified, right justified, or full justified) or to set the color of text.

Hypertext and Multimedia

`<a href="URL"> . . . </a>`
optional attribute:
 `target="_blank"`
	Anchor: a hyperlink to a Web page at the specified URL. If the attribute `target="_blank"` is used, the page will open in a new browser window.

`<img src="URL">`
 optional attributes:
 `alt="DESCRIPTIVE_TEXT"`
 `width=NUMBER_OF_PIXELS`
 `height=NUMBER_OF_PIXELS`
 `id="ELEMENT_ID"`
 `onclick="JAVASCRIPT_CODE"`
 `onmouseover="JAVASCRIPT_CODE"`
 `onmouseout="JAVASCRIPT_CODE"`
	Image: an image that is stored in the file at the specified URL. Alternative text can be specified using `alt`, and the size of the image can be adjusted using `width` and `height`. The image element can be given an identifier for future access using `id`. Also, attributes can specify actions to take place when the user clicks on the image, or moves the mouse on or off.

Tables

`<table> . . . </table>`
optional attribute:
 `style="border:solid"`
	Table: a collection of text or HTML elements organized into rows and columns. By default, the border around the table and between data elements is invisible. It can be made visible by adding a style attribute to the opening TABLE and TD tags.

`<tr> . . . </tr>`	**Table Row:** a sequence of elements that will appear in a row of the table.
`<td> . . . </td>`	**Table Data (column):** a data element that will appear in a column of a particular row in the table.

Lists

`<ul> . . . </ul>`
optional attribute:
`style="list-style-type:square"`
	Unordered List: a sequence of items, each preceded by a round bullet (or a square bullet if the style attribute is used).

`<ol> . . . </ol>`
optional attributes:
`style="list-style-type:lower-alpha"`
`style="list-style-type:upper-alpha"`
`style="list-style-type:lower-roman"`
`style="list-style-type:upper-roman"`
	Ordered List: a sequence of numbered items. The style attribute can be used to specify letters or roman numerals instead of numbers.

`<li> . . . </li>`	**List Item:** an item that appears within an unordered or ordered list.

Programming and Event Handling

`<script type="text/javascript> . . . </script>`	**JavaScript Code:** statements that are to be executed by the browser's built-in JavaScript interpreter.
`<input type="button" value="BUTTON_LABEL" onclick="JAVASCRIPT_CODE">`	**Button:** An element that serves as a clickable button. When clicked, the code specified by the `onclick` attribute is executed.

`<input type="text" id="ELEMENT_ID" size=NUM_CHARS value="INITIAL_TEXT">`
optional attributes:
`onfocus="JAVASCRIPT_CODE"`
`onchange="JAVASCRIPT_CODE"`
	Text Box: An element that displays a single line of text. Attributes can specify actions to take place when the user clicks or types in the box.

`<textarea  id="ELEMENT_ID" rows=NUM_ROWS cols=NUM_COLS>`
`INITIAL_TEXT`
`</textarea>`
optional attributes:
`onfocus="JAVASCRIPT_CODE"`
`onchange="JAVASCRIPT_CODE"`
	Text Area: An element that displays multiple lines of text. Attributes can specify actions to take place when the user clicks or types in the area.

Common HTML Colors

aqua	darkgray	green	navy	royalblue	tan
beige	darkgreen	greenyellow	olive	silver	teal
blue	darkred	lightblue	orange	skyblue	violet
black	fuchsia	lightgreen	pink	slateblue	wheat
brown	gold	lightgrey	purple	slategray	yellow
darkblue	gray	mediumblue	red	steelblue	yellowgreen

Appendix D

JavaScript Reference

Variables

`Legal variable name:` consists of letters, digits and underscores, and must begin with a letter

Reserved words that shouldn't be used as variable names because they are already used by JavaScript or the browser.					
abstract	default	form	length	public	throw
all	delete	frame	link	reset	throws
anchor	do	function	location	return	top
area	document	goto	long	screen	transient
boolean	double	hidden	name	scroll	true
break	element	history	native	select	try
button	else	if	navigator	self	typeof
byte	enum	image	new	short	var
case	event	implements	null	static	void
catch	export	import	open	status	volatile
char	extends	in	option	submit	while
class	false	instanceof	package	super	window
const	final	int	parent	switch	with
continue	finally	interface	password	synchronized	
date	float	java	private	text	
debugger	for	layer	protected	this	

Data Types

Data Type	Examples
Number	1 -1024 18.0 3.14159 1.024e3
String	' ' 'foo' '2 words' 'uses single quotes'
Boolean	true false

Mathematical Operators

Operator	Name	Examples	
+	Addition	2 + 12	evaluates to 14
		4 + 7.432	evaluates to 11.432
−	Subtraction	7 − 2	evaluates to 5
		5 - 3.359	evaluates to 1.641
*	Multiplication	2 * 5	evaluates to 10
		10 * 9.773	evaluates to 97.73
/	Division	10 / 4	evaluates to 2.5
		2.5 / 8	evaluates to 0.3125
%	Remainder	10 % 4	evaluates to 2
		2 % 0.75	evaluates to 0.5

Comparison Operators

Operator	Name	Examples	
==	Equality	3 == 3	evaluates to true
		'foo' == 'bar'	evaluates to false
		false == false	evaluates to true
!=	Inequality	12 != 39	evaluates to true
		'foo' != 'bar'	evaluates to true
		false != false	evaluates to false
<	Less Than	2 < 3.1415	evaluates to true
		'b' < 'a'	evaluates to false*
<=	Less Than or Equal To	17 <= 17	evaluates to true
		'ABD' <= 'ABC'	evaluates to false*
>	Greater Than	12 > −4	evaluates to true
		'bar' > 'foo'	evaluates to false*
>=	Greater Than or Equal To	3.99 >= 3.98	evaluates to true
		'foo' >= 'fool'	evaluates to false*

*Strings follow standard dictionary ordering, i.e.,
```
'A' < 'B' < . . . < 'Z' < 'a' < 'b' . . . < 'z'
'a' < 'aa' < . . . < 'ab' < 'aba' < . . . < 'b'
```

Logical (Boolean) Connectives

Operator	Name	Examples	
&&	AND	true && true	evaluates to true
			true && false	evaluates to false
			false && true	evaluates to false
			false && false	evaluates to false
||	OR	true || true	evaluates to true
			true || false	evaluates to true
			false || true	evaluates to true
			false || false	evaluates to false
!	NOT	!true	evaluates to false
			!false	evaluates to true

Statements

Statement	General Form	Examples
Comment	// Comment. . .	// A one-line comment.
	/* Comment. . . */	/* A comment that spans two lines */

Assignment Statement	VARIABLE = VALUE_OR_EXPRESSION;	x = 7.5;
		firstName = 'Dave';
		done = false;
		y = (x + 1) * 3;
		msg = 'Hi ' + firstName;

If Statement	if (BOOLEAN_TEST) {
	   STATEMENTS_EXECUTED_IF_TRUE
	}
		if (x < 0) {
		  x = 0 − x;
		}

	if (BOOLEAN_TEST) {
	   STATEMENTS_EXECUTED_IF_TRUE
	}
	else {
	   STATEMENTS_EXECUTED_IF_FALSE
	}
		if (user == 'Dave') {
		  found = true;
		}
		else {
		  found = false;
		}

While Loop	while (BOOLEAN_TEST) {
	   STMTS_EXECUTED_AS_LONG_AS_TRUE
	}
		while (x >= 0) {
		  x = x − 5;
		}

```
                                                          reps = 1;
                                                          while (reps < = 10) {
                                                            document.write('Hi');
                                                            reps = reps + 1;
                                                          }
```

| For Loop | `for (INIT; BOOLEAN_TEST; UPDATE)`
`    STMTS_EXECUTED_AS_LONG_AS_TRUE`
`}` | `for (r=1; r<=10; r=r+1) {`
`    document.write('Hi');`
`}` |

Predefined Functions

Function	Description	Input → Output	Examples	
`Math.sqrt`	Square Root	*Number → Number*	`Math.sqrt(9)`	`returns 3`
`Math.abs`	Absolute Value	*Number → Number*	`Math.abs(−23)` `Math.abs(99)`	returns 23 returns 99
`Math.max`	Maximum Value	*2 Numbers → Number*	`Math.max(3, 14)`	returns 14
`Math.min`	Minimum Value	*2 Numbers → Number*	`Math.min(3, 14)`	returns 3
`Math.pow`	Raise to a Power	*2 Numbers → Number*	`Math.pow(2, 3)`	returns 8
`Math.floor`	Round Down	*Number → Number*	`Math.floor(3.14159)` `Math.floor(4.5623)`	returns 3 returns 4
`Math.ceil`	Round Up	*Number → Number*	`Math.ceil(3.14159)` `Math.ceil(4.5623)`	returns 4 returns 5
`Math.round`	Round to Nearest	*Number → Number*	`Math.round(3.14159)` `Math.round(4.5623)`	returns 3 returns 5
`parseFloat`	Convert to Number	*String → Number*	`parseFloat('12.8')` `parseFloat('ABC')`	returns 12.8 returns NaN
`alert`	Open Alert Window	*String → undefined*	`alert("Welcome to my page.")` opens a new window with the message `Welcome to my page.`	

User-Defined Functions

Action	General Form	Examples

Function Definition	```function FUNC_NAME(PARAM1, PARAM2, . . .)```
	```// Assumes: ASSUMPTIONS ABOUT PARAMS```
	```// Returns: VALUE RETURNED BY FUNCTION```
	```{```
	``` var VAR1, VAR2, . . .; // optional```
	
	``` STATEMENTS_TO_BE_EXECUTED```
	
	``` return RETURN_VALUE; // optional```
	```}```
		```function Stars(N)```
		```// Assumes: N > = 0```
		```// Returns: string of N stars```
		```{```
		``` var theStr;```
		
		``` theStr = '';```
		``` while (N > 0) {```
		``` theStr = theStr + '*';```
		``` N = N - 1;```
		``` }```
		``` return theStr;```
		```}```
		
		```function Greet(name)```
		```// Assumes: name is a string```
		```// Results: displays greeting```
		```{```
		``` document.write ('Hi '+ name);```
		```}```

Function Call	```FUNC_NAME(INPUT1, INPUT2, . . .)```	```str = Stars(5);```
		```// Result: str == '*****'```
		
		```Greet('Dave');```
		```// Result: displays Hi Dave```

Strings

Property	Description	Examples (assuming word = 'Foo 2';)	
length	Specifies the number of characters in the string.	word.length	evaluates to 5

Methods	Description	Examples (assuming word = 'Foo 2';)	
+	Concatenation operator: appends two strings end to end	'ab' + 'cd' word + 'U'	evaluates to 'abcd' evaluates to 'Foo 2U'
toUpperCase	Returns a copy of the string with all letters made uppercase	word.toUpperCase()	evaluates to 'FOO 2'

toLowerCase	Returns a copy of the string with all letters made lowercase	`word.toLowerCase()`	evaluates to `'foo 2'`

charAt	Returns the character stored at a particular index	`word.charAt(0)`
		`word.charAt(1)`
		`word.charAt(4)`
		`word.charAt(5)`
			evaluates to `'F'`
			evaluates to `'o'`
			evaluates to `'2'`
			evaluates to `' '`

substring	Returns a sequence of characters from a string, specified by starting and ending indices	`word.substring(0, 3)`
		`word.charAt(4, 5)`
		`word.charAt(1, 3)`
			evaluates to `'Foo'`
			evaluates to `'2'`
			evaluates to `'oo'`

search	Returns the index of the first occurrence of a character, substring, or class of characters	`word.search('F')`
		`word.search('oo')`
		`word.search(/[0-9]/)`
		`word.search('x')`
			evaluates to 0
			evaluates to 1
			evaluates to 4
			evaluates to −1

split	Splits the string based on the specified delimiter, and returns the substrings in an array	`word.split(' ')` `word.split(/[ \t]/)`	evaluates to `['foo', '2']` evaluates to `['foo', '2']`

Arrays

Property	Description	Examples (assuming `arr = [1, 'foo', 3.8];`)	
length	Specifies the number of items in the array	`arr.length`	evaluates to 3

Methods	Description	Examples (assuming `arr = [1, 'foo', 3.8];`)	

[]	Indexing operator: returns the item stored at the specified index	`arr[0]`
		`arr[1]`
		`arr[2]`
		`arr[3]`
			evaluates to 1
			evaluates to `'foo'`
			evaluates to 3.8
			evaluates to `undefined`

sort	Returns a copy of the array, with items sorted into increasing order	`arr.sort()`
		
		`nums = [3, 6, 2.7];`
		`nums.sort()`
		`strs = ['xy','ab','a'];`
		`strs.sort()`
			evaluates to `[1, 3.8, 'foo']`
			
			evaluates to `[2.7, 3, 6]`
			
			evaluates to `['a', 'ab', 'xy']`

Manipulating HTML Elements

Action	General Form	Examples
Accessing the contents of a text box (or text area)	document.getElementById ('ELEMENT_ID').value	document.getElementById ('nameBox').value = 'Alan'; user = document.getElementById ('nameBox').value;
Accessing the source of image	document.getElementById ('ELEMENT_ID').src	document.getElementById ('facePic').src = 'sad.gif'; moodFile = document.getElementById ('facePic').src;
Accessing the contents of a page division, paragraph, or text span	document.getElementById ('ELEMENT_ID').innerHTML	document.getElementById ('outputDiv').innerHTML = 'Welcome!'; contents = document.getElementById ('outputDiv').innerHTML;

Appendix E

random.js Library

```
// File:    random.js
// Author: Dave Reed
//
// This file contains several routines for generating random values.
// Source code is available at http://balance3e.com
///////////////////////////////////////////////////////////////////

function RandomNum(low, high)
// Given   : low <= high
// Returns: a random number in the range [low, high)
{
    return Math.random()*(high-low) + low;
}

function RandomInt(low, high)
// Given   : low <= high
// Returns: a random integer in the range [low, high]
{
    return Math.floor(Math.random()*(high-low+1)) + low;
}

function RandomChar(str)
// Given   : str is a nonempty string
// Returns: a random character from the string
{
    return str.charAt(RandomInt(0, str.length-1));
}

function RandomOneOf(list)
// Given   : list is a nonempty list (array)
// Returns: a random item from the list
{
    return list[RandomInt(0, list.length-1)];
}
```

Appendix F
time.js **Library**

```
// File: time.js
// Author: Dave Reed
//
// Functions for converting units of time.
// Source code is available at http://balance3e.com
/////////////////////////////////////////////////////

function SecondsToString(seconds)
// Assumes: seconds is a number of seconds
// Returns: a string that breaks down that number of
//      seconds; e.g., 10,000 seconds -->
//      '0 days, 2 hours, 46 minutes, 40 seconds'
{
   var days, hours, minutes, seconds;
   days = Math.floor(seconds / (24*60*60));
   seconds = seconds - days*(24*60*60);
   hours = Math.floor(seconds / (60*60));
   seconds = seconds - hours*(60*60);
   minutes = Math.floor(seconds / 60);
   seconds = seconds - minutes*60;
   return days + ' days, ' + hours + ' hours, ' +
       minutes + ' minutes, ' + seconds + ' seconds';
}

function SecondsUntil(dateString)
// Assumes: dateString describes a date and time; e.g.,
//      'May 25, 2020 17:23:00'
// Returns: the number of seconds from now until that time
{
   var goalDate, current, diff;
   goalDate = new Date(dateString);
   current = new Date();
   diff = Math.floor((goalDate - current)/1000);
   return diff;
}

function TimeUntil(dateString)
// Assumes: dateString describes a date and time; e.g.,
//      'May 25, 2020 17:23:00'
// Returns: a string describing the time remaining until
//      the dateString date & time
{
   var seconds, time;
   seconds = SecondsUntil(dateString);
   time = SecondsToString(seconds);
   return time;
}
```

```
function CurrentTime()
// Returns: the current time (in military time); e.g.,
//      17:23:00 for 5:23 pm.
{
    var current, hours, minutes, seconds;
    current = new Date();
    hours = current.getHours();
    minutes = current.getMinutes();
    seconds = current.getSeconds();
    return PadWithZeros(hours, 2) + ':' +
        PadWithZeros(minutes, 2) + ':' +
        PadWithZeros(seconds, 2);
}


function PadWithZeros(number, width)
// Assumes: number is an integer to be formatted,
//      width is the desired format width
// Returns: a string representation of number with
//      leading zeros to achieve the desired width
{
    var str;
    str = '' + number;
    while (str.length < width) {
      str = "0" + str;
    }
    return str;
}
```

Appendix G

`arrays.js` Library

```javascript
// File:   arrays.js
// Author: Dave Reed
//
// Functions for manipulating arrays of values.
// Source code is available at http://balance3e.com
/////////////////////////////////////////////////////

function Acronym(phrase)
// Assumes: phrase is a string of words, separated by whitespace
// Returns: the acronym made up of first letters from the words
{

  var words, acronym, index, nextWord;
  words = phrase.split(/[\t\n]+/);             // CONVERT phrase TO AN ARRAY
  acronym = '';                                // INITIALIZE THE acronym
  index = 0;                                   // START AT FIRST WORD
  while (index < words.length) {               // AS LONG AS WORDS LEFT
    nextWord = words[index];                   //    GET NEXT WORD
    acronym = acronym + nextWord.charAt(0);    //    ADD FIRST CHAR OF WORD
    index = index + 1;                         //    GO ON TO NEXT WORD
  }

  return acronym.toUpperCase();       // RETURN UPPER CASE acronym
}

function ParseArray(strArray)
// Assumes: strArray is an array of strings representing numbers
// Returns: a copy of strArray with items converted to numbers
{

  var numArray, index;
  numArray = [ ];                              // CREATE EMPTY ARRAY TO STORE COPY
  index = 0;                                   // FOR EACH ITEM IN strArray
  while (index < strArray.length) {            //    CONVERT TO NUMBER AND COPY
    numArray[index] = parseFloat(strArray[index]);
    index = index + 1;
  }

  return numArray;                             // FINALLY, RETURN THE COPY
}

function Average(numArray)
// Assumes: numArray is an array of numbers
// Returns: average of the numbers in numArray
{
  var sum, index;
  sum = 0;                                     // INITIALIZE sum
```

```
    index = 0;                       // START AT FIRST NUMBER
    while (index < numArray.length) { // AS LONG AS NUMBERS LEFT
      sum = sum + numArray[index];    //   ADD NUMBER TO sum
      index = index + 1;              //   GO ON TO NEXT NUMBER
    }

    return sum/numArray.length;       // RETURN AVERAGE
}
```

Index

for commerce, 342–343
as communications media, 341–342
defined, 12, 43
as distributed network, 48–49
domain names, 50–52
functioning of, 48–52
growth, 48
history of, 44–48
as information source, 338–340
number of computers on, 114
packet switching, 49
TCP/IP, 50
Web growth and, 55
Internet Corporation for Assigned Names and
    Numbers (ICANN), 51
Internet Society, 47
Internet Software Consortium, 48
interpretation, 150–151
interpreters, 150–151
inventions, greatest, 336
IP (Internet Protocol), 50
IP addresses
    defined, 50
    domain names and, 50–52
ISPs (Internet service providers), 341
italics, 363

J
Jacquard, Joseph-Marie, 102, 103
Java, 37, 114, 148, 274
JavaScript, 37, 147
    arrays, 311–334
    data types, 366
    HTML tag, 365
    identifiers, 68
    name capitalization, 68
    number representation, 90–91
    precedence rules, 89, 98
    program illustration, 148
    program interpretation, 150
    reference, 366–372
    scientific notation, 90
    strings, 69, 273–292
    variables, 83–88, 366
JavaScript data types
    arrays, 311–334
    Booleans, 88
    defined, 88
    numbers, 88
    predefined operators, 88
    strings, 88
JavaScript operators
    %, 132, 367

&&, 205, 239, 368
*, 367
+, 277, 321, 367, 370
<, 196, 367
<= , 196, 367
!, 205, 368
-, 367
/, 367
 =, 89
!=, 196, 367
 ==, 89, 196, 203–204, 367
>, 196, 367
>=, 196, 367
||, 205, 368
comparison, 367
logical, 205, 206, 368
mathematical, 367
relational, 196
JavaScript statements
    alert, 69–70
    assignment, 62, 63, 64, 83, 368
    comment, 368
    control, 233
    defined, 61
    encapsulation, 156
    error types, 72–73
    for, 251–252
    function call, 120
    if, 195–199
    line breaks, 67
    mathematical operations, 93
    syntax errors, 64
    while, 234–239
    with images and buttons, 61
Jobs, Steven, 113
JPEG (Joint Photographic Experts Group) format,
    28, 226

K
Kay, Alan, 1, 113
KB (kilobyte), 6
Kepler, 101
kernel, 10
Kernighan, Brian, 79
Kilby, Jack, 109, 110, 293, 303
Knuth, Donald, 176

L
label alignment, 96
LANs (local area networks), 184, 185
laptop computers, 2
LARC computer, 108
Ledgard, Henry, 95

Credits

Credits and acknowledgments borrowed from other sources and reproduced, with permission, in this textbook are as follows:

Chapter 1

Figure 1.1 (left):	© Alamy
Figure 1.1 (left center, right center, right):	© iStockPhoto
Figure 1.3:	© iStockPhoto
Figure 1.5:	© Intel
Figure 1.8a:	© Shutterstock
Figure 1.8b:	© ThinkStock
Figures 1.8c, 1.8d:	© Shutterstock
Figure 1.9 (left, right):	© iStockPhoto
Figure 1.10:	© 2010 Apple Inc. All rights reserved.
Figure 1.11:	© 2009 Microsoft Corporation. All rights reserved.
Figure 1.12a:	© ThinkStock
Figure 1.12b:	© Alamy
Figure 1.14:	© Mozilla Firefox® is a registered trademark of Mozilla.org. All Rights Reserved.

Chapter 3

Figure 3.1:	© Courtesy of the MIT Museum
Figure 3.2:	© Dr. Lawrence G. Roberts
Figures 3.3, 3.4, 3.5:	© 2010 Martin Dodge. Reprinted with permission.
Figure 3.13:	Photo courtesy of CERN
Figure 3.14:	© AP Images

Chapter 6

Figure 6.2:	© Science Museum/Science Society and Picture Library
Figure 6.3:	© Science Society and Picture Library via Getty Images
Figure 6.4:	© Bettmann/Corbis
Figure 6.5:	© Grant Braught
Figure 6.6:	© iStockPhoto
Figure 6.7:	Photo courtesy of the Computer Museum
Figure 6.8:	Photo courtesy of the United States Army
Figure 6.9:	Photographed by Alan Richards. From the Shelby White and Leon Levy Archives Center, Institute for Advanced Study, Princeton, NJ, USA.
Figure 6.10:	© Corbis
Figure 6.11:	© Astrid and Hanns-Frieder Michler/Photo Researchers, Inc.
Figure 6.12:	© Getty Images
Figure 6.13:	© Michael W. Davidson at Florida State University
Figure 6.15:	© AP Images
Figure 6.16:	Photo Courtesy of the Microsoft Archives

Chapter 8

Figure 8.1:	© Cooking instructions on a box of KRAFT® Macaroni & Cheese (Original). KRAFT is a registered trademark used with permission of Kraft Foods.
Figure 8.2:	© British Museum, London, UK/The Bridgeman Art Library
Figure 8.7:	© Sir Isaac Newton, engraved by W.T. Fry. Library of Congress
Figure 8.12:	© Corbis

Chapter 9

Figure 9.11:	© Magic 8 ball® is a registered trademark of Mattel, Inc. All Rights Reserved.

Chapter 10

Figure 10.3:	© NPG
Figure 10.8:	© Getty Images
Figure 10.9:	© AP Images
Figure 10.10:	Photo courtesy of the Technical Information Department of Lawrence Livermore National Library
Figure 10.11:	© Shutterstock
Figure 10.14:	© AP Images
Figure 10.15:	© iRobot
Figure 10.16:	© National Center for Biotechnology Information

Chapter 11

| Figures 11.9, 12.1a: | © Shutterstock |

Chapter 12

Figure 12.1b:	© Bose Corportation
Figure 12.9:	© Photolibrary
Figure 12.15:	© Dorling Kindersley
Figures 12.13a, 12.13b:	Photo courtesy of the author David Reed

Chapter 16

Figure 16.3:	© Alamy
Figure 16.6:	© AP Images
Figures 16.19, 16.21a, 16.21b:	© Intel
Figure 16.22:	© Photo Disc/Getty Images
Figure 16.23:	© Reprinted with permission of Intel Corporation

Chapter 18

Figure 18.2:	© Alamy
Figure 18.4:	© 2010 HRB Digital LLC. All Rights Reserved.
Figure 18.5:	© 2007 Cable News Network. Turner Broadcasting System, Inc. All Rights Reserved.
Figure 18.6:	© 2007 TheOtherNews.com. All Rights Reserved. Reprinted with permission.
Figure 18.7:	© Google, Inc.
Figure 18.8:	© Microsoft Outlook® is a registered trademark of Microsoft. All Rights Reserved.
Figure 18.9:	© 2010 Facebook, Inc. All Rights Reserved.
Figure 18.9 (right):	Photo courtesy of Joan Reed. All Rights Reserved.
Figure 18.9 (bottom):	Photo courtesy of Owen Astrachan. All Rights Reserved.
Figure 18.9:	Christmas Tree application image courtesy of Kari Ardley.
Figures 18.10, 18.12:	© 2010 Amazon.com

Trademark Information

Adobe Photoshop and FrameMaker are registered trademarks of Adobe, Inc.

AMD Athlon is a trademark of Advanced Micro Devices, Inc.

AOL is a registered trademark and AOL Instant Messenger is a trademark of Time Warner, Inc.

Apple Mac OS X is a registered trademark and SimpleText is a trademark of Apple Computers, Inc.

Bose Wave radio is a registered trademark of Bose Corporation.

Corel WordPerfect is a registered trademark of Corel, Inc.

Cray 20-XMP is a trademark of Cray, Inc.

DEC and Hewlett-Packard are registered trademarks of Hewlett-Packard, Inc.

Dell Dimension 4400 and Dell Axim PDA are a trademarks of Dell.

Doom is a registered trademark of Id Software, Inc.

Emacs is a trademark of UniPress Software, Inc.

Fairchild Semiconductor is a registered trademark of Fairchild Semiconductor Corporation.

GIF (Graphics Interchange Format) (The Graphics Interchange Format© is the Copyright property of CompuServe Incorporated. GIF$^{(sm)}$ is a Service Mark property of CompuServe Incorporated.)

Google is a registered trademark of Google, Inc.

IBM is a registered trademark of International Business Machines, Inc.

Intel, Celeron, and Intel Pentium 4 are registered trademarks of Intel Corporation.

International Data Corporation (IDC) is a registered trademark of International Data Corporation.

KRAFT Macaroni and Cheese is a registered trademark used with the permission of Kraft Foods.

Linux is a registered trademark of Linus Torvalds.

Macromedia Flash is a trademark of Macromedia, Inc.

Magic 8 Ball is a registered trademark owned by and used with permission from Mattel, Inc. ©2003 Mattel, Inc. All Rights Reserved.

MCI WorldCom is a registered trademark of MCI, Inc.

Microsoft Windows XP, Internet Explorer, Microsoft Works, Microsoft Outlook, Microsoft Office XP, NotePad, WordPad, and Word, Visual Studio, PowerPoint, Metrowerks CodeWarrior, Hotmail, and MSN are registered trademarks of Microsoft Corporation.

MITS Altair 8800 is a trademark of Micro Instrumentation Telemetry Systems.

Motorola is a registered trademark of Motorola, Inc.

Motorola PowerPC G4 is a trademark of Motorola.

National Semiconductors is a registered trademark of National Semiconductor Corporation.

Netscape Navigator is a registered trademark of Netscape, Inc.

Norton Anti-Virus is a trademark of Symantec Corporation.

Palm m130 and Handspring Treo are trademarks of PalmOne, Inc.

Quicken New User Edition is a registered trademark of Intuit, Inc.

Sprint is a registered trademark of Sprint Communications Company, L.P.

Sun Microsystems is a registered trademark and Java and JavaScript are trademarks of Sun Microsystems, Inc.

TaxCut is a registered trademark of H&R Block.

Texas Instruments is a registered trademark of Texas Instruments Incorporated.

Unified Modeling Language (UML) is a trademark of Object Management Group.

UNIX is a registered trademark of The Open Group.

Yahoo!News, Yahoo!Search, Yahoo!Mail are registered trademarks of Yahoo, Inc.